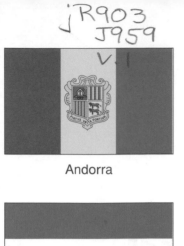

Andorra

Angola

Antigua and Barbuda

Austria

Azerbaijan

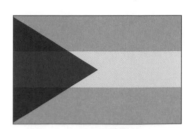

Bahamas

Belarus

Belgium

Belize

Junior Worldmark Encyclopedia of the Nations

Flags of Countries found in Volume 1

Junior Worldmark Encyclopedia of the Nations

Junior Worldmark Encyclopedia of the Nations

U·X·L
An imprint of Thomson Gale,
a part of The Thomson Corporation

Fourth Edition

VOLUME 1

Afghanistan
to Bolivia

THOMSON
GALE

Detroit • New York • San Francisco • San Diego • New Haven, Conn. • Waterville, Maine • London • Munich

Junior Worldmark Encyclopedia of the Nations, Fourth Edition

Project Editor
Julie L. Carnagie

Permissions
Ann Taylor

Imaging and Multimedia
Lezlie Light, Robyn Young

Product Design
Pamela Galbreath

Composition
Evi Seoud

Manufacturing
Rita Wimberley

```
        Library of Congress Cataloging-in-Publication Data
Junior worldmark encyclopedia of the nations / [Timothy L. Gall and Susan Bevan
Gall, editors].-- 4th ed.
      p. cm.
   Includes bibliographical references and index.
   ISBN 0-7876-9215-8 (set : hardcover : alk. paper) -- ISBN 0-7876-9221-2 (v. 1)
-- ISBN 0-7876-9222-0 (v. 2) -- ISBN 0-7876-9223-9 (v. 3) -- ISBN 0-7876-9224-7
(v. 4) -- ISBN 0-7876-9225-5 (v. 5) -- ISBN 0-7876-9226-3 (v. 6) -- ISBN 0-7876-
9227-1 (v. 7) -- ISBN 0-7876-9228-X (v. 8) -- ISBN 0-7876-9229-8 (v. 9) - ISBN
1-4144-0031-4 (v. 10)
   1. Geography--Encyclopedias, Juvenile. 2. History--Encyclopedias, Juvenile. 3.
Political science--Encyclopedias, Juvenile. 4.  United Nations--Encyclopedias,
Juvenile.  I. Gall, Timothy L. II. Gall, Susan B.
   G63.J86 2004
   903--dc22
                                                   2004006311
```

This title is also available as an e-book
ISBN 0-7876-9363-4
Contact your Thomson Gale sales representative for ordering information.

Printed in the United States of America
10 9 8 7 6 5 4 3 2 1

Table of Contents

Reader's Guide

Junior Worldmark Encyclopedia of the Nations, Fourth Edition, presents profiles of 193 countries of the world, arranged alphabetically from Afghanistan to Zimbabwe, in 10 volumes. *Junior Worldmark* is based on the eleventh edition of the reference work, *Worldmark Encyclopedia of the Nations.* The *Worldmark* design organizes facts and data about every country in a common structure. Every profile contains a map, showing the country and its location in the world.

For this fourth edition of *Junior Worldmark,* the pages were redesigned to make the information more accessible to student researchers. Facts were updated and elements were developed or expanded. The profile of the current political leader of each country was expanded; most leader profiles are accompanied by a photo. Approximately 100 new photographs were chosen to illustrate the landscape or society of the countries of the world. Many depict people engaged in activities of everyday life (especially young people or families at home, at school, or at work).

The *Junior Worldmark* structure—35 numbered headings—allows students to compare two or more countries in a variety of ways. To further the opportunity for comparisons, most country profiles feature graphical presentations of data: Geographic Profile, Growth Rate of the Economy, Components of the Economy, Yearly Balance of Trade, and a standard table comparing selected social indicators.

The Geographic Profile table ranks the country in land area among the 193 countries of the world. The highest and lowest points in the country are given, as well as average rainfall and temperature. The table entitled Selected Social Indicators offers a snapshot of the country and its development in relation to the other nations of the world in terms statistics available as of 2004. Included are data for eight key characteristics—per capita gross national product, population growth rate (overall and in urban areas), life expectancy, population per physician, pupils per teacher in primary schools, illiteracy rate, and per capita energy consumption. The country's statistics are compared to the averages for low-income countries, high-income countries, and the United States.

Because of differences in exchange rates, economic systems, government instability or lack of resources, and government reporting procedures, it is difficult—in some cases impossible—to find data for all of the categories listed in the articles. If a country profile lacks any of the graphical elements, in most cases it was due to lack of reliable statistical information.

The statistics, however, are more than complete enough to paint a disturbing picture of the great discrepancy in wealth between the industrialized nations and those of most of the rest of the world. As every Selected Social Indicators table illustrates, nearly half of the world's people live in countries where the yearly per capita gross national product averages $2,110.

Because many terms used in this encyclopedia will be new to students, each volume includes a comprehensive glossary. A keyword index to all ten volumes appears in Volume 10.

Profile Features

Each country profile begins by defining eight ways that the country is known to its neighbors and to the rest of the world:

Country names are reported in three forms. The first, the common name, is the name most English-speaking people use when talking about the country. In smaller type below the common name is the official name, in English. Finally, the name, in the language of the country, appears in italic type below the official name.

Capitals are named in the common English-language form, with the native language (if available) following in parentheses.

National emblems and flags are provided in color on the end pages of each volume, and in black and white accompanying the country's entry; the flag is also described in the text appearing below the flag.

National Anthem. The title of the national anthem is provided in the native language (with English translation in parentheses). Some anthems are untitled. In those cases, the first line of the anthem, or the phrase commonly used to refer to the anthem, is provided in the native language (with English translation in parentheses).

Monetary Unit of the country is described, with information about its history where available. Exchange rates are provided to give the student a relative idea of the value of the currency, and to enable broad comparisons between currencies of different countries. For the twelve European nations that are members of the European Union, conversions are provided for the euro as well. For up-to-the-minute information on exchange rates, the student should consult a newspaper or bank.

Weights and measures vary around the world, and *Junior Worldmark* reports on the system used by each country.

Holidays listed are official public holidays celebrated by the government and its citizens. A movable holiday falls on a different date each year, like Labor Day (first Monday in September) in the United States.

Time is standard time given by time zone in relation to Greenwich mean time (GMT). The world is divided into 24 time zones, each one hour apart. The Greenwich meridian, which is 0 degrees, passes through Greenwich, England, a suburb of London. Greenwich is at the center of the initial time zone, known as Greenwich mean time (GMT). All times given are converted from noon in this zone. The time reported for the country is the official time zone.

The body of each country's profile is arranged in 35 numbered headings.

1　Location and Size. The country is located on its continent in the world. Statistics are given on area and boundary length. Size comparisons are made to states of the United States, and a descriptive location for the capital is provided.

3　Topography. Features of the terrain and major rivers and lakes are described. A geographic profile accompanies this section, and provides information on points of highest and lowest elevation, climate, and ranks the country in land area among the 193 countries of the world.

3　Climate. Temperature and rainfall are given for the various regions of the country in both English and metric units.

4　Plants and Animals. Described here are the plants and animals native the country.

5　Environmental. Destruction of natural resources—forests, water supply, air—is described here. Statistics on solid waste production and endangered and extinct species are also included.

6　Population. Census statistics from the country, from the United Nations, and from the United States are provided. Population density and major urban populations are summarized.

7　Migration. This section describes movements of the country's people, both within the country, and emigration to other nations of the world. Also described is the country's policy on refugees and immigration from other countries.

8　Ethnic Groups. The major ethnic groups are ranked in percents. Where appropriate, some description of the influence or history of ethnicity is provided.

9　Languages. The official language is listed, along with other languages spoken in the country.

10　Religions. The population is broken down according to religion.

11　Transportation. Statistics on roads, railways, waterways, and air traffic, along with a listing of key ports for international trade and travel, are provided.

12　History. Concise summary of the country's history from ancient times (where appropriate) to the present.

13　Government. The form of government is described, and the process of governing is summarized. A brief biographical profile of the current political leader is provided, accompanied by his or her photo.

14　Political Parties. Descriptions of the political parties of significance through history where appropriate, and of influence as of 2004.

15　Judicial System. Structure of the court system and the jurisdiction of courts in each category is provided.

16 ■ Armed Forces. Statistics on troops and weapons are provided, along with description of the structure of the military.

17 ■ Economy. This section summarizes the key elements of the economy and describes key trading alliances. In most countries, two graphical presentations of data accompany the text. These are a bar graph showing the yearly growth rate of the country's economy, and a pie chart illustrating the percentage of the economy devoted to agriculture, industry, and services.

18 ■ Income. Gross national product, total and per person in US$, along with the average inflation rate.

19 ■ Industry. Key industries are listed, and important aspects of industrial development in the country are described.

20 ■ Labor. Statistics on the civilian labor force, including numbers of workers, percent of workers by industry segment, employment outlook including unemployment statistics, wage rates where available.

21 ■ Agriculture. Statistics on key agricultural crops for internal consumption and export are provided.

22 ■ Domesticated Animals. Statistics on livestock—cattle, hogs, sheep, etc.—and the land area devoted to raising them are given.

23 ■ Fishing. The relative significance of fishing to the country is provided, with statistics on fish and seafood products.

24 ■ Forestry. Land area classified as forest is given, along with a listing of key forest products and a description of government policy toward forest land.

25 ■ Mining. Description of mineral deposits and statistics on related mining activity and export are provided.

26 ■ Foreign Trade. Value of exports and imports in US$, with key products, are listed. For most countries, a graph illustrates the trend in balance of trade (exports minus imports).

27 ■ Energy and Power. Description of the country's power resources, including electricity produced and oil reserves and production, are provided.

28 ■ Social Development. Government social programs are described and statistics given. Included are insurance for the elderly, unemployed, disabled, and children. The status of women is summarized.

29 ■ Health. Statistics and description on such public health factors as life expectancy, principal causes of death, access to safe drinking water, numbers of hospitals and medical facilities appear here.

30 ■ Housing. Housing shortages and government programs to build housing are described. Statistics on numbers of dwellings, percentage with water, plumbing, and electricity are provided.

31 ■ Education. Statistical data on literacy, compulsory education, and primary and secondary schools are given. Major universities are listed, and government programs to foster education are described.

32 ■ Media. The state of telecommunications—television, radio, telephone—and print media is summarized.

33 ▮ Tourism and Recreation. A summary of the importance of tourism to the country is given, and factors affecting the tourism industry (such as war or natural disasters) are described. Key tourist attractions are listed.

34 ▮ Famous People. In this section, a few of the best-known citizens of a country are listed. When a person is noted in a country that is not the country of his of her birth, the birthplace is given.

35 ▮ Bibliography. Suggestions are provided as a guide for further reading.

Glossary. Appearing in every volume of *Junior Worldmark Encyclopedia of the Nations, Fourth Edition,* the glossary expands upon information given in the body of the profile.

Index. A keyword index to all ten volumes appears in Volume 10.

Acknowledgments

Junior Worldmark Encyclopedia of the Nations, Fourth Edition, draws on the eleventh edition of the *Worldmark Encyclopedia of the Nations.* Readers are directed to that work for a complete list of contributors, too numerous to list here.

Advisors

The following persons provided insights, opinions, and suggestions that led to many enhancements and improvements in the presentation of the material.

Mary Alice Anderson, Media Specialist, Winona Middle School, Winona, Minnesota

Pat Baird, Library Media Specialist and Department Chair, Shaker Heights Middle School, Shaker Heights, Ohio

Pat Fagel, Library Media Specialist, Shaker Heights Middle School, Shaker Heights, Ohio

Nancy Guidry, Young Adult Librarian, Santa Monica Public Library, Santa Monica, California

Ann West LaPrise, Children's Librarian, Redford Branch, Detroit Public Library, Detroit, Michigan

Nancy C. Nieman, Teacher, U.S. History, Social Studies, Journalism, Delta Middle School, Muncie, Indiana

Madeline Obrock, Library Media Specialist, Woodbury Elementary School, Shaker Heights, Ohio

Ernest L. O'Roark, Teacher, Social Studies, Martin Luther King Middle School, Germantown, Maryland

Ellen Stepanian, Director of Library Services, Shaker Heights Board of Education, Shaker Heights, Ohio

Mary Strouse, Library Media Specialist, Woodbury Elementary School, Shaker Heights, Ohio

Comments and Suggestions

We welcome your comments and suggestions for features to be included in future editions. Please write: Editors, *Junior Worldmark Encyclopedia of the Nations, Fourth Edition,* U•X•L, 27500 Drake Rd., Farmington Hills, Michigan 48331-3535; or call toll-free: 1-800-877-4253.

Photographs of World Leaders

The following sources provided images of the leaders of the nations of the world that appear in most entries. Sources for other photos illustrating the entries are credited in association with the image.

© **Attar Maher/Corbis Sygma:** Equatorial Guinea—Mbasogo, Teodoro Obiang Nguema; **AP/Wide World Photos:** Afghanistan—Karzai, Hamid; Albania—Nano, Fatos Thanas; Angola—Dos Santos, José Eduardo; Antigua—Bird, Lester; Armenia—Kocharyan, Robert; Bahamas—Christie, Perry; Bangladesh—Zia-Ur Rahman, Begum Khaleda; Barbados—Arthur, Owen; Belize—Musa, Said; Bhutan—Wangchuk, Jigme Singye; Botswana—Mogae, Festus; Bulgaria—Saxe-Coburg-Gotha, Simeon; Cambodia—Sen, Hun; Chile—Lagos Escobar, Ricardo; Colombia—Vélez, Álvaro Uribe; Congo-DROC—Kabila, Joseph; Cote d'Ivoire—Gbagbo, Laurent; Cyprus—Papadopoulos, Tassos; Czech Republic—Spidla, Vladimír; Dominica—Skerrit, Roosevelt; East Timor—Alkatiri, Mari; Ecuador—Gutierrez Borbua, Lucio Edwin; El Salvador—Flores Perez, Francisco; Estonia—Rüütel, Arnold; Fiji—Qarase, Laisenia; France—Chirac, Jacques; Gabon—Bongo, Omar; The Gambia—Jammeh, Yahya; Ghana—Kufuor, John Agyekum; Greece—Simitis, Kostas; Guinea—Conté, Lansana; Guyana—Jagdeo, Bharrat; Haiti—Aristide, Jean Bertrand; Honduras—Maduro, Ricardo; Hungary—Medgyessy, Péter; India—Vajpayee, Atal Behari; Iran—Khatami, Mohammed; Israel—Sharon, Ariel; Italy—Berlusconi, Silvio; Kenya—Kibaki, Mwai; North Korea—Kim Jong Il; Lithuania—Paksas, Rolandas; Madagascar—Ravalomanana, Marc; Malawi—Muluzi, Bakili; Mali—Touré, Amadou Toumani; Marshall Islands—Note, Kessai H.; Mauritius—Jugnauth, Anerood; Moldova—Voronin, Vladimir; Monaco—Rainier III; Mongolia—Enkhbayar, Nambaryn; Morocco—Mohamed Vi; Mozambique—Chissano, Joachim Alberto; Namibia—Nujoma, Sam; Nauru—Harris, Rene; Nigeria—Obasanjo, Olusegun; Palau—Remengesau, Tommy; Panama—Moscoso Rodríguez, Mireya Elisa; Philippines—Arroyo, Gloria; Poland—Kwasniewski, Aleksander; Portugal—Durão Barroso, José Manuel; Qatar—AL-Thani, Hamad Bi Khalifa; Romania—Iliescu, Ion; Rwanda—Kagame, Paul; Saint Kitts—Douglas, Denzil; Saint Lucia—Anthony, Kenny; Saint Vincent—Gonsalves, Ralph; Samoa—Malielegaoi, Tuilaepa Sailelel; São Tomé—Menzes, Fradique De; Serbia and Montenegro—Marović, Svetozar; Sierra Leone—Kabbah, Ahmad Tejan; Singapore—Tong, Goh Chok; Slovakia—Dzurinda, Mikulas; Slovenia—Drnovsek, Janez; Suriname—Venetiaan, Runaldo Ronald; Syria—Al-Assad, Bashar; Tajikistan—Rakhmonov, Imomali; Tanzania—Mkapa, Benjamin William; Thailand—Shinawatra, Thaksin; Trinidad—Manning, Patrick; Turkmenistan—Niyazov, Saparmurad; Ukraine—Kuchma, Leonid Danylovich; Uruguay—Batlle Ibáñez, Jorge Luis; Uzbekistan—Karimov, Islam; Vietnam—Nong Duc Manh; Zambia—Mwanawasa, Levy Patrick; **Austrian Press and Information Service:** Austria—Schüessel, Wolfgang; **Bahrain Government:** Bahrain—Al-Khalifa, Hamad Bin Isa; **Consulate General of Jamaica:** Jamaica—Patterson, Percival James; **Corbis:** Australia—Howard, John; Benin—Kérékou, Mathieu; Burkina Faso—Campaoré, Blaise; Burundi—Buyoya, Pierre; Cameroon—Biya, Paul; Central African Republic—Patassé, Ange-Félix; Chad—Deby, Idriss; Denmark—Rasmussen, Anders Fogh; Guinea-Bissau—Yala (Iala), Koumba; Korea, South—Roh Moo Hyun; Lebanon—Lahoud, Emile; Liberia—Taylor, Charles; Luxembourg—Juncker, Jean-Claude; Macedonia—Trajkovski, Boris; Malaysia—Mohamad, Mahathir; Mauritania—Taya, Maaouya Ould Sid Ahmed; Mexico—Fox Quesada, Vicente; Netherlands—Balkenende, Jan Peter; Oman—Said, Qaboos Bin Al; Pakistan—Musharraf, Pervez; Peru—Toledo, Alejandro; Russia—Putin, Vladimir; Senegal—Wade, Abdoulaye; Seychelles—René, France Albert; Sudan—Al-Bashir, Omar Hassan Ahmed; Sweden—Persson, Göran; Togo—Éyadéma, Gnassingbé Étienne; Tonga—Taufa'ahau Tupou IV; **Department of Information, Government of Malta:** Malta—Adami, Eddie Fenech-; **Eastword Publications Development:** Libya—Qadhafi, Mu'ammar Al; **Embassy of Ethiopia:** Ethiopia—Zenawi, Meles; **Embassy of Ireland:** Ireland—Ahern, Bertie; **Embassy of Kyrgystan:** Kyrgyzstan—Akayev, Askar Akayevich; **Embassy of Maldives in Sri Lanka:** Maldives—Gayoom, Maumoon Abdul; **Embassy of South Africa:** South Africa—Mbeki, Thabo; **Embassy of the Lao People's Democratic Republic:** Laos—Siphandone, Khamtay; **Embassy of the Republic of Indonesia:** Indonesia—Sukarnoputri, Megawati; **Embassy** of the Republic of Sri Lanka: Sri Lanka—Kumaratunga, Chandrika Bandaranaike; **Embassy of the Union of Myanmar:** Myanmar—Shwe, Than; **Embassy of Zimbabwe:** Zimbabwe—Mugabe, Robert; **Getty Images:** Algeria—Bouteflika, Abdelaziz; Republic of the Congo—Sassu-Nguesso, Denis; Eritrea—Afwerki, Isaias; Grenada—Mitchell, Keith; Kazakhstan—Nazarbayev, Nursultan; Lesotho—Mosisili, Pakalitha; New Zealand—Clark, Helen; Spain—Aznar, José María; Swaziland—Mswati III; Taiwan—Shui-Bian, Chen; **Government of the Principality of Liechtenstein:** Liechtenstein—Hans Adam II; **Government of United Arab Emirates:** United Arab Emirates—Al-Nuhayyan, Zayid Bin Sultan; **Landov:** Argentina—Kirchner Néstor Carlos; Azerbaijan—Aliyev, Heydar; Belarus—Lukashenko, Alyaksandr; Belgium—Verhofstadt, Guy; Bolivia—Gisbert, Carlos Diego Mesa; Brazil—Lula Da Silva, Luiz Inácio; Brunei—Bolkiah, Hassanal; Canada—Martin, Paul; Croatia—Mesic, Stjepan; Cuba—Castro, Fidel; Djibouti—Guelleh, Ismail Omar; Dominican Republic—Mejía Domínguez, Rafael Hipólito; Finland—Vanhanen, Matti; Georgia—Saakashvili, Mikhail; Germany—Schroeder, Gerhard; Guatemala—Perdomo, Óscar Berger; Japan—Koizumi, Junichiro; Jordan—Abdullah II; Latvia—Vike-Freiberga, Vaira; Micronesia—Urusemal, Joseph; Nepal—Thapa, Surya Bahadur; Nicaragua—Bolaños Geyer, Enrique; Norway—Bondevik, Kjell Magne; Paraguay—Duarte Frutos, Óscar Nicanor; Switzerland—Deiss, Joseph; Tunisia—Ben Ali, Zine El Abidine; Turkey—Erdogan, Recep Tayyip; Uganda—Museveni, Yoweri Kaguta; United Kingdom—Blair, Tony; **Office of the President of Venezuela:** Venezuela—Chavez Friaz, Hugo; **President of Costa Rica:** Costa Rica—Pacheco De La Espreilla, Abel; **Reuters Media:** Kuwait—Jabir III; **Royal Embassy of Saudi Arabia:** Saudi Arabia—Al-SAUD, Fahd Bin Abdul Aziz; **The White House;** United States of America—Bush, George W.

Guide to Country Articles

Every country profile in this encyclopedia includes the same 35 headings. Also included in every profile is a map (showing the country and its location in the world), the country's flag and seal, and a table of data on the country. The country articles are organized alphabetically in ten volumes. A glossary of terms is included in each of the ten volumes. This glossary defines many of the specialized terms used throughout the encyclopedia. A keyword index to all ten volumes appears at the end of Volume 10.

Alphabetical listing of sections

Agriculture	21	Income	18
Armed Forces	16	Industry	19
Bibliography	35	Judicial System	15
Climate	3	Labor	20
Domesticated Animals	22	Languages	9
Economy	17	Location and Size	1
Education	31	Media	32
Energy and Power	27	Migration	7
Environment	5	Mining	25
Ethnic Groups	8	Plants and Animals	4
Famous People	34	Political Parties	14
Fishing	23	Population	6
Foreign Trade	26	Religions	10
Forestry	24	Social Development	28
Government	13	Topography	2
Health	29	Tourism/Recreation	33
History	12	Transportation	11
Housing	30		

Sections listed numerically

1	Location and Size	19	Industry
2	Topography	20	Labor
3	Climate	21	Agriculture
4	Plants and Animals	22	Domesticated Animals
5	Environment	23	Fishing
6	Population	24	Forestry
7	Migration	25	Mining
8	Ethnic Groups	26	Foreign Trade
9	Languages	27	Energy and Power
10	Religions	28	Social Development
11	Transportation	29	Health
12	History	30	Housing
13	Government	31	Education
14	Political Parties	32	Media
15	Judicial System	33	Tourism/Recreation
16	Armed Forces	34	Famous People
17	Economy	35	Bibliography
18	Income		

Abbreviations and acronyms to know

GMT=Greenwich mean time. The prime, or Greenwich, meridian passes through Greenwich, England (near London), and marks the center of the initial time zone for the world. The standard time of all 24 time zones relate to Greenwich mean time. Every profile contains a map showing the country and its location in the world.

These abbreviations are used in references to famous people:

b.=born
d.=died
fl.=flourished (lived and worked)
r.=reigned (for kings, queens, and similar monarchs)
A dollar sign ($) stands for US$ unless otherwise indicated.

Afghanistan

Islamic State of Afghanistan
Dowlat-e Eslami-ye Afghanestan

Capital: Kabul.

Flag: The national flag has three equal vertical stripes of green, white, and black. In the center is the national coat of arms.

Anthem: *Esllahte Arzi (Land Reform),* beginning "So long as there is the earth and the heavens."

Monetary Unit: The afghani (AF) is a paper currency of 100 puls. There are coins of 25 and 50 puls and 1, 2, and 5 afghanis, and notes of 10, 20, 50, 100, 500, and 1,000 afghanis. AF1 = $0.0211 (or $1 = AF47.3; May 2003).

Weights and Measures: The metric system is the legal standard, although some local units are still in use.

Holidays: Now Rooz (New Year's Day), 21 March; May Day, 1 May; Independence Day, 18 August. Movable religious holidays include First Day of Ramadan, 'Id al-Fitr, 'Id al-'Adha', 'Ashura, and Milad an-Nabi. The Afghan calendar year begins on 21 March; the Afghan year 1376 began on 21 March 1997.

Time: 4:30 PM = noon GMT.

1 Location and Size

Afghanistan is a landlocked country in South Asia. Afghanistan is slightly smaller than the state of Texas, with a total area of 647,500 square kilometers (250,001 square miles). Afghanistan shares boundaries with Turkmenistan, Uzbekistan, Tajikistan, China, Pakistan, and Iran, with a total boundary length of 5,529 kilometers (3,436 miles). Afghanistan's capital city, Kabul, is located in the east central part of the country.

2 Topography

The average altitude of Afghanistan is about 1,200 meters (4,000 feet). The Hindu Kush mountain range, where Afghanistan's highest mountain peaks are found, rises to more than 6,100 meters (20,000 feet) in the northern corner of the Wakhan panhandle in the northeast and continues in a southwesterly direction, dividing the northern provinces from the rest of the country. The highest point is Mount Nowshak (7,485 meters/24,557 feet). Central Afghanistan, a plateau with an average elevation of 1,800 meters (6,000 feet), contains many small fertile valleys and provides excellent grazing for sheep, goats, and camels. To the north of the Hindu Kush and the central mountain range, the altitude drops to about 460 me-

Geographic Profile

Geographic Features

Size ranking: 40 of 193

Highest elevation: 7,485 meters (24,557 feet) at Nowshak

Lowest elevation: 258 meters (846 feet) at the Amu Darya

Land Use*

Arable land: 12%

Permanent crops: 0%

Forests: 2%

Other: 86%

Weather**

Average annual precipitation: 37.2 centimeters (14.6 inches)

Average temperature in January: -2.3°c (27.9°F)

Average temperature in July: 24.8°c (76.6°F)

---

* *Arable Land: Land used for temporary crops, like meadows for mowing or pasture, gardens, and greenhouses.*

Permanent crops: Land cultivated with crops that occupy its use for long periods, such as cocoa, coffee, rubber, fruit and nut orchards, and vineyards.

Forests: Land containing stands of trees.

Other: Any land not specified, including built-on areas, roads, and barren land.

** *The measurements for precipitation and average temperatures were taken at weather stations closest to the country's largest city.*

Precipitation and average temperature can vary significantly within a country, due to factors such as latitude, altitude, coastal proximity, and wind patterns.

---

ters (1,500 feet), permitting the growth of cotton, fruits, grains, groundnuts, and other crops. Southwestern Afghanistan is a desert, hot in summer and cold in winter. The four major river systems are the Amu Darya (the longest river at 2,661 kilometers/1,654 miles) in the north, flowing into the Aral Sea; the Harirud and Morghab in the west; the Helmand in the southwest; and the Kabul in the east, flowing into the Indus. The lowest point in the country is along the Amu Darya River (258 meters/846 feet). There are few lakes.

3 ▪ Climate

Wide temperature variations are usual from season to season and from day to night. Summer temperatures in Kabul may range from 16°C (61°F) at sunrise to 38°C (100°F) by noon, while the average January temperature is 0°C (32°F). The maximum summer temperature in Jalalabad is about 46°C (115°F). Rainfall averages about 25 to 30 centimeters (10 to 12 inches).

4 ▪ Plants and Animals

There are over 3,000 plant species, including hundreds of varieties of trees, shrubs, vines, flowers, and fungi. The country is particularly rich in such medicinal plants as rue and wormwood; fruit and nut trees are found in many areas. Native fauna (animals) include the fox, lynx, wild dog, bear, mongoose, shrew, hedgehog, hyena, jerboa, hare, and wild varieties of cats, asses, mountain goats, and mountain sheep. Trout is the most common fish. There are more than 100 species of wildfowl and birds.

AFGHANISTAN

| 0 | 50 | 100 | 150 Miles |
| 0 | 50 | 100 | 150 Kilometers |

Location: 29°28′ to 38°30′ N; 60°30′ to 74°53′ E. **Boundary lengths:** China, 76 kilometers (47 miles); Iran, 936 kilometers (582 miles); Pakistan, 2,430 kilometers (1,511 miles); Tajikistan, 1,206 kilometers (750 miles); Turkmenistan, 744 kilometers (463 miles); Uzbekistan, 137 kilometers (85 miles).

5 ■ Environment

Afghanistan's most significant ecological problems are deforestation, drought, soil degradation, and overgrazing. Neglect and the damage caused by extensive bombardments have destroyed previously productive agricultural areas. The people of Afghanistan use wood for fuel. The country has responded to the fuel needs of its growing population by cutting down many of its already sparse forests. Consequently, by late 2002, only between 1% and 2% of

A refugee boy carries a suitcase to his new home in an apartment building that was abandoned during the war.

Afghanistan's land area was forestland. As of 2002, a four-year drought had emptied rivers and irrigation canals.

By 2002, 11 mammal species, 13 bird species, and 4 plant species were endangered. Endangered species in Afghanistan included the snow leopard, long-billed curlew, Argali sheep, musk deer, tiger, white-headed duck, Afghani brook salamander, Kabul markhor, and the Siberian white crane. There were thought to be fewer than 100 snow leopards in 2002. The country's Caspian tigers have virtually disappeared. In 2002, there was one pair of Siberian white cranes, with one chick.

6 ▪ Population

Two decades of civil war killed as many as 3 million Afghans and made the country's population size hard to assess. As of 2003, the population was estimated at 23.9 million. Afghanistan's estimated population density (excluding nomads) was 43 persons per square kilometer (110 persons per square mile) in 2002. Kabul, the capital, had a population of 2.45 million in 2001.

7 ▪ Migration

In 2001 and 2002, the United States and its allies bombed Afghanistan in conflicts against the government, known as the Taliban. During that time, many Afghans fled to surrounding countries as refugees. There were about 3.7 million Afghan refugees in Pakistan in 2002, and 1.6 million Afghan refugees in Iran and elsewhere to the west. In 2002, approximately 1 million people were internally displaced (they had lost their homes in war) within the country. The UN High Commissioner for Refugees (UNHCR) began helping refugees to return to the country in February 2002. As of October 2002, over 1.5 million had returned to their homes.

In addition to the UNHCR, the International Organization for Migration, the International Committee of the Red Cross, and UNICEF were helping refugees return to their homes. The Return of Qualified Afghans program was launched to bring back Afghan professionals who had left the country to participate in rebuilding the country. The program had returned 227 people by mid-2002.

8 ■ Ethnic Groups

All citizens are called Afghans. The Pashtoons (the name may also be written as "Pushtun" or "Pukhtun," and in Pakistan as "Pathan") account for 44% of the population as of 2003. The Pashtoons have long been divided into two major divisions, the Durranis and the Ghilzais, each with its own tribes and subtribes.

The Tajiks, of Iranian stock, comprise nearly 25% of the population and are mainly concentrated in the north and northeast. The Hazaras (about 10% of the total population) are found in the central mountain ranges. The Uzbeks account for about 8% of the population. Other groups include the Aimaks, Farsiwans (Persians), and Brahiu. In the northeast are the Kafirs. After their conversion to Islam at the end of the nineteenth century, they were given the name of Nuristanis, or "people of the light."

9 ■ Languages

Both Pashtu (or Pushtu) and Dari (Afghan Persian) are the official languages of the country. Pashtu is spoken by about 35% of the population, while approximately 50% speak Dari. Dari has been the principal language of cultural expression, of the government, and of business. Both Pashtu and Dari are written primarily with the Arabic alphabet, with some modifications. The Hazaras speak their own dialect of Dari. The Turkic languages, including Uzbek and Turkmen, are spoken by 11% of the population. The Nuristanis speak some seven different dialects belonging to the Dardic linguistic group. There are about 30 minor languages, primarily Balochi and Pashai, spoken by some 4% of the population. It is common for Afghans to speak two languages.

10 ■ Religions

Islam is the official religion of state. Almost all Afghans are Muslims. About 84% are Sunni Muslims. The rest are Shiites. Others comprise only 1%.

In 1994, an Islamic militant group known as the Taliban ("the Seekers") began to impose a strict form of Islamic observance in areas under their control. The Taliban fell from power in 2001. After that, the country returned to the 1964 constitution for the definition of religious freedom and practices. The 1964 constitution proclaims Islam to be the sacred religion of Afghanistan but tolerates the practice of non-Muslim religions.

11 ■ Transportation

Afghanistan has an estimated 21,000 kilometers (13,000 miles) of roads. However, due to many years of warfare and neglect, the majority of paved roads were unusable by 2002. In 2002 there were 35,000 passenger cars and 32,000 trucks and buses in use.

The Khyber Pass in Pakistan is the best known of the passes providing land access to Afghanistan. However, most of the country's trade moves through the former Soviet Union. There were only three short railway lines in the country in 2001. The only navigable river is the Amu Darya on the border with Turkmenistan. In 2002, there were 46 airports, 10 of which had paved runways, and 2 heliports. Kabul's airport began international flight service to Delhi, India, in early 2002.

12 ■ History

Afghanistan has existed as a nation for less than three centuries. Previously, the area was made up of various kingdoms, going as far back as the Persian rule of Darius I in the sixth century B.C. and, 300 years later, Alexander the Great. Toward the middle of the third century B.C., Buddhism spread to Afghanistan from India.

Beginning in the seventh century A.D., Muslim invaders brought Islam to the region, and it eventually became the main cultural influence. The region came under the control of a series of Arab and Turkic kingdoms until it was invaded by the Mongols under Genghis Khan in 1219. It was then ruled by Mongols and Uzbeks for several centuries.

The formation of a unified Afghanistan under the Persian commander Ahmad Shah Abdali in the eighteenth century marks Afghanistan's beginning as a distinct nation. His descendant, Dost Muhammad, was defeated by the British in the two Afghan Wars (1838–42 and 1877–79). Abdur Rahman Khan, recognized as emir (ruler) by the British in 1880, established a central administration and supported the British interest in a neutral Afghanistan to help prevent the expansion of Russian influence.

In 1907, an agreement between the British and Russians guaranteed the independence of Afghanistan. Afghanistan remained neutral in both World Wars (1914–18 and 1939–45). The Treaty of Rawalpindi (1919) gave the government of Afghanistan the freedom to conduct its own foreign affairs.

Muhammad Zahir Shah, who ascended the throne in 1933, continued the modernization efforts begun by his father, Muhammad Nadir Shah. He governed for the next forty years. In 1964, a new constitution was introduced, converting Afghanistan into a constitutional monarchy. In 1965 the country's first general election was held.

In July 1973, Muhammad Daoud Khan, the king's first cousin, seized power, establishing a republic and appointing himself president and prime minister. He abolished the monarchy, dissolved the legislature, and suspended the constitution. Daoud ruled as a dictator until 1977, when the new Loya Jirga (Grand National Assembly) elected him president for a six-year term.

Afghanistan Under PDPA Rule: On 27 April 1978, Daoud was removed from office and executed in a bloody coup d'état (military takeover). The country became known as the Democratic Republic of Afghanistan, with members of the People's Democratic Party of Afghanistan (PDPA) in charge. Soon after the takeover, rural Afghan groups took up arms against the new government. These groups came to be known as the mujahideen guerrillas.

Meanwhile, two groups within the ruling PDPA became involved in a bitter power struggle. By the end of 1979, two prime ministers had been forcibly removed from power. Thousands of troops from the Soviet Union (a country that broke apart in 1991) arrived in the capital, Kabul, to maintain order.

Throughout the early and mid-1980s, the mujahideen resistance continued to build and violence continued. From 1973 to 2000, more than 3 million Afghans lost their lives in the struggle.

The United Nations tried to find a political solution to the war. In April 1988,

AP Photos/EPA/Olivier Matthys

Afghan children arrive as U.S. military forces of the Parwan Province Provincial Reconstruction Team attend the official opening of a school for girls near the Bagram Air Base, Afghanistan, Wednesday 14 January 2004.

the Soviet Union agreed to pull its troops out of Afghanistan within nine months, but the Afghan leader they supported remained in power until April 1992, when mujahideen forces closed in on the city.

With the fall of the government, the Seven Party Alliance (SPA) of Islamic groups announced plans to set up an Afghan Interim Government (AIG) in charge of preparing the way for elections. Differences within the SPA/AIG leadership prevented the creation of a genuine interim government, and the country remained in a state of civil war.

Rise of the Taliban: By 1994, internal turmoil and fighting between factions brought the economy to a halt. The Pakistani government encouraged Afghan students from the fundamentalist Islamic religious schools along the border to protect Pakistani businessmen in Afghanistan from bandits. Pakistan's government supplied the students with ammunition, fuel, and food. The students freed a convoy from bandits and went on to capture Kandahar, Afghanistan's second-largest city. They called themselves the Taliban (the Arabic word for religious students, literally "the Seekers"). By late 1996 the

Biographical Profile

Hamid Karzai

Name: Hamid Karzai

Position: President of the Afghan Transitional Authority

Took Office: Named chairman of the Afghan Interim Government in December 2001; named president of the Afghan Transitional Authority in June 2002

Birthplace: Karz, a village near Kandahar, Afghanistan

Birthdate: 24 December 1957

Religion: Islam

Education: Studied political science at Himachal Pradesh University, in Simla, India; studied journalism at the École Supérieure de Journalisme de Lille, in Lille, France; received an honorary doctorate in literature from Himachal Pradesh University in 2003

Spouse: Zinat Karzai, a medical doctor

Children: no children

Of interest: Karzai is fluent in six languages— Pushtu, Dari, Urdu, English, French, and Hindu

Taliban had captured the capital, Kabul, and controlled 21 of Afghanistan's 32 provinces. In areas under Taliban control, order was restored.

However, the Taliban enforced a strict interpretation of Islamic law. Afghanistan's non-Pashtun minorities in the north and west part of the country did not accept the Taliban's rules. In May 1997, the Taliban suffered heavy casualties in fighting for the northern town of Mazar-i-Sharif, Afghani-

stan's largest town north of the Hindu Kush. The Taliban's opposition was supported by Iran, Russia, and Afghanistan's other neighbors. They feared that the Taliban might bring instability to the region. Fighting between the Taliban and the opposition continued, and in 2000, the Taliban controlled 90% of the country. An opposition group called the Northern Alliance led by Ahmad Shah Masoud controlled the northeast part of the country. In early September 2001, Masoud was assassinated.

The 11 September 2001 terrorist attacks carried out against the United States by members of the al-Qaeda organization caused the United States to begin a war on terrorism. The war on terrorism was first directed against the Taliban for harboring al-Qaeda leader Osama bin Laden and his forces. U.S.-led forces began a bombing campaign in Afghanistan in October 2001. By November, the Taliban were removed from power in Kabul. In December, an interim government under the leadership of Hamid Karzai was established. In June 2002, a Loya Jirga (Grand National Assembly) was held, and Karzai was elected head of state. At that time, the plan was to have the government in place for 18 months until elections could be held. In 2003, fighting between the remaining 8,000 U.S. troops and forces friendly to the Taliban and al-Qaeda continued.

13 ■ Government

In December 2001, an interim government was created at a meeting held in Bonn, Germany. The new leader was Hamid Karzai. Karzai was elected head of state of the "Islamic Transitional Government of Afghanistan" in June 2002. He named a cabinet, three deputy presidents, and a chief justice to head the country's highest court. A Loya Jirga (Grand National Assembly) was held in December 2003 to approve a new constitution. Elections for a new government were scheduled for June 2004.

14 ■ Political Parties

In September 1996, the Pashtun-dominated fundamentalist Islamic Taliban movement, led by Mullah Muhammad Omar, captured Kabul. Ousted President Rabbani, an ethnic Tajik, claimed that he remained the head of the government, and his delegation retained Afghanistan's United Nations seat. After the Taliban were removed from power in 2001, various warlords, leaders, and political factions emerged in the country. The main political group is the Northern Alliance, which fought alongside U.S. forces against the Taliban. As of 2003, Northern Alliance members held 60% of the cabinet posts in government. Prominent warlords include Rashid Dostum, Ismail Khan, and Gulbuddin Hekmatyar.

15 ■ Judicial System

In areas under Taliban control, justice was based on the interpretation of Islamic law. Murderers were executed in public and thieves had a limb or two (such as one hand, one foot) severed. Adulterers were stoned to death in public.

Until a new constitution is approved, the 1964 constitution serves as the country's legal framework. It is supplemented by laws that follow the Bonn Agreement of 2001, which established the interim government. A Ministry of Justice, Supreme Court, and attorney general's office are part of the judicial system. Because the Taliban burned law books, texts of Afghan laws are for the most part unavailable. Candidates for judge positions must have legal training. Afghan candidates may have received either secular or religious law training, which presents conflicts in naming new judges.

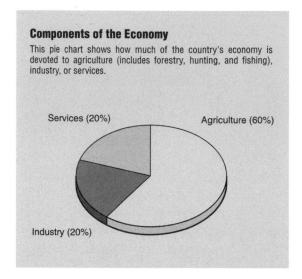

Components of the Economy

This pie chart shows how much of the country's economy is devoted to agriculture (includes forestry, hunting, and fishing), industry, or services.

Services (20%) Agriculture (60%)

Industry (20%)

16 ■ Armed Forces

In 2002–03, the United States was helping to create an Afghan national army. In 2002, Afghanistan asked the United Nations for funds to train 60,000 men for the land army, 8,000 for the air force, and 12,000 border guards.

17 ■ Economy

Afghanistan's economy has been ruined by over 20 years of war. Lack of resources and war have impeded the reconstruction of irrigation systems, repairing of roads, and replanting of orchards. Agriculture is the mainstay of the economy. In 2000, the Taliban announced a ban on growing poppies (used to produce opium). Before the ban, Afghanistan was the world's second-largest producer of poppies. The country remains a large producer of hashish. Many political factions profit from the drug trade.

In 2002, $4.5 billion was raised for a trust fund to rebuild Afghanistan. Planned projects included improving education, health, and sanitation facilities; developing agriculture; and rebuilding roads, energy, and telecommunication links.

18 ■ Income

In 2000 the gross domestic product (GDP) was reported to be $21 billion. Per person GDP was estimated at $800.

19 ■ Industry

Afghan industry was still in an early stage of growth before the outbreak of war in the 1980s. Industry has struggled ever since. The few industries that continued production during the years of civil war were limited to processing local materials.

The main modern industry is cotton textile production. Other important industries include soap, furniture, shoes, fertilizer, cement, natural gas, and copper.

Carpet making is the most important handicraft industry. Other handicrafts include feltmaking and the weaving of cotton, wool, and silk cloth; wood and stone carving; jewelry making; and the making of leather goods.

20 ■ Labor

Afghanistan's labor force was estimated at 10 million in 2002, with about 85% engaged in agriculture and animal husbandry. The textile industry was the largest employer of industrial labor. The vast majority of workers are frequently unemployed. Children as young as six years old work to help sustain their families.

21 ■ Agriculture

About 12% of the land is arable but less than 6% is currently cultivated. Wheat is

AP Photos/EPA/Syed Jan Sabawoon

Afghan farmers in Nahangar province grow poppies. Opium and heroin are derived from poppy buds. The United Nations has declared that Afghanistan is the world's largest producer of poppy-derived opium used to make heroin, bringing the country $2.3 billion in revenue in 2003.

common to several regions and makes up 80% of all grain production. Wheat production in 2002 was estimated at 2.69 million tons. Following wheat, the most important crops were barley (74,000 tons), corn (115,000 tons), rice (232,800 tons), potatoes (235,000 tons), and cotton. Nuts and fruit, including pistachios, almonds, grapes, melons, apricots, cherries, figs, mulberries, and pomegranates, are among Afghanistan's most important exports. In 2001, agricultural products accounted for about 53% of Afghanistan's exports, of

which fruits and nuts were a large portion.

Opium and hashish are also widely grown for the drug trade. Opium is easy to grow and transport and offers a quick source of income for impoverished Afghans. Afghanistan was the world's largest producer of raw opium in 1999 and 2000. In 2000, the Taliban banned opium poppy cultivation but failed to destroy the existing stockpile. After the ban, the prices for opium poppies increased. Even though growing poppies is illegal, many Afghans still grow them because opium from poppies can be sold for high prices. Much of Afghanistan's opium production is refined into heroin and is either consumed by a growing South Asian addict population or exported, primarily to Europe.

22 ▇ Domesticated Animals

In 1998, the northern regions around Mazar-i-Sharif and Maymanah were the home range for about 6 million karakul sheep. Annual production of livestock products includes 300,000 tons of cows' milk, 201,000 tons of sheep's milk, 41,000 tons of goats' milk, 18,000 tons of eggs, 16,000 tons of wool, and 16,000 tons of sheepskins and goatskins. In 2000, the total meat output was 356,840 tons.

23 ▇ Fishing

Some fishing takes place in the lakes and rivers, but fish does not constitute a significant part of the Afghan diet. Using explosives for fishing, called dynamite fishing, is a trend that has become very popular since the 1980s and is common practice in the country. The annual catch was about 1,000 tons in 2000.

24 ▇ Forestry

The natural forests in Afghanistan are mainly of two types. There are dense forests, mainly of oak, walnut, and other species of nuts, which grow in the southeast and on the northern and northeastern slopes of the Sulaiman ranges. There are also sparsely distributed short trees and shrubs on all other slopes of the Hindu Kush. The dense forests of the southeast cover only 2.7% of the country. Significant stands of trees have been destroyed by the ravages of the war. Logging, forest fires, plant disease, insects, and the destruction

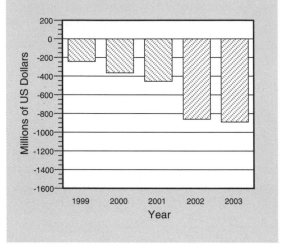

Yearly Balance of Trade

The balance of trade is the difference between what a country sells to other countries (its exports) and what it buys (its imports). If a country imports more than it exports, it has a negative balance of trade (a trade deficit). If exports exceed imports there is a positive balance of trade (a trade surplus).

of the forests to create agricultural land are all causes of the reduction in forest coverage. However, the most important factor in this destructive process is illegal logging and clear-cutting by timber smugglers.

25 ▇ Mining

Afghanistan has valuable deposits of barite, beryl, chrome, coal, copper, iron, lapis lazuli, lead, mica, natural gas, petroleum, salt, silver, sulfur, and zinc. Reserves of high-grade iron ore are estimated to total 2 billion tons. It is estimated that the country has 73 million tons of coal reserves. Coal production in 2000 amounted to 200,000 tons. In 2000, Afghanistan produced 13,000 tons of salt, 3,000 tons of gypsum, 5,000 tons of copper, and 120,000 tons of cement.

Selected Social Indicators

The statistics below are the most recent estimates available as of 2003. For comparison purposes, data for the United States and averages for low-income countries and high-income countries are also given. About 15% of the world's 6.4 billion people live in high-income countries, while 40% live in low-income countries.

Indicator	Afghanistan	Low-income countries	High-income countries	United States
Per capita gross national income (GNI)*	$700	$2,110	$28,480	$36,110
Population growth rate	2.6%	2.1%	0.7%	1.1%
People per square kilometer of land	43	77	31	31
Life expectancy in years: *male*	43	58	75	75
female	44	60	81	80
Number of physicians per 1,000 people	0.1	1.0	3.0	2.8
Number of pupils per teacher (primary school)	43	40	17	15
Literacy rate (15 years and older)	36%	66%	>95%	97%
Television sets per 1,000 people	14	91	735	938
Internet users per 1,000 people	n.a.	10	364	551
Energy consumed per capita (kg of oil equivalent)	111	550	5,366	7,937

* The GNI is the total of all goods and services produced by the residents of a country in a year. The per capita GNI is calculated by dividing a country's GNI by its population and adjusting for relative purchasing power.

n.a. = data not available   > = greater than   < = less than

SOURCES: International Telecommunication Union (ITU). *World Telecommunication Development Report 2003*. Geneva, Switzerland: ITU, 2003; World Bank. *World Development Indicators*. Washington, D.C.: The World Bank, 2004; Central Intelligence Agency. *The World Factbook*. Washington, D.C.: Government Printing Office, 2003.

26 ■ Foreign Trade

Trade with other countries began to increase during the late 1980s; however, the Taliban was unable to attract foreign investment because it was unable to gain international recognition. Exports, including fruits and nuts, carpets, wool, cotton, hides and pelts, and gems, amounted to an estimated $1.2 billion in 2001. Imports, including food, petroleum products, and most commodity items, totaled an estimated $1.3 billion.

In 2000, Afghanistan's main export markets included Pakistan, India, Finland, Belgium, and China. Major import suppliers included Japan, Kenya, Pakistan, Kazakhstan, and Turkmenistan.

27 ■ Energy and Power

In 2000, production of electricity totaled 0.4 billion kilowatt hours, and consumption of energy was 453.8 million kilowatt hours. Natural gas was Afghanistan's only economically significant export, carried by pipeline to Uzbekistan. In 2002, Afghan leader Hamid Karzai was attempting to revive a project to build a 1,430 kilometer (890 mile) pipeline to carry natural gas from Turkmenistan to Pakistan via Afghanistan. Petroleum products such as diesel, gasoline, and jet fuel are imported, mainly from Pakistan and Turkmenistan.

28 ■ Social Development

Social welfare in Afghanistan has traditionally relied on family and tribal organization. Disabled people are cared for in social welfare centers in the provincial capitals.

In 1996, the Taliban imposed limits on women's participation in society. Women were allowed to go out in public only if they wore a burka, a long black garment with a veil covering the face. The Taliban also banned girls from attending school, and prohibited women from working outside the home. Following the fall of the Taliban in 2001, women and girls were permitted to attend school and universities. Women were no longer forced to wear the burka.

The Taliban also applied harsh measures against crime. Theft was punishable by amputation, and public executions were used for more serious crimes. Following the removal of the Taliban from power, respect for human rights and basic freedoms was being restored.

29 ■ Health
Between 1985 and 1995 only 29% of the population had access to health services. As of 2002, Afghanistan had an average of 4 hospital beds for every 10,000 people. Most of the country's health care facilities are in Kabul. Because of the ongoing war, current statistics were not available in 2003, but health care was being provided by international organizations. There are some medical facilities supported by the Red Cross operating in the country. In 24 of 31 provinces there are no hospitals or medical staff.

In 2002, estimated life expectancy was 46.6 years (one of the lowest in the world) and infant mortality was estimated at 145 per 1,000 live births, which is the world's fourth-highest mortality rate for children under age 5. In 2002, 80,000 children a year were dying of diarrheal disease.

30 ■ Housing
The war severely damaged or destroyed countless houses. According to an official report, there were 200,000 dwellings in Kabul in the mid-1980s. In 2002, over 100,000 shelters were needed for people who had lost their homes, returning refugees, and the poor. These dwellings were needed in both rural and urban areas.

31 ■ Education
Education is free at all levels. Primary education lasts for six years and is theoretically required for six years, but only 53% of boys and 5% of girls were enrolled in elementary school in 2002. Boys and girls are schooled separately. A teacher has 58 pupils in an elementary school classroom, but only 28 students in a secondary school classroom. Only 32% of the males and 11% of females graduating from elementary school continue into secondary education. Secondary education lasts for six years. Vocational training is provided in secondary schools and senior high schools, and 6% of students are enrolled in the vocational system.

Children are taught in their native language—Dari (Persian) or Pashtu (Pashto)—during the first three grades. Both are official languages of the country. The second official language is introduced to students in the fourth grade. Children are also taught Arabic so that they may be able to read the Quran. The school year extends from early March to November in the cold areas and from September to June in the warmer regions.

AP/Wide World Photos.

High school students are seated on the floor of a gymnasium as they register for classes.

In addition to the secular public education system, there are traditional Islamic madrassa schools. At the madrassas, children study the Quran, the Hadith (Sayings of the Prophet Muhammad), and popular religious texts.

The University of Kabul, which is now coeducational, was founded in 1932. By 2002 a total of eight universities had been established in Afghanistan along with nine teaching institutes.

The adult illiteracy rate for 1999 (the most recent year for which statistics were available as of 2004) was 64% (males, 49%; females, 79%). This is the highest illiteracy rate in Asia.

32 ■ Media

Prior to 2001, there were some 30,000 telephones in use; however, local telephone networks were not operating reliably in 2002. The first television broadcast took place in 1978. As of 1997, there were 63 radios per 1,000 people. As of 2003 there were 14 television sets per 1,000 people.

Prior to the fall of the Taliban, the major newspapers, all headquartered in Kabul, (with estimated 1999 circulations) were: *Anis* (25,000), published in Dari and Pashtu; *Hewad* (12,200); and *New Kabul Times* (5,000), in English. In January 2002, the independent newspaper *Kabul Weekly* was published after having disappeared when the Taliban seized power. The first issue carried news in Dari, Pashtu, English, and French.

UNESCO, an agency of the United Nations, is providing aid to journalists and technical media staff, including those of national television networks, to strengthen the Afghan News Agency and develop public service broadcasting.

33 ■ Tourism and Recreation

The tourist industry, developed with government help in the early 1970s, has been negligible since 1979 due to internal political instability. In 1999, the daily cost of staying in Kabul was estimated at $70. Travel within the country was highly restricted due to the U.S.-led war against the Taliban and al-Qaeda beginning in 2001.

34 ■ Famous Afghans

The most renowned ruler of medieval Afghanistan was Mahmud of Ghazni (971?–1030). Many important figures of Arab and Persian intellectual history were born or spent their careers in what is now Afghanistan. Al-Biruni (973–1048) was a great Arab encyclopedist. Abdul Majid Majdud Sana'i (1070–1140) was a major Persian poet of mystical verse. Jalal ud-Din Rumi (1207–1273) and Abdur Rahman Jami (1414–1492) were also major Persian poets. Behzad (c.1450–1520) was the greatest master of Persian painting.

The founder of the state of Afghanistan was Ahmad Shah Abdali (1724–1273), who changed his dynastic name to Dur-rani. Dost Muhammad (1789–1863) was the founder of the Muhammadzai (Barakzai) dynasty. Amanullah Khan (1892–1960), who reigned from 1919 to 1929, tried social reforms aimed at Westernizing the country but was forced to abdicate. Muhammad Nadir Shah (d.1933), who was elected king by a tribal assembly in 1929, continued Amanullah's Westernization program. Leaders in the violent years since 1978 have been Nur Muhammad Taraki (1917–1979), founder of the PDPA; Hafizullah Amin (1929–1979), Babrak Karmal (b.1929), and Dr. Mohammad Najibullah (1947–1996), former head of the Afghan secret police who was brutally executed by the Taliban militia after they seized control of Kabul. Hamid Karzai (b.1957) became the head of the government in 2001.

35 ■ Bibliography

Banting, Erinn. *Afghanistan*. New York: Crabtree, 2003.

Behnke, Alison. *Afghanistan in Pictures*. Minneapolis, MN: Lerner, 2003.

Corona, Laurel. *Afghanistan*. San Diego, CA: Lucent Books, 2002.

Englar, Mary. *Afghanistan*. Mankato, MN: Capstone Press, 2003.

Greenblatt, Miriam. *Afghanistan*. New York: Children's Press, 2003.

Gritzner, Jeffrey A. *Afghanistan*. Philadelphia, PA: Chelsea House, 2003.

Kazem, Halima. *Afghanistan*. Milwaukee, WI: Gareth Stevens, 2003.

Rall, Ted. *To Afghanistan and Back: A Graphic Travelogue*. New York: Nantier, Beall, Minoustchine, 2002.

Albania

Republic of Albania
Republika é Shqipërisë

Capital: Tirana.

Flag: The flag consists of a red background at the center of which is a black double-headed eagle.

Anthem: *Hymni i Flamúrit (Anthem of the Flag)* begins "Rreth flamúrit të për bashkuar" ("The flag that united us in the struggle").

Monetary Unit: The lek (L) of 100 qindarka is a convertible paper currency. There are coins of 5, 10, 20, 50 qindarka, and 1 lek, and notes of 1, 3, 5, 10, 25, 50, 100, and 500 leks. L1 = $0.0079 (or $1 = L126.53; as of May 2003).

Weights and Measures: The metric system is the legal standard.

Holidays: New Year's Day, 1 January; Small Bayram, end of Ramadan, 11 February 2003*; International Women's Day, 8 March; Catholic Easter, April**; Orthodox Easter, April**; Great Bayram, Feast of the Sacrifice, 25 November 2003*; Independence Day, 28 November; Christmas Day, 25 December. *Dependent on the Islamic lunar calendar and will vary from the dates given; ** Dependent on religious calendar, and also will vary.

Time: 1 PM = noon GMT.

1 ▪ Location and Size

Albania is located in southeast Europe on the west coast of the Balkan Peninsula opposite the "heel" of the Italian "boot," from which it is separated by the Strait of Otranto and the Adriatic Sea. It is bordered by Serbia and Montenegro, Macedonia, and Greece, with a total boundary length of 720 kilometers (447 miles) and a coastline of 362 kilometers (224.9 miles). Albania is slightly larger than the state of Maryland, with a total area of 28,748 square kilometers (11,100 square miles).

Albania's capital city, Tiranë, is located in the west central part of the country.

2 ▪ Topography

Albania is mostly mountainous, with 70% of the territory at elevations of more than 300 meters (1,000 feet). The rest of the country is made up of a coastal lowland and river valleys opening onto the coastal plain. The Albanian mountains, representing a southern continuation of the Dinaric system, rise abruptly from the plains and are especially rugged along the country's borders. The highest peak, Mount Korabit

Geographic Profile

Geographic Features

Size ranking: 139 of 193

Highest elevation: 2,751 meters (9,026 feet) at Mount Korabit

Lowest elevation: Sea level at the Adriatic Sea

Land Use*

Arable land: 21%

Permanent crops: 4%

Forests: 36%

Other: 39%

Weather**

Average annual precipitation: 118.9 centimeters (46.8 inches)

Average temperature in January: 7.3°C (45.1°F)

Average temperature in July: 25°C (77°F)

---

* *Arable Land: Land used for temporary crops, like meadows for mowing or pasture, gardens, and greenhouses.*

Permanent crops: Land cultivated with crops that occupy its use for long periods, such as cocoa, coffee, rubber, fruit and nut orchards, and vineyards.

Forests: Land containing stands of trees.

Other: Any land not specified, including built-on areas, roads, and barren land.

** *The measurements for precipitation and average temperatures were taken at weather stations closest to the country's largest city.*

Precipitation and average temperature can vary significantly within a country, due to factors such as latitude, altitude, coastal proximity, and wind patterns.

(2,751 meters/9,026 feet), lies in eastern Albania on the Macedonian border. The most important rivers include the Drin (the longest river, 285 kilometers/177 miles), the Buna, the Mat, the Shkumbin, the Seman, and the Vijosë, all of which empty into the Adriatic. Albania shares Lake Scutari (the largest lake, 385 square kilometers/149 square miles) with Serbia and Montenegro, Lake Ohrid with Macedonia, and Lake Prespë with Macedonia and Greece. The lowest point of the country is sea level (0 meters) at the Adriatic Sea.

3 ■ Climate

The average annual temperature is 15°C (59°F). Rainy winters (with frequent cyclones) and dry, hot summers are typical of the coastal plain. Summer rainfall is more frequent and winters are colder in the mountains. Annual precipitation is 118.9 centimeters (46.8 inches), ranging from about 100 centimeters (40 inches) on the coast to more than 250 centimeters (100 inches) in some areas in the mountains.

4 ■ Plants and Animals

The mountainous landscape produces different zones for flora (plants). The dry lowlands are occupied by a bush and shrub type of plant growth known as maquis, which commonly has hairy, leathery leaves. There are some trees in the low-lying regions, but larger forests of oak, beech, and other deciduous species begin at 910 meters (2,986 feet). Black pines and other conifers are found at higher elevations in the northern part of the country. There are few wild animals, even in the mountains, but wild birds still abound in the lowland forests.

5 ▌ Environment

Deforestation remains Albania's principal environmental problem. Forest and woodland account for 38% of the country's land use. Soil erosion is also a cause for concern, as is pollution of the water by industrial and domestic effluents.

Albania produced 1,942 million metric tons (2,140 tons) of carbon dioxide emissions from industrial sources in 1996.

A total of 2.9% of Albania's lands are protected by environmental laws. Of Albania's 3,000-plus plant species, 17 were endangered as of 2001. Two mammal species and seven bird species were also threatened. Endangered species include the Atlantic sturgeon, Mediterranean monk seal, and the hawksbill turtle.

6 ▌ Population

Albania's population in 2003 was estimated at 3.2 million. The population growth was just 1.1% during 1990–2000. The population projection for the year 2005 is 3.6 million. Average population density was 109 persons per square kilometer (282 persons per square mile). Tiranë, the capital and principal city, had a population of 279,000 in 2001.

7 ▌ Migration

Emigration following World War II (1939–45) has occurred on a very limited scale, mainly for political reasons. Between 1945 and 1990, Albania was virtually isolated from the rest of Europe. In the early 1990s, about 2 million Albanians lived in Serbia and Montenegro (formerly Yugoslavia).

Location: 39°38′ to 42°39′N; 19°16′ to 21°4′E.
Boundary Lengths: Yugoslavia, 287 kilometers (178 miles); Macedonia, 151 kilometers (94 miles); Greece, 282 kilometers (175 miles); coastline, 362 kilometers (225 miles). **Territorial Sea Limit:** 15 miles.

Jane Christo

Two Albanian girls, ages ten and eight, enjoy crocheting.

Many ethnic Albanians live in Greece, Italy, and Macedonia.

At the end of 2000, there were only about 500 Kosovo refugees in Albania. As of 2003, Albania had an estimated net migration rate of -1.39 migrants per 1,000 population.

8 ■ Ethnic Groups

Generally regarded as descendants of the ancient Illyrians, the Albanians make up about 95% of the population. Ethnic Greeks comprise as much as 3% of the populace. Other groups, including Gypsies, Vlachs, Bulgarians, and Serbs, make up the remaining 2%. The Albanians themselves fall into two major groups: the Ghegs in the north and the Tosks in the south, divided by the Shkumbin River.

9 ■ Languages

Albanian (Shqip) is an independent language of the Indo-European family of languages. It was not until 1908 that a common Latin alphabet was established for Albanian. There are two distinct dialects: Gheg, spoken in the north, and Tosk, spoken in the south. During the period between World War I (1914–18) and World War II (1939–45), Gheg was officially favored as standard Albanian. After World War II, because the principal leaders of the regime were southerners, Tosk became the standard. Greek is spoken by a minority in the southeast border area.

10 ▪ Religions

Historically, Islam has been the majority religion of Albania. Today, Albania is a self-proclaimed secular state that allows freedom of religion.

In the total population, the percentage of Muslims remains stable at roughly 65% to 70%, including followers of Sunni Islam and members of the Bektashi school (Shi'a Sufism). Since 1925, Albania has been considered the world center of the Bektashi school.

About 20% of the population are members of the Orthodox Autocephalous Church of Albania (Albanian Orthodox) and about 10% are Roman Catholic. There are a few small Protestant groups.

The 1998 constitution calls for freedom of religion; however, the four main groups of Sunnis, Bektashis, Orthodox, and Catholics have maintained a higher degree of social recognition and status due to their historical presence within the country.

11 ▪ Transportation

Many roads are unsuitable for motor transport. Bicycles and donkeys are common. In 2001, there were 18,000 kilometers (11,185 miles) of paved road. The railroads had a total length of 447 kilometers (228 miles).

Albania's rivers are not navigable, but there is some local shipping on lakes Skadarsko, Ohridsko, and Prespanko. Durrës is the principal port for foreign trade. In 2001, the merchant fleet consisted of seven vessels. In 2001, there were 11 airports, 3 of which had paved runways. Tiranë's international airport connects Albania with major cities throughout the world. In 2001, a total of 146,300 passengers were carried on scheduled domestic and international airline flights.

12 ▪ History

Origins and the Middle Ages: The Albanians are descended from ancient Illyrian or Thracian tribes that may have come to the Balkan Peninsula even before the Greeks. An Illyrian kingdom was formed in the third century B.C. and conquered by Rome in 167 B.C. Present-day Albania was raided by Slav invaders in the sixth century A.D. and taken over by Bulgaria in the ninth century. Some independent kingdoms existed briefly during the second half of the fourteenth century.

From the Ottomans to Independence: By 1479, the Turks gained complete control of the area. Over the following centuries Islam spread throughout most of the country. Turkish rule continued through the nineteenth century. However, during this period nationalistic feelings grew, and often erupted into open rebellion against the Turks.

In November 1912, the National Assembly proclaimed Albania's independence. However, Albania became a principal battleground during World War I and by the time the war ended, portions of Albania were under Italian, French, and Yugoslav control. Albania again asserted its independence in 1920. A government was established, as the Italians and French withdrew.

In 1925, after a period of instability, Ahmet Zogu seized power. In 1928 he declared Albania a kingdom and crowned himself King Zog I. However, Italy invaded Albania in 1939, and Zog was forced into exile. Italy occupied Albania during World War II, but communist-led guerrillas under Enver Hoxha resisted Italian and German forces. With the defeat of the Italians and Germans in World War II, Hoxha established a new government based on communist principles.

Under Communist Rule: The constitution of 1946 declared Albania a people's republic. Over the following decades, Albania became more and more isolated from both the West and the other communist countries. Albania allied itself first with the former Soviet Union, and then with China. As the 1980s began, Albania was locked in a bitter internal conflict. Officials who favored increased relations with the West were executed or purged from the government. During this time, Albania was known as the most rigidly communist country in Europe.

On 11 April 1985, Enver Hoxha died. He had ruled Albania with an iron fist for four decades. After his death, Albania took steps to end its isolation, but was still ruled by the communists.

Democracy and Free Market: By 1990, internal unrest led to mass protests and calls for the government's resignation. After multiparty elections in 1991, a coalition government was formed between Albania's Communist (renamed Socialist) Party and the new Democratic Party. New general elections on 22 March 1992 gave the Democratic Party a majority of seats (92 of 140). Sali Berisha, a cardiologist, was elected president.

Berisha pushed hard for radical reforms to create a market economy and democratic institutions after a half century of international isolation. By the end of 1993, barriers to foreign trade had been removed and relations with other nations had been strengthened. Albania joined the Council of Europe in 1995.

In late 1996 and early 1997, several pyramid-scheme investment funds collapsed. (Pyramid-scheme investment funds accept money from investors, but do not actually invest the money. Instead, they use money from new investors to pay interest due to earlier investors.) Many Albanians believed that the government had used funds provided by the schemes to finance election campaigns. Anger over collapse of the funds led to violence and looting in southern Albania. When the government failed to bring the area under control, order broke down throughout the country and looting occurred nationwide. Berisha accepted the creation of a coalition government to restore order. As violence came closer to Tiranë, France and Italy provided 6,000 peacekeepers to patrol the countryside and restore order so that new elections could be held. The ruling Democratic Party lost its parliamentary majority in June 1997 to the Socialist Party (the former Communist Party), which elected Rexhep Mejdani as president.

In 1998 a new, Western-style constitution defining Albania as a democratic republic was approved in a nationwide referendum. In spring 1999, the crisis in neighboring Kosovo sent hundreds of thousands of refugees into Albania, causing an economic crisis. Aid was provided by international sources, and most of the refugees returned

Biographical Profile

Name: Fatos Thanas Nano
Position: Prime minister of a republic
Took Office: 25 July 2002
Birthplace: Tirana, Albania
Birthdate: 16 September 1952
Education: Degree in political economy and
    Ph.D. in economics from the University
    of Tirana
Spouse: Xhoana
Children: Two children
Of interest: In 1993, Nano was imprisoned
    for corruption, but was acquitted of
    those charges in 1999. He is fluent in
    Italian and English, and proficient in
    Russian, French, Serbian, and Spanish

Fatos Thanas Nano

home by the fall. In January 2001, Albania and Yugoslavia reestablished diplomatic relations, which had been severed during the Kosovo crisis.

Fighting between ethnic Macedonians and ethnic Albanian rebels, largely from the former Kosovo Liberation Army (UCK), in the northwest region of Macedonia around the town of Tetovo intensified in March 2001 (it had begun in 2000). Fears in Macedonia of the creation of a "Greater Albania," including Kosovo and parts of Macedonia, were fueled by the separatist movement.

In June 2002, parliament elected former defense minister Alfred Moisiu as president. In August 2002, Fatos Thanas Nano became prime minister for the fourth time after the Socialist Party decided to merge the roles of prime minister and party chairman. In November 2002, NATO announced that of ten countries aspiring to join the organization, seven would be accepted in 2004, leaving Albania, Macedonia, and Croatia to wait until a later round of expansion. In January 2003, Albania and Macedonia agreed to intensify two-way cooperation, especially in the economic sphere, so as to prepare their way to NATO and European Union (EU) membership.

13 ■ Government

Through most of the 1990s, Albania's government was based on the 29 April 1991 Law on Constitutional Provisions. This law was enacted to provide a transition

Yearly Growth Rate

This economic indicator tells by what percent the economy has increased or decreased when compared with the previous year.

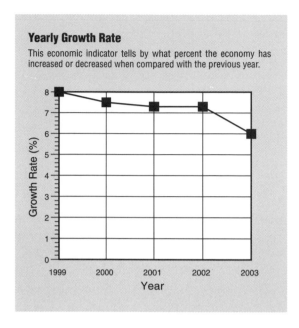

the Party of the Albanian National Front, the Republican Party of Albania, and the Liberal Democratic Union); the Social Democratic Party; the Union for Human Rights Party; the Party of the Democratic Alliance of Albania; and the Albanian-Agrarian Party.

15 ■ Judicial System

The judicial system includes district courts, six courts of appeals, and a supreme court, or Court of Cassation. The district courts are trial-level courts from which appeal can be taken to a court of appeals and then to the Court of Cassation. There also is a Constitutional Court that has authority over how the constitution is interpreted.

16 ■ Armed Forces

In 2002, the estimated strength of the Albanian armed forces was 27,000. This number included 20,000 in the army, 2,500 in the navy, and 4,500 in the air force. As of 2002, the armed forces were being restructured following the 1999 crisis in neighboring Kosovo. Defense spending in 2002 totaled $56.5 million or 1.5% of gross domestic product (GDP).

17 ■ Economy

With the end of communist rule in 1992, farmland was returned to private ownership. But despite significant progress, living standards in Albania are among the lowest in Europe. When socialist-style central planning was abandoned, there was no alternate system to take its place. After falling 45% during 1990–92, Albania's gross domestic product (GDP) began to improve in the mid-1990s and

from a communist form of government to a democratic one. It established the principle of separation of powers, the protection of private property and human rights, a multiparty parliament, and a president with broad powers. In 2002, Alfred Spiro Moisiu of the Socialist Party was elected president, and Fatos Thanas Nano (also of the Socialist Party) was named prime minister that year as well. In 1998 voters approved a new constitution.

Albania is divided into 12 regions (*qarqe*), 36 districts (*rrethe*), 65 cities and towns, and 309 communes.

14 ■ Political Parties

In the elections held in 2001, leading parties were the Socialist Party (the new name of the Communist Party); the Democratic Party-led Union for Victory (an alliance composed of the Democratic Party of Albania, the Movement for Legality Party,

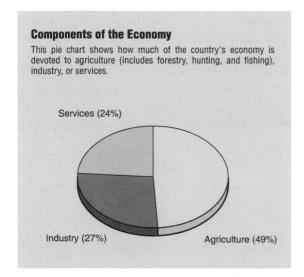

Components of the Economy

This pie chart shows how much of the country's economy is devoted to agriculture (includes forestry, hunting, and fishing), industry, or services.

Services (24%)

Industry (27%)

Agriculture (49%)

annual growth rate of GDP was estimated at 5%. The average inflation rate in 2002 was 6%.

19 ▪ Industry

Major industries include food processing, textiles and clothing, lumber, oil, cement, chemicals, and basic metals. Industrial production fell 44% in 1992 and 10% in 1993, but by 1995 it was growing at a rate of 6%. The return of business to private ownership is proceeding slowly. In 2001, the government privatized a brewery, distillery, dairy, and pharmaceutical company. In 2002, industrial production accounted for 27% of gross domestic product (GDP).

20 ▪ Labor

When communism was abandoned in favor of a free market economy in 1991, a temporary disruption of workers and resources took place, resulting in an estimated unemployment rate of 40% in 1992. By 2001, the official unemployment rate remained high, up to an estimated 30%.

In 1991, workers were granted the legal right to create independent trade unions. All citizens have the right to organize and bargain collectively. As of 2002, unions generally negotiated directly with the government, since all large enterprises were still state owned.

The minimum work age is 16. Minimum wages were approximately $50 per month in 2002, which does not provide a decent living wage for a family.

21 ▪ Agriculture

About 49% of workers are employed in agriculture. Although Albania's moun-

into the twenty-first century. Inflation remained low, the economy was expanding at a rate of approximately 7% a year, and foreign direct investment was growing. As of 2002, nearly all land in Albania was privately owned.

The country's transition to a free-market economy did not come without difficulties, however. Unemployment remained high, and the economy remained based on agriculture (around 50%). Crime and corruption were problems, as were governmental bureaucratic hurdles that hinder business activity. Severe energy shortages caused blackouts and were responsible for small businesses failing. In 2003, the country was increasing its imports of electricity.

The nationwide collapse of pyramid investment schemes in 1997 and a large influx of refugees from Kosovo in 1999 imposed burdens on the Albanian economy.

18 ▪ Income

Albania's gross domestic product (GDP) was estimated at $14 billion in 2002. The

Ceramist Mira Kuçuku decorates pottery in her studio in Tiranë.

tainous terrain limits the amount of land available for agriculture, the cultivated and arable area was about 26% of the total in the mid-1990s. Albania claims to be 95% self-sufficient in food production. Nearly two-thirds of the population is rural, and agriculture provided 49% of GDP in 2001.

Wheat is the principal crop, and corn, oats, sorghum, and potatoes are also important. Greater emphasis is being placed on the production of cash crops, such as cotton, tobacco, rice, sugar beets, vegetables, sunflowers, and fruits and nuts. Estimates of annual crop output include 272,000 tons of wheat, 206,000 tons of corn, 40,000 tons of sugar beets, 640,000 tons of vegetables and melons, 162,000 tons of potatoes, 70,000 tons of grapes, 13,000 tons of oats, and 14,000 tons of sorghum.

22 ■ Domesticated Animals

The major challenge for Albanian animal husbandry (raising of livestock) has been a shortage of feed. The estimated number of livestock is 1.94 million sheep, 4 million

Yearly Balance of Trade

The balance of trade is the difference between what a country sells to other countries (its exports) and what it buys (its imports). If a country imports more than it exports, it has a negative balance of trade (a trade deficit). If exports exceed imports there is a positive balance of trade (a trade surplus).

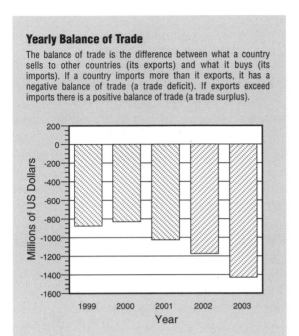

total land area. As a result of exploitation, erosion, and neglect, about 70% of the forested area consists of little more than shoots and wild shrubs. Roundwood production in 2000 totaled 443,000 cubic meters (15,644 cubic feet) with about 73% used for firewood.

poultry, 1.12 million goats, 720,000 cattle, 81,000 hogs, and 65,000 horses. Annual estimates of livestock products include 761,000 tons of cows' milk, 73,000 tons of sheep's milk, 73,000 tons of goats' milk, 34,000 tons of beef and veal, 5,000 tons of pork, 12,000 tons of mutton and lamb, and 20,000 tons of eggs.

23 ▪ Fishing

Fishing is an important occupation along the Adriatic coast. Annual fish production was estimated at 3,320 tons in 2000, of which 995 tons came from marine fishing. Exports of fish products amounted to almost $5.4 million in 2000.

24 ▪ Forestry

Forests cover 1,046,000 hectares (2,585,000 acres), or about 38% of the

25 ▪ Mining

Mineral deposits traditionally associated with Albania include chromite, copper ore, and nickeliferous iron ore. In 2000, chromite production was 80,000 tons. Copper ore concentrate production was 9,000 tons and production of bauxite was 5,000 tons. Albania is one of the few countries producing natural asphalt. Production of asphalt in 2000 was 17,000 tons. Recent cement output has not exceeded the 243,000 tons produced in 1995 and imports have ranged from 500,000 to 600,000 tons per year.

26 ▪ Foreign Trade

Albania exports leather products, apparel, footwear components, tobacco products, and metal ores. The production of chromium ore, formerly an important export product, has plummeted in recent years. Imports include raw materials, machinery, transportation equipment, fuel, minerals, metals, and food.

Italy, Greece, and Germany are the major destinations for Albania's exports. The chief sources of Albania's imports are Italy, Greece, Germany, Bulgaria, Turkey, and Macedonia.

27 ▪ Energy and Power

Albania has both thermal and hydroelectric power stations to generate electricity.

Hydroelectric sources accounted for 97% of the total production in 2000. That year, total power production totaled 4.7 billion kilowatt hours.

Petroleum production was 6,000 barrels per day in 1998. Oil refineries are located at Ballësh, Stalin, Fier, and Cërrik.

28 ■ Social Development

The Act on State Social Insurance provides benefits for disability, old age, survivors, and retirement. Unemployment benefits were introduced in 1993.

Albania's constitution prohibits discrimination based on sex, and women make up roughly half the labor force.

29 ■ Health

In 1992, Albania had 16 hospitals. In 1993, there were also almost 1,000 health centers staffed by primary care physicians and nurses and more than 2,300 walk-in clinics staffed by nurses or midwives. In 1998, there were an estimated 1.3 physicians and 3.8 nurses per 1,000 people. There is a medical school in Tiranë (part of the Enver Hoxha University), and some Albanians receive medical training abroad.

In 2000, the mortality rate was an estimated 6.49 deaths per 1,000 people. Average life expectancy was estimated at 74 years. Albania's infant mortality rate was estimated at 20 per 1,000 live births.

The leading causes of death are cardiovascular disease, trauma, cancer, and respiratory disease.

30 ■ Housing

At the time of the 2001 census, there were about 520,936 residential buildings in the country containing about 783,640 dwellings. As of 1998, about 74% of rural households did not have an indoor toilet and 54% did not have access to running water. In comparison, 18% of urban households were without an indoor toilet and 5% lacked running water. In 2001, about 30% of the dwelling spaces were block flats constructed and owned by the government during the communist era.

31 ■ Education

Preschool training for children ages three through six is general but not obligatory. The basic compulsory school program, extending for eight years (ages 6 to 14), combines practical work with study. Secondary education lasts from three to five years, depending on the type of school attended. These include comprehensive and vocational schools as well as schools specializing in the arts, sports, and foreign languages. The student-to-teacher ratio as of 2003 (the most recent year for which statistics were available) was 22 to 1 for primary education and about 17 to 1 for secondary schools.

Other institutes of higher learning include two agricultural schools, one institute for fine arts, one institute of physical culture, and three teacher-training institutes. All institutions of higher education have a combined enrollment of 30,000 to 40,000 students. The University of Shkodër was established in 1991.

As of 2000, the government claims that complete literacy has been achieved; however, Western estimates put the adult illiteracy rate at 13.5% in 2003 (7% for males, 21% for females).

Selected Social Indicators

The statistics below are the most recent estimates available as of 2003. For comparison purposes, data for the United States and averages for low-income countries and high-income countries are also given. About 15% of the world's 6.4 billion people live in high-income countries, while 40% live in low-income countries.

Indicator	Albania	Low-income countries	High-income countries	United States
Per capita gross national income (GNI)*	$4,960	$2,110	$28,480	$36,110
Population growth rate	0.7%	2.1%	0.7%	1.1%
People per square kilometer of land	115	77	31	31
Life expectancy in years: *male*	72	58	75	75
female	76	60	81	80
Number of physicians per 1,000 people	1.3	1.0	3.0	2.8
Number of pupils per teacher (primary school)	22	40	17	15
Literacy rate (15 years and older)	86.5%	66%	>95%	97%
Television sets per 1,000 people	318	91	735	938
Internet users per 1,000 people	4	10	364	551
Energy consumed per capita (kg of oil equivalent)	284	550	5,366	7,937

* The GNI is the total of all goods and services produced by the residents of a country in a year. The per capita GNI is calculated by dividing a country's GNI by its population and adjusting for relative purchasing power.

n.a. = data not available   > = greater than   < = less than

SOURCES: International Telecommunication Union (ITU). *World Telecommunication Development Report 2003*. Geneva, Switzerland: ITU, 2003; World Bank. *World Development Indicators*. Washington, D.C.: The World Bank, 2004; Central Intelligence Agency. *The World Factbook*. Washington, D.C.: Government Printing Office, 2003.

32 ▪ Media

Most communications organizations are owned and operated by the state. In 2001, there were 120,000 mainline telephones and 250,000 mobile cellular phones. Some villages do not have telephone service at all. Seventeen radio stations (13 AM and 4 FM) were operated by Radiotelevizioni Shqiptar (Albanian Radio and Television-RTVSh). As of 2000, there were 2 national and 50 local television stations. In the same year, there were 1,000,000 radios and 700,000 television sets.

There are several daily newspapers published in Tiranë. In 2002, the four major ones were *Koha Jone* (*Our Time*, circulation 400,000); *Zërii Popullit* (*People's Voice*, circulation 105,000), published by the Socialist Party; *Rlindia Demokratike* (*The Democratic Revival*, circulation 50,000), published by the Democratic Party; and *Bashkimi Kombetar* (circulation 30,000), published by the Democratic Front.

There are about 200 publications overall, including daily and weekly newspapers, magazines, newsletters, and pamphlets. About 15 Greek papers and magazines are distributed, primarily throughout the south. *Albanian Newspaper* (circulation 30,000) is published in Italian and *Albanian Daily News* is a daily paper published in English. Agjensia Telegrafike Shqiptare (Albanian Telegraphic Agency) is the official news agency.

Though the law protects freedom of speech and press, nearly all news stories are biased toward the political and economic interests of the publisher.

As of 2001, there were 10 Internet service providers and about 12,000 Internet users.

33 ■ Tourism and Recreation

Albania slowly became accessible to tourists following the advent of democracy. In promoting travel to Albania, the official tourist agency cites the Adriatic beaches, especially at Durrës, Vlorë, and Sarandë, and the picturesque lakes. In 2000, 317,000 foreign tourists visited Albania.

The most popular sports are soccer, gymnastics, volleyball, and basketball.

34 ■ Famous Albanians

Much Albanian popular lore is based on the exploits of the national hero Gjergj Kastrioti (known as Scanderbeg, 1405–1468), who led his people against the Turks. Ahmet Bey Zogu (1895–1961) was elected first president of the new republic in 1925. In 1928, when Albania became a kingdom, he ascended the throne as Zog I. Two major political leaders were Enver Hoxha (1908–1985), postwar Albania's first premier, minister of foreign affairs, and defense minister; and Mahmet Shehu (1913–1981), who replaced Hoxha as premier in 1954.

Naim Erashëri (1846–1900) was Albania's national poet. His most highly regarded works are *Bagëti e Bujqësi (Cattle and Land), Histori e Skenderbeut (History of Scanderbeg),* and a collection of short poems called *Lulet e Verës (Spring Flowers).* Kostandin Kristoforidhi (K. Nelko, 1827–1895) translated the Old and New Testaments into Albanian and compiled a standard Albanian-Greek dictionary. Faik Konitza (1875–1942), prewar Albanian minister to Washington, D.C. edited a literary review, *Albania,* which became the most important publication for Albanian writers living abroad. Gjergj Fishta (1871–1940), a Franciscan friar who was active in the nationalist movement, wrote a long epic poem, *Lahuta e Malcís (The Lute of the Mountains),* which is regarded as a masterpiece of Albanian literature. Bishop Fan Stylian Noli (1882–1965), a political leader in the early 1920s, was Albania's foremost translator of Shakespeare, Ibsen, Cervantes, and other world classics. Lasgush Poradeci (1899–1987) was a highly regarded lyric poet.

35 ■ Bibliography

Elsie, Robert. *The Dictionary of Albanian Religion, Mythology, and Folklore.* New York: New York University Press, 2000.

Lear, Aaron. *Albania.* Philadelphia, PA: Chelsea House, 2000.

Marx, Trish. *One Boy from Kosovo.* New York: Lothrop, Lee and Shepard, 2000.

Mead, Alice. *Girl of Kosovo.* New York: Farrar Straus Giroux, 2001.

Wright, David K. *Albania.* Chicago, IL: Children's Press, 1997.

Algeria

Democratic and Popular Republic of Algeria
Al-Jumhuriyah al-Jaza'iriyah ad-Dimuqratiyah ash-Sha'biyah

Capital: Algiers (Alger).

Flag: The national flag consists of two equal vertical stripes, one green and one white, with a red crescent enclosing a five-pointed red star in the center.

Anthem: *Kassaman (We Pledge).*

Monetary Unit: The Algerian dinar (DA) is a paper currency of 100 centimes. There are coins of 1, 2, 5, 10, and 50 centimes and 1, 5 and 10 dinars, and notes of 10, 20, 50, 100, and 200 dinars. DA1 = $0.0127 (or $1 = DA78.46; as of May 2003).

Weights and Measures: The metric system is the legal standard.

Holidays: New Year's Day, 1 January; Labor Day, 1 May; Overthrow of Ben Bella, 19 June; Independence Day, 5 July; Revolution Day, 1 November. Muslim religious holidays include 'Id al-Fitr, 'Id al-'Adha', 1st of Muharram (Muslim New Year), and Milad an-Nabi. Christians observe their own religious holidays.

Time: GMT.

1 ▪ Location and Size

Situated in northwestern Africa along the Mediterranean Sea, Algeria is the second-largest country on the continent. Comparatively, it is slightly less than 3.5 times the size of Texas, with a total area of 2,381,740 square kilometers (919,595 square miles). The country shares borders with Tunisia, Libya, Niger, Mali, Mauritania, the Western Sahara, and Morocco. The total boundary length is 6,343 kilometers (3,933 miles). The total coastline is 998 kilometers (620 miles).

Land boundary and claims disputes with Libya and Tunisia are unresolved.

Algeria's capital city, Algiers, is located on the northern boundary of the country along the Mediterranean Sea.

2 ▪ Topography

The parallel mountain ranges of the Tell (or Maritime Atlas) and the Saharan Atlas divide Algeria into three basic zones running generally east-west: the Mediterranean zone, or Tell; the High Plateaus, including the regions of Great and Small Kabylie; and the Sahara Desert, which accounts for at least 80% of Algeria's total land area. The highest point is Mount Tahat (2,918 meters/9,753 feet), in the Ahaggar Range of the Sahara. The lowest

Geographic Profile

Geographic Features

Size ranking: 11 of 193

Highest elevation: 2,918 meters (9,753 feet) at Mount Tahat

Lowest elevation: -40 meters (-131 feet) at Chott Melrhir

Land Use*

Arable land: 3%

Permanent crops: 0%

Forests: 1%

Other: 96%

Weather**

Average annual precipitation: 69.1 centimeters (27.2 inches)

Average temperature in January: 10.3°C (50.5°F)

Average temperature in July: 24.4°C (75.9°F)

---

* *Arable Land: Land used for temporary crops, like meadows for mowing or pasture, gardens, and greenhouses.*

Permanent crops: Land cultivated with crops that occupy its use for long periods, such as cocoa, coffee, rubber, fruit and nut orchards, and vineyards.

Forests: Land containing stands of trees.

Other: Any land not specified, including built-on areas, roads, and barren land.

** *The measurements for precipitation and average temperatures were taken at weather stations closest to the country's largest city.*

Precipitation and average temperature can vary significantly within a country, due to factors such as latitude, altitude, coastal proximity, and wind patterns.

point is Chott Melrihr (-40 meters/-131 feet), located in the north region of the country.

Only the main rivers of the Tell have water all year round, but the summer flow is generally small. None of the rivers are navigable. The longest river is the Chelif (230 kilometers/143 miles), which empties into the Mediterranean Sea.

The mountainous areas of the High Plateaus are poorly watered. In the High Plateaus are many salt marshes and dry or shallow salt lakes (*sebkhas* or *chotts*). Farther south, the land becomes increasingly arid, merging into the completely dry desert.

Algeria lies on the African Tectonic Plate. Northwestern Algeria is a seismically active area.

3 ■ Climate

Northern Algeria lies within the temperate zone, and its climate is similar to that of other Mediterranean countries, although the variety of the land provides sharp contrasts in temperature. The coastal region has a pleasant climate, with winter temperatures averaging from 10 to 12°C (50 to 54°F) and average summer temperatures ranging from 24 to 26°C (75 to 79°F).

Farther inland, the climate changes. Winters average 4 to 6°C (39 to 43°F), with considerable frost and occasional snow on the mountains; summers average 26 to 28°C (79 to 82°F). In the Sahara Desert, temperatures range from -10 to 34°C (14 to 93°F), with extreme highs of 49°C (120°F). There are daily variations of more than 44°C (80°F). Winds are frequent and violent and rainfall is irregular and unevenly distributed.

ALGERIA

0   100   200   300 Miles

0   100   200   300 Kilometers

MEDITERRANEAN SEA

Alboran Sea

Golfe de Bejaïa

Algiers

Annaba

Blida   Bejaïa   Skikda

Oran   Mostaganem   Setif   **Constantine**

Sidi Bel Abbès   Batna

Oujda   **Tlemcen**   Djelfa   Biskra

Taza   Redeyef   *Golfe de Gabès*

A T L A S   M O U N T A I N S   Laghouat   Touggourt   **T U N I S I A**

A T L A S   S A H A R I E N

Ghardaïa

Béchar   Ouargla

Zagora   **Grand Erg Occidental**

Oued Draa   El Golea   Dirg

M O R O C C O

Oued Saoura   **Grand Erg Oriental**

Akka   Tabelbala   Plateau du Tademaït   I-n-Amenas

Tindouf   Adrar   I-n-Belbel

WESTERN SAHARA   El Mansour   Titaf

Chenachane   Tarat   **L I B Y A**

MAURITANIA   *Erg Chech*   Ghat

I-n-Amguel   Djanet

A H A G G A R   M T S .

Silet   Mt. Tahat   9,573 ft.   2918 m.

Tamanrasset

S A H A R A   D E S E R T

Algeria

M A L I   Ti-n-Zaouâtene   **N I G E R**

N   W   E   S

Location: 18°57′ to 37°5′N; 8°44′W to 12°E. **Boundary Lengths:** Mediterranean coastline, 1,104 kilometers (686 miles); Tunisia, 958 kilometers (595 miles); Libya, 982 kilometers (610 miles); Niger, 956 kilometers (594 miles); Mali, 1,376 kilometers (855 miles); Mauritania, 463 kilometers (288 miles); Morocco, 1,637 kilometers (1,017 miles). **Territorial Sea Limit:** 12 miles.

Gordon Barbery

A vast majority of Algerians follow the Muslim faith in mosques such as this.

4 ▪ Plants and Animals

Characteristic trees of northern Algeria are the olive and the cork oak. The mountain regions contain large forests of evergreens (Aleppo pine, juniper, and evergreen oak) and some deciduous trees. The forests are inhabited by boars and jackals, which are all that remain of the many wild animals once common. Fig, eucalyptus, agave, and various palm trees grow in the warmer areas. Esparto grass, alfa, and drinn are common in the semiarid regions. On the coastal plain, the grape vine is indigenous.

Vegetation in the Sahara is sparse and widely scattered. Animal life is varied but scarce. Camels are used extensively. Other mammals are jackals, jerboas, and rabbits. The desert also abounds with poisonous and nonpoisonous snakes, scorpions, and numerous insects.

5 ▪ Environment

Algeria's principal environmental problem is desertification. Soil erosion from overgrazing adds to the effect. Other significant environmental problems include water shortages and pollution. The small amount of water available in Algeria is threatened by regular droughts. The problem is further complicated by lack of sewage control and pollutants from the oil industry, as well as other industrial effluents. The Mediterranean Sea has also been contaminated by the oil industry, fertilizer runoff, and soil erosion.

Endangered or extinct species include the Barbary hyena, Barbary leopard, Barbary macaque, and Mediterranean monk seal. Of the 92 species of mammals, 15 were threatened as of late 2001, as well as 8 of the 192 species of birds.

6 ▪ Population

The population of Algeria was estimated at 31.8 million in 2003. The projected population for the year 2005 is 35.1 million. The population is concentrated in the cultivated areas of the north (more than 90% live in the northern eighth of the country) and thinly distributed in the plateau and desert regions. In 2001, greater Algiers had about 4.4 million people.

7 ▪ Migration

In 1999 there were 165,000 refugees from Western Sahara in the Tindouf region of southwestern Algeria. As of 2000, there were a total of 169,500 refugees remaining in Algeria. In 2003, the net migration rate for Algeria was estimated at -0.4 migrants per 1,000 population, which was a loss of 52,000 people.

8 Ethnic Groups

The citizens of Algeria, called Algerians, consist almost entirely of Arabs. The Berbers (an Arab group) are descendants of the original inhabitants of Algeria and are divided into many subgroups. They account for 99% of the population. The Kabyles (Kaba'il), mostly farmers, live in the compact mountainous section in the northern part of the country between Algiers and Constantine. The Chaouia (Shawiyyah) live in the Aurès Mountains of the northeast. The Mzab, or Mozabites, include sedentary date growers in the Ued Mzab oases. Desert groups include the Tuareg, Tuat, and Wargla (Ouargla).

Europeans are of French, Corsican, Spanish, Italian, and Maltese ancestry. Algeria's European population was estimated at less than 1% of the population in 2003. About half the Jews in Algeria are descended from converted Berbers and the remainder are mainly descendants of Spanish Jews.

9 Languages

The sole official and majority language is Arabic, with many variations and dialects. Many Algerians also speak French. About one-fifth of the population speaks a wide variety of Berber dialects, particularly in Kabylie, in the Aurès, and in smaller, relatively protected areas in the mountains and the Sahara. Berber is a distinct branch of the Hamitic language group.

10 Religions

About 99% of the population adheres to Islam, which is the state religion. Most Muslims are adherents of the Maliki rite of the Sunni sect, with a few Hanafi adherents. The law prohibits assemblies to practice any faith other than Islam. However, there are Roman Catholic churches that conduct services without government interference. Non-Muslims usually meet in private homes for worship services.

Many citizens who practice non-Muslim faiths have fled the country because of the civil war. The number of Christians and Jews is thus significantly lower than in the early 1990s. The small Christian community, which is mostly Roman Catholic, has approximately 25,000 members and the Jewish community numbers fewer than 100.

11 Transportation

In 2002, Algeria's nationally owned railroad had about 4,772 kilometers (2,965 miles) of track. The system consists of a main east-west line linked with the railways of Tunisia and Morocco. It also links with lines serving the mining regions of Béchar (formerly Colomb Béchar); the High Plateaus; the date-producing areas of Biskra, Touggourt, and Tebessa; and the main port cities.

In 2002, there were 104,000 kilometers (64,625 miles) of roads, of which about 75% were paved, used by 589,000 passenger cars and 396,200 commercial vehicles. The French colonial government built a good road system, partly for military purposes, which has not been well maintained since independence. However, new roads have been built linking the Sahara oil fields with the coast. Algeria's portion of the trans-Sa-

Gordon Barbery

A stone head found in a Roman ruin. The region that is now Algeria was an important center of Roman culture.

12 ■ History

Before the period of recorded history, the North African coastal area now known as Algeria was inhabited by Berber tribal groups, from whom many present-day Algerians are descended. Phoenician sailors established coastal settlements. After the eighth century B.C., the territory was controlled by Carthage, the largest Phoenician settlement. Roman dominance dates from the fall of Carthage in 146 B.C. Completely annexed in A.D. 40, the region (known as Numidia) became a center of Roman culture. Christianity flourished, as did agriculture and commerce. Despite the prosperity of the Roman cities and the cereal-growing countryside, there were frequent Berber revolts. The Roman influence gradually declined, especially after the Vandal invasion of 430–31. The Byzantine Empire conquered eastern Numidia in the sixth century.

After the Arab conquest began in 637, the area was known as Al-Maghrib al-Awsat, or the Middle West. Arabs from the east attacked in the eleventh century. The Almoravid dynasty from Morocco also took possession of part of the region during this period. They were followed by Almohads a century later. Although these and other dynasties and individuals united the territory and consolidated it with Morocco and Spain, local rulers retained considerable power.

Spain conquered part of the coast in the early sixteenth century, and Algerians asked for aid from 'Aruj, known as Barbarossa, a Turkish pirate. He expelled the Spaniards from some of their coastal footholds, made himself sultan, and conquered additional territory. Spain held a small area around Oran until 1708 and controlled it again from 1732 to 1791.

haran highway, formally known as the Road of African Unity, stretches about 420 kilometers (260 miles) from Hassi Marroket to the Niger border south of Tamanrasset. It was completed in 1985.

Algiers is the principal seaport. Algeria's merchant fleet numbered 73 ships totaling 903,944 gross registered tons as of 2002.

An extensive air service uses 136 airports and airstrips. The main international airport is about 20 kilometers (12 miles) from Algiers. Air Algérie, the national airline, provides international service, and carried 3.24 million people in 2001.

Algiers became increasingly independent and, joining with other states along the coast, thrived on piracy. At this time, it had diplomatic and trade relations with many European countries, including France. But with the defeat (though not suppression) of the pirates by United States and European fleets during 1815–16, and with the growing European interest in acquiring overseas colonies, Algiers was seen as a possible addition to either the British or the French empire. In 1830, the French took over the principal ports, gained control of the northern regions, and set up a system of fortified posts. Thereafter, revolts often broke out, notably the guerrilla war from 1830 to 1847 led by the legendary hero Abd al-Qader, and the Kabyle rebellion in 1871. Other sections, however, remained independent of France until the first decade of the twentieth century.

Al-Jazair, as it was called in Arabic, became, in French, Algérie, a name that France applied to the territory for the first time in 1839. In 1848, northern Algeria was proclaimed a part of France and was organized into three provinces. Following the Franco-Prussian War of 1870–71, large numbers of French colonizers settled the most fertile lands, as did other Europeans at the invitation of France. Muslims had no political rights except for limited participation in local financial decisions.

Following World War I (1914–18), France took the first steps toward making all of Algeria an integral part of France. In 1919, voting rights were given to a few Muslims, based on education and military service qualifications. (French citizenship had previously been open to Muslims who renounced their religious status.)

During World War II (1939–45), in exchange for loyalty to France, many

EPD Photos

Abd al-Qader, a political leader and marabout (a member of a Muslim religious order believed to have supernatural powers), led the Muslim resistance against the French during the 1840s.

Muslims hoped for increased rights, and moderates believed that France might be persuaded to grant Algeria a separate status while retaining close diplomatic, economic, and defense ties. In 1957, all Muslims became French subjects, but about 9 million Muslims and 500,000 Europeans voted in separate elections for a joint assembly.

The Rise of the FLN: Meanwhile, younger nationalists had formed what would become known as the National Liberation Front (Front de Libération Nationale-

FLN), and a guerrilla war was launched on 1 November 1954. The FLN's National Liberation Army (Armée de Libération Nationale; ALN) carried out acts of terrorism and sabotage throughout Algeria and gained increasing mass support. Eventually, France was forced to maintain at least 450,000 troops in Algeria. During more than seven years of civil war, more than 100,000 Muslim guerrillas and civilians and 10,000 French soldiers lost their lives.

The war in Algeria toppled several French governments before causing the downfall of the Fourth Republic in May 1958. General Charles de Gaulle was then brought to power by French rightists and military groups in Algeria. To their surprise, however, he pursued a policy of preparing for Algerian independence. He offered self-determination to Algeria in September 1958. Independence was formally proclaimed on 3 July 1962, despite a program of counterterrorism by the French Secret Army Organization operating in Algeria.

With independence achieved, a seven-man Political Bureau, set up as the policymaking body of the FLN, took over control of the country on 5 August 1962. Ahmed Ben Bella became the first premier, and Ferhat Abbas was chosen speaker of the Assembly. The Assembly adopted a constitution, which was endorsed in September 1963.

Elected president in October, Ben Bella began to nationalize foreign-owned land and industry. Opposition to his authoritarian leadership led to an outbreak of armed revolts in July 1964 and to open attacks by leading political figures. On 19 June 1965, the Ben Bella government was overthrown in a bloodless takeover directed by Colonel Houari Boumedienne, first deputy premier and defense minister. The 1963 constitution was suspended, and a revolutionary council headed by Boumedienne took power.

Bendjedid and Government Reform: The new government shifted to a more gradual approach to national development, with deliberate economic planning and an emphasis on financial stability. During the 1970s, the council nationalized the oil industry and initiated farm reforms. Boumedienne was officially elected president in December 1976 but died two years later.

The FLN Central Committee, with strong army backing, chose Colonel Chadli Bendjedid as the party's leader, and he became president on 7 February 1979. After a period of transition, the Bendjedid government moved toward more moderate policies, expanding powers for the provinces and state enterprises.

Serious internal trouble developed in 1988 when young Algerians rioted over high prices, unemployment, and the dictatorship of an aging and corrupt revolutionary government. Shocked by the 500 deaths in the streets, Bendjedid moved to liberalize his government. New political parties were allowed to form outside the FLN. In addition, the prime minister and cabinet were made responsible to the National Assembly.

Burdened by heavy debts and low oil prices, Bendjedid was forced to follow tight economic policies and to abandon socialism for the free market-actions that further inflamed his opposition, now led by the Islamic Salvation Front (FIS). In 1989, the FIS won 55% of urban election seats while the FLN maintained power in the countryside. Elections to the National Assembly, postponed six months, were held in December 1991 under relatively free conditions. FIS candidates

Gordon Barbery

A view of the main marketplace of an Algerian city.

won 188 out of 231 contested seats, needing only 28 more places in a second vote to control the 430-member Assembly. The FLN won only 16 seats.

The army, disappointed with the election results, arrested FIS leaders and postponed the second-stage vote indefinitely. Bendjedid resigned under pressure from the army. Mohammed Boudiaf, a hero of the revolution, returned from exile to lead the High State Council that the army established. A harsh crackdown on Islamists began. The FIS was banned and its local councils were closed. As acts of terrorism continued by both sides in 1992 and 1993, the regime declared a state of emergency, set up special

security courts, and arrested more than 5,000 persons. Boudiaf was assassinated in June 1992, to be replaced by Ali Kafi with Redha Malek as prime minister in August 1993. In January 1994, Defense Minister Liamine Zeroual was named president and the five-man presidential council was abolished.

Parties accounting for 80% of the vote in the 1991 parliamentary elections were excluded from participating, but the government claimed that 75% of registered voters participated in the 1994 election. Zeroual's first act as president was to pass a new constitution that greatly expanded presidential powers. Voters approved the new constitution in an effort to give the government

Biographical Profile

Name: Abdelaziz Bouteflika
Position: President of a republic
Took Office: 28 April 1999
Birthplace: Oujda, Morocco
Birthdate: 2 March 1937
Religion: Islam
Of interest: Bouteflika has often been called the "consensus candidate," referring to his strong interests in finding solutions to international crises rather than domestic problems

Abdelaziz Bouteflika

the power to stop civil conflict, which had claimed between 60,000 and 100,000 lives since 1992. The elections did not stop the terrorist activity, and by 1997 bombings and massacres had become common. Despite the political instability, pro-government parties won the parliamentary elections of June 1997. Three nighttime massacres in Algiers killed hundreds of civilians in September 1997.

Algeria made an appeal to the UN Human Rights Commission in March 1998 for help with its domestic terrorism problem. However, the government refused to allow international observers to investigate the mass killings.

Boudiaf unexpectedly stepped down in February 1999, and new elections were held in April. Amid allegations of massive electoral fraud, Abdelaziz Bouteflika was elected president. Before the year ended, he opened a dialogue with opposition groups and took steps to fight corruption.

In April 2001, a Berber youth taken into custody by the police was killed, sparking months of demonstrations and rioting in the northeastern region of Kabylie. More than 90 people died in the unrest. In May, the mainly Berber party, the Rally for Culture and Democracy, withdrew from the government in protest against the government's handling of the unrest. In October, Bouteflika agreed to a constitutional amendment granting national recognition to the Berber language, Tamazight. However, the language would not be granted "official" status, like Arabic.

In parliamentary elections held on 30 May 2002, the FLN won 199 of 389 seats in the National Assembly; it was one of 23 parties participating. Four parties, including two Berber parties, boycotted the elections, which were marred by violence and low voter turnout (47%).

On 3 March 2003, French president Jacques Chirac visited Algiers, the first state visit by a French president since Algeria won independence in 1962. He laid flowers at a monument for Algerians who fought the French during the war, which was regarded as an act of reconciliation. Chirac also called on the government to use dialogue to end the Islamic revolt that has been ongoing since 1992.

13 ■ Government

Algerian voters approved a new constitution in 1996 that strengthened the already dominant role of the president. Under the new constitution, a second legislative body called the Council of the Nation would join the National Assembly. One-third of the Council is appointed by the president, and the rest are elected by local and regional governments. The Council must approve any legislation from the National Assembly with a three-fourths majority. The 389 deputies of the National Assembly are elected to five-year terms.

The commune is the basic unit of local government, and there were 1,541 communes in 2002.

14 ■ Political Parties

In September 1989 the government approved a multiparty system. By December 1990, more than 30 legal political parties existed, including the Islamic Salvation Front (FIS), the National Liberation Front (FLN), and the Socialist Forces Front (FFS).

Twenty-three parties participated in the May 2002 parliamentary elections. Two Berber parties boycotted the elections, including the Rally for Culture and Democracy and the Socialist Forces Front. The FLN took a majority of seats in the National Assembly. Also winning seats were Islah, the National Democratic Rally, the Movement for a Peaceful Society, the Workers' Party, the Algerian National Front, the Islamic Renaissance Movement, the Party of Algerian Renewal, and the Movement of National Understanding.

15 ■ Judicial System

The judicial system includes civil and military courts. Within each *wilayat* (district) is a court for civil and some criminal cases. At the head of the system is the Supreme Court. The Special Court of State Security was abolished in 1995.

Algeria's legal codes, adopted in 1963, are based on the laws of Islam and of other North African and Socialist states, as well as on French laws.

A Constitutional Council reviews the constitutionality of treaties, laws, and regulations. It is not a part of the judiciary, but it can nullify unconstitutional laws.

16 ■ Armed Forces

Six months of military service is compulsory for males. In 2000, the army had 105,000 officers and men, plus reserves of up to 150,000. The navy had 7,000 men. Vessels included 2 submarines, 3 frigates, 5 corvettes (frigates and corvettes are types of warships), and 11 missile patrol

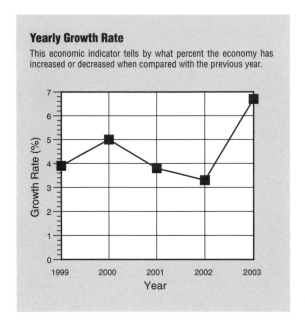

Yearly Growth Rate

This economic indicator tells by what percent the economy has increased or decreased when compared with the previous year.

craft. The air force had 10,000 men, about 242 combat aircraft, and 60 combat helicopters.

17 ▪ Economy

Saharan oil and natural gas have been important export items since 1959, and they dominate Algeria's economy, accounting for more than 95% of total export value and 30% of gross domestic product (GDP). Algeria is the largest supplier of natural gas to the European Union (EU). The real growth rate in 1998 was 3.2%, and it was forecast at 5.3% in 2004. These healthy growth rates in the early twenty-first century were driven by real export growth, based on expanding oil production. As of 2003, Algeria had a large trade surplus and high foreign exchange reserves and had reduced its foreign debt.

Agriculture produces only about 10% of Algeria's GDP every year, and meets only a small portion of the country's needs. In the late 1990s and into the 2000s, challenges to the Algerian economy included terrorism, inefficient agricultural methods, and an unemployment rate of 34% in 2001 that extended into the ranks of professionals, engineers, and highly trained workers.

18 ▪ Income

In 2001 Algeria's gross domestic product (GDP) was $177 billion, or an estimated $5,600 per person. The annual growth rate of GDP was estimated at 3.8%. The average inflation rate in 2001 was 3%.

19 ▪ Industry

Industries, which are concentrated around Algiers and Oran, include carpet mills, cement factories, chemical plants, automobile assembly plants, food-processing plants, oil refineries, soap factories, and textile plants. Other major industries produce bricks and tiles, rolled steel, farm machinery, electrical supplies, machine tools, phosphates, sulfuric acid, paper and cartons, matches, and tobacco products. As of 2000, industry accounted for about 33% of the nation's gross domestic product (GDP). The hydrocarbons sector (mostly petroleum and natural gas) alone accounted for 30% of GDP in 2003 and over 95% of income from exports.

20 ▪ Labor

The minimum age for employment is 16 years. Child labor remains a problem in agriculture and in the informal economy. In 2001, the estimated workforce stood at 9.4 million. About 34% of the workforce was unemployed in 2001. As of 2002, the minimum wage was $105 per month. This amount does not provide a family with a decent standard of living. Approximately two-thirds of Algerian workers were unionized as of 2002.

21 ▌ Agriculture

Although almost 25% of the population is engaged in agriculture (including subsistence farming), only 3% of Algeria's land is cultivated. The soil is poor and subject to erosion, and the water supply is generally irregular and insufficient. In 2003, agriculture contributed 8% to the gross domestic product (GDP).

The main agricultural products continue to be wheat, barley, pulses, fresh vegetables, dates, table and wine grapes, figs, olives, and citrus. Estimated agricultural output annually includes 1.1 million tons of wheat, 410,000 tons of barley, 996,000 tons of potatoes, 955,000 tons of tomatoes, 307,000 tons of oranges, 78,000 tons of grapes, and 428,000 tons of dates. In 2001, nearly 6.6 million tons of cereals were imported, including 4.5 million tons of wheat. The total cost for imported cereals was nearly $996 million. Algeria is one of the world's largest agricultural import markets. Imports of food and agricultural products amount to about $2.8 billion per year.

Government policy aims at increased use of fertilizers and improved seeds, conversion of vineyards to the production of cereals and other staple foods, and achievement of self-sufficiency in food production.

22 ▌ Domesticated Animals

About half of the livestock is owned by only 5% of the herdsmen. There are an estimated 16.75 million sheep, 3.4 million goats, 1.65 million head of cattle, 200,000

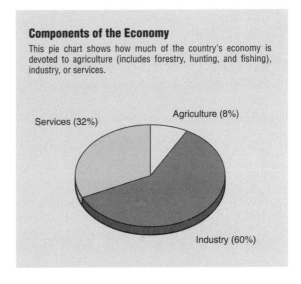

Components of the Economy

This pie chart shows how much of the country's economy is devoted to agriculture (includes forestry, hunting, and fishing), industry, or services.

Services (32%) Agriculture (8%)

Industry (60%)

donkeys, 150,000 camels, 70,000 mules, and 55,000 horses. There were also 105 million chickens. Algeria is self-sufficient in poultry meat and eggs, but must import everything needed to produce them (chicks, hatching eggs, feed, veterinary products, equipment). Algeria has a severe shortage of milk, meat, and cheese and must therefore rely on imports. Algeria produces about 1 billion liters (264 million gallons) of milk annually, while consumption amounts to 3 billion liters (792 million gallons).

23 ▌ Fishing

Fishing is fairly extensive along the coast, but the industry is relatively undeveloped. Sardines, bogue, mackerel, anchovies, and shellfish are caught. The 2000 catch was 100,000 tons, up from the 1997 catch of 99,337 tons.

Yearly Balance of Trade

The balance of trade is the difference between what a country sells to other countries (its exports) and what it buys (its imports). If a country imports more than it exports, it has a negative balance of trade (a trade deficit). If exports exceed imports there is a positive balance of trade (a trade surplus).

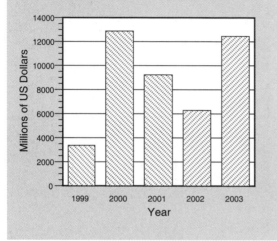

24 ■ Forestry

Only 1.6% of the land is forested. The mountain ranges contain dense forests of evergreens (evergreen oak, Aleppo pine, and cedar) and deciduous trees, whereas the warmer regions contain large numbers of fruit and palm trees. Algeria is an important producer of cork. Other forestry products are firewood, charcoal, and wood for industrial use. In 2000, roundwood production was estimated at 7.5 million cubic meters (94.7 million cubic feet).

25 ■ Mining

Algeria's phosphate deposits at Djebel Onk, in the northeast, are among the largest in the world, with an output of 877,000 tons in 2000. There are deposits of high-grade iron ore at Ouenza, near the Tunisian border. Production of iron ore totaled 1.65 million tons in 2000. Other mineral production in 2000 included zinc concentrate (10,452 tons), bentonite (22,708 tons), lead concentrate (818 tons), mercury (215,625 kilograms/475,371 pounds), crude barite (51,925 tons), salt (182,000 tons), hydraulic lime (96,000 tons), and marble (700,000 tons). Silver, kaolin, sulfur, fuller's earth, and strontium are also mined.

Two gold projects, Amesmessa and Tirek, in the southern Hoggar region, are under development by the South African Council for Mineral Technology.

26 ■ Foreign Trade

Crude oil and natural gas account for nearly all of Algeria's exports. Industrial equipment, semifinished goods, and foodstuffs dominate the country's imports. In 1986, because of a severe drop in oil prices, exports declined and Algeria experienced a trade deficit for the first time since 1978. It was the largest ever. Rising oil prices during 1999 brought back a trade surplus.

The majority of Algerian exports go to Italy, France, the United States, and Spain. The majority of imports come from France, the United States, and Italy.

27 ■ Energy and Power

Natural gas and petroleum dominate the economy. In 2003, their exports were valued at more than 90% of total exports, and around 30% of gross domestic product (GDP). Algeria's natural gas reserves are among the world's 10 largest, totaling an estimated 4.5 trillion cubic meters (158.9 trillion cubic feet) as of 2002. Proven reserves of crude oil amounted to 9.2 billion barrels in 2002.

A busy street in an Algerian city.

Installed electrical generating capacity in 2001 totaled 6 million kilowatts.

28 ▮ Social Development

A social insurance system for old age, disability, sickness, and death covers all employees and self-employed persons. Only salaried workers are entitled to unemployment benefits.

The Family Code, based on Islamic principles, basically treats women as legal minors for life, under the authority of the father, husband, or other male head of the family. The code permits polygamy (having more than one wife) and does not allow marriage between a Muslim woman and a non-Muslim man, while allowing a Muslim man to marry outside the faith. In a court of law, a woman's testimony is not considered equal to a man's, and women do not have full legal guardianship of their children. The father is required to sign all official documents.

Ethnic tensions exist between Arabs and Berbers, who were Algeria's original inhabitants. In 1995, the government created the High Commission for Berber Affairs to protect and promote Berber language and culture.

As of 2002, the government's human rights record remained poor. Abuses included torture and massacres of suspected Islamic militants.

29 ▦ Health

In 1990, Algeria had 284 hospitals with 60,124 beds. There were also 1,309 health centers, 510 polyclinics, and 475 maternity hospitals. Medical personnel included 23,550 doctors, 2,134 pharmacists, and 7,199 dentists.

Free medical care was introduced in 1974 under a Social Security system that reimburses 80% of private consultations and prescription drugs.

In 2000, the average life expectancy was 71 years. Infant mortality was 33 per 1,000 live births.

The principal health problems have been tuberculosis, malaria, trachoma, and malnutrition. In 2000, malnutrition was present in an estimated 18% of all children under the age of five. In 2000 fewer than 1 in every 100 adults was infected with the human immunodeficiency virus (HIV), which causes acquired immunodeficiency syndrome (AIDS).

30 ▦ Housing

The need for adequate housing is a serious problem in Algeria. The government, predicting a need for almost 2 million new homes, launched programs in the late 1990s to support housing construction and home ownership. In 2000, about 94% of the population had access to clean water; 73% had access to improved sanitation systems.

31 ▦ Education

Education is officially required for children between the ages of 6 and 15. The public schools are regulated jointly by the Ministry of Education and the Ministry of Religious Affairs, and the study of Islam is a required part of the curriculum. Arabic is the official language, although French and Berber are also in widespread usage. The primary pupil-teacher ratio averages 28 to 1.

There are 10 universities, along with 5 centers, 7 colleges, and 5 institutes for higher learning. The University of Algiers (founded in 1909), its affiliated institutes, and other regional universities enroll between 260,000 and 280,000 students. The universities provide a varied program of instruction. Many technical colleges also are in operation.

The adult illiteracy rate for the year 2003 was estimated at 30% (males, 22%; females, 39%).

32 ▦ Media

President Bouteflika has maintained that the media should ultimately be at the service of the state. Radio and television remain under government control. Though there are independent newspapers, it is difficult for them to operate, since the government controls imports of paper and of equipment needed for printing.

As of 2002, there were five daily newspapers: *Al-Moudjahid* (in French and Arabic), *An-Nasr* (*The Victory,* in Arabic), *Ach-Chaab* (in Arabic), *Al-Joumhouria* (in Arabic), and *Le Jeune Independent* (in French).

Algeria had Arabic and French radio networks with an estimated total of 25 AM, 1 FM, and 8 shortwave radio stations in 1999 and a total of 46 television stations in 1995, all operated by the national television network. As of 2000, there were about 244 radios and 110 television sets for every 1,000 people. Two Internet service providers served about 180,000 customers in 2001. Telephones numbered 2.3 mil-

Selected Social Indicators

The statistics below are the most recent estimates available as of 2003. For comparison purposes, data for the United States and averages for low-income countries and high-income countries are also given. About 15% of the world's 6.4 billion people live in high-income countries, while 40% live in low-income countries.

Indicator	Algeria	Low-income countries	High-income countries	United States
Per capita gross national income (GNI)*	$5,530	$2,110	$28,480	$36,110
Population growth rate	2.4%	2.1%	0.7%	1.1%
People per square kilometer of land	13	77	31	31
Life expectancy in years: *male*	69	58	75	75
female	72	60	81	80
Number of physicians per 1,000 people	1.0	1.0	3.0	2.8
Number of pupils per teacher (primary school)	28	40	17	15
Literacy rate (15 years and older)	70%	66%	>95%	97%
Television sets per 1,000 people	114	91	735	938
Internet users per 1,000 people	16	10	364	551
Energy consumed per capita (kg of oil equivalent)	898	550	5,366	7,937

* The GNI is the total of all goods and services produced by the residents of a country in a year. The per capita GNI is calculated by dividing a country's GNI by its population and adjusting for relative purchasing power.

n.a. = data not available   > = greater than   < = less than

SOURCES: International Telecommunication Union (ITU). *World Telecommunication Development Report 2003*. Geneva, Switzerland: ITU, 2003; World Bank. *World Development Indicators*. Washington, D.C.: The World Bank, 2004; Central Intelligence Agency. *The World Factbook*. Washington, D.C.: Government Printing Office, 2003.

lion main lines in 1998, with an additional 33,500 cellular subscribers recorded in 1999. Satellite, cable, and radiotelephone services link Algeria with most other parts of the world.

Though the constitution ensures freedom of speech and press, a 1990 law restricts such speech in the name of national and domestic security. The government has broad powers to restrict information.

33 ■ Tourism and Recreation

Among popular tourist attractions are the Casbah and Court of the Great Mosque in Algiers, as well as the excellent Mediterranean beaches, Atlas Mountains resorts, and tours of the Sahara Desert. The government has encouraged tourism as an increasingly important source of income.

In 2000, there were 865,984 visitor arrivals, with the vast majority from France and Tunisia.

The most popular Algerian sport is soccer, which is played throughout the country by professionals and amateurs alike. Tennis is widely played as well.

34 ■ Famous Algerians

The most famous Algerian of ancient times was Saint Augustine (Aurelius Augustinus, A.D. 354–430), a Christian priest and theologian who was born in eastern Numidia. Abd al-Qader (1807–1883) was an Algerian political leader and marabout (a person thought to have supernatural powers) who led the Muslim resistance against French imperialism in central and western Algeria during the second quarter of the nineteenth century. Other important nationalist leaders include Messali Hadj (c.1898–1974), who organized several political movements, and Ferhat Abbas (1900–1986), who led the first provisional government and was elected first speaker of the National Assembly in 1962. Ahmed Ben Bella (b. 1916) was the first premier of independent Algeria.

The renowned French Algerian novelist, playwright, and essayist Albert Camus (1913–1960) won the Nobel Prize for literature in 1957. Frantz Fanon (b.Martinique, 1925–1961), a psychiatrist, writer, and revolutionary, was a leading critic of colonialism.

35 ◼ Bibliography

Brill, M. *Algeria.* Chicago, IL: Children's Press, 1990.

Entelis, John P. *Algeria.* Boulder, CO: Westview, 1985.

Heggoy, Alf A., and Robert R. Crout. *Historical Dictionary of Algeria.* Metuchen, NJ: Scarecrow, 1981.

Kagda, Falaq. *Algeria.* New York: Marshall Cavendish, 1997.

Sebbar, Leila, ed. *An Algerian Childhood: A Collection of Autobiographical Narratives.* St. Paul, MN: Ruminator Books, 2001.

Andorra

Principality of Andorra
Principat d'Andorra

Capital: Andorra la Vella.

Flag: The national flag is a tricolor of blue, yellow, and red vertical stripes. On the state flag (shown here) the yellow stripe bears the coat of arms.

Anthem: The *Himne Andorra* begins "El gran Carlemany mon pare" ("Great Charlemagne my father").

Monetary Unit: Andorra has no currency of its own; the euro, adopted by both Spain and France, is used. There are coins of 1, 5, 10, 20, and 50 cents and 1 euro and 2 euros. There are notes of 5, 10, 20, 50, 100, 200, and 500 euros. As of May 2003, €1 = $1.0977 (or $1 = €0.911 euro).

Weights and Measures: The metric system and some old local standards are used.

Holidays: New Year's Day, 1 January; National Festival, 8 September; Christmas, 25 December. Movable religious holidays include Good Friday and Easter Monday.

Time: 1 PM = noon GMT.

1 ▪ Location and Size

The landlocked nation of Andorra lies in southwestern Europe on the southern slopes of the Pyrenees between France and Spain, with a total boundary length of 125 kilometers (77.7 miles).

Andorra is slightly more than 2.5 times the size of Washington, D.C., with a total area of 450 square kilometers (174 square miles).

Andorra's capital city, Andorra la Vella, is located in the southwestern part of the country.

2 ▪ Topography

Most of the country's terrain is rough and mountainous, and there is little level surface. All the valleys are at least 900 meters (3,000 feet) high, and the mean altitude is over 1,800 meters (6,000 feet).

The highest point is the mountain peak, Coma Pedrosa (2,942 meters/9,665 feet). The lowest point is on the Riu Valira (Valira River) at 840 meters (2,755 feet), located near the intersection of the Runer and Valira Rivers.

Geographic Profile

Geographic Features

Size ranking: 177 of 193
Highest elevation: 2,942 meters (9,652 feet) at Coma Pedrosa
Lowest elevation: 840 meters (2756 feet) at Riu Valira

Land Use*

Arable land: 2%
Permanent crops: 0%
Forests: 22%
Other: 76%

Weather**

Average annual precipitation: 97 centimeters (38 inches)
Average temperature in January: 0°c (32°F)
Average temperature in July: 16°c (61.5°F)

---

* *Arable Land: Land used for temporary crops, like meadows for mowing or pasture, gardens, and greenhouses.*

  Permanent crops: Land cultivated with crops that occupy its use for long periods, such as cocoa, coffee, rubber, fruit and nut orchards, and vineyards.

  Forests: Land containing stands of trees.

  Other: Any land not specified, including built-on areas, roads, and barren land.

** *The measurements for precipitation and average temperatures were taken at weather stations closest to the country's largest city.*

  Precipitation and average temperature can vary significantly within a country, due to factors such as latitude, altitude, coastal proximity, and wind patterns.

3 Climate

Because of its high elevation, Andorra has severe winters. The northern valleys are completely filled with snow for several months. Most rain falls in April and October. Summers are warm or mild, depending on the altitude. There are wide variations between the maximum day and night temperatures.

4 Plants and Animals

The plant and animal life is similar to that found in the neighboring areas of France and Spain. Chestnut and walnut trees grow only in the area around Sant Julía de Lòria, the lowest village. Elsewhere, evergreen oaks still are common. Higher regions and many valleys have pines, firs, and various forms of subalpine and alpine plant life. At the highest altitudes there are no trees, but grass is plentiful during the summer. There are carnations, violets, bellflowers, and daisies, as well as blackberries, wild strawberries, and moss. Bears, wolves, foxes, martens, Pyrenean chamois, rabbits, hares, eagles, vultures, wild ducks, and geese may be found in isolated areas. The mountain streams contain trout, brochet, and crayfish.

5 Environment

Andorra was once heavily forested, but the forested area has been decreasing steadily. Overgrazing of mountain meadows by sheep, with consequent soil erosion, is another environmental problem. The Apollo butterfly, the European otter, and the lesser horseshoe bat are vulnerable species.

6 ■ Population

The population in 2003 was estimated at 68,000, with a density of 136 persons per square kilometer (352 persons per square mile). The population is concentrated in the seven urbanized valleys that form Andorra's political districts. Andorran citizens are outnumbered three to one by other ethnic groups, the majority of whom are of Spanish descent. The capital, Andorra la Vella, had a population of 25,000 in 2002.

7 ■ Migration

Immigration consists mainly of Spanish, Portuguese, and French people who intend to work in Andorra. Spanish nationals account for the largest group of foreign residents. There is also a small but rapidly growing group of African immigrants, especially from North Africa, working mostly in agriculture and construction. Immigrant workers are supposed to hold temporary work authorization permits, which are valid only as long as the job exists for which the permit was obtained. However, more than 4,000 immigrants did not have work permits in 1999, due to the fact that the quota for immigration is not as high as the number of workers needed in the country. In 2003, the net migration rate was estimated at 6.67 migrants per 1,000 population. In 2000, approximately 81% of the population were not born in Andorra.

8 ■ Ethnic Groups

Native Andorrans made up only about 33% of the total population in 1998. They are of Catalan stock. About 43% of the population was Spanish, 11% were Portu-

Location: 42°25' to 42°40'N; 1°25'E. **Boundary Lengths:** France, 60 kilometers (37.3 miles); Spain, 65 kilometers (40.4 miles).

guese, and about 7% were French. About 6% were from other groups.

9 ■ Languages

The official language is Catalan. French and Spanish also are spoken.

10 ■ Religions

Traditionally, over 90% of all Andorrans are Roman Catholic. Though Catholicism is not an official state religion, the consti-

Anne Kalosh

The capital, Andorra la Vella, is tucked between the mountains.

tution acknowledges a special relationship with the Roman Catholic Church. The Muslim community (about 2,000 people) consists primarily of North African immigrants. Other Christian denominations include the Anglican Church, Jehovah's Witnesses, the Reunification Church, the New Apostolic Church, and the Church of Jesus Christ of Latter-day Saints.

11 ■ Transportation

A north-south highway links Andorra la Vella with the Spanish and French borders. There are 269 kilometers (167 miles) of surfaced roads, and as of 2001, Andorra had 40,127 motor vehicles. Among several cable cars, the most important operates between Encamp and Engolasters Lake. Most merchandise is transported by vehicles from neighboring countries.

Andorra does not have railways or commercial airports. The nearest international airports are at Barcelona, Spain, and Toulouse, France.

12 ■ History

According to one tradition, Charlemagne (742–814) gave the region the name Andorra for its supposed likeness to the biblical town of Endor. Tradition also asserts that Charlemagne granted the Andorran people a charter in return for their help in fighting the Moors, and that Charlemagne's son Louis I, king of France, confirmed the charter.

It is generally agreed that Charles the Bald, the son of Louis, appointed the count of Urgel overlord of Andorra and gave him the right to collect the imperial tribute (tax). The bishop of Urgel, however, also claimed Andorra as part of the endowment of his cathedral. In 1226, the lords of the countship of Foix, in present-day south-central France, became heirs to the counts of Urgel by marriage. The quarrels between the Spanish bishop and the French counts over rights in Andorra led in 1278 to their adoption of a *pareage,* a feudal institution recognizing equal rights of two lords.

Joint rule continued until 1793, when the French revolutionary government renounced its claim to Andorra, despite the wish of the Andorrans to enjoy French protection and avoid being under only Spanish influence. Napoleon restored joint rule in 1806 after the Andorrans asked him to do so. French rule of Andorra later passed from the kings to the president of France.

Long an impoverished land having little contact with any nations other than adjoining France and Spain, Andorra achieved prosperity through tourism after World War II (1939–45). It formally became a parliamentary democracy in May 1993.

Its new constitution retained the French and Spanish coprinces, although with reduced powers. Civil rights were greatly expanded, including the legalization of political parties and trade unions. Andorra was admitted to the United Nations on 28 July 1993.

At the start of the twenty-first century, the country was seeking ways to improve its export potential and increase its economic ties with its European neighbors. The financial services sector of the economy is highly important, given Andorra's status as a tax haven and its banking secrecy laws.

13 ■ Government

The governmental system of Andorra is unique. Authority is shared equally by the president of France and the (Spanish) bishop of Urgel as coprinces. Legislation is enacted by the General Council, consisting of 28 members.

As of 2003, the president of the General Council was Marc Forné Molné, who was elected in December 1997 and reelected in 2001.

Andorra is divided into seven parishes or districts. Voters elect members of the parish council, which usually consists of 8 to 14 members.

Biographical Profile

Name: Marc Forné Molné
Position: Executive Council President of a parliamentary democracy
Took Office: 21 December 1994
Birthplace: 1947
Religion: Roman Catholic
Education: Educated as an attorney
Of interest: Forné is typically viewed by the public as a well-educated moderate who believes in reform

14 ■ Political Parties

Prior to 1993, political parties were illegal in Andorra. In the general election of 2001, three main parties won seats in the 28-seat General Council: the conservative Liberal Party, the left-of-center Social Democratic Party, and the centrist Democratic Party. The local Lauredian Union won 2 seats in the 2001 election.

15 ■ Judicial System

A Superior Council of Justice oversees and administers the judicial system. Appeals from lower courts are decided by a Supreme Court in France or an Ecclesiastical Court in Spain. The current system provides a hearing for civil and criminal cases, with different appeals systems for each. Sentenced criminals have the choice of French or Spanish jails.

16 ■ Armed Forces

France and Spain are pledged to defend Andorra, which has no defense force.

Anne Kalosh

An Andorran policewoman directs city traffic.

17 ■ Economy

The Andorran economy is primarily based on trade and tourism, with the traffic between France and Spain providing most of the revenue. Andorra also is a tax haven because there are no direct taxes. Before the European Union (EU) passed new trade policies in the mid-1990s, there was an active trade in consumer goods, which were duty-free in Andorra. With more open trade policies between European countries, Andorra lost its unique duty-free status.

18 ■ Income

In 2000, Andorra's gross domestic product (GDP) was $1.3 billion, or $19,000 per person. The annual growth rate of GDP was estimated at 3.8%. The average inflation rate in 2000 was 4.3%.

19 ■ Industry

Andorran industry produces cigars, cigarettes, textiles, leather, building materials, and furniture. There also are distilleries for the production of anisette, vermouth, liqueurs, and brandy. Several firms manufacture woolen goods.

20 ■ Labor

Total employment as of 2001 was 33,000, of which fewer than 1% were employed in agriculture, about 21% in industry, and more than 78% in services. There is virtually no unemployment in Andorra. Under a new constitution passed in 1993, workers are permitted to form unions. It is unclear whether strikes are legal under the constitution. There is a government-set minimum wage, which was $3.65 per hour in 2002. The minimum working age is 18.

21 ■ Agriculture

Because of Andorra's mountainous character, only about 2% of the land is suitable for crops. Most of the cropped land is devoted to hay production for animal feed. Since there is insufficient sunlight on northward-facing slopes and the lands in shadow are too cold for most crops, some southward-facing fields high in the mountains must be used even though they are a considerable distance from the farmers' homes.

Tobacco, the most distinctive Andorran crop, is grown on the best lands. Andorran tobacco is usually mixed with eastern tobaccos, because of its strong quality. Other farm products include cereals, potatoes, and garden vegetables. Grapes are used mainly for raisins and for the making of anisette. Most food is now imported.

22 ■ Domesticated Animals

For many centuries sheep raising was the basis of Andorra's economy. Now tourism and service industries are more important to the economy. However, Andorran mules are still greatly prized. Cattle, sheep, and goats are raised both in the valleys and in some of the higher areas. Cattle are raised mainly for their meat, and there are few dairy cows. When the cattle move upward in the spring, entire families move to temporary villages in the mountains to herd, mow, and plant. Large droves of sheep and goats from France and Spain feed in Andorra in the summer. The Spanish-owned animals in particular are looked after by Andorran shepherds. On their way back to their native land, many of the animals are sold at annual fairs. The Spanish fairs are usually held in Andorra in September and the French in November. Andorra's own animal fairs are also held in the fall.

Livestock includes an estimated 9,000 sheep, 1,100 cattle, and 200 horses. Meat production has increased in recent years, but imports account for about 90% of total meat consumption. The milk produced is sufficient for domestic consumption and some milk has been exported to Spain.

23 ■ Fishing

The streams are full of trout and other freshwater fish, but Andorra imports most fish for domestic consumption from Spain.

24 ■ Forestry

About 10,000 hectares (24,700 acres), or 22% of the total land area, are forested. Fuel wood may be freely gathered by anyone, but it may not be bought or sold. Wood needed for building purposes is cut in rotation from a different district each year. For centuries logs have been shipped to Spain. Most newly planted trees are pines.

25 ■ Mining

For hundreds of years, Andorran forges were famous in northern Spain. There are still iron ore deposits in the valley of Ordino and in many of the mountain areas, but access to them is difficult. In addition to iron, small amounts of lead are still mined, and alum and building stones are extracted. The sulfurous waters of Les Escaldes are used in washing wool.

26 ■ Foreign Trade

Owing to the heavy traffic in smuggled goods across Andorra's borders, official statistics do not reflect the true volume of transactions. Of recorded trade, close to half is with Spain and over one-quarter with France. The majority of imports consists of consumer goods sold to visitors.

27 ■ Energy and Power

Hydroelectric power provides about 40% of Andorra's electric power needs. There are four gas companies, with Andor Gas supplying propane and the others butane.

28 ■ Social Development

There is a social welfare system, expanded in 1968 to cover the entire population. Women have only enjoyed full suffrage (the right to vote) since 1970. There is no governmental department specifically designated to address women's issues, but in 2001 a Secretariat of State for the Family was created.

Foreigners account for over 40% of the population. Although they are accorded the same rights and freedoms as citizens, they lack access to some of the social benefits provided by law.

29 ■ Health

In 1999, infant mortality was estimated at 4 per 1,000 births. Life expectancy was estimated at 85 years in 2003. In 1998, Andorra had 2.5 physicians, 2.8 nurses, 0.09 midwives, 0.5 dentists, and 0.9 pharmacists per 1,000 people.

30 ■ Housing

Most Andorran houses are made of stone. Because the flat land is used for farm crops, the rural houses are frequently built against the mountainsides. All residents have access to safe water and sanitation systems.

31 ■ Education

By law, students must attend school until age 16. Education is provided by both French- and Spanish-language schools. The French government partially subsidizes education in Andorra's French-language schools. Schools in the southern section, near Spain, are supported by the church. About 50% of Andorran children attend French primary schools, and the rest attend Spanish or Andorran schools. In general, Andorran schools follow the Spanish curriculum, and their diplomas are recognized by Spain.

The University of Andorra was established in July 1997. It has a small enrollment and mostly offers long-distance courses through universities in Spain and France. The majority of secondary graduates who continue their education attend schools in France or Spain. Andorra also has a nursing school and a school of computer science. Nearly 100% of the adult population are literate.

32 ■ Media

In 1998, there were 32,946 mainline and 14,117 mobile cellular phones in use. Postal and telegraph services are handled by the Spanish and French administrations.

As of 1998, there were 15 FM radio stations. Andorra does not have its own television stations. Television transmission is provided through technical agreements with the Spanish and French government networks. In 1997 there were 16,000 radios and 27,000 television sets in use throughout the country.

The two main daily papers are the independent publications of *Diari D'Andorra* (*Andorra Daily*, 2002 circulation 3,000) and *El Peridico de Andorra. Poble Andorra* is a major weekly publication with a circulation of about 3,000. Other newspapers, with smaller circulations, are the dailies *Independent* and *Informacions Diari*, and the weeklies *Correu Andorra* and *Informacions*. French and Spanish newspapers are also widely available.

As of 2000, there was only one Internet service provider with an estimated 24,500 Internet users in 2001.

Selected Social Indicators

The statistics below are the most recent estimates available as of 2003. For comparison purposes, data for the United States and averages for low-income countries and high-income countries are also given. About 15% of the world's 6.4 billion people live in high-income countries, while 40% live in low-income countries.

Indicator	Andorra	Low-income countries	High-income countries	United States
Per capita gross national income (GNI)*	**$19.000**	$2,110	$28,480	$36,110
Population growth rate	**1.1%**	2.1%	0.7%	1.1%
People per square kilometer of land	**136**	77	31	31
Life expectancy in years: *male*	**81**	58	75	75
female	**87**	60	81	80
Number of physicians per 1,000 people	**n.a.**	1.0	3.0	2.8
Number of pupils per teacher (primary school)	**n.a.**	40	17	15
Literacy rate (15 years and older)	**100%**	66%	>95%	97%
Television sets per 1,000 people	**403**	91	735	938
Internet users per 1,000 people	**354**	10	364	551
Energy consumed per capita (kg of oil equivalent)	**n.a.**	550	5,366	7,937

* The GNI is the total of all goods and services produced by the residents of a country in a year. The per capita GNI is calculated by dividing a country's GNI by its population and adjusting for relative purchasing power.

n.a. = data not available   > = greater than   < = less than

SOURCES: International Telecommunication Union (ITU). *World Telecommunication Development Report 2003.* Geneva, Switzerland: ITU, 2003; World Bank. *World Development Indicators.* Washington, D.C.: The World Bank, 2004; Central Intelligence Agency. *The World Factbook.* Washington, D.C.: Government Printing Office, 2003.

33 ■ Tourism and Recreation

Tourism has brought considerable prosperity to Andorra and now constitutes the principal source of income. Visitors, mostly from France and Spain, come to Andorra each summer to attend the fairs and festivals, to buy consumer items at lower prices than are obtainable in the neighboring countries, and to enjoy the pleasant weather and beautiful scenery. There is skiing at Pas de la Casa and Soldeu in winter.

Romanesque churches and old houses of interest are located in Ordino, Encamp, Sant Julía de Lória, Les Escaldes, Santa Coloma, and other villages. Pilgrims come from France and Spain to pay homage on 8 September, the festival day of Andorra's patroness.

An estimated 10,000 tourists visit Andorra each year.

34 ■ Famous Andorrans

Some famous Andorrans include Bonaventura Riberaygua i Argelich (1892–1950), secretary of parliament from 1935 to 1950 and a writer who published the book *Les Valls d'Andorra,* a geographical, historical, and political documentary about Andorra. Philippe Wolff (1913–2001) was an author and a member of the French Académie des Inscriptions et Belles-Lettres. Jacques Tremoulet (1896–1971), French radio and press magnate, was the founder of Radio Andorra.

35 ■ Bibliography

Cameron, Peter. *Andorra.* New York: Farrar, Straus and Giroux, 1997.

Deane, Shirley. *The Road to Andorra.* New York: Morrow, 1961.

De Cugnac, Pascal. *Pyrenees and Gascony: Including Andorra.* London: Hachette UK, 2000.

Taylor, Barry. *Andorra.* Santa Barbara, CA: Clio Press, 1993.

Angola

Republic of Angola
República de Angola

Capital: Luanda.

Flag: The upper half is red, the lower half black; in the center, a five-pointed yellow star and half a yellow cogwheel are crossed by a yellow machete.

Anthem: *Angola Avanti..*

Monetary Unit: The Angolan escudo (AE) was the national currency until 1977, when the kwanza (Kw) of 100 lwei replaced it. There are coins of 50 lwei and 1, 2, 5, 10, and 20 kwanza, and notes of 20, 50, 100, 500, and 1,000 kwanza. Kw1 = $0.0141 (or $1 = Kw70.77; as of May 2003).

Weights and Measures: The metric system is used.

Holidays: New Year's Day, 1 January; Anniversary of Outbreak of Anti-Portuguese Struggle, 4 February; Victory Day, 27 March; Youth Day, 14 April; Workers' Day, 1 May; Armed Forces Day, 1 August; National Heroes' Day, 17 September; Independence Day, 11 November; Pioneers' Day, 1 December; Anniversary of the Foundation of the MPLA, 10 December; Family Day, 25 December.

Time: 1 PM = noon GMT.

1 ▪ Location and Size

Angola is located on the west coast of Africa, south of the equator. Angola is slightly less than twice the size of Texas, with a total area of 1,246,700 square kilometers (481,353 square miles), including Cabinda (7,270 square kilometers/2,810 square miles), a small coastal section to the north that is separated from the main part of the country and completely surrounded by the Democratic Republic of the Congo (DROC) and the Republic of the Congo. Angola's total boundary length, including Cabinda's, is 6,798 kilometers (4,224 miles). The country has a coastline on the Atlantic Ocean that extends for 1,600 kilometers (994 miles).

2 ▪ Topography

Topographically, Angola consists mainly of broad tablelands above 1,000 meters (3,300 feet) in altitude. A high plateau (*planalto*) in the center and south ranges up to 2,400 meters (7,900 feet). The highest point in Angola is Mount Moco, at 2,620 meters (8,596 feet). The lowest point is at sea level (Atlantic Ocean).

Rivers are numerous, but few are navigable. There are three types of rivers in Angola: constantly fed rivers (such as the

Geographic Profile

Geographic Features

Size ranking: 22 of 193
Highest elevation: 2,620 meters (8,596 feet) at Mount Moco
Lowest elevation: Sea level at the Atlantic Ocean

Land Use*

Arable land: 2%
Permanent crops: 0%
Forests: 56%
Other: 42%

Weather**

Average annual precipitation: 36.7 centimeters (14.4 inches)
Average temperature in January: 25.9°C (78.6°F)
Average temperature in July: 20.2°C (68.4°F)

* *Arable Land: Land used for temporary crops, like meadows for mowing or pasture, gardens, and greenhouses.*

  Permanent crops: Land cultivated with crops that occupy its use for long periods, such as cocoa, coffee, rubber, fruit and nut orchards, and vineyards.

  Forests: Land containing stands of trees.

  Other: Any land not specified, including built-on areas, roads, and barren land.

** *The measurements for precipitation and average temperatures were taken at weather stations closest to the country's largest city.*

  Precipitation and average temperature can vary significantly within a country, due to factors such as latitude, altitude, coastal proximity, and wind patterns.

Zaire River), seasonally fed rivers, and temporary rivers and streams. Only the Cuanza, in central Angola, and the Zaire, in the north, are navigable by boats of significant size. The Cuanza is also the longest river that flows entirely within the country. Its length is about 966 kilometers (600 miles).

3 ■ Climate

Angola's climate varies considerably from the coast to the central plateau, and even between the north coast and the south coast. There are two seasons: a dry, cool season from June to late September, and a rainy, hot season from October to April or May. The average temperature is 20°C (68°F). However, temperatures are warmer along the coast and cooler on the central plateau.

4 ■ Plants and Animals

Thick forests (especially in Cabinda and in the Uíge area in the north) cover the wet regions, and in the drier areas there is a thinner savanna vegetation. Fauna includes the lion, impala, hyena, hippopotamus, rhinoceros, and elephant. There are thousands of types of birds and a wide variety of insects.

5 ■ Environment

The existing environmental problems in Angola have been aggravated by a 30-year war. The main problems are land abuse, desertification, loss of forests, and impure water. The productivity of the land is continually threatened by drought and soil erosion, which contributes to water pollution and deposits silt in rivers and dams. The cutting of tropical rain forests for international timber sale and domestic

Location: Angola proper: 5°49' to 18°3's; 11°40' to 24°5'ᴇ. Cabinda: 4°21' to 5°46's; 12°2' to 13°5' ᴇ. **Boundary Lengths:** Democratic Rep. of the Congo, 2,291 kilometers (1,423 miles); Zambia, 1,110 kilometers (690 miles); Namibia, 1,376 kilometers (855 miles); Atlantic coastline, 1,600 kilometers (995 miles). Cabinda: Democratic Rep. of the Congo, 220 kilometers (136 miles); Republic of the Congo, 201 kilometers (125 miles). **Territorial Sea Limit:** 20 miles.

Corel Corporation

A view of the Atlantic coast at Benguela, Angola.

use as fuel contributes to the destruction of the land.

Endangered species in Angola include the black-faced impala, three species of turtle (green, olive ridley, and leatherback), the giant sable antelope, the African slender-snouted (or long-snouted) crocodile, the African elephant, Vernay's climbing monkey, and the black rhinoceros. Threatened species in Angola include 17 of the 276 species of mammals; 13 of the 765 species of birds; and 20 of the 5,185 species of plants.

6 ▇ Population

Angola's population was estimated at 13.6 million in 2000. A total population of 13.1 million is projected for the year 2005. Lu-

anda, the capital, had 2.7 million people in 2002.

7 ▇ Migration

Although the civil war ended in 1994, at the start of 1997 there were still 200,000 Angolan refugees in the Democratic Republic of the Congo (DROC), 96,000 in Zambia, 12,000 in the Republic of the Congo, 1,000 in Namibia, and 15,000 other Angolan refugees in 15 other countries. As of May 1997, there were still 1.2 million Angolans displaced within their country as a result of the civil war. Angola still hosted some 12,000 refugees, most from DROC, as of 2000. In 2003, the net migration rate was estimated at 0 migrants per 1,000 population.

8 ▇ Ethnic Groups

The overwhelming majority of the population consists of Bantu, who are divided into groups based on their native tribal languages. The main ones are the Ovimbundu, who account for about 37% of the population as of 2003, the Kimbundu, totaling 25% of the population, and the Bakongo with 13%.

The *mestiços* (mixed European and Native African) make up about 2% of the population. Since *mestiços* are generally better educated than the black population, they exercise influence in government disproportionate to their numbers. Europeans, mostly of Portuguese extraction, constitute 1% of the population. Other varied groups account for the remaining 22%.

Some Congolese use sleek low boats to travel on the country's rivers, especially on the Cuanza and the Zaire rivers, both of which flow constantly.

9 ▪ Languages

Portuguese remains the official language, although African languages (and their dialects) are used at the local level.

10 ▪ Religions

Christianity is the major religion in the country. About 5 million people, or 38% of the population, were Roman Catholic as of 1998. About 15% of the population belonged to Protestant denominations, including Methodists, Baptists, Congregationalists (United Church of Christ), and Assemblies of God.

The largest native religious group is the Kimbanguist Church, whose followers believe that the mid-twentieth-century Congolese pastor Joseph Kimbangu was a prophet. Almost half the population (47%) follow African traditional beliefs either exclusively or in combination with other faiths. Communities in rural areas of the country practice animism and other indigenous religions. There is also a small Islamic community.

11 ▪ Transportation

In 2002, there were 76,626 kilometers (47,615 miles) of roads, of which 19,156

Biographical Profile

Name: Jose Eduardo dos Santos

Position: President of a transitional government

Took Office: 21 September 1979

Birthplace: Luanda, Angola

Birthdate: 28 August 1942

Education: Institute of Oil and Gas in Baku, USSR, petroleum engineer, 1969

Spouse: Ana Paula

Children: Two children

Of interest: Dos Santos received a scholarship to study in the USSR

Jose Eduardo dos Santos

kilometers (11,904 miles) were paved. There were 117,200 passenger cars and about 118,300 commercial vehicles.

The rail network had a total extension in 2002 of about 2,771 kilometers (1,722 miles), of which 2,648 kilometers (1,645 miles) were 1.067-meter-gauge track. The merchant marine had 9 ships of 1,000 gross registered tons (GRT) or over in 2002, totaling 39,305 GRT. Angola had a total of 244 airports in 2001, 32 of which had paved runways. There is an international airport at Luanda.

12 ■ History

Originally inhabited by people of the Khoisan group (Bushmen), Angola was occupied by various Bantu peoples from farther north and east between A.D. 1300 and 1600.

The Portuguese arrived on the coast in the late fifteenth century. The first European to reach Angola was the Portuguese explorer Diogo Cao, who landed at the mouth of the Congo River in 1483. Luanda, the current capital, was founded as a trading settlement in 1575. The slave trade assumed great importance during the seventeenth century, when slaves were carried to Portuguese plantations in Brazil. From the late sixteenth through the mid-nineteenth century, Angola may have provided the New World with as many as 2 to 3 million slaves. Slavery was formally abolished in 1836, although under Portuguese rule forced labor was common until the early 1950s.

European domination spread and, in 1951, Angola was made an overseas province of Portugal. Increasing numbers of Portuguese settlers came to Angola, and by 1960 there were about 160,000 Europeans in the country.

Organized armed resistance to Portuguese rule began on 4 February 1961, when urban partisans of the Popular Movement for the Liberation of Angola (MPLA) attacked the police headquarters in Luanda. The National Front for the Liberation of Angola (FNLA), headed by Holden Roberto, set up a revolutionary government-in-exile in Zaire (now the Democratic Republic of the Congo-DROC) on 3 April 1962. A third movement, the National Union for the Total Independence of Angola (UNITA), came into being as the consequence of a split in the government-in-exile. This group was headed by Jonas Savimbi.

The three movements were divided by political beliefs, ethnic makeup, and personal rivalries. All three movements fought the Portuguese. On 11 November 1975 the Portuguese decided to end their African empire and granted complete independence to Angola. An agreement between the Portuguese and the three movements established a coalition government headed by the leaders of all three parties. As independence day approached, however, the coalition government fell apart and the three groups fought among themselves for control of the government. The MPLA was a Marxist-oriented party that received military as well as financial assistance from the Soviet Union and Cuba. The FLNA and UNITA parties had a pro-Western orientation and were aided by South Africa and the United States.

On 11 February 1976, the Organization of African Unity formally recognized the MPLA government as the legitimate government of Angola. With the help of Cuban troops, the MPLA was able to gain control of most of the country. However, the losing parties continued to wage war against the MPLA government for the next sixteen years. During this period, thousands of blacks were killed, most whites left the country, and the economy was totally ruined.

Finally, in April 1991, there was a UN-supervised cease-fire. All parties agreed to hold national elections on 29 and 30 September 1992. The resulting elections were won by the MPLA. However, UNITA leader Savimbi, upset by his unexpected defeat, charged fraud and threatened to take up arms again. Fighting broke out in Luanda. UNITA gained control of about 75% of Angola. Pressure for peace continued and on 20 November 1994 the Angolan government signed a peace treaty with UNITA, supported by 6,000 UN peacekeepers, known as the Lusaka Peace Accord.

In mid-1997, the government and UNITA were on opposite sides of the civil war in the DROC. The United Nations (UN) imposed new sanctions that further weakened UNITA. In mid-1998, UN officials uncovered a mass grave in northern Angola, indicating that despite the peace treaty of 1994, civil violence had continued. Full-scale warfare resumed at the end of 1998. In February 1999, the UN Security Council voted to end peacekeeping operations because there was no longer any hope of carrying out the 1994 Lusaka agreement.

In February 2002, prospects for peace changed dramatically when the army announced that it had killed Savimbi in an attack in southeastern Angola. In March 2002 UNITA commanders issued a joint communiqué with the Angolan army (FAA) confirming a halt to hostilities and restating unwavering support for a political settlement based on the 1994 Lusaka Peace Accord. A peace accord between the government and UNITA followed in April. In February 2003, a UN mission overseeing the peace process finished its operations. By June 2003, UNITA had been transformed into a political party and had elected a new leader.

13 ■ Government
The president of the republic is the president of the MPLA-Workers' Party. The president may rule by decree, exercising legislative functions delegated to him by the People's Assembly. A transitional government was set up in December 1992, dominated by the MPLA. UNITA had six cabinet posts and four other parties were represented. In 1997, an agreement was reached regarding UNITA's participation in the Government of National Unity and Reconciliation. However, the resumption of warfare in 1998 doomed the prospects for a national unity government. The civil war ended in August 2002, with the death of Jonas Savimbi that February. José Eduardo dos Santos is president. There are currently 220 seats in the National Assembly, and elections are slated for 2004.

Angola consists of 18 provinces, which are divided into districts and communes.

14 ■ Political Parties
The three leading political organizations at the time of independence were the Popular Movement for the Liberation of Angola (Movimento Popular de Libertação de Angola; MPLA), founded in 1956; the National Front for the Liberation of Angola (Frente Nacional de Libertação de Angola; FNLA), founded in 1962; and the National Union for the Total Independence of Angola (União Nacional para a Independência Total de Angola; UNITA), founded in 1966. Some eighteen parties contested the 1992 elections.

15 ■ Judicial System
The judicial system currently consists of municipal and provincial courts at the trial level and a Supreme Court at the appellate level. Provincial court judges are nominated by the Supreme Court. The judge of the provincial court, along with two laymen, acts as a jury. Many seats on the Supreme Court remain vacant. The judiciary system was largely destroyed during the civil war and was not functioning properly throughout much of the country as of 2003.

16 ■ Armed Forces
National defense is the responsibility of the Armed Popular Forces for the Liberation of Angola (Forças Amadas Populares de Libertação de Angola; FAPLA). In 2002, the army had 90,000 active soldiers with 400 main battle tanks and other combat vehicles, the navy had 4,000 sailors and 7 vessels, and the air force had 6,000 personnel and 104 combat aircraft.

17 ■ Economy
Angola is a potentially rich country with abundant natural resources, a surplus-producing agricultural sector, and a sizable manufacturing potential. This promise has remained unfulfilled due to the effects of the twenty-seven-year-long civil war that only ended in April 2002.

Cassava is the staple food crop. Petroleum production and diamond mining lead Angola's mineral industry. Angola also has significant deposits of high-grade iron ore, copper, manganese, phosphates, and uranium. Angola was the second-largest oil producer in sub-Saharan Africa in 2002, and oil exports accounted for 45% of the country's gross domestic product (GDP) that year. Inflation, always a problem, ran at approximately 150% in 2001.

18 ■ Income

In 2001 Angola's gross domestic product (GDP) was $13.3 billion. The GDP per person was estimated at $1,330. The annual growth rate of GDP was estimated at 5.4%. The average inflation rate in 2001 was 110%.

19 ■ Industry

Industrial production consists of food processing and the production of textiles, soap, shoes, matches, paint, plastic bottles, and glues. Heavy industry (cement, steel, oil refining, vehicle assembly, and tire production) accounts for approximately 15% of manufacturing output. Angola is now an importer of machinery, vehicles, and spare parts.

The diamond mining industry is also important, but during the twenty-seven-year-long civil war, many of the gemstones had been sold on the black market and were referred to as "conflict diamonds" because the parties in the civil war used diamond sales to fund their military campaigns. Since the civil war ended in 2002, Angola began to restructure its diamond industry. The government in 2003 ended the monopoly of the state-controlled diamond marketing company,

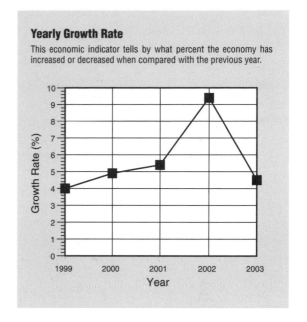

Yearly Growth Rate

This economic indicator tells by what percent the economy has increased or decreased when compared with the previous year.

Ascorp. It now competes with other private companies to buy diamonds from miners and small producers. The government also planned to develop a diamond-cutting industry in Angola.

20 ■ Labor

The minimum legal age for employment is fourteen, but the government has been unable to enforce this standard. Although the legal minimum wage in 2002 was $30 per month, average earnings were considerably less. In 2001, it was estimated that more than half of the population was unemployed or underemployed.

21 ■ Agriculture

Agriculture has long been the backbone of the Angolan economy. Even though an abundance of arable land is available, less than 3% is cultivated. Agriculture employs

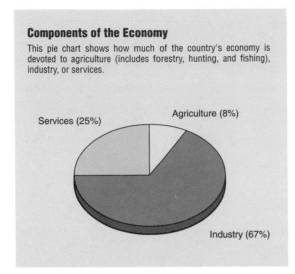

Components of the Economy

This pie chart shows how much of the country's economy is devoted to agriculture (includes forestry, hunting, and fishing), industry, or services.

Services (25%)

Agriculture (8%)

Industry (67%)

over 70% of the population but accounts for 8% of gross domestic product (GDP).

Cash crops marketed annually include 6,000 tons of coffee, 1,000 tons of cotton, and 1,000 tons of sisal. The principal food crops include an annual 3.1 million tons of cassava, 428,000 tons of corn, 182,000 tons of sweet potatoes, 290,000 tons of bananas, 75,000 tons of citrus fruit, 102,000 tons of millet, 68,000 tons of dry beans, 50,000 tons of palm oil, 19,000 tons of potatoes, 32,000 tons of raw sugar, 16,000 tons of rice, and 11,000 tons of peanuts (in shell).

22 ■ Domesticated Animals

What little there was of the livestock industry was virtually destroyed in the 1976–91 civil war. Estimated livestock include 3.9 million cattle, 2 million goats, 800,000 hogs, and 336,000 sheep. There are 7 million chickens. Livestock products include an estimated 85,000 tons of beef and veal annually and 191,000 tons of milk. Honey production totals approximately 22,000 tons, among the highest yields in Africa.

23 ■ Fishing

Fresh fish, fish meal, dried fish, and fish oil are produced for the domestic market and for export. In 2000, the Angolan catch was 238,351 tons (up from 122,781 tons in 1995), 97% from marine fishing. Exports of fish products in 2000 totaled $10.8 million. About 22% of the 2000 catch consisted of cunene horse mackerel.

24 ■ Forestry

About 18.4% of the country is classified as forest and woodland. Angola's abundant timber resources include the great Maiombe tropical rain forest north of Cabinda. In addition, eucalyptus, pine, and cypress plantations cover 140,000 hectares (346,000 acres). In 2000, roundwood production was estimated at 4.27 million cubic meters (150 million cubic feet), of which 6,000 cubic meters (211,888 cubic feet) were exported.

25 ■ Mining

In 1999, diamonds accounted for 8.7% of the country's gross domestic product. Official reported diamond production in 2000 was 4.35 million carats. The United Nations has issued sanctions against "conflict diamonds." Profits from the sale of these diamonds have been used to support terrorist activities and civil war. Many of the diamonds are illegally smuggled out of the country, primarily to Portugal. Diamond smugglers gained $250 million in 2000.

Large iron ore deposits have been discovered in many areas. Salt production has remained steady at 30,000 metric tons per year. Clay, granite, marble, and crushed stone were also reportedly mined throughout the country. The country is also rich in nickel, platinum-group metals, magnetite, copper, phosphates, gypsum, uranium, gold, asphalt, and feldspar, but some areas have been off limits to exploration during the civil war.

26 ■ Foreign Trade

Angola is a major exporter of crude oil and diamonds. Principal imports include food and food products, civil engineering equipment, motor vehicles and parts, metal products, and medicines and pharmaceuticals. Angola's principal export markets were the United States, Belgium, Taiwan, and China. Imports came primarily from South Africa, Portugal, and the United States.

27 ■ Energy and Power

Total electric power production in 2000 was 1.4 billion kilowatt hours, of which 60% was hydroelectric. Crude oil, in the production of which Angola ranks second in sub-Saharan Africa, has been Angola's chief export since 1973. It also accounts for 95% of government revenue. Total natural gas reserves were estimated at 45 billion cubic meters (1.6 trillion cubic feet) as of 2002.

28 ■ Social Development

Until recently, social services for most Angolans were almost entirely the responsibility of the various tribal groups. The Roman Catholic Church also played an important part in welfare, health, and educational programs. Women and children are often at high risk for mutilation by land mines as they tend crops and gather

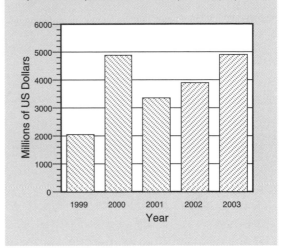

Yearly Balance of Trade

The balance of trade is the difference between what a country sells to other countries (its exports) and what it buys (its imports). If a country imports more than it exports, it has a negative balance of trade (a trade deficit). If exports exceed imports there is a positive balance of trade (a trade surplus).

firewood. There are an estimated 5,000 children living on the street in Luanda.

29 ■ Health

Yellow fever is common in Angola, and the levels of cholera and tuberculosis are also high. Only about 30% of the population receive even basic medical attention. As of 2003, the ratio of physicians per population was estimated at 0.1 per 1,000 people.

In 2000, average life expectancy was estimated at only forty-one years and infant mortality was estimated at 128 per 1,000 live births. Malnutrition affected an estimated 53% of children under five years of age as of 1999. As of 2001, there were an estimated 350,000 adults and children living with human immunodeficiency virus/acquired immunodeficiency syndrome (HIV/AIDS).

Selected Social Indicators

The statistics below are the most recent estimates available as of 2003. For comparison purposes, data for the United States and averages for low-income countries and high-income countries are also given. About 15% of the world's 6.4 billion people live in high-income countries, while 40% live in low-income countries.

Indicator	Angola	Low-income countries	High-income countries	United States
Per capita gross national income (GNI)*	$1,840	$2,110	$28,480	$36,110
Population growth rate	2.8%	2.1%	0.7%	1.1%
People per square kilometer of land	11	77	31	31
Life expectancy in years: *male*	45	58	75	75
female	48	60	81	80
Number of physicians per 1,000 people	0.1	1.0	3.0	2.8
Number of pupils per teacher (primary school)	n.a.	40	17	15
Literacy rate (15 years and older)	42%	66%	>95%	97%
Television sets per 1,000 people	52	91	735	938
Internet users per 1,000 people	3	10	364	551
Energy consumed per capita (kg of oil equivalent)	595	550	5,366	7,937

* The GNI is the total of all goods and services produced by the residents of a country in a year. The per capita GNI is calculated by dividing a country's GNI by its population and adjusting for relative purchasing power.

n.a. = data not available   > = greater than   < = less than

SOURCES: International Telecommunication Union (ITU). *World Telecommunication Development Report 2003.* Geneva, Switzerland: ITU, 2003; World Bank. *World Development Indicators.* Washington, D.C.: The World Bank, 2004; Central Intelligence Agency. *The World Factbook.* Washington, D.C.: Government Printing Office, 2003.

The disease was affecting 5.5% of the adult population. There were an estimated 24,000 deaths from AIDS in 2001.

30 ▪ Housing

The rapid growth of Angola's industrial centers has meant the rapid growth of urban slums. A recent United Nations (UN) report shows that about 90% of urban residents live in settlements that don't legally belong to any one city. Most live in multifamily dwellings that were constructed in the 1960s. Since then, these homes have become so run down that basic utilities are limited or unavailable.

The government has tried to ease the situation. It was estimated that by the end of 2003, about 800 houses and 1,664 flats would have been built.

31 ▪ Education

Education for children between the ages of seven and fifteen years is required and free. Primary education is for four years and secondary for seven years. While Portuguese was the language of instruction in earlier times, local African languages are more commonly used now in schools.

The University Agostinho Neto in Luanda was established in 1963 and offers courses in science, engineering, law, medicine, economics, and agriculture. In 1998 the adult illiteracy rate was estimated at 58% (males, 44%; females, 72%). This is the most

Cory Langley

Women returning from the market carry some of their goods on their heads.

recent year for which statistics were available as of 2004.

32 ▪ Media

There were 69,700 mainline telephones in 1997, with telephone service being limited to government and business use. There were 25,800 mobile cellular phones in the country in 2000.

Most of the media is controlled by the state. In 2000, there were 36 AM and 7 FM radio stations and 7 television stations. Rádio Nacional de Angola broadcasts in Portuguese, English, French, Spanish, and major local languages. In 2000, there were about 74 radios for every 1,000 people. In 2003 there were about 52 television sets for every 1,000 people. There is one Internet service provider, which served about 30,000 subscribers in 2001.

There were five daily newspapers as of 2002: *Jornal de Angola,* with a circulation of 41,000; *Provincia de Angola,* 35,000; *Diario da Luanda,* 18,000; *ABC Diario de Angola,* 8,500; and *Diario da Republica,* circulation unknown. All were published in Portuguese in Luanda. The official government newspaper is the *Diario da Republica.*

33 ■ Tourism and Recreation

Tourism was an important activity until 1972, when an increase in warfare led to a sharp drop in the number of tourists and in tourism revenues. Since the mid-1980s, the government has severely restricted the number of foreigners allowed into the country. Records for 2000 show that 50,765 visitors arrived in Angola that year.

34 ■ Famous Angolans

António Agostinho Neto (1922–1979), a poet and physician who served as the president of MPLA (1962–79) and president of Angola (1975–79), was Angola's dominant political figure. Jonas Malheiro Savimbi (1934–2002), the son of a pastor, founded UNITA in 1966.

35 ■ Bibliography

Africa on File. New York: Facts on File, 1995.

Africa South of the Sahara. London: Europa Publishers, 1997.

Black, Richard. *Angola.* Santa Barbara, CA.: Clio Press, 1992.

Broadhead, Susan Herlin. *Historical Dictionary of Angola.* 2nd ed. Metuchen, NJ: Scarecrow Press, 1992.

Laurè, J. *Angola.* Chicago, IL: Children's Press, 1990.

McKissack, Pat. *Nzingha, Warrior Queen of Matamba.* New York: Scholastic, 2000.

Antigua and Barbuda

Capital: St. John's.

Flag: Centered on a red background is a downward-pointing triangle divided horizontally into three bands of black, light blue, and white, the black stripe bearing a symbol of the rising sun in yellow.

Anthem: Begins "Fair Antigua and Barbuda, I salute thee."

Monetary Unit: The East Caribbean dollar (EC$) is a paper currency of 100 cents, pegged to the US dollar. There are coins of 1, 2, 5, 10, 25 cents and 1 dollar, and notes of 5, 10, 20, and 100 dollars. EC$1 = US$0.3704 (or US$1 = EC$2.70; as of January 2003).

Weights and Measures: Imperial measures are used, but the metric system is being introduced.

Holidays: New Year's Day, 1 January; Labor Day, 1st Monday in May; CARICOM Day, 3 July; State Day, 1 November; Christmas, 25 December; Boxing Day, 26 December. Movable holidays include Good Friday, Easter Monday, and Whitmonday.

Time: 8 AM = noon GMT.

1 ▪ Location and Size

The state of Antigua and Barbuda is part of the Leeward Islands chain in the eastern Caribbean. The total land area, which includes the uninhabited island of Redonda, is 440 square kilometers (170 square miles), slightly less than 2.5 times the size of Washington, D.C. The total coastline is 153 kilometers (95 miles). Redonda is located about 40 kilometers (25 miles) southwest of Antigua. The capital city, Saint John's, is located on the northwestern edge of the island of Antigua.

2 ▪ Topography

Partly volcanic and partly coral in origin, Antigua has deeply indented shores lined by reefs and shoals. There are many natural harbors and beaches. Boggy Peak (402 meters/1,319 feet), in southwestern Antigua, is the nation's highest point. The lowest point of the country is at sea level (Caribbean Sea). Antigua's northeastern coastline is dotted by numerous tiny islets, while the central area is a fertile plain. Barbuda is a coral island with a large harbor on the west side. Redonda is a low-lying rocky islet.

Geographic Profile

Geographic Features
Size ranking: 180 of 193
Highest elevation: 402 meters (1,318
   feet) at Boggy Peak
Lowest elevation: Sea level at the
   Caribbean Sea

Land Use*
Arable land: 18%
Permanent crops: 0%
Forests: 11%
Other: 71%

Weather**
Average annual precipitation: 117
   centimeters (46 inches)
Average temperature in January: 24°C
   (75°F)
Average temperature in July: 29°C
   (84°F)

* *Arable Land: Land used for temporary crops, like meadows for mowing or pasture, gardens, and greenhouses.*

Permanent crops: Land cultivated with crops that occupy its use for long periods, such as cocoa, coffee, rubber, fruit and nut orchards, and vineyards.

Forests: Land containing stands of trees.

Other: Any land not specified, including built-on areas, roads, and barren land.

** *The measurements for precipitation and average temperatures were taken at weather stations closest to the country's largest city.*

Precipitation and average temperature can vary significantly within a country, due to factors such as latitude, altitude, coastal proximity, and wind patterns.

3 ▪ Climate
Temperatures average 24°C (75°F) in January and 29°C (84°F) in July. Rainfall averages 117 centimeters (46 inches) per year.

4 ▪ Plants and Animals
Most of the vegetation is scrub, but there is luxuriant tropical growth where fresh water is available. Many varieties of fruits, flowers, and vegetables are grown. Palmetto and seaside mangrove trees are native to the islands. About 1,600 hectares (4,000 acres) of red cedar, white cedar, mahogany, whitewood, and acacia forests have been planted. Barbuda is heavily wooded, with an abundance of deer, wild pigs, guinea fowl, pigeons, and wild ducks. Pineapple plantations can be found throughout Antigua.

5 ▪ Environment
Water management is the principal environmental concern. The existing water supply is threatened by pollution from distilleries, food-processing facilities, and other industrial operations. Deforestation contributes to soil erosion as rainfall, which is concentrated into a short season, quickly runs off, adding to the water shortage problem on the islands.

The nation's main city, Saint John's, has developed a problem with waste disposal. Untreated sewage from resort hotels travels in open sewage lines across the land and empties into the sea.

There are four main protected areas, including Barbuda's offshore islands of North Sound and Codrington Lagoon. Endangered species in the nation include the Antiguan ground lizard, the West Indian whistling duck, and the Antiguan racer.

6 ▪ Population

The population in 2003 was estimated at 64,461, and is projected to be 76,000 by the year 2015. The overall population density was 152 persons per square kilometer (394 persons per square mile). Saint John's, the capital, has an estimated population of 25,000.

7 ▪ Migration

The United Kingdom has been the traditional destination of people leaving Antigua (emigrants). In recent years emigrants have moved to other Caribbean islands, such as Saint Martin, Barbados, the U.S. Virgin Islands, and the U.S. mainland. The primary motive for emigration is the search for work. The net migration rate in 2003 was estimated at -6.19 migrants per 1,000 population.

8 ▪ Ethnic Groups

Antiguans are almost entirely of African descent. There are small numbers of persons of British, Portuguese, Lebanese, and Syrian ancestry.

9 ▪ Languages

English is the official language. An English patois (dialect) is in common use.

10 ▪ Religions

The dominant religion is Christianity, and the Church of England is the dominant denomination. Other Protestant groups, including Baptists, Methodists, Pentecostals, Seventh-day Adventists, Moravians, and Nazarenes, account for the next largest group. Roman Catholics make up a small percentage of the Christians. Minority religions include Islam, Baha'i, and Rastafarianism.

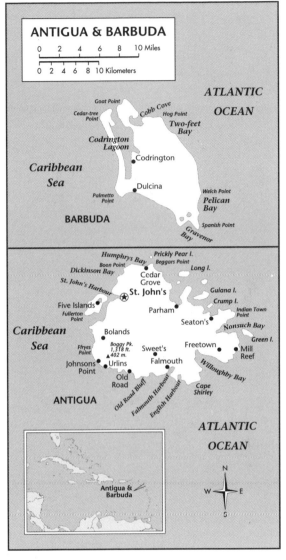

Location: Antigua: 17°9′N; 61°49′W. Barbuda: 17°41′N; 61°48′W. **Total Coastline:** 153 kilometers (95 miles). **Territorial Sea Limit:** 12 miles.

11 ▪ Transportation

In 2002, there were 1,165 kilometers (724 miles) of highways, of which 384 kilome-

Biographical Profile

Name: Lester Bird

Position: Prime Minister of a constitutional monarchy with Westminster-style parliament

Took Office: 8 March 1994

Birthplace: 21 February 1938

Education: University of Michigan, studied law and played track and field

Of interest: Between 1956 and 1957, Bird represented Antigua and the Leeward Islands in cricket. He also won a bronze medal for the long jump at the Pan American Games

Lester Bird

ters (239 miles) were paved. There were about 15,000 motor vehicles registered. The railway consists of 77 kilometers (48 miles) of narrow-gauge track. The merchant fleet in 2002 consisted of 762 ships with a cargo capacity of 4.5 million gross registered tons. Vere Cornwall Bird International Airport, outside Saint John's, accommodates the largest jet aircraft. Domestic and international scheduled flights carried 1,369,100 passengers in 2001.

12 ■ History

Arawak and Carib Indians inhabited the islands in 1493, the year that Christopher Columbus made his second voyage. Antigua formally became a British colony in 1667. In 1674, Sir Christopher Codring-

ton established the first large sugar estate, leasing Barbuda to raise slaves and provide supplies for Antigua. In 1860, Barbuda was annexed to the island of Antigua. The islands were governed under the Federation of the Leeward Islands from 1871 to 1956, and under the Federation of the West Indies from 1958 to 1962.

Antigua achieved full self-government as of 27 February 1967. Antigua and Barbuda became an independent state within the Commonwealth of Nations on 1 November 1981.

In the mid-1990s, the United States and Antigua signed several laws to counteract narcotics trafficking in Antigua and Barbuda.

In late September 1998, Antigua was hit by high winds from Hurricane Georges. Building roofs and landscape plantings were damaged.

By 1999, Antigua and Barbuda had held four general elections since independence. That year, Lester Bird was elected prime minister. New elections were to be held in March 2004.

13 ▪ Government

The British monarch, as head of state, is represented in Antigua and Barbuda by a governor-general. The two-chamber legislature consists of a seventeen-member House of Representatives, elected for up to five years, and a seventeen-member Senate, appointed by the governor-general. The prime minister, who must have the support of a majority of the House, is appointed by the governor-general, as is the cabinet.

As of 2003, the prime minister was Lester Bird. Elections were scheduled for March 2004.

The island of Antigua has six parishes and two dependencies, Barbuda and Redonda. Twenty-nine community councils conduct local government affairs.

14 ▪ Political Parties

The Antigua Labour Party (ALP) has held power since 1946, except for a period from 1971 to 1976 when the Progressive Labour Movement (PLM) held a parliamentary majority. Other political groups include the United Progressive Party and the Barbuda's People's Movement, a coalition of three small opposition political parties.

15 ▪ Judicial System

Antigua and Barbuda is under the jurisdiction of the Eastern Caribbean Supreme Court, based in Saint Lucia, which also provides a High Court and Court of Appeals. Final appeals may be made to the Queen's Privy Council in the United Kingdom. A court of summary jurisdiction on Antigua deals with civil cases.

In 2003, Caribbean leaders met in Jamaica to establish a Caribbean Court of Justice (CCJ). Antigua and Barbuda was planning to use the court for appeals.

16 ▪ Armed Forces

There is a Royal Antigua and Barbuda Defense Force of some 170 personnel that forms a part of the Eastern Caribbean Regional Security System.

17 ▪ Economy

Since the 1960s, tourism has dominated the economy. It now accounts for well over half of the gross domestic product (GDP). Antigua and Barbuda has the largest tourism industry in the Windward and Leeward Islands. In spite of the growth of tourism, the country hasn't reduced its large foreign debt and trade deficit.

18 ▪ Income

In 2000, Antigua and Barbuda's gross domestic product (GDP) was $674 million, or $10,000 per person. The annual growth rate of the GDP was estimated at 3.5%. The average inflation rate in 2000 was 0.4%.

19 ▪ Industry

Industrial activity has shifted from the processing of local agricultural products to consumer and export industries that

Yearly Growth Rate

This economic indicator tells by what percent the economy has increased or decreased when compared with the previous year.

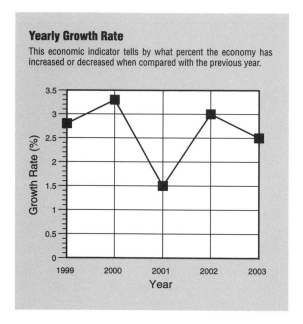

21 ■ Agriculture

About 30% of the land on Antigua is potential farmland, with 18% in use. Sea-island cotton is a profitable export crop. A modest amount of sugar is harvested each year and there are plans for production of ethanol from sugarcane. Vegetables, including beans, carrots, cabbage, cucumbers, plantains, squash, tomatoes, and yams, are grown mostly on small family plots for local markets. The Ministry of Agriculture is encouraging self-sufficiency in certain foods to cut dependence on food imports. (Food imports account for about 25% of all imports in terms of value.) Crops suffer from drought and insect pests, and cotton and sugar plantings suffer from soil depletion and the unwillingness of the population to work in the fields. Annual mango production is approximately 1,000 tons.

use imported raw materials. Industrial products include rum, refined petroleum, pottery, paints, garments, furniture, and electrical components. Industry accounted for 19% of gross domestic product (GDP) in 2001.

20 ■ Labor

The total labor force was estimated at 30,000 in 2002. About 82% of the employed labor force worked in occupations connected with tourism or other services; 7% in industry; and 11% in agriculture, hunting, forestry, and fishing. In 2002, the minimum wage averaged $93.63 per week.

The minimum working age is 16, and the law is enforced by the Ministry of Labour, which conducts periodic workplace inspections. Around 75% of the workforce is unionized.

22 ■ Domesticated Animals

Antigua and Barbuda has an estimated 16,000 head of cattle, 12,000 sheep, 12,000 goats, and 2,000 hogs. Most livestock is owned by individual households. Milk production is an estimated 6,000 tons. The government has sought to increase grazing space and to improve stock, breeding Nelthropp cattle and Black Belly sheep. There is a growing poultry industry.

23 ■ Fishing

Most fishing is for local consumption, although there is a growing export of the lobster catch to the United States and of some fish to Guadeloupe and Martinique. Antiguans annually consume the most fish per person per year (46 kilograms/ 101.4 pounds) of any Caribbean nation or territory. The main fishing waters are

Components of the Economy

This pie chart shows how much of the country's economy is devoted to agriculture (includes forestry, hunting, and fishing), industry, or services.

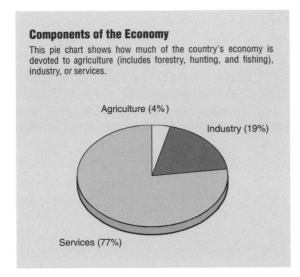

Agriculture (4%)

Industry (19%)

Services (77%)

Yearly Balance of Trade

The balance of trade is the difference between what a country sells to other countries (its exports) and what it buys (its imports). If a country imports more than it exports, it has a negative balance of trade (a trade deficit). If exports exceed imports there is a positive balance of trade (a trade surplus).

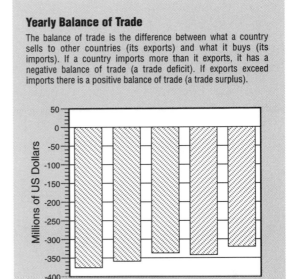

near shore or between Antigua and Barbuda. There are also shrimp and lobster farms. The Smithsonian Institution has a Caribbean king crab farming facility for the local market. The government has encouraged modern fishing methods and supported mechanization and the building of new boats. Fish landings in 2000 were 1,481 tons. The lobster catch was 42 tons. Exports of fish commodities in 2000 were valued at $1.5 million.

24 ■ Forestry

About 11% of the land is forested, mainly by plantings of red cedar, mahogany, white cedar, and acacia. A reforestation program was begun in 1963 to improve soil and water conservation.

25 ■ Mining

Few of the islands' mineral resources, including limestone, building stone, clay, and barite, were exploited until recently. Limestone and volcanic stone have been extracted from Antigua for local construc-

tion. The manufacture of bricks and tiles from local clay has begun on a small scale. Barbuda produced a small amount of salt, while phosphate has been collected from Redonda.

26 ■ Foreign Trade

Primary exports include petroleum products, manufactured goods and materials, and machinery and transport equipment. Imports include food, live animals, machinery and transport equipment, manufactured goods, chemicals, and oil.

The country exports mostly to the OECS (Organization of Eastern Caribbean States), Barbados, and Trinidad and Tobago. Its major import providers are the United States, United Kingdom, and the nations of the OECS.

AP/Wide World Photos

Nine-year-old Mahasha Johnson carries a water bottle through the streets of St. John's. Antigua was hit by Hurricane Luis in 1995 and by Hurricane Georges in 1998.

27 ▪ Energy and Power

Electric power produced in 2000 totaled 100 million kilowatt hours. Gas is produced and refined locally. All primary energy consumption is petroleum based.

28 ▪ Social Development

A social security fund provides compulsory coverage of persons between the ages of sixteen and sixty years. Medical insurance includes maternity benefits. The government operates daycare centers for children under five years of age. Domestic

violence legislation was passed by parliament in 1999.

29 ▪ Health

There are 4 hospitals to care for the sick and aged. In addition, 9 health centers and 18 dispensaries are located throughout the country. In 1995 there were 11 doctors and 218 nurses.

The infant mortality rate in 2002 was estimated at 22 per 1,000 live births. The average life expectancy was 71 years.

The leading causes of death between 1996 and 1999 included cancer, cardiovascular disease, and trauma. By the end of 1999, there had been 271 cases of human immunodeficiency virus/acquired immunodeficiency syndrome (HIV/AIDS) reported.

30 ▪ Housing

The Central Housing and Planning Authority (CHAPA) rehabilitates houses in the event of disaster, develops new housing tracts, and redevelops deteriorating areas. In March 2003, the government announced that plans were in place for CHAPA to build a number of affordable housing developments on private lands. CHAPA also planned to institute a Housing Improvement Mortgage program to make it easier for citizens to purchase these homes.

31 ▪ Education

Education is required for children between the ages of 5 and 16 years. Primary education begins at the age of 5 years and normally lasts for 7 years. Secondary education lasts for five years. As of 2000, there were 72 primary and secondary schools. There were 9,298 students enrolled at the

Selected Social Indicators

The statistics below are the most recent estimates available as of 2003. For comparison purposes, data for the United States and averages for low-income countries and high-income countries are also given. About 15% of the world's 6.4 billion people live in high-income countries, while 40% live in low-income countries.

Indicator	Antigua and Barbuda	Low-income countries	High-income countries	United States
Per capita gross national income (GNI)*	$11,000	$2,110	$28,480	$36,110
Population growth rate	0.6%	2.1%	0.7%	1.1%
People per square kilometer of land	157	77	31	31
Life expectancy in years: *male*	69	58	75	75
female	74	60	81	80
Number of physicians per 1,000 people	3	1.0	3.0	2.8
Number of pupils per teacher (primary school)	21	40	17	15
Literacy rate (15 years and older)	89%	66%	>95%	97%
Television sets per 1,000 people	466	91	735	938
Internet users per 1,000 people	73	10	364	551
Energy consumed per capita (kg of oil equivalent)	2,025	550	5,366	7,937

* The GNI is the total of all goods and services produced by the residents of a country in a year. The per capita GNI is calculated by dividing a country's GNI by its population and adjusting for relative purchasing power.

n.a. = data not available   > = greater than   < = less than

SOURCES: International Telecommunication Union (ITU). *World Telecommunication Development Report 2003.* Geneva, Switzerland: ITU, 2003; World Bank. *World Development Indicators.* Washington, D.C.: The World Bank, 2004; Central Intelligence Agency. *The World Factbook.* Washington, D.C.: Government Printing Office, 2003.

primary schools and 5,845 students at the secondary schools. The primary pupil-teacher ratio is an estimated 21 to 1.

There currently are three colleges. The University of Health Sciences, Antigua, was founded in 1982. The University of the West Indies School of Continuing Studies (Antigua and Barbuda), founded in 1949, offers adult education courses, secretarial skills training programs, summer courses for children, and special programs for women. In 1972, the technical and teacher's training colleges merged and formed the Antigua State College.

The University of the West Indies has campuses in Barbados, Trinidad, and Jamaica, and it maintains facilities on several other islands, including Antigua. Those interested in higher education also enroll at schools in the United Kingdom, the United States, Europe, and Canada. Antigua's illiteracy rate (estimated at 11%: males, 10%; females, 12%) is among the lowest in the Eastern Caribbean.

32 ▪ Media

The islands' automatic telephone system had approximately 28,000 mainline telephones and 1,300 cellular phones in use as of 1996. International telephone and telex services are supplied by Cable and Wireless (West Indies), Ltd.

Eight broadcasting stations—4 AM, 2 FM, and 2 television—were in operation in 1999. In 2001, the first independent radio station, Observer, began operations. This station is operated by the owners of the *Observer* newspaper. In 1997 there were about 36,000 radios and 31,000 television sets in use throughout the country. With 16 Internet service providers, 5,000 people subscribed to Internet service in 2001.

The *Workers' Voice,* the official publication of the ALP and the Antigua Trades and Labour Union, appears weekly and has a circulation of 6,000 as of 2002. The *Outlet,* published weekly by the Antigua Caribbean Liberation Movement, has a circulation of 5,000. The *Nation,* with a circulation of about 1,500, is published by the government and appears weekly.

33 ■ Tourism and Recreation

Tourism is the main source of income in Antigua and Barbuda. Antigua's abundance of beaches, as many as 365, and its charter yachting and deep-sea fishing facilities have created the largest tourist industry in the Windward and Leeward Islands. The international regatta and Summer Carnival are popular annual events. Cricket is the national pastime. A wide range of hotels and restaurants served 232,000 tourists in 1999.

34 ■ Famous Antiguans and Barbudans

The first successful colonizer of Antigua was Sir Thomas Warner (d. 1649). Vere Cornwall Bird Sr. (1910–1999) was prime minister from 1981 until 1994. (Isaac) Vivian Alexander ("Viv") Richards (b. 1952) is a famous cricketer.

35 ■ Bibliography

Berleant-Schiller, Riva. *Antigua and Barbuda.* Oxford: ABC Clio, 1995.

Etherington, Melanie. *The Antigua and Barbuda Companion.* Brooklyn, NY: Interlink Books, 2003.

Jinkins, Dana. *Antigua and Barbuda: A Photographic Journey.* Waitsfield, VT: Concepts, 1999.

Kincaid, Jamaica. *A Small Place.* New York: Farrar, Straus, Giroux, 2000.

Kozleski, Lisa. *The Leeward Islands: Anguilla, St. Martin, St. Barts, St. Eustatius, Guadeloupe, St. Kitts and Nevis, Antigua and Barbuda, and Montserrat.* Philadelphia, PA: Mason Crest Publishers, 2004.

Philpott, Don. *Antigua and Barbuda.* Edison, NJ: Hunter, 2000.

Argentina

Argentine Republic
República Argentina

Capital: Buenos Aires.

Flag: The national flag consists of a white horizontal stripe between two light blue horizontal stripes. Centered in the white band is a radiant yellow sun with a human face.

Anthem: *Himno Nacional*, beginning "Oíd, mortales, el grito sagrado Libertad" ("Hear, O mortals, the sacred cry of Liberty").

Monetary Unit: The peso (A$) is a paper currency of 100 centavos. There are coins of 1, 5, 10, 25 and 50 centavos, and notes of 1, 2, 5, 10, 20, 50, and 100 pesos. The rate of exchange is about A$0.3597= US$1 (or US$1= A$2.78; as of May 2003).

Weights and Measures: The metric system is the legal standard.

Holidays: New Year's Day, 1 January; Labor Day, 1 May; Anniversary of the 1810 Revolution, 25 May; Occupation of the Islas Malvinas, 10 June; Flag Day, 20 June; Independence Day, 9 July; Anniversary of San Martín, 17 August; Columbus Day, 12 October; Immaculate Conception, 8 December; Christmas, 25 December. Movable religious holidays include Carnival (two days in February or March) and Good Friday.

Time: 9 AM = noon GMT.

1 ■ Location and Size

Shaped like a wedge with its point in the south, Argentina is the second-largest country in South America. Argentina is slightly less than three-tenths the size of the United States, with a total area of 2,766,890 square kilometers (1,068,302 square miles). Argentina shares boundaries with Bolivia, Paraguay, Brazil, Uruguay, and Chile, with a total land boundary length of 9,665 kilometers (6,006 miles). The coastline is 4,989 kilometers (3,100 miles).

Argentina's capital city, Buenos Aires, is located along the eastern edge of the country on the Atlantic coast.

Argentina lays claim to a section of Antarctica that has an area of about 1,235,000 square kilometers (477,000 square miles). Both Argentina and the United Kingdom claim the Falkland Islands, which the United Kingdom currently occupies.

2 ■ Topography

Except for the mountainous western area, Argentina is generally a lowland country.

Geographic Profile

Geographic Features

Size ranking: 8 of 193

Highest elevation: 6,960 meters (22,834 feet) at Mount Aconcagua

Lowest elevation: -40 meters (-131 feet) at Salinas Chicas

Land Use*

Arable land: 12%

Permanent crops: 1%

Forests: 13%

Other: 74%

Weather**

Average annual precipitation: 103 centimeters (40 inches)

Average temperature in January: 23.7°C (74.7°F)

Average temperature in July: 10.6°C (51.1°F)

---

* Arable Land: Land used for temporary crops, like meadows for mowing or pasture, gardens, and greenhouses.

Permanent crops: Land cultivated with crops that occupy its use for long periods, such as cocoa, coffee, rubber, fruit and nut orchards, and vineyards.

Forests: Land containing stands of trees.

Other: Any land not specified, including built-on areas, roads, and barren land.

** The measurements for precipitation and average temperatures were taken at weather stations closest to the country's largest city.

Precipitation and average temperature can vary significantly within a country, due to factors such as latitude, altitude, coastal proximity, and wind patterns.

It is divided into four topographical regions: the Andean region, Patagonia, the subtropical plain of the north, and the pampas. The Andean region covers almost 30% of the country. It runs from the high plateau of the Bolivian border southward into western Argentina. Patagonia consists of all the area from the Río Negro to the southern extremity of the continent. Patagonia is a semiarid, sparsely populated region. It includes the barren island of Tierra del Fuego, part of which belongs to Chile. A portion of the Gran Chaco, covering the area between the Andean piedmont and the Paraná River, consists of an immense lowland plain, rain forests, and swampland, little of which is habitable.

Argentina's best-known topographical feature is a huge area of lush, well-watered, level plains known as the pampas. Stretching from the east coast, the pampas spread in a semicircle from the Buenos Aires area to the foothills of the Andes, to the Chaco, and to Patagonia. They form the heartland of Argentina, the source of its greatest wealth, and the home of 80% of its people.

The major Argentine rivers flow eastward into the Atlantic Ocean. The Paraná, Uruguay, Paraguay, and Alto Paraná rivers all flow into the Río de la Plata. The Paraná is the longest river, with a length of 4,900 kilometers (3,060 miles). There is a region of snow-fed lakes in the foothills of the Andes in western Patagonia. Many small lakes are found in the Buenos Aires, La Pampa, and Córdoba provinces. The largest lake is Lake Buenos Aires (which is shared with Chile) with an area of 2,240 square kilometers (860 square miles).

The highest peak in Argentina is Mount Aconcagua (6,960 meters/22,835 feet), which is also the highest mountain in

South America. The lowest point is Salinas Chicas (on Peninsula Valdes) at -40 meters (-131 feet) below sea level.

3 ▊ Climate

Argentina's climate is generally temperate, but there are many variations due to the great range in altitude and the vast extent of the country. The highest temperature, 49°C (120°F), was recorded in the extreme north, and the lowest, -16°C (3°F), in the southern tip of the country. Rainfall at Buenos Aires averages 94 centimeters (37 inches) annually, and the mean annual temperature is 16°C (61°F).

Throughout Argentina, January is the warmest month, and June and July are the coldest. The pampas, despite their immensity, have an almost uniform climate, with much sunshine and adequate precipitation. The coldest winters occur not in Tierra del Fuego, which is warmed by ocean currents, but in Santa Cruz Province, where the July average is 0°C (32°F).

4 ▊ Plants and Animals

More than 10% of the world's flora varieties are found in Argentina. The magnificent grasslands have had a prominent role in the development of Argentina's world-famous cattle industry. Evergreen beeches and Paraná pine are common.

Many tropical animals thrive in the forests and marshes of northern Argentina. Among them are the capybara, coypu, puma, and various wildcats. In the grasslands and deserts are the guanaco, rhea, and many types of rodents. The cavy, viscacha, tuco tuco, armadillo, pichiciago, otter, weasel, nutria, opossum, various types of fox, and hog-nosed skunk are common. The ostrich,

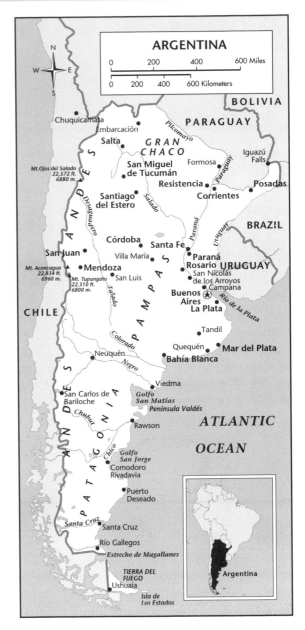

Location: 21°47' to 55°16's; 53°38' to 73°35'w.
Boundary Lengths: Bolivia, 832 kilometers (517 miles); Paraguay, 1,880 kilometers (1,168 miles); Brazil, 1,224 kilometers (761 miles); Uruguay, 579 kilometers (360 miles); Atlantic coastline, 4,989 kilometers (3,100 miles); Chile, 5,150 kilometers (3,200 miles).
Territorial Sea Limit: 200 miles.

A view of Perito Moreno Glacier in Argentina's Glacier National Park.

crested screamer, tinamou, and ovenbird are a few of the many species of birds. Caimans, frogs, lizards, snakes, and turtles are present in great numbers. The dorado, a fine game fish, is found in larger streams, and the pejerrey, corvina, palameta, pacu, and zurubi abound in the rivers.

Argentina is richly endowed with fossil remains of dinosaurs and other creatures.

5 ■ Environment

The major environmental issues in Argentina are pollution and the loss of agricultural lands. The soil is threatened by erosion, salinization, and deforestation. Air pollution is also a problem due to chemicals from industrial sources. The water supply is threatened by uncontrolled dumping of pesticides, hydrocarbons, and heavy metals.

Endangered species in Argentina include the ruddy-headed goose, Argentinian pampas deer, South Andean huemul, Puna rhea, tundra peregrine falcon, black-fronted piping guan, glaucous macaw, spectacled caiman, broad-nosed caiman, Lear's macaw, guayaquil great green macaw, and American crocodile. Of the 320 species of mammals in Argentina, 27 are considered endangered. Forty-one of the 897 species of birds are threatened. Out of a total of 234 reptiles, 5 are also threatened. Of the nation's 9,000-plus plant species, 83 were endangered as of 2001.

6 ■ Population

Argentina's population was estimated at 38.4 million in 2003. The projected population for the year 2005 is 39.6 million. Average population density was 13 persons per square kilometer (34 persons per square mile) in 2002. Around one-third of all Argentines live in or around Buenos Aires. The estimated populations of Argentina's largest metropolitan areas in 2000 were Buenos Aires, 12.4 million; Córdoba, 1.4 million; and Rosario, 1.2 million.

7 ■ Migration

Migration to Argentina has been heavy in the past, especially from Spain and Italy. More recently, immigrants have also come from Paraguay, Bolivia, Chile, Uruguay, and Brazil. As of September 2000, there were 3,000 refugees and asylum seekers in the country. Most were from Peru and Cuba, but there were also more than 30 other nationalities from Latin America, Eastern Europe, Africa, and Asia.

Of much greater significance to Argentina has been the tendency for workers in rural areas to move to the cities. The growth in the urban population has led to a host of economic and social problems. Both the federal government and provincial governments have vainly encouraged aged workers to return to rural areas. In 2003 there were an estimated 0.62 migrants per 1,000 population.

8 ■ Ethnic Groups

Argentina's population is overwhelmingly European in origin (principally from Spain and Italy); there is little mixture of indigenous peoples. An estimated 97% of

©Greta De Meyer/EPD Photos

Giant cacti grow on the dry plains in parts of Patagonia.

the people are of European extraction, and 3% are mestizo, Amerindian, or of other nonwhite groups. The pure Amerindian population has been increasing slightly through immigration from Bolivia and Paraguay. Citizens of Argentina are called Argentines.

9 ■ Languages

The national language of Argentina is Spanish. The most distinctive sound in Argentine Spanish is the yeísmo, in which the *ll* and *y* are pronounced like the *z* in *azure*. Also, the meaning of many words has been changed from their original definition in Castilian Spanish. The Porteños, as the inhabitants of Buenos Aires are called, rely heavily upon different tones of voice to express shades of meaning.

English has become increasingly popular as a second language, especially in metropolitan areas and in the business and professional community. There are pockets of Italian and German immigrants speaking their native languages. Some Amerindian languages are still spoken, including a version of Tehuelche in the pampas and Patagonia, Guaraní in Misiones Province, and Quechua in some parts of the Jujuy and Salta provinces.

10 ▧ Religions

Statistics submitted by nongovernment organizations in 2001 indicate that the Roman Catholic religion continues to claim the largest number of members, at about 88% of the population. Argentina retains national patronage over the Roman Catholic Church. Under this system, bishops are appointed by the president of the republic. The government also provides the Catholic Church with some monetary support. However, the constitution does provide for freedom of religion, and the government encourages tolerance and understanding between social and religious groups.

In 2001, Protestants accounted for about 7% of the population. About 1.5% of the population were Muslims and about 1% were Jewish.

11 ▧ Transportation

Argentina has the largest railway system in South America, with 33,744 kilometers (20,968 miles) of track as of 2002. The number of passengers carried dropped from 445 million in 1976 to 300 million in 1991. The subway system in Buenos Aires consists of 5 lines totaling 36 kilometers (22 miles). Millions of passengers ride the subway each year.

By 2001, the nation had 215,434 kilometers (133,871 miles) of roads. The road system still is far from adequate, especially in view of Argentina's rapidly growing automotive industry. In 2000, the total number of registered vehicles reached 4,785,189 (including 3,722,992 passenger cars).

The main river system of Argentina consists of the Río de la Plata and its tributaries, the Paraná, Uruguay, Paraguay, and Alto Paraná (located in Brazil) Rivers. There is a total of 10,950 kilometers (6,800 miles) of navigable waterways, offering vast possibilities for efficient water transportation. The La Plata ports (Buenos Aires and La Plata) account for more than half of all maritime cargo.

The port of Buenos Aires handles about four-fifths of the country's imports and exports, and it is the focus of river traffic on the La Plata system. Other major ports are Rosario, Quequén, Bahía Blanca, Campana, and San Nicolás.

Buenos Aires is the most important air terminal in South America. Ezeiza Airport, about 40 kilometers (25 miles) from Buenos Aires, is one of the largest in the world and services several million passengers each year. In 2001 Argentina had a total of 145 airports and landing fields with paved runways. The government line is Aerolíneas Argentinas. Scheduled civil aviation services

Susan D Rock

Avenida 9 de Julio in Buenos Aires is the world's widest street at 130 meters (425 feet).

fly more than 15 billion passenger-kilometers (9.3 billion passenger-miles) per year.

12 ■ History

Before the Spaniards arrived in 1515, about 20 Amerindian groups totaling some 300,000 people lived in the region now called Argentina. Spanish colonists from Chile, Peru, and Paraguay created the first permanent settlements in Argentina, including Buenos Aires in 1580.

In 1776, Spain created the Viceroyalty of Río de la Plata from its territories in southeastern South America, with Buenos Aires as its main port and capital. During the colonial period, there was little interest in Argentina. The region had no mineral wealth, and Spaniards overlooked its fertile soil and temperate climate.

In May 1810, Buenos Aires held an open town meeting *(cabildo abierto)*, deposed the viceroy, and set up an independent government to rule the Viceroyalty. Argentina formally declared its independence on 9 July 1816. A long period of disorder followed until 1862 when Bartolomé Mitre finally unified the nation with Buenos Aires at its center. A period of rapid economic development followed, and the fertile pampas began to shift from livestock to agricultural production. During this time, the country came under the control of a powerful team of wealthy landowners and the military. Although social reforms were enacted in the 1920s, an economic crisis caused by the world depression led to a military takeover in 1930.

For the next thirteen years, Argentina was ruled by the old military-landowner alliance, which brought economic recovery, political corruption, and a worsening of social tensions. Argentina's careful neutrality in World War II (1939–45) masked strong Fascist sympathies, further dividing the nation.

The Presidencies of the Peróns: Another military takeover in 1943 launched a new era in Argentine politics. With Argentina's war-related industrial expansion, a large blue-collar workforce had been created. This new power base supported Colonel Juan Domingo Perón in his successful 1946 bid for the presidency. His supporters also won majorities in both houses of Congress.

Perón then began sweeping political, economic, and social changes. Perón combined industrialism, nationalism, and dictatorship. His strong personal appeal was enhanced by the charm of his wife Eva ("Evita"), who captivated the masses with her work on behalf of the poor. Perón also sought to act as a protector of weaker Latin American nations against U.S. and British "imperialists."

After reelection in 1951, Perón became more dictatorial and unpredictable, especially after the death of Evita a year later. Finally, a disillusioned military group took over in September 1955. Perón went into exile in Spain. For the next twenty years, Argentina felt the shadow of Perón, who held veto powers from exile in Spain. Under the military's watchful eye, a succession of governments attempted unsuccessfully to create a new political order.

Perón returned to Argentina in June 1973 and ran for the presidency. He won 61.9% of the vote in a special election in September. His running mate was his third wife, María Estela ("Isabel") Martínez de Perón. However, there was no magic left in the elderly Perón, and the economy continued to decline. When Perón died in July 1974, his widow, Isabel, succeeded to the presidency.

Isabel had none of Evita's appeal, and her administration plunged Argentina more deeply into chaos. In March 1976, she was arrested in a bloodless takeover, and a military group took over.

For seven years, the military attempted to "purify" Argentina by removing all traces of the influence of the Peróns, leftism, and trade unionism. During this period, the military killed more than 5,000 people and jailed and tortured many others. It also was during this time that between 6,000 and 15,000 antigovernment activists "disappeared." Major economic reforms included the turning of banking and industry over to private ownership. However, the military was never able to solve the problem of inflation, which remained in triple digits for most of this period.

Troubled by economic woes, the government attempted to gain the support of the people by asserting Argentina's rights to the Falkland Islands. The Falkland Islands lie about 550 kilometers (340 miles) due east of Río Gallegos and were claimed by the United Kingdom. In April 1982, Argentina invaded the Falkland Islands, claiming possession of them. In the war with the United Kingdom that followed, Argentina's armed forces were defeated, and were forced to surrender in June.

In elections for a civilian president held in October 1983, the surprise winner was a human rights activist, Dr. Raúl Alfonsín. Alfonsín called for a new inquiry of the thousands who had "disappeared" between 1975 and 1979 and ordered the prosecution of members of the former government. Several were convicted. However, the human rights trials of leading military officers angered the military, and in 1987 Alfonsín was forced to ease his prosecutions.

The Alfonsín administration also acted to halt runaway inflation with the "Austral Plan" of mid-1985. This plan froze wages and prices and created a new unit of currency, the austral, to replace the peso. The initial success of the plan was weakened by renewed inflation and wage demands.

With the failure of the Alfonsín administration to stabilize the economy or bring military leaders to justice, Argentines sought change from an old source: the Perónists. In May 1989, Carlos Saul Menem, running under the Perónist banner, was elected president in May 1989 and reelected in 1994. Abandoning his party's traditional support of state enterprises, Menem cut government spending, reduced the role of government in the economy, and abruptly introduced capitalist reforms. Following allegations of corruption in 1997, support for Menem weakened in spite of his administration's economic successes.

As the Argentine economy slipped into recession, Fernando de la Rúa Bruno, the former mayor of Buenos Aires, defeated Eduardo Duhalde in the 1999 presidential election. Declaring a national economic emergency, by March 2000 de la Rúa had pushed through a new budget that cut the country's fiscal deficit in half. Because he had failed to restrict spending by provincial governors and had trouble stimulating economic growth, de la Rúa could not overcome the economic crisis. The government was forced to devalue the currency against the dollar.

Social and political chaos followed, with the economy going into its worst recession in decades. After protests turned violent in Buenos Aires in December 2001, looting and chaos erupted, followed by police repression. De la Rúa was forced to resign from the presidency. After a few weeks of political instability, the Senate chose Eduardo Duhalde as temporary president. Duhalde governed until May 2003, when Néstor Kirchner, elected in April, was inaugurated president.

Kirchner became president of a country in the midst of an economic, social, and political crisis. The economy shrank by 14% in 2002 and official unemployment remained at 25%. With a mounting foreign debt and financial obligations to foreign lenders that were difficult to meet, President Kirchner faced the challenge of assuring Argentines and the world that he had the leadership skills, political muscle, and will needed to lead his country out of turmoil.

13 ■ Government

Argentina is a federation of twenty-three provinces and the federal capital of Buenos Aires.

There is separation of powers among the executive, legislative, and judicial branches, but the president is powerful within this arrangement. The president can draw up and introduce his own bills in Congress and appoint cabinet members and other officials without the consent of the Senate. The president also possesses broad powers to declare a state of siege and suspend the constitution.

The president is commander-in-chief of the army, navy, and air force. The president

Biographical Profile

Name: Néstor Carlos Kirchner
Position: President of a republic
Took Office: 25 May 2003
Birthplace: Rio Gallegos, Argentina
Birthdate: 25 February 1950
Spouse: Cristina Fernandez, a senator
Children: Two children
Of interest: Before becoming president, Kirchner was a little-known governor of Santa Cruz, an oil-rich southern province of Argentina

Néstor Carlos Kirchner

and vice president are directly elected for a four-year term and cannot be reelected beyond a second consecutive term. They or their parents must be native-born citizens. Voting is compulsory for all citizens eighteen to seventy years of age.

The constitution calls for a National Congress consisting of a 72-member Senate and a 257-member Chamber of Deputies.

14 ■ Political Parties

Due to the frequency of military takeovers, parties have often been banned. Still, several parties were formed in the 1980s and continued be active in the 1990s and into the twenty-first century.

Traditionally, the alignment of Argentine political parties has been along socioeconomic and religious lines. The landowners, the high clergy, and the more conservative lower-class supporters have formed an alliance that defends the Roman Catholic Church and the status quo. On the other side have been the advocates of change: merchants and professionals who resent the dominance of the aristocracy and who tend also to be opposed to the influence of the Roman Catholic Church. This second group has supported separation of church and state and decentralization (the dispersion of power and authority). However, more recently, new parties have emerged to represent the working class, small farmers, and intellectuals.

As of 2003, the Justicialist Party (a Peronist umbrella organization) and the Radical Civic Union Party were the predominant political parties, although the Alternative for a Republic of Equals (ARI) and the Front for a Country in Solidarity, or FREPASO (a four-party coalition), also held seats in the National Congress.

15 ▉ Judicial System

The Supreme Court supervises and regulates all other federal courts. Other federal courts include nine appeals courts; single-judge district courts, at least one for each province; and one-judge territorial courts. Provincial courts include supreme courts, appeals courts, courts of first instance, and minor courts.

In 2003, President Néstor Kirchner announced his plan to strengthen the judiciary by undoing some of former President Menem's policies that turned the Supreme Court into a political ally of the president.

16 ▉ Armed Forces

From 1930 through 1983, fourteen of Argentina's eighteen presidents were military officers. The military remained one of the most powerful political forces in Argentina until it suffered defeat by the British in the Falklands War in 1982.

The Argentine armed forces, after being reduced and reorganized, numbered 70,000 in 2002. The navy had 16,000 personnel including 2,500 marines. The air force numbered 12,500 with 130 combat aircraft and 29 armed helicopters. Defense spending for 1999 was $4.3 billion or 1.3% of the gross domestic product (GDP). Required military service ended in 1995.

17 ▉ Economy

Argentina has one of the most highly developed economies and richest natural

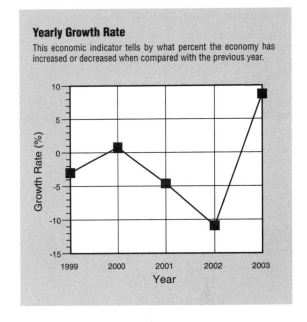

Yearly Growth Rate

This economic indicator tells by what percent the economy has increased or decreased when compared with the previous year.

resource bases in Latin America. However, political instability has kept the economy from reaching its full potential. The country has almost overcome its dependence on imported machinery and finished products. There is a great demand for parts and raw materials that are assembled or finished within Argentina.

The inflation rate for 1983 was 434%, the highest in the world. By 1998, inflation had been reduced to about 1%.

In 1991, President Carlos Menem introduced an original stabilization and reform program. During the period from 1988 to 1999, average annual growth reached 4.4%, due largely to successful planning and political stability.

The Argentine economy experienced a serious financial crisis in 2001–02. Doubts were raised as to Argentina's ability to repay its debts. Unpopular steps taken by the government, such as tax increases, spending cuts, and restrictions on bank withdraw-

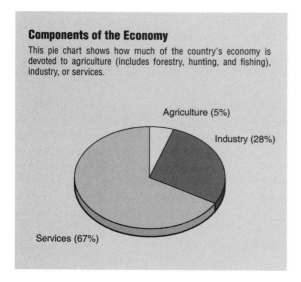

Components of the Economy

This pie chart shows how much of the country's economy is devoted to agriculture (includes forestry, hunting, and fishing), industry, or services.

Agriculture (5%)

Industry (28%)

Services (67%)

als, did not stop the decline in investor and consumer confidence. At the end of 2001, street violence broke out. The country went through an extraordinary five presidents in two weeks. The third president took the step of defaulting on payments due on $132 billion of bonds in late December 2001. The fifth broke the one-to-one relationship between the peso and the dollar in January 2002. With the devalued currency, external debt jumped from 56% of the gross domestic product (GDP) to over 130%.

In 2003, the government negotiated an agreement with the International Monetary Fund (IMF) for loans in the amount of $6.87 billion.

18 ▪ Income

In 2002, Argentina's gross national product (GNP) was $391 billion, or $10,200 per person. The annual growth rate of GNP was estimated at -14.7%. The average inflation rate in 2001 was 4%.

19 ▪ Industry

Córdoba is Argentina's major industrial center. It is the center of metalworking, especially for motor vehicle production. Argentina's other principal industrial enterprises are heavily concentrated in and around the city of Buenos Aires. The plants are close to both the many raw materials imported by ship and the vast productive area of the pampas. The major industries in Buenos Aires are meat packing, food processing, motor vehicles, machinery manufacturing and assembly, flour milling, tanning and leather goods manufacturing, oil refining, oilseed milling, and textile, chemical, pharmaceutical, and cement manufacturing.

The packing and processing of food products is the oldest and most important industry in Argentina. The textile industry also was developed quite early, making use of wool from the vast herds of sheep and the cotton from Chaco Province in the northeast. In addition to these traditional products, a variety of synthetic fibers are produced.

Argentina's automotive industry manufactured 235,577 motor vehicles in 2001. Argentina also produces electric appliances, communications equipment—including radios and television sets—motors, watches, and numerous other items. Output of cement, trucks, machinery, plastics, petrochemicals, and other chemicals all rose in the 1990s.

Industry accounted for 16% of the gross domestic product (GDP) in 2001; it was 20% of the GDP in 2002, and was expected to be at least 25% of the GDP in 2003. Industrial goods represented approximately 31% of exports in 2002.

In 1985, exports of petroleum fuels exceeded imports for the first time, and by

1999 Argentina was self-sufficient in oil and gas. A recession that began in 1998 was worsened by the economic crisis of December 2001. Industrial production began to increase in late 2002, however, and the best-performing sectors were textiles, automobile tires, and oils.

20 ■ Labor

The labor force is estimated to be divided as follows: about 18% in manufacturing, 18% in commerce, 10% in transport and communications, 10% in public administration and defense, 2% in agriculture, and the remainder in other sectors.

Organized labor has probably had a greater effect on the modern history of Argentina than any other group. Long-time dictator Juan Perón used the labor movement as his chief means of achieving and holding dictatorial power. In 2002, an estimated 35% of laborers were unionized.

Argentine law specifies that all workers are entitled to a minimum wage (about $200 per month in 2001). It does not provide a living wage for a family, but most workers earn considerably more.

The law prohibits children under the age of fifteen from working full-time, as they are required to attend school. However, child labor continues to be a problem.

21 ■ Agriculture

Agriculture and agroindustry in Argentina focus on the production of cereal, oil grains and seeds, sugar, fruit, wine, tea, tobacco, and cotton. Argentina is one of the greatest food-producing and food-exporting countries of the world. As of 2001, agriculture made up 5% of the GDP.

Agricultural products also accounted for 41% of exports by value.

The principal agricultural region consists of the humid pampas, one of the world's greatest reaches of arable land. Citrus fruit, tobacco, cotton, and sugarcane are cultivated outside the pampas. Wheat is the leading crop. Argentina accounts for about 75% of all wheat produced in South America and is one of the world's leading wheat exporters. Argentina is also one of the largest corn-growing countries in the world, with production at 13.2 million tons. Barley is favored as the grain of greatest yield and resistance to disease. The barley harvest produces about 400,000 tons annually.

Rice is a major crop, with annual production of approximately 1.57 million tons. Argentina was also one of the world's biggest producers of flaxseed (linseed), with production at 85,000 tons. Most of the crop is exported in the form of linseed oil. The province of Tucumán dominates the sugar-raising industry. Sugarcane production is about 19.4 million tons annually.

Cotton growing is concentrated in Chaco Province. Annual production of cotton fiber is approximately 227,000 tons. Production of sunflower seeds, used primarily to make oil, is about 6.5 million tons. Tobacco is raised in several northern provinces, especially Misiones, with production at an estimated 113,000 tons. Annual soybean production is about 18 million tons.

Estimates of annual fruit production are 1 million tons of apples, 780,000 tons of oranges, 1 million tons of lemons and limes, 250,000 tons of peaches and nectarines, 230,000 tons of grapefruit, and 175,000 tons of bananas. The province of Mendoza is the center for the nation's vineyards. Annual grape production is approximately 2.5 million tons. Argentina is one of the world's leading producers of wine, accounting for about 1.26 million tons annually, or between 4% and 5% of the world's total production.

22 ▪ Domesticated Animals

Argentina is one of the world's preeminent producers of cattle and sheep, possessing approximately 4% of the entire world's stock of cattle and 2% of the total stock of sheep. Thus, livestock and meat exports play an essential part in the nation's international trade. In 2001, total meat production was 3.7 million tons, of which 2.45 million tons consisted of beef. Beef exports for 2001 were valued at $528 million.

Argentina has about 55 million head of cattle. Cattle were introduced into Argentina by Pedro de Mendoza in 1536. The most important beef-producing breeds are Shorthorn, introduced in 1823; Hereford, 1858; Aberdeen Angus, 1879; and in recent years, zebu and Charolais. The dairy industry produces about 9.75 tons of milk, 425,000 tons of cheese, and 55,000 tons of butter annually. The most important dairy breeds are Holstein-Friesian, Jersey, and Holando Argentino. Córdoba, Santa Fe, and Buenos Aires are the three major dairy provinces. Egg production is about 236,000 tons and the number of poultry reaches about 60 million.

In sheep raising, Argentina ranks third in South America after Uruguay and Brazil, with an estimated 14 million sheep. Production includes 65,000 tons of wool clip (greasy basis) and 45,000 tons of mutton and lamb. Patagonia has approximately 40% of all the sheep in Argentina.

Argentina has 3.3 million horses, placing it among the top five countries in the world for number of horses. Argentine horses, especially favored as polo ponies and racehorses, have won many international prizes. Other livestock includes 3.2 million pigs and 3.4 million goats. Argentina is South America's largest producer of honey, with an annual output of approximately 85,000 tons.

23 ▪ Fishing

Fishing has not been a significant industry in Argentina. The catch fell from 1,256,000 tons in 1996 to 917,725 tons in 2000. The most favored saltwater fish are the pejerrey, a kind of mackerel; the dorado, resembling salmon but of a golden color; and the zurubí, an immense yellow and black spotted catfish. The principal species in the 2000 catch were Argentine shortfin squid, southern hake, and Argentine hake.

24 ▪ Forestry

Argentina's forests, estimated at about 50.9 million hectares (125.8 million acres), or 18.6% of the total area, are among its greatest underused natural resources. A major reason for the industry's lack of development is the great distance of most forests from the markets and the high cost of transportation. Woods currently harvested include softwoods, such as the elm and willow; white quebracho, used as a fuel and in the refining of coal; and red quebracho, from which tannin is extracted; as well as cedar, oak, pine, cypress, and larch.

In 2000, production of roundwood was 10.6 million cubic meters (374 million cubic feet). Exports of forest products totaled $293.9 million that year.

The most important tree is the red quebracho, which contains 21% tannin, the extract used for tanning. Argentina possesses four-fifths of the world's supply of this wood.

25 ■ Mining

The value of mineral exports in 2001 was $754.2 million, with 90% of that value from metals. Metal production accounted for 57.5% of mineral production. In 2001, Argentina was the third-largest Latin American producer of aluminum (255,000 tons of primary aluminum), the second-largest producer of lead, and the fourth-largest producer of silver. Copper production in 2001 was at about 91,566 tons and gold production was at 30,630 kilograms (67,527 pounds). The country's total silver mine output for 2001 was 152,802 kilograms (336,870 pounds). The same year, mining production included about 39,703 tons of zinc and 12,334 tons of lead. Platinum, palladium, and uranium deposits are being explored.

In 2001, Argentina produced 500,000 tons of crude boron materials, ranking third in the world, after the United States and Turkey. Other industrial minerals included limestone, dolomite, crushed quartz, talc, bentonite, diatomite, crude gypsum, kaolin, and salt. The country also produced marble, clays, sodium carbonate, asbestos, barite, and vermiculite. There are also deposits of lithium, beryllium, and columbium.

26 ■ Foreign Trade

Argentina has removed practically all non-tariff barriers to trade. The creation of the North American Free Trade Agreement (NAFTA) was viewed as an extremely positive development. Argentina is a member of MERCOSUR (a common market incor-

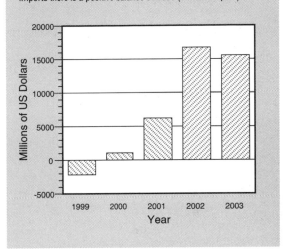

Yearly Balance of Trade

The balance of trade is the difference between what a country sells to other countries (its exports) and what it buys (its imports). If a country imports more than it exports, it has a negative balance of trade (a trade deficit). If exports exceed imports there is a positive balance of trade (a trade surplus).

porating Argentina, Brazil, Uruguay, and Paraguay), formed on 1 January 1995.

In 1998, Argentina's leading export markets were Brazil, the United States, Chile, and Spain. Imports came primarily from Brazil, the United States, China, Germany, France, Italy, and Japan.

27 ■ Energy and Power

Despite a shortage of energy resources, production of electric power has steadily increased since 1958. In 2000, electrical energy production totaled 82.8 billion kilowatt hours, and 41% of generating capacity was hydroelectric.

Argentina was the first country in Latin America to install nuclear-powered electric generating plants. Nuclear energy accounted for 7% of total electricity production in 2000. Argentina is rich in uranium.

Selected Social Indicators

The statistics below are the most recent estimates available as of 2003. For comparison purposes, data for the United States and averages for low-income countries and high-income countries are also given. About 15% of the world's 6.4 billion people live in high-income countries, while 40% live in low-income countries.

Indicator	Argentina	Low-income countries	High-income countries	United States
Per capita gross national income (GNI)*	$10,190	$2,110	$28,480	$36,110
Population growth rate	1.2%	2.1%	0.7%	1.1%
People per square kilometer of land	36	77	31	31
Life expectancy in years: *male*	71	58	75	75
female	78	60	81	80
Number of physicians per 1,000 people	2.7	1.0	3.0	2.8
Number of pupils per teacher (primary school)	20	40	17	15
Literacy rate (15 years and older)	97.1%	66%	>95%	97%
Television sets per 1,000 people	326	91	735	938
Internet users per 1,000 people	112	10	364	551
Energy consumed per capita (kg of oil equivalent)	1,726	550	5,366	7,937

* The GNI is the total of all goods and services produced by the residents of a country in a year. The per capita GNI is calculated by dividing a country's GNI by its population and adjusting for relative purchasing power.

n.a. = data not available   > = greater than   < = less than

SOURCES: International Telecommunication Union (ITU). *World Telecommunication Development Report 2003*. Geneva, Switzerland: ITU, 2003; World Bank. *World Development Indicators*. Washington, D.C.: The World Bank, 2004; Central Intelligence Agency. *The World Factbook*. Washington, D.C.: Government Printing Office, 2003.

Oil production was 818,000 barrels per day in 2002. The natural gas industry has expanded rapidly. As of 2002, Argentina had the third-largest proven natural gas reserves in South America, exceeded only by Venezuela and Mexico. Production in 2002 was 37.4 billion cubic meters (1.3 trillion cubic feet). In 2002, known reserves were estimated at 779 billion cubic meters (27.5 trillion cubic feet). There is a network of more than 9,900 kilometers (6,150 miles) of gas pipelines. Coal production was reported at 330,000 tons in 2002.

28 Social Development

In his early years in office, longtime leader Juan Perón took aggressive steps to enact far-reaching social legislation, although his social policies broke down in many ways after 1953. In the 1940s, new provisions established salary increases, paid holidays, sick leave, job security, and many other benefits. Perón's wife Eva joined him in extending legislation to working women and to the poorer classes, called the "shirtless ones," or *descamisados*. By 1945, a National Social Security Institute administered social insurance programs and a pension system. In the early 1950s, these measures continued and also were extended to the rural sector. Most of the social legislation enacted during the Perón years has remained in effect.

Although guaranteed equality under the Constitution, women are fighting for equal advancement and pay in the labor force. Although wage discrimination is prohibited by law, women earn less than men for

©Greta De Meyer/EPD Photos

In the densely populated cities and towns of Argentina, there is a shortage of housing.

the same work. A law establishing protection against family violence was passed in 1994. For disabled people, handicapped access to public places is specified by law. A constitutional amendment recognizes the ethnic and cultural identities of Argentina's indigenous people.

29 ■ Health

In the field of health and medical care, Argentina compares favorably with other Latin American countries. In 1998 Argentina had an estimated 108,800 physicians, 28,900 dentists, 15,300 pharmacists, 29,000 nurses, and 11,100 medical

technicians. Health and medical services for workers are provided by union clinics. Employers are usually required to provide free medical and pharmaceutical care for injured workers. Funding for health services comes from employee payroll taxes and contributions.

In 2000, the infant mortality rate was 17 per 1,000 live births. In 1999, life expectancy averaged 75 years (79 years for females and 71 years for males). Of the major infectious diseases, smallpox, malaria, and diphtheria have been practically eliminated and polio has been greatly reduced. By the end of

Susan D Rock

Iguazu Falls is a popular tourist site on Argentina's border with Paraguay and Brazil.

the year 2000, a total of 18,824 cases of AIDS had been reported in the country.

30 ■ Housing

Housing in Argentina reflects the Italian and Spanish ethnic backgrounds of the population. Concrete, mortar, and brick are generally favored as the principal construction materials. Wood is generally considered less durable and feared as a fire hazard. The total number of dwellings in the mid-1990s was more than 9 million, but there was a housing shortage of roughly 2.5 million houses.

31 ■ Education

Education is free, secular, and compulsory for all children at the primary level. In 1993 Argentina switched from seven years of primary and five years of secondary education to a system known as EGB, consisting of nine compulsory years divided into three-year stages. This is followed by a three-year "multimodal" course of study offering either general or specialized training.

The pupil-teacher ratio at the primary level averages 20 to 1.

Argentina has forty-six officially accredited universities. The largest is the University of Buenos Aires.

Private, foreign, and religious schools are permitted, but they must conform to a nationally prescribed pattern of teaching in the Spanish language. Argentina has one of the lowest illiteracy rates in Latin America, estimated at 3% for the year 2003 (males, 3%; females, 3%).

32 ■ Media

In 1998 there were 7.5 million mainline telephones in the nationalized system. An additional 3 million cellular phones are in use, according to 1999 figures.

As of 1999 there were 260 AM and an unspecified number of unlicensed FM radio stations. There were 42 television stations the same year. Many of the stations are privately owned. In 2003, there were about 681 radios and 326 television sets for every 1,000 people. In 2000, there were 33 Internet service providers, serving 3.88 million subscribers by 2001.

Buenos Aires is one of the principal editorial centers of the Spanish-speaking world, with more than fifty publishing houses in the 1980s and 1990s. Numerous literary magazines and reviews, as well as books, are published there. Press coverage in Argentina is among the most thorough in the hemisphere. Four news agencies (Noticias Argentinas, TELAM, Diarios y Noticias, and Interdiarios) were operating in 1995, and the major international news services were also represented. Two of the great dailies of Buenos Aires, *La Nación* and *La Prensa,* enjoy international reputations and *La Prensa* is probably the most famous newspaper in Latin America.

The largest dailies, with their estimated daily circulation figures in 2002, were: *La Nación,* 630,000; *Clarín,* 560,000; *Pagina 12,* 280,000; *Diario Popular,* 145,000; and *Tiempo Argentino,* 75,000.

33 ■ Tourism and Recreation

In 2000, 2,949,139 foreign tourists visited Argentina, about 70% of them from other countries in South America. As of 2000, there were 166,087 hotel rooms with 378,246 beds.

Mar del Plata, on the South Atlantic, about 400 kilometers (250 miles) from Buenos Aires, is the most popular ocean resort. San Carlos de Bariloche, at the entrance to Nahuel Huapi National Park in the Andean lake region of western Patagonia, has become famous as a summer and winter resort, with some of the best skiing in the Southern Hemisphere. The Iguazú Falls, in the province of Misiones, on the border with Paraguay and Brazil, is a major tourist attraction.

The most popular sport is football (soccer). Tennis, rugby, basketball, and golf also are played.

©Greta De Meyer/EPD Photos

The architecture of Argentina reflects the Italian and Spanish backgrounds of the population.

34 ■ Famous Argentines

The most famous Argentine is José de San Martín (1778–1850), known as the Protector of the South, who was principally responsible for freeing southern South America from Spanish rule. The tyrannical dictator Juan Manuel de Rosas (1793–1877) ruled Argentina from 1829 to 1852. The political tactics and the pen of the statesman and essayist Domingo Faustino Sarmiento (1811–1888) did much to undermine him. While in exile, Sarmiento wrote some of his best works, including *Facundo,* the story of a rival caudillo.

The most famous Argentine political figures of modern times have been Juan Domingo Perón Sosa (1895–1974) and his second wife, Eva Duarte de Perón (1919–1952), known as "Evita." José Hernández (1834–1886), one of the first Argentine literary figures to use the uncultured language of the gaucho in his writings, is the author of *Martín Fierro,* considered the greatest of gaucho poems. The works of the poet Leopoldo Lugones (1874–1938) form a panorama of all Argentine life and landscape. Enrique Rodríguez Larreta (1875–1961) wrote the first Latin American novel to win international fame, *La gloria de Don Ramiro,* a reconstruction of Spanish life during the reign of Philip II. The leading modern writer of Argentina is Jorge Luis Borges (1899–1986), best known for his essays and collections of tales such as *Historia universal de la infamia.* Outstanding in the visual arts are the sculptor Rogelio Irurtia (1879–1950) and the painters Miguel Carlos Victorica (1884–1955) and Emilio Pettoruti (1892–1971). Argentina's foremost composers are Alberto Williams (1862–1952), founder of the Buenos Aires Conservatory; Juan José Castro (1895–1968); Juan Carlos Paz (1901–1972); and Alberto Ginastera (1916–1983).

The most famous Argentine scientist, Bernardo Alberto Houssay (1887–1971), was awarded the 1947 Nobel Prize in medicine for his work on diabetes. Notable philosophers include Alejandro Korn (1860–1936), whose work marked a reaction against positivism. Carlos Saavedra Lamas (1878–1959), an authority on international law, received the Nobel Prize for peace in 1936. Adolfo Pérez Esquivel (b. 1931), a sculptor and professor of architecture, received the Nobel Peace Prize in 1980 for his work in the Argentine human rights movement.

35 ◼ Bibliography

Dalai, Anita. *Argentina.* Austin, TX: Raintree Steck-Vaughn, 2001.

Frank, Nicole. *Argentina.* Milwaukee, WI: Gareth Stevens, 2000.

Gofen, Ethel, and Leslie Jermyn. *Argentina.* New York: Marshall Cavendish, 2002.

Nickles, Greg. *Argentina: The Culture.* New York: Crabtree, 2001.

Nickles, Greg. *Argentina: The Land.* New York: Crabtree, 2001.

Shields, Charles J. *Argentina.* Philadelphia, PA: Mason Crest Publishers, 2003.

Armenia

Republic of Armenia
Hayastani Hanrapetut 'Yun

Capital: Yerevan.

Flag: Three horizontal bands of red (top), blue and gold.

Anthem: *Mer Hayrenik.*

Monetary Unit: The dram (introduced 22 November 1993) is a paper currency in denominations of 10, 25, 50, 100, 200, and 500 drams. The dram (D) replaced the Armenian ruble and the Russian ruble (R). Currently D1 =$0.0017 (or $1 = D591.00; as of May 2003).

Weights and Measures: The metric system is in force.

Holidays: New Year, 1–2 January; Christmas, 6 January; Easter, 1–4 April; Day of Remembrance of the Victims of the Genocide, 24 April; Peace Day, 9 May; Anniversary of Declaration of First Armenian Republic (1918), 28 May; Public Holiday, 21 September; Day of Remembrance of the Victims of the Earthquake, 7 December.

Time: 4 PM = noon GMT.

1 ▪ Location and Size

Armenia is a landlocked nation located in southeastern Europe. Comparatively, the area occupied by Armenia is slightly larger than the state of Maryland with a total area of 29,800 square kilometers (11,506 square miles). Armenia shares boundaries with Georgia, Azerbaijan, and Turkey and has a total boundary length of 1,254 kilometers (780 miles). The capital city, Yerevan, is located in the west-central portion of the country on the Hrazdan River.

2 ▪ Topography

Armenia is located in what geographers call the Aral Caspian Lowland. The country has broad sandy deserts and low grassy plateaus. The topography features the high Armenian Plateau, with mountains (many peaks are above 10,000 feet), fast-flowing rivers, and the Aras River Valley. The highest point is Mount Aragats at 4,090 meters (13,419 feet). The lowest point is in the Debed River valley at 400 meters (1,320 feet). The Aras is the longest river with a length of 914 kilometers (568 miles). Lake Sevan is the largest lake with an area of 1,244 square kilometers (480 square miles).

3 ▪ Climate

The mean temperature is 25°C (77°F) in August and -3°C (27°F) in January. Yerevan, the capital city, receives 33 centime-

Geographic Profile

Geographic Features

Size ranking: 138 of 193
Highest elevation: 4,090 meters (13,419 feet) at Mount Aragats
Lowest elevation: 400 meters (1,312 feet)

Land Use*

Arable land: 18%
Permanent crops: 2%
Forests: 12%
Other: 68%

Weather**

Average annual precipitation: (Yerevan): 33 centimeters (13 inches)
Average temperature in January: 3°C (27°F)
Average temperature in July: 25°C (77°F)

---

* *Arable Land: Land used for temporary crops, like meadows for mowing or pasture, gardens, and greenhouses.*

Permanent crops: Land cultivated with crops that occupy its use for long periods, such as cocoa, coffee, rubber, fruit and nut orchards, and vineyards.

Forests: Land containing stands of trees.

Other: Any land not specified, including built-on areas, roads, and barren land.

** *The measurements for precipitation and average temperatures were taken at weather stations closest to the country's largest city.*

Precipitation and average temperature can vary significantly within a country, due to factors such as latitude, altitude, coastal proximity, and wind patterns.

---

ters (13 inches) of rain annually, though more rainfall occurs in the mountains.

4 ■ Plants and Animals

Armenia has broad sandy deserts and low grassy plateaus. The region is home to European bison, snow leopards, cheetahs, and porcupines.

5 ■ Environment

In 2000, Armenia's chief environmental problems resulted from natural disasters, pollution, and warfare. The nation's soil has also been polluted by chemicals including DDT, and the Hrazdan and Aras Rivers have also been polluted. The war between Armenia and Azerbaijan has strained the country's economy, limiting the resources that can be devoted to environmental preservation. It has also led to an energy blockade that has caused deforestation as trees are cut for firewood. Yet another environmental hazard is the restarting of the Metsamor nuclear power plant, which has been brought online without the safety systems recommended by international groups.

As of 2001, 7.6% of the total land area in Armenia was protected. Also as of 2001, four of the nation's eight species of mammal were endangered, as were five species of bird and three species of reptile. Endangered species include the Barbel sturgeon, Dahl's jird, and the field adder.

6 ■ Population

The population of Armenia was estimated at 3.0 million in 2003. A population of 3.35 is estimated for the year 2005. Yerevan, the capital, had an estimated population of 1.3 million in 2002.

7 ▪ Migration

There are Armenian communities in Turkey, Iran, Azerbaijan, Russia, Georgia, Lebanon, Syria, and the United States. Armenia has a net migration rate of -9.0 migrants per 1,000 population as of 2000. This numbered 300,000 people, or 7.9% of the population.

8 ▪ Ethnic Groups

A 2002 report indicates that Armenians comprise an estimated 93% of the population. Minority groups include the Azeri (1%), Russians (2%), and Yezidi Kurds (4%). As of 1993, most of the Azeris had emigrated from Armenia.

9 ▪ Languages

Armenian is spoken by some 96% of the population. Armenian belongs to an independent branch of the Indo-European linguistic family. Its vocabulary includes many Persian loan words. There are two main dialects: East Armenian, the official language of Armenia, and West, or Turkish, Armenian. The alphabet, patterned after Persian and Greek letters, has thirty-eight characters. Armenian literature dates from the early fifth century A.D. Russian is spoken by 2% of the population. Various other languages are spoken by the remaining 2%.

Location: 40°0'N to 45°0'E **Boundary Lengths:** Total boundary lengths, 1,254 kilometers (780 miles); Azerbaijan (east), 566 kilometers (352 miles); Azerbaijan (south), 221 kilometers (137 miles); Georgia, 164 kilometers (102 miles); Iran, 35 kilometers (22 miles); Turkey, 268 kilometers (167 miles).

10 ▪ Religions

Christianity became the state religion in the fourth century, making Armenia one of the first Christian countries. In 1991 the Law on Freedom of Conscience established the separation of church and state but granted the Armenian Apostolic Church status as the national church. The Armenian Apostolic Church is not subject to some of the restrictions imposed on other faiths. For instance, only the Armenian Apostolic Church is allowed to proselytize (to convert members from other faiths).

AP/Wide World Photos

An Armenian boy dances on the roof of a car in downtown Yerevan after a referendum on Armenian independence. The vote was overwhelmingly for independence.

In 2002, the vast majority of the population (90%) claimed to be Armenian Apostolics.

There are small communities of Roman Catholics, Mekhitarists (Armenian Uniate), Pentecostals, Greek Orthodox, Armenian Evangelicals, Baptists, Seventh-day Adventists, Mormons, Jews, Muslims, Baha'is, and Hare Krishnas. There is also a small Kurdish community that practices Yezidi, a faith combining elements of Zoroastrianism, Islam, and animism.

11 ■ Transportation

As of 2002, there were 825 kilometers (513 miles) of one-meter gauge railroad. The highway system includes 11,300 kilometers (5,332 miles) of surfaced roads. Four-lane highways connect the major cities.

In 2001 there were twelve airports, seven of which had paved runways. The airport at Yerevan receives scheduled flights from Moscow, Paris, New York, and Sofia. In 2001, scheduled domestic and international flights carried 369,200 passengers.

12 ■ History

Armenia existed as an independent kingdom long before the birth of Christ. In the first century B.C., Armenian rule extended into what is now Syria and Iraq. Defeated by the Roman general Pompey in 67 B.C., Armenia came under the dominance of the Roman Empire. Armenia adopted Christianity at the beginning of the fourth century A.D.

Although there were periods of relative independence (notably from 809 to 1045), over the centuries Armenia came under the control of several empires, including the Roman, Byzantine, Persian, Arab, and Ottoman. In 1639, Armenia was divided between the Ottoman and Persian empires. In 1828, Russia seized what had been Persian Armenia.

With the collapse of the Russian and Ottoman empires, Armenia declared its independence on 28 May 1918. The August 1920 Treaty of Sevres gave international recognition to Armenian independence, but shortly afterwards both Turkey and Soviet Russia invaded.

The Soviet Republic of Armenia was declared on 29 November 1920. During the

Biographical Profile

Name: Robert Kocharyan
Position: President of a republic
Took Office: 30 March 1998
Birthplace: Nagorno Karabakh, Armenia
Birthdate: 31 August 1954
Education: Yerevan Polytechnical Institute,
    electrical engineering degree, 1982
Spouse: Bella Aloyan (doctor)
Children: Sons Sedrak and Levon, and
    daughter Gayane
Of interest: Kocharyan's favorite music is jazz

Robert Kocharyan

1920s, the Soviet government separated the Armenian region of Nagorno-Karabakh from the rest of Soviet Armenia. Nagorno-Karabakh had the status of an "autonomous republic" within the Soviet Republic of Azerbaijan.

When Armenia decided to seek independence from the Soviet Union on 23 August 1990, Armenia and Azerbaijan began fighting over who would control Nagorno-Karabakh. The Armenians think of Nagorno-Karabakh as the cradle of their race, and their traditional last sanctuary when their country has been invaded. Fighting between mostly Christian Armenia and mostly Muslim Azerbaijan continued until May 1994 when a cease-fire was announced. Despite Armenian military success, the war

resulted in a prolonged economic crisis for the new republic, and the status of Nagorno-Karabakh remains unresolved.

On 27 October 1999 gunmen motivated by personal and clan grievances entered the legislative chamber and opened fire, killing the prime minister and eight other government officials and taking dozens of hostages.

In September 2001, Russian president Vladimir Putin visited Armenia, the first Russian president to do so since independence. Armenia and Russia negotiated a ten-year economic cooperation package, and an agreement was reached on expanding a Russian military base in Armenia.

Presidential elections were held on 19 February 2003, with no candidate receiving 50% of the votes; a runoff election was held in March. Robert Kocharyan took 48.3% of the first-round vote, with Stepan Demirchyan—son of Karen Demirchyan, the former parliamentary speaker assassinated in 1999—taking 27.4% of the vote. Kocharyan won in the second round of voting and was reelected president. In August 2003, the death penalty was abolished.

13 ■ Government

Armenia adopted its first post-Soviet constitution in July 1995, based on the French model with a strong presidency. Armenia has two branches of government, the executive and legislative, with elections held every five years. As of 2003, the single-chamber legislature had 131 members. Armenia is divided into eleven provinces; each has its own legislative and executive bodies that control the provincial budget as well as residential and commercial affairs.

14 ■ Political Parties

In March 1998, Prime Minister Robert Kocharyan was elected president. Elections to a new 131-seat single-chamber legislature were held in May 1999. Of twenty-one parties, only six gained the 5% vote needed to field candidates.

Kocharyan was reelected in a runoff election in March 2003. In elections held in May 2003, the main parties gaining seats in the legislature were the Republican Party, the Justice Bloc, the Rule of Law Party, the Armenian Revolutionary Federation (or "Dashnak" Party), the National Unity Party, and the United Labor Party.

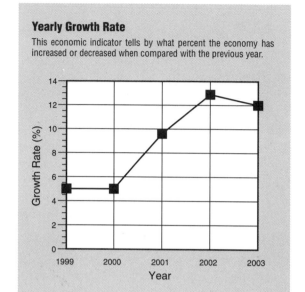

Yearly Growth Rate

This economic indicator tells by what percent the economy has increased or decreased when compared with the previous year.

15 ■ Judicial System

A new judicial system went into effect in January 1999. It provides for district courts, an Appeals Court, and a Court of Cassation. Criminal procedures include the right to an attorney, a public trial, and the right to appeal. A Constitutional Court reviews the constitutionality of legislation and approves international agreements.

16 ■ Armed Forces

The armed forces numbered 44,610 in 2002. There were 38,900 personnel in the army. There are as many as 300,000 reservists. Equipment includes 110 main battle tanks. Military expenditures for 2001 were $135 million, or 6.5% of the gross domestic product (GDP).

17 ■ Economy

The Armenian economy is mainly agricultural. In December 1988, a severe earthquake seriously damaged the economy, which also was severely disrupted by the breakup of the former Soviet Union in 1991. Economic growth has improved; it stood at 10% in 2001.

Telecommunications, the assembly of electric and electronic appliances, agriculture and food processing, energy generation and distribution, construction, coal and gold mining, and international air communications are some areas of the economy that are experiencing growth in the twenty-first century.

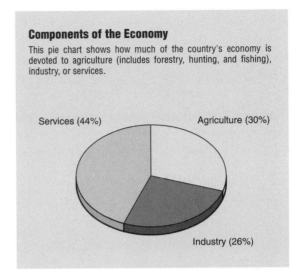

Components of the Economy

This pie chart shows how much of the country's economy is devoted to agriculture (includes forestry, hunting, and fishing), industry, or services.

Services (44%)

Agriculture (30%)

Industry (26%)

18 ▪ Income

In 2001, the gross domestic product (GDP) was $11.2 billion, or about $3,350 per person. The annual GDP growth rate was estimated at 9.6%. The average inflation rate in 2000 was 3.1%.

19 ▪ Industry

The main industries in 2002 were metal-cutting machine tools, forging-pressing machines, electric motors, tires, knitted wear, hosiery, shoes, silk fabric, chemicals, trucks, instruments, microelectronics, gem cutting, jewelry manufacturing, software development, food processing, and brandy. Since the collapse of the former Soviet Union, industrial production has been severely disrupted by political instability and power shortages. A severe earthquake in December 1988 destroyed about one-tenth of the country's industrial capacity.

Armenia is moving to privatize (transfer from government to private ownership) its major industries. About 70% of the larger operations had been privatized by 1998. In 2000, industry accounted for

32% of the gross domestic product (GDP), but employed about 42% of the labor force. In 2002, with 12.5% overall GDP growth, industry grew 16%, including a 42% growth in construction.

20 ▪ Labor

The labor force numbered approximately 1.4 million in 2001. About 42% were involved in industry and construction, 44% in forestry and agriculture, and 14% in services and other sectors. The unemployment rate was estimated at 20% in 2001. Armenians are guaranteed a minimum wage, which was set at $9.00 per month as of 2002. Children under the age of sixteen are prohibited by law from full-time labor.

21 ▪ Agriculture

About 20% of the total land area is cultivated and agriculture employs about 13.2% of all workers. Annual production includes approximately 457,000 tons of

Armenian schoolgirls pose for a photographer. Education is compulsory and free for students to age fifteen.

vegetables and melons, 425,000 tons of potatoes, 220,000 tons of wheat, and 106,000 tons of grapes.

22 ▦ Domesticated Animals
More than one-fifth of the total land area is permanent pastureland. The livestock population includes 575,000 sheep, 512,000 cattle, 57,000 pigs, 13,000 goats, 12,000 horses, and 3 million chickens. About 51,000 tons of meat are produced annually, including 35,000 tons of beef and veal, 5,000 tons of mutton and lamb, 5,000 tons of poultry, and 6,000 tons of pork. About 452,000 tons of milk, 18,000

tons of eggs, 10,000 tons of cheese, and 1,000 tons of greasy wool are also produced. Meat, milk, and butter are the chief agricultural imports.

23 ▦ Fishing
Fishing is limited to the Arpa River and Sevana Lich. Commercial fishing is not a significant part of the economy. The total catch in 2000 was about 1,105 tons. Carp and whitefish are the principal species.

24 ▦ Forestry
In 2000, forests covered an estimated 12.4% of Armenia. Previous mismanage-

ment, the 1988 earthquake, hostilities with Azerbaijan, and fuel shortages have impaired forest growth. Available timber is used for firewood during the harsh winters. In 2000, imports of forestry products totaled $14.4 million.

25 ▪ Mining

Mineral resources in Armenia are concentrated in the southern region, where several operating copper and molybdenum mines were located. Perlite is mined southeast of Yerevan. In 2000, Armenia produced industrial minerals such as clays, diatomite, dimension stone, limestone (1.7 million tons), salt (30,000 tons), and semiprecious stones. It mined copper (14,000 tons of copper concentrate), copper-zinc, and native gold deposits. Significant byproducts among the nonferrous ores included barite, gold, lead, rhenium, selenium, silver, tellurium, and zinc.

26 ▪ Foreign Trade

Exports include gold and diamonds, aluminum, transport equipment, electrical equipment, and scrap metal. Imports consist mostly of grain and other foods, and fuel and energy.

Armenia's main trading partners are Belgium, Iran, Russia, Israel, Georgia, the United States, and European Union nations.

27 ▪ Energy and Power

With only very limited reserves of oil, natural gas, and coal, and with no production, Armenia must rely heavily on foreign imports. Electricity production in 2000 totaled 6.2 billion kilowatt hours. Of total electricity generated in 2000, roughly 31% came from hydroelectric plants, 32% from

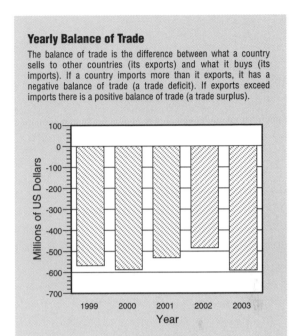

Yearly Balance of Trade

The balance of trade is the difference between what a country sells to other countries (its exports) and what it buys (its imports). If a country imports more than it exports, it has a negative balance of trade (a trade deficit). If exports exceed imports there is a positive balance of trade (a trade surplus).

nuclear power, and 36% from thermal power.

28 ▪ Social Development

Pension, disability, unemployment, sickness, and maternity benefits and family allowances are provided under Armenian law. Women in Armenia largely occupy traditional roles defined by their families despite an employment law that prohibits discrimination based on gender. The government allows ethnic minorities the right to preserve their own cultures and languages.

29 ▪ Health

In 2000, the infant mortality rate was 15 per 1,000 live births. Life expectancy averaged seventy-four years.

Selected Social Indicators

The statistics below are the most recent estimates available as of 2003. For comparison purposes, data for the United States and averages for low-income countries and high-income countries are also given. About 15% of the world's 6.4 billion people live in high-income countries, while 40% live in low-income countries.

Indicator	Armenia	Low-income countries	High-income countries	United States
Per capita gross national income (GNI)*	$3,230	$2,110	$28,480	$36,110
Population growth rate	0.0%	2.1%	0.7%	1.1%
People per square kilometer of land	109	77	31	31
Life expectancy in years: *male*	71	58	75	75
female	79	60	81	80
Number of physicians per 1,000 people	3.2	1.0	3.0	2.8
Number of pupils per teacher (primary school)	19	40	17	15
Literacy rate (15 years and older)	98.6%	66%	>95%	97%
Television sets per 1,000 people	229	91	735	938
Internet users per 1,000 people	16	10	364	551
Energy consumed per capita (kg of oil equivalent)	511	550	5,366	7,937

* The GNI is the total of all goods and services produced by the residents of a country in a year. The per capita GNI is calculated by dividing a country's GNI by its population and adjusting for relative purchasing power.

n.a. = data not available   > = greater than   < = less than

SOURCES: International Telecommunication Union (ITU). *World Telecommunication Development Report 2003*. Geneva, Switzerland: ITU, 2003; World Bank. *World Development Indicators*. Washington, D.C.: The World Bank, 2004; Central Intelligence Agency. *The World Factbook*. Washington, D.C.: Government Printing Office, 2003.

As of 1999, there were an estimated 3.2 physicians and 0.7 hospital beds per 1,000 people. The incidence of heart disease is high compared to other moderately developed countries. There is nearly a 50% chance of dying of heart disease after age sixty-five for both women and men. As of 1999, the number of people living with human immunodeficiency virus/acquired immunodeficiency syndrome (HIV/AIDS) was estimated at fewer than five hundred.

30 ■ Housing

The 1988 earthquake is estimated to have destroyed up to 10% of the housing in Armenia. In 1990, Armenia had 15 square meters (161 square feet) of housing space per person. Between 1993 and 1996, about 3,700 new housing units were under construction each year. In 2000, however, there were about 4,565 buildings that were incomplete due to lack of funds. As of 1999, there were an estimated 880,000 families in Armenia, but only about 771,285 dwelling structures. About 46% of dwellings were single-family homes. In the earthquake zone, an estimated 33,000 families were living in trailers without water or sanitation facilities as of 2000. About 14,000 refugee families were homeless, residing in hostels and nonresidential buildings.

31 ■ Education

Education is compulsory between the ages of seven and fifteen years and free at both the primary and secondary levels. Elementary education lasts three years and inter-

Cory Langley

Armenian boys relax after school. There are about 10 students per class in Armenian elementary schools, with slightly larger classes in secondary schools.

mediate education lasts five years. This is followed by two years of general secondary education. Since the early 1990s, increasing emphasis has been placed on Armenian history and culture. The official language for education is Armenian.

There are two universities in Yerevan: the Yerevan State University and the State Engineering University of Armenia. Seven other educational institutions are located in the capital.

The secondary pupil-teacher ratio averages 10 to 1.

In 2003, the adult illiteracy rate was estimated at 1.4% (males, 0.6%; females, 2%).

32 ▪ Media

In 1997, there were 568,000 mainline telephones. As of 2001, there were also 25,000 mobile cellular phones. Communications are operated by Armental, a 90% Greek-owned company.

As of 1998, there were nine AM and six FM radio stations and three television stations. In addition, programs were relayed by Russian television. Television is the most accessible medium. In 1997, there were

850,000 radios and 825,000 televisions in the country.

The three largest newspapers as of 2002 were: *Golos Armenii* (*The Voice of Armenia,*) circulation 20,000, *Hayastani Hanrapetutyun* (a joint publication of the parliament and the newspaper's staff), and *Respublika Armenia.*

Armenia's constitution provides for freedom of speech and the press. However, journalists seem to follow an unspoken rule of self-censorship, particularly when reporting on political issues, since they traditionally depend on the government for funding and access to facilities.

In 2001, there were 9 Internet service providers serving about 30,000 Internet users.

33 ■ Tourism and Recreation

Armenia has attempted to increase tourism in recent years. Lake Sevan, the world's largest mountain lake, is a popular summer tourist spot, and the Tsakhador Ski Resort is open year round for skiing in the winter and hiking and picnicking the rest of the year. Mount Ararat, the traditional site of the landing of Noah's Ark, is located along the border with Turkey. In 2000, there were 45,000 tourist arrivals.

34 ■ Famous Armenians

Levon Ter-Petrossyan was president of Armenia from 1991 to 1998. Gregory Nare Katzi, who lived in the tenth century, was Armenia's first great poet. Nineteenth-century novelists include Hakob Maliq-Hakobian, whose pen name was "Raffi," and the playwright Gabriel Sundukian. Soviet aircraft designer Artem Mikuyan served as head of the MiG design bureau.

35 ■ Bibliography

Abrahamian, Levon, and Nancy Sweezy, eds. *Armenian Folk Arts, Culture, and Identity.* Bloomington, IN: Indiana University Press, 2001.

Adalian, Rouben Paul. *Historical Dictionary of Armenia.* Lanham, MD: Scarecrow Press, 2002.

Karanian, Matthew. *Edge of Time: Traveling in Armenia and Karabagh.* Washington, DC: Stone Garden Productions, 2002.

Wilson, Neil. *Georgia, Armenia & Azerbaijan.* London: Lonely Planet, 2000.

Streissguth, Thomas. *The Transcaucasus.* San Diego, CA: Lucent Books, 2001.

Australia

Commonwealth of Australia

Capital: Canberra.

Flag: The flag has three main features: the red, white, and blue Union Jack in the upper left quarter, indicating Australia's membership in the Commonwealth of Nations; the white five-star Southern Cross in the right half; and the white seven-pointed federal star below the Union Jack. The flag has a blue ground. Of the five stars of the Southern Cross, four have seven points and one has five points.

Anthem: *God Save the Queen* is reserved for regal and state occasions and whenever singing is appropriate; the national tune is *Advance Australia Fair.*.

Monetary Unit: The Australian dollar (A$) is a paper currency of 100 cents. There are coins of 5, 10, 20, and 50 cents and 1 and 2 dollars, and notes of 5, 10, 20, 50 and 100 dollars. A$1 = US$0.6173 (US$1 = A$1.62; as of May 2003).

Weights and Measures: Metric weights and measures are used. The Australian proof gallon equals 1.37 US proof gallons.

Holidays: New Year's Day, 1 January; Australia Day, last Monday in January; Anzac Day, 25 April; Queen's Birthday, second Monday in June; Christmas, 25 December; Boxing Day, 26 December. Numerous state holidays also are observed. Movable religious holidays include Good Friday, Easter Saturday, and Easter Monday.

Time: Western Australia, 8 PM = noon GMT; South Australia and Northern Territory, 9:30 PM; Victoria, New South Wales, Queensland, and Tasmania, 10 PM. Summer time is 1 hour later in all states except Western Australia, Queensland, and the Northern Territory.

1 ■ Location and Size

Lying southeast of Asia, between the Pacific and Indian Oceans, Australia is the world's smallest continent. Australia is slightly smaller than the United States, with a total area of 7,686,850 square kilometers (2,967,909 square miles) and a total coastline of 25,760 kilometers (16,007 miles). Australia's capital city, Canberra, is located in the southeastern part of the country.

2 ■ Topography

The continent of Australia is divided into four general topographic regions: (1) a low, sandy eastern coastal plain; (2) the eastern highlands extending from Cape York Peninsula in northern Queensland southward to Tasmania; (3) the central plains, including the Great Artesian Basin; and (4) the western plateau, covered with great deserts and "bigger plains" (regularly spaced sand ridges and rocky wastes).

Geographic Profile

Geographic Features

Size ranking: 6 of 193

Highest elevation: 2,228 meters (7,310 feet) at Mount Kosciusko

Lowest elevation: -15 meters (-49 feet) at Lake Eyre

Land Use*

Arable land: 7%

Permanent crops: 0%

Forests: 21%

Other: 72%

Weather**

Average annual precipitation: 120.5 centimeters (47.4 inches)

Average temperature in January: 21.9°C (71.4°F)

Average temperature in July: 12.3°C (54.1°F)

---

* *Arable Land: Land used for temporary crops, like meadows for mowing or pasture, gardens, and greenhouses.*

Permanent crops: Land cultivated with crops that occupy its use for long periods, such as cocoa, coffee, rubber, fruit and nut orchards, and vineyards.

Forests: Land containing stands of trees.

Other: Any land not specified, including built-on areas, roads, and barren land.

** *The measurements for precipitation and average temperatures were taken at weather stations closest to the country's largest city.*

Precipitation and average temperature can vary significantly within a country, due to factors such as latitude, altitude, coastal proximity, and wind patterns.

The average elevation is less than 300 meters (1,000 feet). The highest point is Mount Kosciusko, 2,228 meters (7,310 feet), in the Australian Alps of the southeastern corner of New South Wales. The lowest point is Lake Eyre in South Australia, -15 meters (-49 feet) below sea level.

The most important river system, and the only one with a permanent, year-round flow, is formed by the Murray, Darling, and Murrumbidgee Rivers in the southeast. The Darling River, a tributary of the Murray, is the longest in the country with a length of 2,739 kilometers (1,702 miles). The Murray, with a length of 2,589 kilometers (1,609 miles), rises in the Australian Alps of New South Wales and empties into the sea below Adelaide, South Australia. Several other rivers are important, but for the most part they carry great amounts of water in the wet season and are dry for the rest of the year.

The largest lakes have no outlet and are usually dry. The largest lake is Lake Eyre with an area of 9,500 square kilometers (3,668 square miles). The coastline is smooth, with few bays or capes. The two largest sea inlets are the Gulf of Carpentaria in the north, between Arnhem Land and the Cape York Peninsula, and the Great Australian Bight in the south. The Great Barrier Reef, the longest coral reef in the world, extends for about 2,000 kilometers (1,243 miles) off the east coast of Queensland.

3 ■ Climate

Although it has many different climatic conditions, Australia is generally warm and dry, with no extreme cold and little frost. July mean temperatures average 9°C (48°F) in Melbourne in the southeast and 25°C (77°F) in Darwin in the north. January mean temperatures average 20°C

AUSTRALIA

0   200   400   600 Miles

0   200   400   600 Kilometers

INDONESIA

NEW GUINEA   PAPUA NEW GUINEA

Arafura Sea

Torres Strait   Port Moresby ⊛

Timor Sea

Melville I.   Cape Arnhem   Bamaga   Cape York

Van Diemen Gulf   **Darwin**   Arnhem Land   Gulf of Carpentaria   Cape York Peninsula

INDIAN OCEAN

BONAPARTE ARCHIPELAGO   Joseph Bonaparte Gulf   Pine Creek   Katherine   Groot Eylandt I.   Edward River

Kimberley Plateau   Bullo River   Borroloola   Mornington I.   Cairns   Coral Sea

Beagle Bay   Derby   Lake Argyle   Great Barrier Reef

Dampier Land   NORTHERN TERRITORY   Burketown   Townsville

Eighty Mile Beach   GREAT SANDY DESERT   Balgo   Tanami Desert   Barkley Tableland   Mount Isa   Mackay

Barrow I.   Port Hedland   MACDONNELL RANGES   QUEENSLAND   Rockhampton

North West Cape   HAMERSLEY RANGE   Alice Springs   Great   Bundaberg

Exmouth   Gibson Desert   Ayers Rock 2,844 ft. 867 m.   Simpson Desert   Artesian   Gympie

Red Bluff   Mt. Newman 3,451 ft. 1053 m.   WESTERN AUSTRALIA   Mt. Sir Thomas 2,536 ft. 773 m.   Channel Country   Basin   Toowoomba   Brisbane

Carnarvon   Lake Eyre   Hungerford   Gold Coast

Dirk Hartog I.   Denham   GREAT VICTORIA DESERT   SOUTH AUSTRALIA   Lake Torrens   Darling   Tamworth

Geraldton   Nullarbor Plain   Yalata   Broken Hill   NEW SOUTH WALES   Orange   Newcastle

Kalgoorlie   Whyalla   Murrumbidgee   Sydney

DARLING RANGE   John Eyre Motel   Scorpion Bight   Point Brown   Wollongong

Esperance   Point Culver   Port Lincoln   Adelaide   Albury   Canberra   Tasman Sea

Perth   Fremantle   Bunbury   Cape Naturaliste   Hood Point   Cape Pasley   Great Australian Bight   Spencer Gulf   Meningie   Murray   Mt. Kosciusko 7,310 ft. 2228 m.

Flinders Bay   Walpole   Albany   Kangaroo I.   Bendigo   VICTORIA

Cape Jaffa   Ballarat   Melbourne

Geelong   Bass Strait

Christmas I.   Ashmore & Cartier Is.   King I.   Flinders I.

Cocos Is.   Coral Sea Islands Territory   Devonport   Launceston

Islands administered by Australia   AUSTRALIA   Norfolk I.   Tasmania   Hobart

Heard & McDonald Is.   Macquarie I.   South West Cape   Cape Pillar

N   W   E   S

Location: (including Tasmania): 113°09' to 153°39' E; 10°41' to 43°39'S. **Territorial Sea Limit:** 3 miles. NOTE: Dotted outlines indicate lake beds that are dry except during rainy seasons.

(68°F) in Melbourne and 30°C (86°F) in Darwin.

Except for a few areas where rainfall is heavy, rainfall is insufficient. Mean annual rainfall is 42 centimeters (17 inches), much less than the world mean of 66 centimeters (26 inches). (The average annual rainfall for Australia is much higher, due to the heavy rainfall experienced in certain smaller regions of the country.) Droughts and floods occur frequently.

4 ▪ Plants and Animals

Many distinctive forms of plant and animal life are found, especially in the coastal and tropical areas. There are some 500 species of eucalyptus and 600 species of acacia (wattle). Other outstanding trees are the baobab, blackwood, red cedar, coachwood, jarrah, Queensland maple, silky oak, and walnut. Native trees shed bark instead of leaves. Numerous types of wildflowers grow in the bush country, including boronia, Christmas bush, desert pea, flanner flower, Geraldton wax plant, kangaroo paw, pomaderris, and waratah. There are 470 varieties of orchids.

About 200 kinds of mammals, 200 kinds of lizards, and 350 kinds of birds are indigenous (native to Australia). Apart from marsupials (bandicoots, kangaroos, koalas, possums, Tasmanian devils, tree kangaroos, and wallabies), the most unusual animals are the dingo, echidna, flying fox (fruit bat), platypus, and wombat. Birds include the anhinga, bellbird, bowerbird, cassowary, emu, galah, kookaburra (laughing jackass), lyrebird, fairy penguin, rosella, and many types of cockatoos, parrots, hawks, and eagles.

Many species of trees, plants, and domestic animals have been imported, often thriving at the expense of indigenous types. Herds of wild buffalo, camels, donkeys, horses, and pigs, descendants of stock that strayed from herds imported by pioneers, roam the sparsely settled areas. The proliferation of rabbits created a menace to the country's sheep, and in 1907, 1,000-mile-long fence was built to keep rabbits out of Western Australia. Subsequently, a similar fence was erected in the east to prevent the incursion of dingos.

5 ▪ Environment

Water being a scarce resource in Australia, problems of water quality and availability are a constant concern, even though safe drinking water is generally available to all urban and rural dwellers. A cause for concern has been the increased salinity (amount of salt in the water) in the Murray Valley, caused by diverting water inland from the coast for irrigation. Another significant environmental problem is inland damage due to soil erosion. The quality of the soil is also affected by salinization. In the mid-1990s Australia was among the top twenty world producers of carbon dioxide emissions from industry.

In 2001, 58 species of mammals, 45 species of birds, and 1,871 species of plants were threatened. Endangered species include the banded anteater, greater rabbit-eared bandicoot, Leadbeater's opossum, northern hairy-nosed wombat, woylie, bridled nailtail wallaby, five species of turtle (western swamp, green sea, hawksbill, leatherback, and olive ridley), Tasmanian freshwater limpet, granulated Tasmanian snail, African wild ass, western ground parrot, paradise parakeet, helmeted honey eater, noisy scrubbird, western rufous bristlebird, Lord Howe wood rail, Lord Howe currawong, small hemiphlebia damselfly, Otway stonefly, giant torrent midge, and Tasmanian torrent midge. The Lord Howe stick insect, Gray's marble toadlet, the dusky flying fox, the Tasmanian wolf, and the banded hare wallaby are among the country's 42 extinct species.

IPB, Department of Foreign Affairs and Trade, Australia

A street in Chinatown, Sydney, Australia. Australia is one of the world's most culturally diverse nations.

6 ■ Population

One-third of Australia is practically uninhabited, and another third is sparsely populated. Most of the people live in the southeast section and in other coastal areas. The population in 2003 was 19.7 million, with a projected population for 2015 of 21.7 million. The population density in 2002 was 3 per square kilometer (7 per square mile). Canberra, the national capital, had a 2000 population of 341,000.

Populations of the six state capitals in 2000 were as follows: Sydney (New South Wales), 3.7 million; Melbourne (Victoria), 3.1 million; Brisbane (Queensland), 1.5 million; Perth (Western Australia), 1.2 million; Adelaide (South Australia), 1 million; and Hobart (Tasmania), 183,838.

7 ■ Migration

In 2001, the Migration Program allowed 80,610 entry visas, most granted under the family and skill-based categories. The main countries of origin of those who come as skilled workers seeking jobs are the United Kingdom, Italy, and Greece. As of 2002, Australia had 57,800 refugees and 13,015 asylum-seekers, primarily from Afghanistan, Iraq, China, and Indonesia. The majority of illegal immigrants are those who entered the country legally but remained beyond the expiration of their visas. The government is undertaking stricter measures to identify and remove illegal aliens. As of 2003, the net migration rate was estimated at 4.05 per 1,000 population.

8 ▉ Ethnic Groups

Most Australians are of British or Irish ancestry. Approximately 92% of the population is Caucasian. The Asian-born population tally stood at 7% while aboriginal and other groups comprised only 1% of the population.

In the 1991 census, 265,492 people identified themselves as being of aboriginal or Torres Strait Islander origin. Many of them live in tribal conditions on government reservations in the north and northwest. Their social organization is among the most complex known to anthropologists. They are nomadic hunters and food gatherers, without settled communities. There seems to be a sprinkling of Australoid groups in India, Sri Lanka, Sumatra, Timor, and New Guinea. In 1963, aboriginals were given full citizenship rights, although as a group they continued to suffer from discrimination and a lower living standard than European Australians generally.

9 ▉ Languages

More than 99% of the population speaks English. There are no class variations of speech, and few if any local dialects. Many different languages or dialects are spoken by the aboriginal tribes. There is no written aboriginal language, but markings on "letter sticks," sometimes carried by messengers from one tribe to another, are readily understood by tribal chiefs. Aboriginal languages are in use in certain schools in the Northern Territories and, to a lesser extent, in schools of other states.

10 ▉ Religions

According to the 2001 census, 67% of Australian citizens considered themselves Christians, including 26% Roman Catholic and 20% Anglican. About 15% of Australians considered themselves to have no religion. Less than 0.03% claimed to practice aboriginal religions. A 1996 census indicated that almost 72% of Aborigines practiced some form of Christianity while 16% claimed no religion. By 2002, increased immigration from Southeast Asia and the Middle East resulted in growth in the numbers of those practicing Buddhism, Islam, Hinduism, and Judaism.

The constitution protects freedom of religion and prohibits the formation of a state religion.

11 ▉ Transportation

As of 2002, government-operated railways totaled about 33,819 kilometers (21,015 miles). There also are some private railways, mainly for the iron ore industry in Western Australia. Australian railway systems do not interconnect well, and rail travel between principal cities involves changing trains.

Highways provide access to many districts not served by railroads. As of 2001, there were 913,000 kilometers (567,338 miles) of roads, of which 353,331 kilometers (219,569 miles) were paved. Motor vehicles in 2000 totaled about 10.6 million, including 8.3 million passenger cars, and 2.3 million commercial trucks, buses, and taxis.

In addition to the fine natural harbors of Sydney and Hobart, many other harbors have been artificially developed. There are about seventy commercially significant ports.

The Australian overseas airline, Qantas, carries more than 3 million passengers per year to and from Australia, nearly 40% of the total carried by all airlines serving

Australia. There are international airports at Adelaide, Brisbane, Cairns, Darwin, Hobart, Melbourne, Perth, Sydney, and Townsville. In 2001, Australian air carriers had 33,477,400 passengers.

12 ■ History

Human beings may have inhabited what is now Australia as long as 100,000 years ago. The aboriginals, the first inhabitants, migrated to Australia from Southeast Asia at least 40,000 years before the first Europeans arrived on the island continent. The aboriginals developed a rich, complex culture and numbered about 300,000 by the eighteenth century. However, with the onset of European settlement, conflict and disease reduced their numbers significantly.

The first recorded explorations of the continent by Europeans took place early in the seventeenth century. It was then that Dutch, Portuguese, and Spanish explorers sailed along the coast and discovered what is now Tasmania. However, none took formal possession of the land until 1770, when Captain James Cook claimed possession in the name of Great Britain.

The first settlement was a British penal colony at Port Jackson (now Sydney), founded in 1788. As the number of free settlers grew, the country developed, the interior was penetrated, and six colonies were created: New South Wales in 1786, Van Diemen's Land in 1825 (renamed Tasmania in 1856), Western Australia in 1829, South Australia in 1834, Victoria in 1851, and Queensland in 1859.

Sheep raising and wheat growing were introduced and soon became the backbone of the economy. The discovery of gold in Victoria in 1851 attracted thousands of prospectors, and in a few years the population had quadrupled.

Until the end of the nineteenth century, Australia's six self-governing colonies remained separate. However, the obvious advantages of common defense and irrigation, and many other joint functions, led to the federation of the states into the Commonwealth of Australia in 1901.

Australian forces fought along with the British in Europe during World War I (1914–18). In World War II (1939–45), the Australian forces supported the United Kingdom in the Middle East between 1940 and 1942 and, after the Japanese attack on Pearl Harbor, Hawaii, in December 1941, played a major role in the war in the Pacific. In the decades following World War II, Australia supported the U.S. military presence in Asia. Australian troops served in Vietnam between 1965 and 1971. However, in 1972, the government began the process of dissociating Australia from U.S. and UK policies and strengthening ties with non-communist Asian nations. In addition, diplomatic relations with the People's Republic of China were established.

In July 1998, the government passed amendments to the 1993 Native Title Act removing time limits for land claims by native groups. In September 1999, Australian troops led UN-sanctioned peacekeeping forces into East Timor in response to violence following a referendum on independence from Indonesia.

A November 1999 referendum on transforming Australia from a commonwealth into a republic was defeated in all six states.

On 12 October 2002, two popular nightclubs in Kuta on the Indonesian island of Bali were bombed, killing more than two

Biographical Profile

Name: John Howard
Position: Prime Minister of a democracy
Took Office: 11 March 1996
Birthplace: Earlwood, Australia
Birthdate: 26 July 1939
Education: University of Sydney, law degree, 1961
Spouse: Janette (teacher)
Children: Melanie, Tim, and Richard
Of interest: Howard's father was an automobile mechanic who taught him the importance of small business

John Howard

hundred people, eighty-eight of them Australians. The bombings were linked to the terrorist organization Jamaah Islamiah. They have been referred to as "Australia's September 11th."

13 ▪ Government

Australia is divided into six states and two territories. The government consists of the British sovereign, represented by a governor-general, and the Australian Parliament. Officially, executive power belongs to the governor-general and an executive council. In practice, however, it is normally exercised by a cabinet chosen and presided over by a prime minister, representing the political party or coalition with a majority in the House of Representatives.

Legislative power is exercised by the Parliament, which is composed of a 76-member Senate, representing the states and territories, and a 150-member House of Representatives, representing electoral districts. Twelve senators are elected from each state and two senators each from the Northern Territory and Capital Territory. House membership is not quite double that of the Senate, with a minimum of five representatives for each state. There are two members from the Australian Capital Territory and one from the Northern Territory. Parliament must meet at least once a year.

In February 1998, a constitutional convention voted to institute a republican form of government in Australia, replacing the British monarch as head of the government. However, a November 1999 popular referendum on the issue failed to carry even a single state.

Voting is universal for all persons eighteen years of age and older. Voting is compulsory in national and state parliamentary elections.

14 ■ Political Parties

The Labour Party is a trade union party, officially socialist in policy and outlook. The Liberal Party represents business interests, while the National Party (formerly the Country Party) is allied with farmers. Smaller parties include the Democratic Labour Party, the Communist Party, the Australian Democrats Party, and the Green Party.

In the elections of 1996, the Labour Party lost majority control over parliament to a coalition between the Liberal Party and the National Party.

Since its formation in 1997, the One Nation Party has focused on racial issues. In 1998, its national platform called for an end to Asian immigration. The Green Party increased its strength in the 2001 elections, while the One Nation Party lost some of its strength.

15 ■ Judicial System

The High Court of Australia consists of a chief justice and six associate justices appointed by the governor-general. It is the supreme authority on interpreting the Australian constitution and has the authority to decide whether state and federal legislation is constitutional. Special cases may be referred to a twenty-five-member federal court that deals with commercial

law, copyright law, taxation, and trade practices. There also is a family court.

States and territories have their own court systems. Cases receive their first hearing in local or circuit courts, magistrates' courts, children's courts, or higher state courts.

16 ■ Armed Forces

The Australian armed forces numbered 50,920 in 2002. The army consisted of 25,150; the navy, 12,570; and the air force, 13,200. Reserve forces numbered 20,300 for all three services. The active forces include approximately 7,000 women. Australia's estimated defense expenditure in 2001–02 was $9.3 billion, 2% of the gross domestic product (GDP).

17 ■ Economy

Wool, food, and minerals provide raw materials for industry at home and around two-thirds of foreign earnings. Australia grows all needed basic foodstuffs and has large surpluses for export. Australia is the world's largest wool-producing country, as well as one of the world's great wheat exporters. It also exports large quantities of meat and dairy products. The country also is a major world supplier of iron ore, bauxite, lead, zinc, and copper. Coal, beach sand minerals, and nickel have become major industries as well.

During the 1990s, Australia had an average annual economic growth rate of nearly 4% a year, the second-fastest growth rate among developed countries, behind only Ireland. Real gross domestic product (GDP) growth fell to 2.6% in 2001, largely due to a downturn in the global economy in 2001.

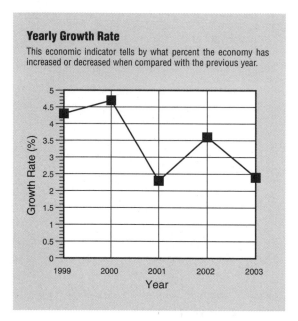

Yearly Growth Rate

This economic indicator tells by what percent the economy has increased or decreased when compared with the previous year.

Growth was expected to recover to about 3.5% in 2004 and 2005.

18 ■ Income

In 2002, Australia's gross domestic product (GDP) was $528 billion, or about $27,000 per person. The annual growth rate of the GDP was estimated at 3.6%. The average inflation rate in 2002 was 2.8%.

19 ■ Industry

In proportion to its total population, Australia is one of the world's most highly industrialized countries. The manufacturing sector has undergone significant expansion in recent years and turns out goods ranging from automobiles to chemicals and textiles. The leading manufacturing industries in 2001 were food and beverage manufacturing; machinery and equipment manufacturing; metal product manufacturing; and petroleum, coal, chemical, and associated product manufacturing. In 2002 and 2003, printing, publishing, food processing, petroleum products, and machinery and equipment industries were also strong growth areas. In 2000, manufacturing accounted for only 13% of the gross domestic product (GDP), or $45.5 billion, showing Australia's transformation to a service-based economy.

Australia produces most of its own foods, as well as its beverages, building materials, many common chemicals, some domestic electrical appliances, radios, plastics, textiles, and clothing. In addition, most of its needed communications equipment, farm machinery (except tractors), furniture, leather goods, and metal products are domestically produced. Recent years have seen the rapid growth of high-tech industries including aircraft, communications and other electronic equipment, electrical appliances and machinery, pharmaceuticals, and scientific equipment.

20 ■ Labor

As of 2001, the Australian work force numbered 9.42 million people. In 1997, services accounted for 73% of employment, industry 22%, and agriculture 5%. The unemployment rate stood at 6.3% in 2002.

Historically, the Australian workforce has been highly unionized, although union membership declined at the end of the twentieth century. About 25% of all wage and salary earners belonged to trade unions in 2000, down from 53% in 1980. The standard workweek is under forty hours. Nearly all Australian workers receive four weeks of annual vacation, many at rates of pay 17.5% above regular pay.

21 ■ Agriculture

Australia is an important producer and exporter of agricultural products and a major world supplier of cereals, sugar, and fruit. The area actively cultivated for crops is 6.9% of the total land area. In 2001, agriculture accounted for about 3% of the gross domestic product (GDP). Agricultural exports accounted for 25% of the GDP.

Production of wheat in 1999–2000 was an estimated 24.8 million tons. Western Australia and New South Wales are the chief wheat-producing states. Australia produces about 4.36 million tons of barley, 1.5 million tons of oats, and 1.4 million tons of rice per year. In 1999–2000, 1.2 million tons of potatoes were produced.

About 95% of sugar production comes from Queensland. The estimated annual harvest yields about 36.9 million tons of sugarcane; about 7,000 tons of tobacco are produced. Cotton has been grown in the coastal river valleys of Queensland for more than a century but on a limited scale, with production at about 716,000 tons.

Australia's wide climate differences permit the cultivation of a range of fruits, from pineapples in the tropical zone to berry fruits in the cooler areas of temperate zones. Annual production of fruit includes approximately 470,000 tons of oranges, 230,000 tons of bananas, 123,000 tons of pineapples, 165,000 tons of pears, 90,000 tons of peaches, 61,000 tons of tangerines, 31,000 tons of lemons and limes, 20,000 tons of apricots, 18,000 tons of grapefruit, 37,000 tons of mangoes, and 27,000 tons of plums. Australia's wine industry is also growing. There are 1.1 million tons of grapes produced for winemaking, drying, and other uses.

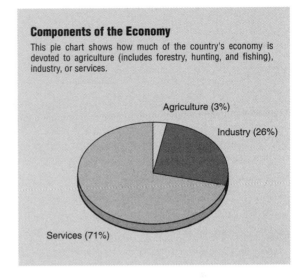

Components of the Economy

This pie chart shows how much of the country's economy is devoted to agriculture (includes forestry, hunting, and fishing), industry, or services.

Agriculture (3%)

Industry (26%)

Services (71%)

22 ■ Domesticated Animals

More than 54% of Australia's land is used in stock raising. Sheep raising has been a mainstay of the economy since the 1820s. Australia's flocks, which include about 119.6 million sheep, constitute approximately 11% of the world's sheep and produce about 30% of the world's supply of wool. Annual wool production is an estimated 931,000 tons. About 95% is exported (mostly to China). Large, scientifically managed sheep stations have produced some of the world's finest stock. Sheep of the Merino breed, noted for its heavy wool yield, make up about three-quarters of Australian flocks.

There are an estimated 2.7 million hogs and 26.7 million head of cattle. Meat production totals an estimated 3.6 million tons. Of these, there are 2 million tons of beef and veal, 603,000 tons of poultry, 608,000 tons of mutton and lamb, and 362,000 tons of ham, pork, and bacon. Beef exports in 2001 were $2.38 billion. Nearly 60% of total beef production is exported annually, most of it going to the United States, South Korea, and Taiwan.

Butter production (in factories) amounts to an estimated 161,000 tons per year, whole milk is estimated at 9.7 million tons, and cheese (factory production) is about 308,000 tons. Egg production is around 190,000 tons per year, predominantly for domestic consumption. Australia produces some 25,000 to 30,000 tons of honey per year, half of which is exported.

23 ■ Fishing

Fishing is relatively unimportant, even though the Australian Fishing Zone is the third largest in the world. Even with a low per capita fish consumption, Australia must import about half its normal requirements. Pearl and other shell fishing are relatively significant. The 2000 catch of fish, crustaceans, and mollusks totaled 211,391 tons. Exports of fishery products in 2000 were valued at $1 billion.

24 ■ Forestry

Forests and woodlands cover 165.9 million hectares (410 million acres), or about 22% of the total land area. Native forests consist principally of hardwood and other fine cabinet and veneer timbers. Eucalyptus trees cover about 35 million hectares (86.5 million acres). Softwood plantations supply more than half the timber harvested annually. About 26.6% of all forest areas are designated as state forest. About 60% of the state forest areas are available for sustainable logging. Roundwood production in 2000 totaled about 30.5 million cubic meters (1.08 billion cubic feet), with exports of 969,000 cubic meters (34.2 million cubic feet).

25 ■ Mining

Australia is the world's leading exporter of alumina, bauxite, coal, diamond, ilmenite, iron ore, refined lead, rutile, and zircon. In 2000, the country was the world's leading producer of alumina, bauxite (for the thirtieth consecutive year), chrysoprase, ilmenite, mined lead, precious opal, rutile, and zircon. The country ranked second in iron ore, mined cobalt, and mined zinc and third in mined gold (with 10% of the world's output) and mined nickel.

Gold production in 2000 was 296,410 kilograms (653,472 pounds). Gold accounted for $2.73 billion of the country's total mineral export value and reserves were estimated at 5,018 tons. Australia produced 2,060 tons of silver in 2000 and reserves were estimated at 31,000 tons. The same year, Australia produced 14.7 million carats of gem diamond and 12 million carats of industrial diamond. Reserves were estimated at 82.4 million carats of gem and near-gem diamond and 85.5 million of industrial diamond. Lightning Ridge, in New South Wales, is the world's major source of black opal. Australia also produced 30% of the world's rough sapphire. Australia produces most of the world's chrysoprase, known as Australian jade. Other gemstones produced in the country include agate, amethyst, emerald (aquamarine), garnet (25,000 tons in 2000), rhodonite, topaz, tourmaline, turquoise, and zircon. The value of gemstones produced in 2000 was over $16 million.

Iron ore production in 2000 was 171 million tons and bauxite production was 5.38 million tons. The country also produced 830,000 tons of contained copper, 1.4 million tons of zinc, 1.6 million tons of manganese ore, 678,000 tons of lead (23% of world production), 168,000 tons of nickel, and 9,146 tons of tin. Australia is also one of the world's leading producers of titanium and zirconium. Other industrial minerals produced in Australia in 2000 included clays, diatomite, gypsum, limestone, magnesite, phosphate rock, salt, sand and gravel, silica, and dimension stone.

26 ▪ Foreign Trade

Measured by foreign trade volume per capita, Australia is one of the great trading nations of the world, and it continues to show a steady rise in trade volume. Fossil, mineral, and plant minerals, wheat, textile fibers, and meat are the main exports. Consumer goods, food, fuels, industrial supplies, machinery, and transportation equipment are the major import items.

Japan is Australia's chief trading partner. In the last two decades, Australia's foreign trade has shifted from European markets to developing Asian nations, which buy nearly 60% of Australia's exports.

27 ▪ Energy and Power

Because of its relatively modest hydroelectric resources and only recently discovered oil, Australia has had to rely on coal-burning steam plants for about three-quarters of its public power requirements. The remainder has been supplied by hydro-electricity, gas turbines, and internal combustion generators. Net installed electrical capacity in 2001 was 42.7 million kilowatt hours. Power generation totaled 200 billion kilowatt hours.

As of 2002, Australia was the world's fourth-largest coal producer. Australia has been the world's leading exporter of coal since 1986. In 2000, production totaled 337.2 million tons. Natural gas reserves were 2.5

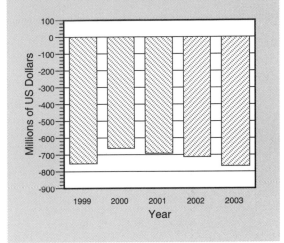

Yearly Balance of Trade

The balance of trade is the difference between what a country sells to other countries (its exports) and what it buys (its imports). If a country imports more than it exports, it has a negative balance of trade (a trade deficit). If exports exceed imports there is a positive balance of trade (a trade surplus).

trillion cubic meters (88 trillion cubic feet) at the beginning of 2002. Oil production in 2001 was 633,000 barrels per day.

28 ▪ Social Development

The Commonwealth Social Services Act of 1947, as amended, provides for invalid and old age pensions and a variety of other benefits. The government provides allowances to families for every child born. Widows' pensions also are provided. The Sex Discrimination Act of 1984 bars discrimination on the basis of gender, marital status, or pregnancy. Although discrimination on the basis of race, color, descent, or national or ethnic origin is prohibited by law, aboriginal Australians have poorer standards of living, are imprisoned more often, and die younger than white Australians.

Selected Social Indicators

The statistics below are the most recent estimates available as of 2003. For comparison purposes, data for the United States and averages for low-income countries and high-income countries are also given. About 15% of the world's 6.4 billion people live in high-income countries, while 40% live in low-income countries.

Indicator	Australia	Low-income countries	High-income countries	United States
Per capita gross national income (GNI)*	$27,440	$2,110	$28,480	$36,110
Population growth rate	1.3%	2.1%	0.7%	1.1%
People per square kilometer of land	3	77	31	31
Life expectancy in years: *male*	76	58	75	75
female	82	60	81	80
Number of physicians per 1,000 people	2.5	1.0	3.0	2.8
Number of pupils per teacher (primary school)	n.a.	40	17	15
Literacy rate (15 years and older)	100%	66%	>95%	97%
Television sets per 1,000 people	731	91	735	938
Internet users per 1,000 people	482	10	364	551
Energy consumed per capita (kg of oil equivalent)	5,600	550	5,366	7,937

* The GNI is the total of all goods and services produced by the residents of a country in a year. The per capita GNI is calculated by dividing a country's GNI by its population and adjusting for relative purchasing power.

n.a. = data not available   > = greater than   < = less than

SOURCES: International Telecommunication Union (ITU). *World Telecommunication Development Report 2003*. Geneva, Switzerland: ITU, 2003; World Bank. *World Development Indicators*. Washington, D.C.: The World Bank, 2004; Central Intelligence Agency. *The World Factbook*. Washington, D.C.: Government Printing Office, 2003.

29 ▪ Health

Australia is one of the healthiest countries in the world. The common cold and other respiratory infections are the most prevalent forms of illness; arteriosclerosis is the most common cause of death. Under the Medicare system (the national health insurance program established in 1984), all Australians have access to free care at public hospitals. Since 1950, certain drugs have been provided free of charge when prescribed by a medical practitioner.

Health services are efficient and hospitals are generally modern and well equipped. In 1998, there were more than 1,015 acute care hospitals, of which 734 were public hospitals. Most private hospitals tend to be fairly small and there are a large number of private hospitals run by religious groups.

Hospital facilities are concentrated in the states of New South Wales and Queensland, which together account for about half the country's hospitals and hospital beds.

In 1998, Australia had 48,934 employed physicians, of which 20,852 were primary care providers. General physicians and specialists are available in most cities. The Royal Flying Doctor Service provides medical care and treatment to people living in remote areas.

In 2000, infant mortality was 5 per 1,000 live births. The estimated life expectancy in 2000 was 79 years. As of 1999, the number of people living with human immunodeficiency virus/acquired immunodeficiency syndrome (HIV/AIDS) was estimated at 14,000.

Homes in a suburb of Paddington near Sydney, Australia.

30 ▤ Housing

According to 2001 national census figures, there were about 7,810,352 dwellings in the nation. About 90.5% were occupied private dwellings. Central heating, formerly found only in the most modern and expensive homes and apartments, is now generally available in the coldest areas of the country. Most apartments and houses are equipped with hot water, refrigeration, and indoor bath and toilet facilities.

31 ▤ Education

Education is compulsory for children from the age of six to fifteen (sixteen in Tasmania). Primary education generally begins at six years of age and lasts for six or seven years, depending on the state. Free education is provided in municipal kindergartens and in state primary, secondary, and technical schools.

Secondary education lasts for five or six years; four years of lower secondary, followed by another one or two years of upper

The Sydney Opera House with its striking contemporary architecture and seaside location is a well-known Australian landmark.

secondary. There are also state-regulated private schools, which are attended by approximately one-third of Australian children.

Correspondence courses and educational broadcasts are given for children living in the remote "outback" areas and unable to attend school because of distance or physical handicap. One-teacher schools also satisfy these needs. Although most aboriginal and Torres Strait Islander students use the regular school system, there are special programs to help them continue on to higher education.

Although each state controls its own system, education is fairly uniform throughout Australia. Education is the joint responsibility of the federal government and each state government and territory. The federal government directly controls schools in the Northern Territory and in the Australian Capital Territory.

Australia has approximately twenty universities in addition to more than two hundred technical institutes. There is a state university in each capital city and each provincial area, a national postgraduate research institute in Canberra, and a university of technology in Sydney with a branch at Newcastle. There are also a number of privately funded higher-education institutions including theological and teacher training colleges. Adult education includes both vocational and nonvocational courses. Most universities offer education programs for interested persons. There are a total of between 1 million and 1.3 million students in higher-level educational institutes.

Illiteracy is practically nonexistent except among the aboriginals.

32 ■ Media

As of 2000, there were 10 million mainline telephones in use, about 1 for every 2 Australians. The same year, there were about 8.6 million cellular phones in use nationwide.

As of 1999, there were 262 AM and 345 FM radio stations and 104 television stations. In 2000, there were 1,908 radios for every 1,000 people. In 2003, there were 731 television sets for every 1,000 people. In 2001, there were 603 Internet service providers serving 10 million subscribers.

In general, news is presented straightforwardly, and political criticism is considered fair and responsible. The *Australian,* one of only two national newspapers, is published in all state capitals. It is independent and had an estimated daily circulation of 153,000 in 1999. The other national daily, the *Australian Financial Review,* had a Monday-Friday average circulation of 78,000 in the same year.

Other leading dailies and their estimated 2002 circulation figures were: *Herald-Sun,* 575,320; *Daily Telegraph-Mirror,* 442,000; and *Sydney Morning Herald,* 231,510. Major Sunday newspapers include the *Sun-Herald* (613,000) and the *Sunday Mail* in Brisbane (598,070).

The major news agency is the Australian Associated Press. Many international news services have bureaus in Sydney.

33 ■ Tourism and Recreation

Among Australia's natural tourist attractions are the Great Barrier Reef, a mecca for scuba divers; the varied and unusual plants and animals; and the sparsely inhabited outback regions, which in some areas may be toured by camel. Other attractions include Ballarat and other historic gold-rush towns near Melbourne. Arts festivals held in Perth every year and in Adelaide every two years, featuring foreign as well as Australian artists, are also popular. In 2000, Australia attracted 4,946,200 foreign visitors.

Among the sports that lure tourists are surfing, sailing, fishing, golf, tennis, cricket, and rugby. Melbourne is famous for its horse racing (Australia's most celebrated race is the Melbourne Cup) and for its 120,000-capacity cricket ground, perhaps the biggest in the world. Sydney, Australia, hosted the Summer Olympic Games in 2000.

34 ■ Famous Australians

The most highly regarded contemporary Australian writer is Patrick White (1912–1990), author of *The Eye of the Storm* and other works of fiction and winner of the 1973 Nobel Prize for literature. Henry Lawson (1867–1922) was a leading short-story writer and creator of popular ballads. Germaine Greer (1939–) is a writer on feminism. A prominent Australian-born publisher of newspapers and magazines, in the United Kingdom and the United States as well as Australia, is Keith Rupert Murdoch (1931–).

Three renowned Australian scholars are Sir Gilbert Murray (1866–1957), a classicist and translator of ancient Greek plays; Samuel Alexander (1859–1938), an influential scientific philosopher; and Eric Partridge (1894–1979), authority on English slang. An outstanding bacteriologist was Sir Frank Macfarlane Burnet (1899–1985), director of the Melbourne Hospital and co-winner of the 1960 Nobel Prize for medicine. Sir John Carew Eccles (1903–1997) shared the 1963 Nobel Prize for medicine for his work on ionic mechanisms of the nerve cell membrane. John Warcup Cornforth (1917–) shared the 1975 Nobel Prize for chemistry for his work on organic molecules.

Among Australia's most prominent film directors are Fred Schepisi (1939–), Peter Weir (1944–), and Gillian Armstrong (1950–). Film stars have included Australian-born Errol Flynn (1909–1950), Paul Hogan (1940–), and U.S.-born Mel Gibson (1956–). Musicians of Australian birth include Dame Joan Sutherland (1926–) and the composer Percy Grainger (1882–1961). Popular singers include Helen Reddy (1941–) and Olivia Newton-John (UK, 1948–). The aviator Sir Charles Edward Kingsford-Smith (1897–1935) pioneered flights across the Pacific Ocean. A popular figure of folklore was the outlaw Ned (Edward) Kelly (c.1855–1880).

In recent decades, the tennis world was dominated by such Australian players as Lewis Hoad (1934–1994), Rod (George) Laver (1938–), John David Newcombe (1944–), and Evonne Goolagong Cawley (1951–). Sir Donald George Bradman (1908–) was one of the outstanding cricket players of modern times. Dawn Fraser (1937–) was the first woman to swim 100 meters in less than a minute.

35 ■ Bibliography

Darian-Smith, Kate. *Exploration into Australia.* Philadelphia, PA: Chelsea House, 2001.

Einfeld, Jann. *Life in the Australian Outback.* San Diego, CA: Lucent Books, 2003.

Fowler, Allan. *Australia.* New York: Children's Press, 2001.

Israel, Fred, ed. *Australia: The Unique Continent.* Philadelphia, PA: Chelsea House, 2000.

Rajendra, Vijeya, and Sundran Rajendra. *Australia.* New York: M. Cavendish, 2002.

Richardson, Margot. *Australia.* Austin, TX: Raintree Steck-Vaughn Publishers, 2003.

Rickard, John. *Australia, A Cultural History.* London: Longman, 1996.

Sammis, Fran. *Australia and the South Pacific.* New York: Benchmark, 2000.

Austria

Republic of Austria
Republik Österreich

Capital: Vienna (Wien).

Flag: The flag consists of a white horizontal stripe between two red stripes.

Anthem: *Land der Berge, Land am Ströme (Land of Mountains, Land on the River).*

Monetary Unit: The euro replaced the schilling as the national currency in 2002. The euro is divided into 100 cents. There are coins in denominations of 1, 2, 5, 10, 20, and 50 cents and 1 euro and 2 euros. There are notes of 5, 10, 20, 50, 100, 200, and 500 euros. As of May 2003, €1 = $1.0977 (or $1 = €0.911).

Weights and Measures: The metric system is in use.

Holidays: New Year's Day, 1 January; Epiphany, 6 January; May Day, 1 May; Assumption, 15 August; National Day, 26 October; All Saints' Day, 1 November; Immaculate Conception, 8 December; Christmas, 25 December; St. Stephen's Day, 26 December. Movable religious holidays include Easter Monday, Ascension, Whitmonday, and Corpus Christi. In addition, there are provincial holidays.

Time: 1 PM = noon GMT.

1 Location and Size

Austria, with an area of 83,858 square kilometers (32,378 square miles), is a landlocked country in Central Europe. It is slightly smaller than the state of Maine and has a total boundary length of 2,562 kilometers (1,588 miles). It shares borders with Germany, the Czech Republic, Hungary, Slovenia, Italy, Liechtenstein, and Switzerland. Austria's capital city, Vienna, is located in the northeastern part of the country.

2 Topography

Most of western and central Austria is mountainous and much of the flatter area to the east is hilly, but a series of passes and valleys permits travel within the country and has made Austria an important bridge between various sections of Europe. The principal topographic regions are the Alps, covering 62.8% of Austria's land area; the Alpine and Carpathian foothills; the Pannonian lowlands of the east; the granite and gneiss highlands of the Bohemian Massif; and the Vienna Basin.

The highest point of the Austrian Alps is the Grossglockner, at 3,797 meters (12,457 feet). The Danube River, fully navigable along its 350-kilometer (217-mile) course through northeastern Austria, is the longest river. The total length of the Danube, which originates

Geographic Profile

Geographic Features

Size ranking: 112 of 193

Highest elevation: 3,797 meters (12,457 feet) at Grossglockner

Lowest elevation: 115 meters (377 feet) at Neusiedler See

Land Use*

Arable land: 17%

Permanent crops: 1%

Forests: 47%

Other: 35%

Weather**

Average annual precipitation: 66 centimeters (26 inches)

Average temperature in January: -2°C (28°F)

Average temperature in July: 19°C (66°F)

---

* *Arable Land: Land used for temporary crops, like meadows for mowing or pasture, gardens, and greenhouses.*

Permanent crops: Land cultivated with crops that occupy its use for long periods, such as cocoa, coffee, rubber, fruit and nut orchards, and vineyards.

Forests: Land containing stands of trees.

Other: Any land not specified, including built-on areas, roads, and barren land.

** *The measurements for precipitation and average temperatures were taken at weather stations closest to the country's largest city.*

Precipitation and average temperature can vary significantly within a country, due to factors such as latitude, altitude, coastal proximity, and wind patterns.

in Germany and is the second-longest river in Europe, is 2,857 kilometers (1,775 miles). Included within Austria are many Alpine lakes. The largest is the Neusiedler See with an area of 320 square kilometers (124 square miles). This lake is shared with Hungary and marks the lowest point in Austria, at 115 meters (377 feet). Lake Constance (Bodensee) is another major lake.

3 ■ Climate

Climatic conditions depend on location and altitude. Temperatures range from an average of about -7 to -1°C (20 to 30°F) in January to about 18 to 24°C (65 to 75°F) in July. Rainfall ranges from more than 102 centimeters (50 inches) annually in the western mountains to less than 66 centimeters (26 inches) in the driest region, near Vienna.

4 ■ Plants and Animals

Austria is one of Europe's most heavily wooded countries, with 44% of its area under forests. Deciduous trees (particularly beech, birch, and oak) and conifers (fir) cover the mountains up to about 1,200 meters (4,000 feet); above that point fir predominates and then gives way to larch and stone pine. There is a large variety of wildlife. Although chamois are now rare, deer, hare, fox, badger, marten, Alpine chough, grouse, marmot, partridge, and pheasant are still plentiful. The birds of the reed beds around the Neusiedler See include purple heron, spoonbill, and avocet. The ibex, once threatened, has begun breeding again. Hunting is strictly regulated.

Location: 46°22' to 49°1'N; 9°22' to 17°10'E **Boundary Lengths:** Germany, 784 kilometers (487 miles); Czech Republic, 362 kilometers (225 miles); Slovakia, 91 kilometers (57 miles); Hungary, 366 kilometers (227 miles); Slovenia, 330 kilometers (205 miles); Italy, 430 kilometers (267 miles); Liechtenstein, 37 kilometers (23 miles); Switzerland, 164 kilometers (102 miles).

5 ▪ Environment

In 1992, Austria was among the 50 countries with the highest levels of industrial carbon dioxide emissions. Austrians continue to fight the problem of acid rain, which has damaged 25% of the country's forests.

Of the country's 83 species of mammals, 7 are threatened. Five of Austria's 213 breeding bird species are endangered. There were 6 endangered plant species from a total of 3,000-plus as of 2001. Endangered species include Freya's damselfly, slender-billed curlew, bald ibis, Danube salmon, and European mink.

6 ▪ Population

Austria's population was estimated at 8.1 million in 2003. The population density in 2002 was 97 persons per square kilometer (252 persons per square mile). Around 65% of the population lives in urban communities. Vienna, the capital, had an estimated population of 2.1 million in 2001. Other large cities include Graz, 237,810; Linz, 203,000; Salzburg, 144,000; and Innsbruck, 118,000.

7 ■ Migration

For several years after the end of World War II (1939–45), fairly large numbers of Austrians emigrated, mostly to Australia, Canada, and the United States, but as the economy recovered from war damage, emigration became insignificant. Between 1945 and 1983, 1,942,782 refugees from more than 30 countries came to Austria, of whom about 590,000 became Austrian citizens. In 2001, there were 30,140 asylum applications. The majority of those seeking asylum were from Afghanistan, Iraq, Turkey, India, and Yugoslavia (which became Serbia and Montenegro in 2003). In 2001, there were 15,500 refugees in Austria. There were 32,000 foreign workers in the country in 2001, primarily from Germany. As of 2003, Austria had an estimated net migration rate of 2.44 migrants per 1,000 population.

8 ■ Ethnic Groups

Austrians are a people of mixed Dinaric, Nordic, Alpine, and East Baltic origin. Germans constitute about 99.4% of the total population. Ethnic minorities include Croatians in the Burgenland, making up about 0.3% of the population, and Slovenes in southern Carinthia, accounting for about 0.2%. Other groups comprise the remaining 0.1%, including Hungarians, Czechs, Slovaks, Serbians, and Italians.

9 ■ Languages

The official language is German, and nearly 99% of the inhabitants speak it as their mother tongue. People in Vorarlberg Province speak German with an Alemannic accent, similar to that in Switzerland. In other provinces, Austrians speak various Bavarian dialects. There are also Croatian- , Slovene- , and Hungarian-speaking minorities, and small groups of Czech, Slovak, and Polish speakers in Vienna.

10 ■ Religions

About 78% of the people are Roman Catholic, 5% are Lutheran, and 17% belong to other or no religious groups. About 2% of the population are Muslim, 0.09% are Jewish, and 1.5% are Eastern Orthodox. Other denominations include the Church of Jesus Christ of Latter-day Saints (Mormons), the New Apostolic Church, the Syrian Orthodox Church, the Armenian Apostolic Church, the Methodist Church of Austria, and a Buddhist community. These are the only religions that are officially recognized. More than 8% of Austrians profess atheism. A number of groups defined as "sects" by the government are active in the country, including the Church of Scientology and the Unification Church.

11 ■ Transportation

The Federal Railway Administration controls 90% of Austria's 5,849 kilometers (3,635 miles) of railways. In 2002, paved highways totaled 133,361 kilometers (82,870 miles), including 1,613 kilometers (1,002 miles) of expressways. In 2000, there were 4,097,145 passenger cars and 779,651 trucks, buses, and taxis.

Susan D Rock

A view of Vienna, Austria, from St. Stephen's Cathedral.

Austria has 446 kilometers (277 miles) of inland waterways. Most of Austria's overseas trade passes through the Italian port of Trieste. The rest is shipped from German ports.

Of the six major airports in Austria—Schwechat (just outside Vienna), Graz, Innsbruck, Klagenfurt, Linz, and Salzburg—Schwechat is by far the most important. In 2001, Austrian air carriers provided flights for 6,514,300 passengers.

12 ■ History

Human settlements have existed in what is now Austria since prehistoric times. In 14 B.C., the region was conquered by the Romans, who founded several towns that survive today, including Vienna (Vindo-bona) and Salzburg (Juvavum). After the fall of the Roman Empire, Austria became a province of the French leader Charlemagne's empire from around A.D. 800 until the tenth century, when it was joined to the Holy Roman Empire as Österreich ("Kingdom of the East").

From the late thirteenth to the early twentieth centuries, the history of Austria was tied to that of the ruling Habsburg family. Great Habsburg rulers included King Charles I of Spain, who ruled over Austria, Spain, the Netherlands, and much of Italy. Holy Roman Emperor Joseph II (reigned 1765–90) sought to abolish serfdom and introduce religious freedom. Joseph II's rule spanned the careers of the composers Franz Joseph Haydn and Wolfgang Amadeus Mozart. One of the last Habsburg rulers was Franz Josef I. He occupied the Austrian throne for sixty-eight years until his death in 1916. During his reign, Austria attempted to set up a strong central government that would unify all the Habsburg possessions under its leadership. But nationalist tensions persisted, and Austrian dominance was challenged in Italy, Germany, and Hungary.

On 28 June 1914, at Sarajevo, Serbian nationalists assassinated Archduke Francis Ferdinand, a nephew of the emperor and heir to the Austrian throne. Their act set off World War I (1914–18), in which Austria-Hungary was joined by Germany, Italy, and Turkey. They became known as the Central Powers. However, in 1915, Italy went over to the side of the Allies—France, Russia, the United Kingdom, and the United States. The Central Powers were defeated, the Austrian empire collapsed, and Austria became a republic.

During the decade after the war, Austria was hit by inflation, food shortages, unemployment, financial scandals, and growing political unrest. As the political climate deteriorated, Austria struggled to remain independent in the face of the growing military threat from Germany. The Nazi Party, headed by Adolf Hitler, had taken over Germany and had set a course for world domination.

On 11 March 1938, German troops entered Austria, and two days later Austria was proclaimed a part of the German Reich. In 1939, Austria, now known as Ostmark, entered World War II (1939–45) on the side of Germany.

Germany lost the war and Allied troops entered Austria. The country was divided into U.S., British, French, and Soviet zones of occupation. The occupying powers permitted Austrians to set up a provisional government, but limited its powers.

On 15 May 1955, after more than eight years of negotiations, representatives of Austria and the four powers signed the Austrian State Treaty. This treaty reestablished an independent and democratic Austria. In October, all occupation forces withdrew from the country.

Although Austria is now a neutral nation, it has not been able to escape its Nazi past. On 8 July 1986, former UN Secretary-General Kurt Waldheim was sworn in as president of Austria. During the presidential campaign, Waldheim was accused of having belonged to Nazi organizations during World War II and of having taken part in war crimes while serving with the German army. Waldheim denied the charges. After his inauguration, many diplomats made a point of avoiding public contact with the new president. Because of the controversy, Waldheim declined to run for a second term.

In 1998, the Austrian government agreed to return works of art that Nazis had stolen from Jews during the war.

The economic recession in Germany during the early 1990s caused Austria to look for trade ties not only with Europe but also with the East. At the beginning of 1995, Austria joined the European Union.

The growing strength of the right-wing Freedom Party, headed by Jörg Haider, in the 1990s was evidence of a turn to the right in Austrian politics. The Freedom Party scored a triumph in the general election of October 1999 with 27% of the vote. In early 2000, the Freedom Party joined with the conservative People's Party to form a new coalition government, provoking widespread protests both within Austria and among the countries of the European Union.

Biographical Profile

Name: Dr. Wolfgang Schuessel
Position: Chancellor of a federal republic
Took Office: 4 February 2000
Birthplace: Vienna, Austria
Birthdate: 7 June 1945
Education: University of Vienna, Doctorate in Law, 1968
Of interest: Schuessel's administration has stated: "We have a declaration where everything is enshrined 'a yes' to human rights, 'a yes' to Europe, 'a yes' to guarantees for our minorities."

Dr. Wolfgang Schuessel

Haider resigned as Freedom Party chairman in April 2000. In 2002, the People's Party/Freedom Party coalition government collapsed, and new elections were called. In those elections, the People's Party made wide gains; the Freedom Party suffered a major defeat. Despite these results, and after failed negotiations with the Social Democratic Party and the Green Party, another coalition government between the People's Party and the Freedom Party was formed, which was sworn in on 1 April 2003.

After the new government took office in 2003, it implemented strict economic measures to save the government 8 billion euros. Early retirement was to be cancelled, cuts were planned in public services, the health care system was to be reformed, and,

most controversially, drastic cuts were proposed in the nation's pension system. As a result, around 500,000 Austrians took part in nationwide strikes in May 2003, the largest in fifty years.

Following the 11 September 2001 terrorist attacks on the United States, Austria passed a Security and Defense Doctrine, representing a shift in the country's longstanding policy of neutrality. Although Austria will not participate in military alliances requiring mutual defense commitments, the country is gradually moving toward closer integration with European security structures.

13 ■ Government

Austria is a federal republic with a democratically elected parliament. The presi-

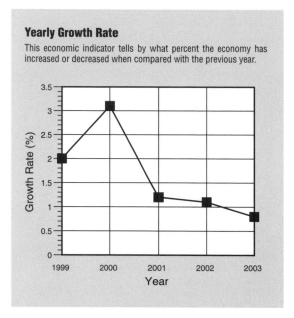

Yearly Growth Rate

This economic indicator tells by what percent the economy has increased or decreased when compared with the previous year.

dent, elected by popular vote for a six-year term, appoints a federal chancellor (*Bundeskanzler*), usually the leader of the largest party in parliament. The president is limited to two terms of office.

The parliament, known as the Federal Assembly (*Bundesversammlung*), consists of the National Council (*Nationalrat*) and Federal Council (*Bundesrat*). The Bundesrat has 64 members, elected by the country's provincial legislatures (*Landtage*). The Nationalrat has 183 members, elected directly in 9 election districts for 4-year terms. All citizens 19 years of age or older may vote. Voting is compulsory for presidential elections.

Austria is divided into 9 provinces (*Länder*). Each province has its own legislature. The provincial governor, elected by the provincial legislature, is assisted by a cabinet. Each province is divided into several administrative districts (*Bezirke*). There are also communal councils, which

elect a mayor and his or her deputies. There are some 2,300 communities in Austria, and 14 cities that fall directly under provincial authority rather than that of the districts.

14 ■ Political Parties

The Austrian People's Party (*Österreichische Volkspartei*-ÖVP), also referred to as Austria's Christian Democratic Party, favors free enterprise, competition, and the reduction of class differences. It advocates provincial rights and strongly supports the Catholic Church.

The SPÖ, also known as the Social Democratic Party, advocates moderate reforms through democratic processes. It favors continued nationalization of key industries, economic planning, and widespread social welfare benefits.

The Freedom Party of Austria (*Freiheitliche Partei Österreichs*-FPÖ), an anti-socialist group, favors individual initiative over collective security. In June 1992, FPÖ dissidents founded the Free Democratic Party.

The legislative election of October 1999 was a watershed event that ended the traditional "grand coalition" between the Social Democrats and the People's Party. The SPÖ took 65 of the National Council's 183 seats; ÖVP, 52; FPÖ, 52; and other parties, 14. In early 2000, the People's Party and the Freedom Party formed a controversial new coalition government.

Following the November 2002 elections, the ÖVP held 79 seats in parliament; the SPÖ 69 seats; FPÖ 18 seats; and the Greens 17 seats. The People's Party and the Freedom Party once again formed a government.

15 ▪ Judicial System

Austria has about two hundred local courts (*Bezirksgerichte*) with civil jurisdiction. There also are nineteen provincial and district courts (*Landesgerichte* and *Kreisgerichte*) with civil and criminal jurisdiction and four higher provincial courts (*Oberlandesgerichte*) with criminal jurisdiction, located in Vienna, Graz, Innsbruck, and Linz.

The Supreme Court (*Oberster Gerichtshof*) in Vienna acts as the final appeals court for criminal and civil cases. The Constitutional Court (*Verfassungsgerichtshof*) has supreme jurisdiction over constitutional and civil rights issues. The Administrative Court (*Verwaltungsgerichtshof*) ensures the legal functioning of public administration.

Criminal defendants are afforded a presumption of innocence, public trial, and jury trial for major offenses.

16 ▪ Armed Forces

In 2002, the Austrian armed forces totaled 34,600. Active reserve strength is 72,000 receiving annual training. Another 990,000 have had military training. The 2001–02 defense budget was $1.5 billion or 0.8% of the gross domestic product (GDP).

17 ▪ Economy

The government plays a large role in the Austrian economy, although private enterprise continues to occupy a central position. Basic industries, including mineral production, heavy industry, rail and water transport, and utilities, were taken over by the government during 1946 and 1947. In 1970, they were reorganized under the Austrian Industrial Administration.

From the 1950s through the early 1970s, the economy was characterized by a high rate of growth and modest price increases. By 1975, Austrian industry, the single most important sector of the economy, had more than quadrupled in value over 1945. But the general economic slowdown that followed the oil price hike of late 1973 affected Austria, as it did other European countries.

In 1982, Austria endured its most prolonged recession since World War II (1939–45). Unemployment reached 6.8% in 1993. Inflation was moderate, and the cost of living rose 17.7% between 1986 and 1992.

Following a mild recession in 1993, Austria's economy rebounded in 1994 and 1995. Membership in the European Union (EU) eased inflation, which was 2.2% in 1995, and by 1998 had dropped to 0.9%. Real gross domestic product (GDP) growth rose to 2.9% in the same year.

Due in large part to a global economic downturn the previous year, in 2002 Austria was experiencing its worst slowdown in over a decade. Following severe flooding in Central Europe during August 2002, extra funds were needed for flood damage.

Austria has a high rate of productivity. It has also been successful in privatizing most of its large manufacturing firms. In the early twenty-first century, Austria invested in high-growth industries such as telecommunications, biotechnology, medical and pharmaceutical research, and electronics.

18 ▪ Income

In 2002, Austria's gross domestic product (GDP) was $226 billion, or about $27,700 per person. The annual growth rate of the GDP was estimated at 0.6%. The average inflation rate in 2002 was 1.8%.

Components of the Economy

This pie chart shows how much of the country's economy is devoted to agriculture (includes forestry, hunting, and fishing), industry, or services.

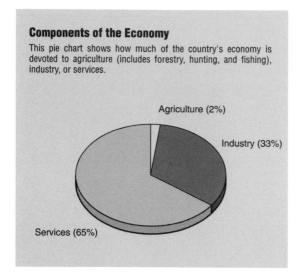

Agriculture (2%)

Industry (33%)

Services (65%)

19 ■ Industry

Industrial output has increased vastly since the beginning of World War II (1939–45) and contributed 33% of the gross domestic product (GDP), including mining, in 2002. Major parts of the electric and electronics, chemical, iron and steel, and machinery industries were government controlled until the 1990s, but as of 2002, the steel, aluminum, and petroleum industries were majority owned by private shareholders.

In the mid-1990s, 4.4 million tons of crude steel and 3.5 million tons of semi-manufactured steel were produced annually. A total of 155,403 automobiles were manufactured in 2001, and 24,988 heavy trucks were produced in 2000.

The most important areas of the textile industry are embroidery, spinning, weaving, and knitting.

The chemical industry, which was relatively unimportant before World War II, now ranks third in value of production. Petroleum refinery products in 1994 (in

barrels) included fuel oil, 23.8 million, and gasoline.

Other leading industries are electrical and electronic machinery and equipment, pulp and paper, ceramics, and especially foodstuffs and allied products. Austria has always been famous for its skilled glassblowers, goldsmiths, jewelers, lacemakers, potters, stonecutters, and woodcarvers.

In 2003, the electronics, biotechnology, and medical and pharmaceutical sectors of the economy held potential for high growth.

20 ■ Labor

In 2001, there were 4.3 million employed persons. Foreign laborers, mainly from Serbia and Montenegro and Turkey, constitute a significant portion of the total work force. Unemployment rose from 3.6% in 1994 to 4.8% in 2002.

In 2002, 52% of the work force was unionized. Most Austrian workers put in thirty-eight hours per week. Every employee is entitled to a paid vacation of thirty to thirty-six workdays annually, depending on length of employment. There is no national minimum wage. The unofficial accepted minimum is $10,928 per year, which provides a family with a decent standard of living. The minimum legal working age is fifteen.

21 ■ Agriculture

Although small, the agricultural sector is highly diversified and efficient. Most production is oriented toward local consumption. Of Austria's total area, about 17% is arable (suitable for farming). The best cropland is in the east, which has the most level terrain. Farms are almost exclusively family owned. Agriculture employs about

5% of the labor force. In 2001, agriculture (together with forestry) contributed 2.2% to Austria's total gross domestic product (GDP).

Chief crops are wheat, rye, oats, barley, potatoes, and sugar beets. Austria is near self-sufficiency in wheat, oats, rye, fruits, vegetables, sugar, and a number of other items. Major annual crop yields include 3 million tons of sugar beets, 1.2 million tons of barley, 1.28 million tons of wheat, 660,000 tons of potatoes, 223,000 tons of rye, and 150,000 tons of oats. Vineyards yield 270,000 tons of grapes crushed for wine.

22 ▓ Domesticated Animals

Dairy and livestock breeding are traditionally the major agricultural activities. Austrian milk, butter, cheese, and meat are excellent. Austria is able to supply all its own dairy products and most of its own meats. Annual livestock production includes 3.8 million hogs, 2.1 million head of cattle, 384,000 sheep, 74,000 horses, and 14 million poultry. Meat and poultry production totals 821,000 tons per year. In 2001, exports of beef and veal were valued at almost $86 million and milk products, $129 million.

Austrian dairy farms produce approximately 3,256,000 tons of milk, 135,000 tons of cheese, and 42,000 tons of butter annually. Some 99,000 tons of eggs are produced, satisfying over 90% of domestic demand. By specializing in quality strains of cattle, hogs, and horses, Austrian breeders have gained wide international recognition.

23 ▓ Fishing

Fishing is not important commercially and fish do not constitute a large part of the Austrian diet. Commercial catches consist mainly of carp and trout. The total catch in 1997 was 3,486 tons. Aquacultural production in 1997 was 3,021 tons, of which rainbow trout comprised 2,160 tons. A sizable part of the population engages in sport fishing.

24 ▓ Forestry

Austria has the largest percentage of forest in the European Union. About 46% of Austria's total area is forested, mostly in the foothills and mountains. About four-fifths of the trees are coniferous, primarily spruce. Beech is the most important broadleaf type. To prevent overcutting, export restrictions have been introduced and reforestation is widely promoted. Exports of raw timber and cork are supplemented by exports of such forestry products as paper, cardboard boxes, prefabricated houses, toys, matches, and turpentine.

In 2000, about 7.75 million cubic meters (274 million cubic feet) of roundwood were processed, almost entirely softwood lumber. Particleboard production in 2000 was estimated at 1.7 million cubic meters (60 million cubic feet). In 2001, exports of wood products totaled $4.18 billion, eighth in the world. Sawed lumber output was at 10,260 cubic meters (362,200 cubic feet).

25 ▓ Mining

Austria produces 2.5% of the world's graphite, ranking tenth in the world, and is one of the world's largest sources of high-grade graphite. In 2000, estimated output was 12,000 tons. The country also produces 1.6% of the world's talc, ranking ninth, with a reported output in 2000 of 133,060 tons of crude talc and soapstone. Other

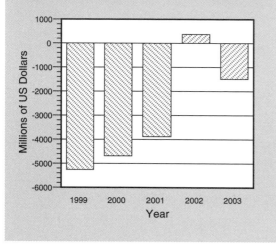

minerals in 2000 included limestone and marble (23 million tons), dolomite (7 million tons), gypsum and anhydrite (946,000 tons), brine salt (400,000 tons), tungsten (1,600 tons), pumice (3,961 tons), and crude kaolin (119,000 tons). Gold production in 2000 was 100 kilograms (220 pounds). Crude magnesite production was reported at 726,000 tons.

26 ■ Foreign Trade

Austria depends heavily on foreign trade, and the government consistently maintains strong ties with the West while being careful to preserve the country's neutrality.

The major industry and export commodity in Austria is the automobile and its components, which account for roughly 10% of Austrian exports.

Germany is by far Austria's most important trade partner. In 2000, the principal countries receiving Austria's exports were Germany, Italy, Switzerland, the United States, and the United Kingdom. Austria received most of its imports from Germany, Italy, the United States, and France.

27 ■ Energy and Power

Austria is one of the foremost producers of hydroelectric power in Europe. In 2000, total power production amounted to 58.8 billion kilowatt hours. That year, 68.6% of Austria's electricity was produced by hydroelectric plants and 28.5% by thermal plants. Oil and gas production fall far short of domestic needs.

28 ■ Social Development

Austria has one of the most advanced and comprehensive systems of social legislation in the world. Health insurance is available to industrial and agricultural workers, federal and professional employees, and members of various other occupational groups. For those without insurance or adequate means, treatment is paid for by public welfare funds.

Family allowances are paid monthly, depending on the number of dependent children, with the amount doubled for any child who is severely handicapped. The state provides school lunches for more than 100,000 children annually.

The state also grants a special birth allowance and a payment for newlyweds setting up their first home. Unmarried people establishing a common household may apply for tax relief.

While the number of women in government is low in relation to the overall pop-

Selected Social Indicators

The statistics below are the most recent estimates available as of 2003. For comparison purposes, data for the United States and averages for low-income countries and high-income countries are also given. About 15% of the world's 6.4 billion people live in high-income countries, while 40% live in low-income countries.

Indicator	Austria	Low-income countries	High-income countries	United States
Per capita gross national income (GNI)*	$28,910	$2,110	$28,480	$36,110
Population growth rate	0.3%	2.1%	0.7%	1.1%
People per square kilometer of land	97	77	31	31
Life expectancy in years: *male*	76	58	75	75
female	82	60	81	80
Number of physicians per 1,000 people	3.1	1.0	3.0	2.8
Number of pupils per teacher (primary school)	13	40	17	15
Literacy rate (15 years and older)	98%	66%	>95%	97%
Television sets per 1,000 people	637	91	735	938
Internet users per 1,000 people	409	10	364	551
Energy consumed per capita (kg of oil equivalent)	3,567	550	5,366	7,937

* The GNI is the total of all goods and services produced by the residents of a country in a year. The per capita GNI is calculated by dividing a country's GNI by its population and adjusting for relative purchasing power.

n.a. = data not available   > = greater than   < = less than

SOURCES: International Telecommunication Union (ITU). *World Telecommunication Development Report 2003.* Geneva, Switzerland: ITU, 2003; World Bank. *World Development Indicators.* Washington, D.C.: The World Bank, 2004; Central Intelligence Agency. *The World Factbook.* Washington, D.C.: Government Printing Office, 2003.

ulation, there are female members of parliament, cabinet ministers, state secretaries, town councilors, and mayors. Women earn only 70% as much as men. A 1975 federal law provides for complete equality between husband and wife in maintaining the household and raising children. Women were allowed in the military for the first time in 1998.

A growing problem is right-wing extremism and the emergence of neo-Nazi groups. Racial violence against ethnic minorities in Austria is evident.

29 ■ Health

Nearly everyone in the country is entitled to free health care at facilities provided by Austria's health service. The costs are paid by the social insurance plan or, in cases of hardship, by the social welfare program.

In 1998, there were 330 hospitals, with 72,078 beds. There were 33,734 doctors and dentists and 1,534 midwives in 1998, and 5,193 psychiatrists in 1999. Life expectancy at birth in 2000 was 78 years. The infant mortality rate was 5 per 1,000 live births.

In 1999 there were 16 cases of tuberculosis per 100,000 people. By 1997, reported cases of acquired immunodeficiency syndrome (AIDS) totaled 7,500.

Vienna's medical school and research institutes are world famous. Spas (with thermal springs), health resorts, and sanatoriums are popular among Austrians as well as foreigners.

30 ■ Housing

The Housing Improvement Act of 1969 provides for government support for

Susan D Rock

This hotel along the River Inn in Innsbruck is an example of traditional Austrian architecture.

modernization of outdated housing. In 1990, 25% of Austria's housing stock had been built before 1919, and 19% between 1971 and 1980. About 53,000 new dwellings were completed in 2000.

31 ■ Education

All schools are coeducational and education at state schools is free of charge. Financial support is provided for postsecondary schooling. Primary education lasts for four years. Disabled students either attend special schools or are mainstreamed into regular classrooms. After primary education, pupils may either attend a general secondary school (*Hauptschule*) or an academic secondary school, which covers two four-year courses of study.

Students may also attend an intermediate or higher vocational school for a period of 5 years. Those who complete their studies at secondary or higher vocational school are qualified to attend the universities. Student-to-teacher ratio averages 13 to 1.

Austria maintains a vigorous adult education system. There are 12 university-level institutions and 6 fine-arts colleges offering 430 subjects and about 600 possible degrees. There are between 240,000 and 300,000 students enrolled full time in universities and all higher-level institutions.

As of 2002, the adult illiteracy rate was estimated at 2%.

32 ■ Media

The Austrian Post and Telegraph Administration operates all telephone, telegraph, teletype, and postal services. In 2001, 4 million mainline telephones were in use. The same year, there were about 6 million mobile cellular phones.

The Austrian Broadcasting Corp. administers the nation's broadcasting system. It broadcasts nationally over 3 radio and 2 television networks, and also provides a shortwave news service in German, English, French, and Spanish. As of 2001, there were a total of about 2 AM and 160 FM radio stations in the country and 45 television stations. As of 1997, there were about 6,800,000 radios and 4,250,000 television sets.

As of 2002, Austria had about twenty-two major papers distributed four times a week or more. Vienna accounts for about half of total readership. Many dailies are affiliated with political parties. The leading newspapers (with their average midweek circulations for 2002) are: *Neue Kronen Zeitung,*

© Corel Corporation

A view of the Austrian Alps.

510,000; *Kurier,* 334,000; *Kleine Zeitung,* 177,000; *Oberösterreichische Nachrichten,* 123,000; and *Tiroler Tageszeitung,* 103,600. The leading periodicals include the weeklies *Wochenpresse-Wirtschaftswoche* and *Profil* and the monthly *Trend,* which had a circulation of 95,000 in 1995.

As of 2000, there were 37 Internet service providers serving about 3 million customers.

Freedom of the press is constitutionally guaranteed and there is no state censorship.

33 ■ Tourism and Recreation

Austria ranks high among European tourist destinations. It has a year-round tourist season. In winter, tourists come to the famous skiing resorts and attend outstanding musical events in Vienna. In summer, visitors are attracted by scenery, sports, and cultural festivals, notably in Vienna and Salzburg. Mountaineering is an Austrian specialty, and soccer and cycling are popular. Motor racing, motorcycle racing, and speedway racing are also extremely popular sports in Austria. Tourist attractions in the capital include 15 state theaters and the Vienna State Opera (which also houses the Vienna Philharmonic); the Vienna Boys' Choir; Saint Stephen's Cathedral; the Schönbrunn and Belvedere palaces; and the Spanish Riding Academy, with its famous Lippizaner stallions. Of the 4,000 communities in Austria, nearly half are considered tourist centers.

Tourism is a major contributor to the Austrian economy. An estimated 17.9 million foreign tourists arrived in Austria in 2000. In the same year, receipts from tourism amounted to $10 billion. There were 304,928 rooms in hotels, inns, and pensions.

34 ▪ Famous Austrians

Monarchs who played a leading role in Austrian and world history include Rudolf I of Habsburg (1218–1291), founder of the Habsburg dynasty and Holy Roman emperor from 1273. Joseph II (1741–1790), the "benevolent despot," became Holy Roman emperor in 1765. Franz Josef (1830–1916) was emperor of Austria at the outbreak of World War I and his brother Maximilian (Ferdinand Maximilian Josef, 1832–1867) became emperor of Mexico in 1864. Adolf Hitler (1889–1945), born in Braunau, was dictator of Germany from 1933 until his death. Kurt Waldheim (1918–), an Austrian diplomat and foreign minister, was UN secretary-general from 1971 to 1981 and was elected to the presidency in June 1986.

Beginning in the eighteenth century and for the next 200 years, Vienna was the center of European musical culture. Among its great masters were Franz Joseph Haydn (1732–1809), Wolfgang Amadeus Mozart (1756–1791), and Franz Schubert (1797–1828). Composers of light music, typical of Austria, are Johann Strauss Sr. (1804–1849) and Johann Strauss Jr. (1825–1899).

Novelists and short-story writers of interest are Marie von Ebner-Eschenbach (1830–1916), Arthur Schnitzler (1862–1931), Hermann Bahr (1863–1934), Hermann Broch (1886–1952), and Peter Handke (1942–). Although born in Czechoslovakia, the poet Rainer Maria Rilke (1875–1926) and the novelist and short-story writer Franz Kafka (1883–1924) are usually identified with Austrian literary life. Film directors of Austrian birth include Max Reinhardt (Maximilian Goldman, 1873–1943), Erich von Stroheim (Erich Oswald Stroheim, 1885–1957), and Billy Wilder (1906–2002).

Psychoanalysis was founded in Vienna by Sigmund Freud (1856–1939). A renowned geneticist was Gregor Johann Mendel (1822–1884). Christian Johann Doppler (1803–1853), a physicist and mathematician, described the wave phenomenon known today as the Doppler shift. Lise Meitner (1878–1968) was the physicist who first identified nuclear fission.

Arnold Schwarzenegger (1947–), once the foremost bodybuilder in the world, went on to become a successful Hollywood film star and governor of California.

35 ▪ Bibliography

Ake, Anne. *Austria.* San Diego, CA: Lucent, 2001.

Allport, Alan. *Austria.* Philadelphia, PA: Chelsea House Publishers, 2002.

Sheehan, Sean. *Austria.* New York: Benchmark Books, 2003.

Stein, R. Conrad. *Austria.* New York: Children's Press, 2000.

What Life Was Like at Empire's End: Austro-Hungarian Empire, a.d. 1848–1918. Alexandria, VA: Time-Life Books, 2000.

Azerbaijan

Azerbaijan Republic
Azarbaichan Respublikasy

Capital: Baku.

Flag: Three equal horizontal bands of blue (top), red, and green; a crescent and eight-pointed star in white are centered in the red band.

Anthem: *Azerbaijan National Anthem,* composed by Uzeyir Hajibeyov.

Monetary Unit: The manat, consisting of 100 gopik, was introduced in 1992 and remains tied to the Russian ruble with widely fluctuating exchange rates.

As of May 2003, 1 manat = $0.000204 (or $1 = 4,909 manat).

Weights and Measures: The metric system is in force.

Holidays: New Year's Day, 1 January; International Women's Day, 8 March; Novruz Bayrom (Holiday of Spring), 22 March; Day of the Republic, 28 May; Day of Armed Forces, 9 October; Day of State Sovereignty, 18 October; Day of National Revival, 17 November; Universal Azeri Solidarity Day, 31 December.

Time: 4 PM = noon GMT.

1 ▪ Location and Size

Azerbaijan is located in southeastern Europe, between Armenia and the Caspian Sea. Comparatively, it is slightly smaller than the state of Maine, with a total area of 86,600 square kilometers (33,436 square miles), including the Nakhichevan Autonomous Republic and the Nagorno-Karabakh Autonomous Oblast. Azerbaijan shares boundaries with Russia, Iran, Armenia, and Georgia. Azerbaijan's boundary length totals 2,013 kilometers (1,251 miles). Azerbaijan's capital city, Baku, is located on the Apsheron Peninsula that juts into the Caspian Sea.

2 ▪ Topography

The main features of the land are the large, flat Kura-Aras Lowland (much of it below sea level) and the Great Caucasus Mountains to the north. The Lesser Caucasus Mountains are to the southwest and the Talish Mountains are in the south along the border with Iran. The Karabakh Upland lies in the west. The nation's highest point is Mount Bazar Dyuzi in the north with a height of 4,466 meters (14,652 feet). The lowest point is at the Caspian Sea, -28 meters (-92 feet) below sea level.

The Nakhichevan exclave (a region completely surrounded by the territory of

Geographic Profile

Geographic Features

Size ranking: 111 of 193
Highest elevation: 4,466 meters
(14,652 feet) at Mount Bazar Dyuzi
(Bazarduzu Dagi)
Lowest elevation: -28 meters (-92 feet)
at Caspian Sea

Land Use*

Arable land: 20%
Permanent crops: 3%
Forests: 13%
Other: 64%

Weather**

Average annual precipitation: (Baku)
23.9 centimeters (9.4 inches)
Average temperature in January: (Baku):
1–4°C (34–39°F)
Average temperature in July: (Baku):
22–28°C (72–82°F)

---

* *Arable Land: Land used for temporary crops, like meadows for mowing or pasture, gardens, and greenhouses.*

Permanent crops: Land cultivated with crops that occupy its use for long periods, such as cocoa, coffee, rubber, fruit and nut orchards, and vineyards.

Forests: Land containing stands of trees.

Other: Any land not specified, including built-on areas, roads, and barren land.

** *The measurements for precipitation and average temperatures were taken at weather stations closest to the country's largest city.*

Precipitation and average temperature can vary significantly within a country, due to factors such as latitude, altitude, coastal proximity, and wind patterns.

---

another country) lies to the west, separated from the rest of Azerbaijan by Armenia. Nakhichevan also shares borders with Turkey and Iran.

The longest river is the Kura, with a length of 1,514 kilometers (941 miles). The largest lake is the Mingacevir Reservoir of the Kura River, with a total area of 605 square kilometers (234 square miles).

3 ■ Climate

The country's climate ranges from subtropical in the eastern and central parts to alpine-like in the mountains. The average temperature in the capital, Baku, in July is 25°C (77°F). In January the average temperature is 4°C (39°F). Rainfall varies according to the nine climate zones in the country.

4 ■ Plants and Animals

The country's plants and animals are rich and varied. There are sixteen nature reserves and more than twenty-eight forest reserves and hunting farms.

5 ■ Environment

UN agencies report severe air and water pollution in Azerbaijan, which ranks among the 50 nations with the world's highest level of carbon dioxide emissions. The combination of industrial, agricultural, and oil-drilling pollution has created an environmental crisis in the Caspian Sea. These sources of pollution have contaminated 100% of the coastal waters in some areas and 45.3% of Azerbaijan's rivers. The pollution of the land through the indiscriminate use of agricultural chemicals such as the pesticide DDT is also a serious problem.

Azerbaijan's war with Armenia has hampered the government's ability to improve the situation. Due to the severity of pollution on all levels, the country's wildlife and vegetation are also seriously affected. From the mid-1980s to mid-1990s, the amount of forest and woodland declined by 12.5%. As of 2001, the endangered list included eleven species of mammals, eight species of birds, five species of fish, and thirteen species of reptile. Endangered species include the Barbel sturgeon, beluga, the Azov-Black Sea sturgeon, the Apollo butterfly, and the Armenian birch mouse.

6 ■ Population

The population of Azerbaijan was estimated at 8.37 million in 2000. A population of 8.2 million is projected for the year 2005. The population density was estimated at 94 persons per square kilometer (244 per square mile) in 2002. Baku, the capital, had an estimated population of 1.8 million as of 2000. Gyanja (formerly Kirovabad) had a population of 287,000, and Sumgait had 235,000.

7 ■ Migration

As a result of the war with Armenia, which started in 1988, more than 1 million people have been forced to leave the region. According to government estimates, there were 616,546 internally displaced persons as of 1999. Also as of 1999, Azerbaijan hosted 233,682 refugees. Most are Azeri refugees from Armenia. The Law on Citizenship allows for the automatic acquisition of Azerbaijani citizenship by refugees from Armenia. As of 2001 there were 148,000 migrants living in Azerbaijan, with less than 1% of these being refugees.

Location: 40°30′N; 47°0′E **Boundary Lengths:** Total boundary lengths, 2,013 kilometers (1,251 miles); Armenia (west), 566 kilometers (352 miles); Armenia (south), 221 kilometers (137 miles); Georgia, 322 kilometers (200 miles); Iran (south), 432 kilometers (268 miles); Iran (southeast), 179 kilometers (111 miles); Russia, 284 kilometers (177 miles); Turkey, 9 kilometers (6 miles).

As of 2003, the net migration rate was estimated at -5.16 per thousand.

8 ■ Ethnic Groups

According to 1998 estimates, 90% of the population was Azeri, about 3.2% were

Dagestani peoples, 2.5% were Russian, another 2% were Armenian, and 2.3% were of other ethnic origins. Almost all Armenians live in the separatist Nagorno-Karabakh region. Residents of Azerbaijan are called Azerbaijanis.

9 ▦ Languages

Azerbaijani, or Azeri, is a language related to Turkish and is also spoken in northwestern Iran. It is traditionally written in Arabic script. In 1995, an estimated 89% of the population spoke Azeri, 3% spoke Russian, 2% spoke Armenian, and 6% spoke other languages.

10 ▦ Religions

About 93% of the population are Muslim, 3% are Russian Orthodox, 2% are Armenian Orthodox, and 2% are of other religions.

Islam (both Shi'a and Sunni), Russian Orthodox, and Judaism are considered to be traditional religions of the country. There are small communities of Evangelical Lutherans, Roman Catholics, Baptists, Molokans (an older branch of Russian Orthodox), Seventh-day Adventists, Baha'is, Wahhabist Muslims, Jehovah's Witnesses, and Hare Krishnas.

11 ▦ Transportation

Railroads in Azerbaijan extend over some 2,125 kilometers (1,320 miles). Suburban trains carry 150,000 passengers each day. In 2002, the highway system totaled 36,700 kilometers (22,805 miles), of which 31,800 kilometers (19,760 miles) were paved. Ships from the Caspian fleet have called at some 125 ports in more than 30 countries. There are flights from Baku's Bina Airport to more than 70 cities of the former Soviet Union. In 2001, a total of 543,800 passengers were carried on scheduled domestic and international airline flights.

12 ▦ History

The territory of present-day Azerbaijan has been continuously inhabited since the Paleolithic era. Starting around 1000 B.C., it was ruled by groups including the Medians, Persians, and Greeks. In the third and fourth centuries A.D., battles between Rome and the Sassanid state in Persia inflicted great damage, leaving Azerbaijan open to raids by Turkic nomadic tribes from the north. New invaders appeared in the seventh and eighth centuries, when Arabs conquered much of the area.

In the 1230s, Azerbaijan was conquered by the famous Mongol warrior Genghis Khan. In the sixteenth and seventeenth centuries, the Safawid state emerged, rebuilding agriculture and commerce destroyed under the Mongols. In the eighteenth century Azerbaijan became the intersection of the Turkish, Persian, and Russian empires, as well as the focus of British and French attempts to block Russian expansion. The northern part of the territory was incorporated into Russia in the first third of the nineteenth century. However, the area did not become important until the 1880s, when its plentiful oil gained commercial importance.

After the 1917 revolution in Russia, communist Bolsheviks overthrew the government in Azerbaijan and declared the country a Soviet state. In the 1920s, the Soviet Union changed the borders between Azerbaijan and its neighbor Armenia and placed the Armenian region of Nagorno-Karabakh within Azerbaijan's borders. This move would eventually lead to war between Azerbaijan and Armenia. The Armenians in

Biographical Profile

Name: Heydar Aliyev. Due to ill health,
Aliyev appointed his son, Ilham, as
prime minister, in August 2003. Ilham
won a landslide victory in presidential
elections held on 15 October. Heydar
Aliyev died on 12 December 2003
Position: President of a republic
Religion: Islam

Heydar Aliyev

Nagorno-Karabakh are mostly Christians, while the Azerbaijanis are mostly Muslims.

In 1988, the ethnic Armenians living in Azerbaijan's Nagorno-Karabakh region declared their intent to leave Azerbaijan and become part of the Armenian republic. This led to a civil war. Inability to solve the conflict was one of the problems that brought down former Soviet leader Mikhail Gorbachev and broke apart the Soviet Union.

Azerbaijan declared itself independent of the Soviet Union on 30 August 1991. In December of that year, the Armenians of Nagorno-Karabakh voted to secede from Azerbaijan. They were helped by Armenian soldiers. Fighting between Armenia and Azerbaijan escalated in 1992 and continued until May 1994, when a cease-fire was announced. At the time of the cease-fire, Armenian forces were in control of Nagorno-Karabakh, which occupies 20% of Azerbaijan's territory.

A new parliament was formed in 1995 by the ruling New Azerbaijan Party, which banned most opposition groups from participating. The conflict with Armenian separatists is still a source of political and economic tension in Azerbaijan. As of 2003, the chances of reaching a negotiated settlement of the conflict remained small, although peace talks between Armenia and Azerbaijan were held in Paris and Florida in 2001.

In September 2002, construction began on a multibillion-dollar pipeline to

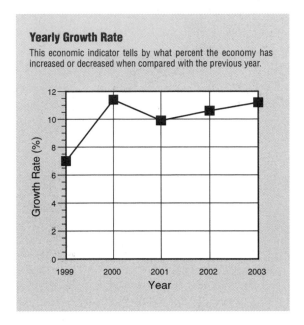

Yearly Growth Rate

This economic indicator tells by what percent the economy has increased or decreased when compared with the previous year.

carry Caspian oil from Azerbaijan to Turkey via Georgia.

13 ■ Government

Azerbaijan adopted its present constitution on 12 November 1995. Its system of government is based on a division of powers between a strong presidency, a legislature with the power to approve the budget and impeach the president, and a judiciary. The Soviet-era legislature has been replaced by a 125-member National Assembly. The country is divided into 59 districts and 11 cities. Ilham Aliyev was elected president in October 2003.

14 ■ Political Parties

As of 2003, almost three dozen political parties were registered in Azerbaijan. The largest and most influential is the New Azerbaijan Party (NAP) of President Ilham Aliyev. Opposition parties include the Azerbaijan Popular Front, the Milli Istiglal (National Independence Party), and the Musavat. Other political parties include the Civil Solidarity Party (CSP), Civic Union Party, Compatriot Party, Justice Party, Liberal Party of Azerbaijan, and the Social Democratic Party of Azerbaijan (SDP).

In the November 2000 National Assembly elections, the NAP and its allies won 108 of 125 seats. The National Independence Party, Musavat, and Azerbaijan Popular Front "Classic Faction" representatives refused to take their seats.

15 ■ Judicial System

The 1995 constitution provides for a judiciary with limited independence. The court system includes district courts and municipal courts that hear cases for the first time, and a Supreme Court that hears appeals. Criminal defendants have the right to an attorney and to an appointed lawyer, the right to a public trial, the right to be present at trial, and the right to confront witnesses. Lower-level judges are appointed directly by the president. Constitutional Court and Supreme Court judges also are appointed by the president, with confirmation by parliament.

16 ■ Armed Forces

Azerbaijan has a total of 72,100 active personnel in its armed forces and 300,000 reservists. The navy has 2,200 personnel, the army has 62,000, and the air force has 7,900. Personnel in two separate paramilitary units number 15,000. The defense budget for 1999 was $121 million, or 2.6% of the gross domestic product (GDP).

17 ■ Economy

Azerbaijan is one of the oldest oil-producing regions of the world. Remaining oil reserves were estimated in 2002 at 7 billion barrels, and gas reserves about 15 trillion cubic feet. In addition, the country has ample deposits of iron, aluminum, zinc, copper, arsenic, molybdenum, marble, and fire clay.

Azerbaijan has varied industry and agriculture and a well-developed transport network. Like those of other post-Soviet republics, Azerbaijan's economy was severely affected by the breakup of its traditional trading arrangements within the former Soviet Union, a steep drop in consumer buying power, and the decline in military-related industrial activity. Conflicts over the provinces of Nagorno-Karabakh and Nakhichevan have added to the republic's economic troubles. In 1994, Russia closed all rail service to Azerbaijan. Between 1991 and 1995, the economy declined by about 60%. However, investment in the oil sector led to gross domestic product (GDP) growth of 10% in 1998 and 7% in 1999. In 2001, the economy registered its fifth straight year of real GDP growth.

18 ■ Income

In 2002, Azerbaijan's gross domestic product (GDP) was $27 billion, or $3,300 per person. The annual growth rate of the GDP was estimated at 6.1%. The average inflation rate in 2002 was 2.6%.

19 ■ Industry

The oil and gas industry has traditionally been important to the wider industrial sector in Azerbaijan. In 2001, refined oil production accounted for more than 14.9% of

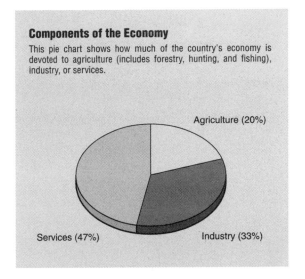

Components of the Economy

This pie chart shows how much of the country's economy is devoted to agriculture (includes forestry, hunting, and fishing), industry, or services.

Agriculture (20%)

Services (47%)

Industry (33%)

total industrial production, second only to the 58.6% accounted for by the extraction of crude oil and natural gas.

Other important industrial sectors in the Azeri economy include electrical power production (12.1% of total industrial production in 2001), chemicals (3.4%), food processing (3.2%), cars and other transport equipment (2.9%), and tobacco goods (1.6%), as well as various kinds of light manufacturing. However, output in almost all of these sectors declined or stagnated in the 1990s due to the conflict with Armenia. In 2001, total industrial production rose 5.1% over 2000.

20 ■ Labor

There were 3.7 million people in the Azerbaijani labor force in 2001. Agriculture accounted for 40% of employment; industry, 7%; and services, 53%. As of 2001, the estimated unemployment rate stood at 16%. There is a nationwide minimum wage, and the legal workweek is forty hours. The minimum age for employment is sixteen.

Cory Langley

Two Azerbaijani women prepare to sell their produce at an open-air market.

Children aged fourteen are allowed to work during vacations.

The constitution provides for the right to form labor unions, but in practice this right is limited and unions are generally not effective in wage negotiations.

21 ■ Agriculture

About 20% of Azerbaijan's area is cultivated or considered arable (suitable for farming). There are fifty-nine agricultural regions in ten geographic zones. The principal crops are grapes, cotton, and tobacco.

In 2001, agriculture accounted for 20% of the gross domestic product (GDP).

Annual crop production amounts to approximately 810,000 tons of wheat, 101,000 tons of seed cotton, and 9,000 tons of tobacco. Also produced annually are 140,000 tons of grapes, 39,000 tons of cotton (lint), 390,000 tons of fruit, 816,000 tons of vegetables, and 932,000 tons of grain.

Since independence, former state-owned farms have become more productive, and private fruit and vegetable farming is increasing. Azerbaijan has an expanding wine-producing industry whose wines have frequently won awards at international exhibitions. Wine production amounts to about 65,000 tons per year.

22 ■ Domesticated Animals

Azerbaijan has about 2.2 million hectares (5.4 million acres) of permanent pasture. The livestock population includes approximately 13 million chickens, 5.1 million sheep, 1.9 million cattle, 371,000 goats, 21,000 pigs, and 56,000 horses. Meat production amounts to about 103,000 tons annually, almost three-fourths of which is beef and mutton. About 991,000 tons of cow's milk, 29,000 tons of eggs, and 10,000 tons of greasy wool are produced per year.

23 ■ Fishing

The Caspian Sea is Azerbaijan's principal fishing resource. Commercial fishing centers on caviar and sturgeon. The total catch was 18,797 tons in 2000, primarily Azov sea sprat.

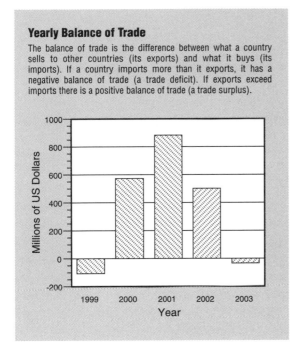

24 ■ Forestry

In 2000, about 13% of the land area consisted of forests and woodlands. The State Committee for Ecology and Use of Natural Resources has recently introduced new regulations to protect forest resources. Roundwood production in 2000 totaled 14,000 cubic meters (494,000 cubic feet).

25 ■ Mining

Besides significant reserves of natural gas and petroleum, Azerbaijan has iron ore reserves near the disputed Nagorno-Karabakh region and lead-zinc and copper-molybdenum deposits in the Nakhichevan area. Production of metallic and industrial minerals in 2000 included alumina (200,000 tons), bromine, clays, gypsum (60,000 tons), iodine, limestone, marble, sand and gravel, decorative building stone, and precious and semiprecious stones.

26 ■ Foreign Trade

Oil and gas, chemicals, oilfield equipment, textiles, and cotton are the predominant exports. The leading imports are machinery and parts, consumer goods, food, and textiles.

The major trading partners are Italy, France, Israel, Turkey, Russia, Georgia, Switzerland, Ukraine, the United Kingdom, the United States, Germany, and Iran.

27 ■ Energy and Power

Almost all production now comes from offshore in the Caspian Sea. Proven oil reserves at the beginning of 1998 totaled between 3.6 and 12.5 billion barrels. Production in 2001 totaled 311,200 barrels per day. Estimated natural gas reserves amount to 440 billion cubic meters (15.5 trillion cubic feet). Production of natural gas in 2000 totaled 5.7 billion cubic meters (201 billion cubic feet).

Electricity production in 2000 totaled 17.7 billion kilowatt hours.

28 ■ Social Development

The minimum wage does not provide adequately for a worker and family. A decent living can only be assured by the "safety net" of the extended family structure. Health and safety standards often are ignored in the workplace. Unemployment compensation and old age, disability pension, and survivor benefits are provided. Women have the same legal status as men.

Ethnic tensions and anti-Armenian sentiment are still strong. Many Armenians have either been expelled or emigrated.

Selected Social Indicators

The statistics below are the most recent estimates available as of 2003. For comparison purposes, data for the United States and averages for low-income countries and high-income countries are also given. About 15% of the world's 6.4 billion people live in high-income countries, while 40% live in low-income countries.

Indicator	Azerbaijan	Low-income countries	High-income countries	United States
Per capita gross national income (GNI)*	$3,010	$2,110	$28,480	$36,110
Population growth rate	1.3%	2.1%	0.7%	1.1%
People per square kilometer of land	94	77	31	31
Life expectancy in years: *male*	62	58	75	75
female	69	60	81	80
Number of physicians per 1,000 people	3.6	1.0	3.0	2.8
Number of pupils per teacher (primary school)	16	40	17	15
Literacy rate (15 years and older)	97%	66%	>95%	97%
Television sets per 1,000 people	332	91	735	938
Internet users per 1,000 people	37	10	364	551
Energy consumed per capita (kg of oil equivalent)	1,564	550	5,366	7,937

* The GNI is the total of all goods and services produced by the residents of a country in a year. The per capita GNI is calculated by dividing a country's GNI by its population and adjusting for relative purchasing power.

n.a. = data not available   > = greater than   < = less than

SOURCES: International Telecommunication Union (ITU). *World Telecommunication Development Report 2003*. Geneva, Switzerland: ITU, 2003; World Bank. *World Development Indicators*. Washington, D.C.: The World Bank, 2004; Central Intelligence Agency. *The World Factbook*. Washington, D.C.: Government Printing Office, 2003.

Other minorities, such as the Kurds and the Turks, also report problems with discrimination.

29 ▪ Health

In 2000, Azerbaijan's infant mortality rate was 13 per 1,000 live births.

In 1999, the total number of people living with human immunodeficiency virus/acquired immunodeficiency syndrome (HIV/AIDS) was under 500. Diphtheria, tuberculosis, hepatitis A, and diarrheal and acute respiratory infections have been serious public health problems. There have also been outbreaks of anthrax, botulism, cholera, tetanus, and malaria. Measles and tuberculosis still remain in this country despite a high incidence of vaccination for one-year-old children.

30 ▪ Housing

Azerbaijan has 12.5 square meters of housing space per person. As of 1 January 1991, there were 138,000 households (or 15.6%) on waiting lists for housing in urban areas. The housing shortage still remained as of 2001. About 32% of all privately owned urban housing had running water, 7% had sewer lines, and 6% had bathtubs. Nearly all had access to gas.

In 1996, there were about 60,000 refugees or other displaced persons living in tent communities. Another 300,000 were living in public, nonresidential buildings. At least 5% of homeless families had been waiting for housing for ten years or more.

31 ▥ Education

Education is free. The usual language of instruction is Azerbaijani, although Russian, Armenian, and Georgian are also offered by some schools. The pupil-teacher ratio at the primary level averages 16 to 1.

Russian is more commonly used at higher-level institutions, but this is slowly changing with a growing demand for the use of Azerbaijani.

Azerbaijan's most important institutes of higher learning are the Azerbaijan Polytechnic Institute, located in Baku, with seven departments and an enrollment of more than 12,000 students, and the State University, also located at Baku. It has an enrollment of over 15,000 students in 11 departments. Other institutions include the Medical University, Technological University, the Economic Institute, and the Oil and Chemistry Academy. In total, between 110,000 and 140,000 students are enrolled in institutions of higher learning. In 1995 (the most recent year for which statistics were available as of 2004), the adult illiteracy rate was estimated at 0.4%.

Baku is sometimes referred to as an "oil academy" because of its ongoing research in the areas of turbine drilling, cementation of oil wells, and the development of synthetic rubber from natural gas.

32 ▥ Media

In 1998, there were 1.4 million mainline telephones in use. Service is said to be of poor quality and inadequate. In 1997, there were about 40,000 cellular phones in use nationwide.

In 2002, there were several newspapers, most of them published in Azerbaijani. *Azerbaijan Ganjlari* (*Youth of Azerbaijan*)

AP/Wide World Photos

An Azerbaijani mother holds her baby.

had a circulation of 161,000 in 2002. More than one hundred periodicals are published, more than half in Azerbaijani.

As of 1999, there were ten AM and seventeen FM radio stations and 2 television stations. Domestic and Russian television programs are received locally, while Iranian television is received via satellite through a receive-only earth station. In 2000, there were 22 radios for every 1,000 people. In 2003, there were 332 television sets for every 1,000 people. In 2001, 2 providers served 12,000 Internet subscribers.

The Constitution of Azerbaijan specifically outlaws press censorship; however, it is said that the government does not always respect freedom of the press in practice.

33 ▪ Tourism and Recreation

The capital city of Baku is one of the prime tourist destinations of the Caucasus region. Its Old Town, with the Shirvanshah palace dating back to the fifteenth century, is especially popular with sightseers. Elsewhere in Azerbaijan, the Gobustan Museum displays prehistoric dwellings and cave paintings. The village of Surakhani attracts visitors to the Atashgah Fire-Worshipper's Temple. Visitors also are welcome at the carpet-weaving factory in the village of Nardaran. Azerbaijan had about 681,000 tourist arrivals in 2000.

34 ▪ Famous Azerbaijanis

The poet Nizami Ganjavi (1141–1204) is celebrated for his *Khamsa,* a collection of five epic poems. Muhammed Fizuli (1438–1556) based his poems on traditional folktales, and his poetic versions provide the bases for many twentieth-century plays and operas. The composer Uzeyir Hajibeyov (1885–1948) wrote the first Azerbaijani opera, founded the Azerbaijani Symphonic Orchestra, and composed Azerbaijan's national anthem. Vagif Mustafa Zadeh (1940–1979) is considered the founder of the Azerbaijani music movement of the 1960s that mixed jazz with the traditional style known as *mugam.* His daughter, Aziza Mustafa Zadeh (1969–), is a noted jazz pianist.

Prominent modern Azerbaijani scientists include Lofti Zadeh (1921–), pioneer of the "fuzzy logic" concept, and Iranian-born Ali Javan (1928–), inventor of the gas laser.

35 ▪ Bibliography

Elliot, Mark. *Azerbaijan with Georgia.* Cincinnati, OH: Seven Hills, 2001.

Leeuw, Charles van der. *Azerbaijan: A Quest for Identity.* New York: St. Martin's Press, 2000.

Roberts, Elizabeth. *Georgia, Armenia, and Azerbaijan.* Brookfield, CT.: Millbrook Press, 1992.

Streissguth, Thomas. *The Transcaucasus.* San Diego, CA: Lucent Books, 2001.

Wilson, Neil. *Georgia, Armenia & Azerbaijan.* London: Lonely Planet, 2000.

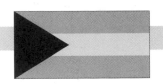

Bahamas

Commonwealth of the Bahamas

Capital: Nassau.

Flag: Three horizontal stripes of blue, gold, and blue, with a black triangle at the hoist.

Anthem: *March on Bahamaland..*

Monetary Unit: The Bahamas dollar (B$) of 100 cents has been in use since May 1966. As of June 1972, the Bahamas dollar ceased to be part of the sterling area and was set on a par with the US dollar. There are coins of 1, 5, 10, 15, 25, and 50 cents, and 1, 2, and 5 dollars, and notes of 50 cents and 1, 3, 5, 10, 20, 50, and 100 dollars. B$1=US$1 (or US$1=B$1).

Weights and Measures: Imperial weights and measures are in use.

Holidays: New Year's Day, 1 January; Labor Day, first Friday in June; Independence Day, 10 July; Emancipation Day, first Monday in August; Discovery Day, 12 October; Christmas Day, 25 December; Boxing Day, 26 December. Movable religious holidays include Good Friday, Easter Monday, and Whitmonday.

Time: 7 AM = noon GMT.

1 ▒ Location and Size

The Commonwealth of the Bahamas occupies a 13,940-square-kilometer (5,382-square-mile) group of islands in the North Atlantic Ocean between southeast Florida and northern Hispaniola. The area occupied by the Bahamas is slightly smaller than the state of Connecticut. There are nearly 700 islands, of which about 30 are inhabited. The total coastline is 3,542 kilometers (2,201 miles).

The Bahamas' capital city, Nassau, is located on New Providence Island in the center of the island group.

2 ▒ Topography

The islands are for the most part low and flat, rising to a peak elevation of about 63 meters (206 feet) at Mount Alvernia on Cat Island. The lowest point is at sea level. The terrain is broken by lakes (though none of them are major) and mangrove swamps, and the shorelines are marked by coral reefs.

3 ▒ Climate

Temperatures average 23°C (73°F) in winter and 27°C (81°F) in summer. Rainfall averages 127 centimeters (50 inches), and there are occasional hurricanes.

Geographic Profile

Geographic Features

Size ranking: 155 of 193
Highest elevation: 63 meters (206 feet)
    at Mount Alvernia on Cat Island
Lowest elevation: Sea level at the
    Atlantic Ocean

Land Use*

Arable land: 1%
Permanent crops: 0%
Forests: 32%
Other: 67%

Weather**

Average annual precipitation: 121.6
    centimeters (47.9 inches)
Average temperature in January: 20.3°C
    (68.5°F)
Average temperature in July: 27.4°C
    (81.3°F)

* Arable Land: Land used for temporary crops, like meadows for mowing or pasture, gardens, and greenhouses.

Permanent crops: Land cultivated with crops that occupy its use for long periods, such as cocoa, coffee, rubber, fruit and nut orchards, and vineyards.

Forests: Land containing stands of trees.

Other: Any land not specified, including built-on areas, roads, and barren land.

** The measurements for precipitation and average temperatures were taken at weather stations closest to the country's largest city.

Precipitation and average temperature can vary significantly within a country, due to factors such as latitude, altitude, coastal proximity, and wind patterns.

4 ◾ Plants and Animals

The islands abound in such tropical plants as bougainvillea, jasmine, oleander, orchid, and yellow elder. Native trees include the black olive, casuarina, cascarilla, cork tree, manchineel, pimento, and seven species of palm. There are 218 species and subspecies of birds, including flamingos, hummingbirds, and other small birds and waterfowl.

5 ◾ Environment

The government's environmental priorities include monitoring industrial operations, providing drinkable water and regular garbage collection throughout the country, maintenance and beautification of public parks and beaches, and removal of abandoned vehicles. Other significant environmental issues are the impact of tourism on the environment, coral reef decay, waste disposal, and water pollution. Land clearing for agricultural purposes is a significant environmental problem because it threatens the habitats of the nation's wildlife.

Endangered species include Kirtland's warbler, Bachman's warbler, green sea turtle, hawksbill turtle, Allen Cays rock iguana, and Watling Island ground iguana. The Caribbean monk seal and American crocodile are extinct. Of seventeen species of mammals, two are endangered. Four species of birds are also threatened. Four species of reptiles in a total of 204 are threatened. One amphibian out of 124 species is also considered endangered.

6 ◾ Population

The population in 2003 was estimated at 295,000. Some two-thirds of the people reside on the island of New Providence, the site of Nassau, the largest city. Nassau's population was estimated at 214,000 in 2001.

7 ■ Migration

Some Bahamians migrate to the United States in search of employment. There is also inter-island migration, chiefly to New Providence and Grand Bahama islands.

The country's location between the United States and other Caribbean islands has made it a transit point for migrants, including asylum seekers, trying to reach the United States. An estimated 100 Cuban nationals seek asylum in the Bahamas each month. As of 2000, there were 30,000 migrants living in the Bahamas, including 100 refugees. The net migration rate of the Bahamas was estimated at -2.21 migrants per 1,000 population in 2003.

8 ■ Ethnic Groups

Descendants of slaves brought to the Western Hemisphere from Africa make up about 85% of the population. About 12% of the total is white, largely of British origin. About 3% are Asian or Hispanic. Residents of the Bahamas are called Bahamians.

9 ■ Languages

English is the spoken and official language of the Bahamas. Haitian immigrants speak French or a Creole patois (dialect).

10 ■ Religions

The population is overwhelmingly Christian, with Baptists comprising about 32% of the people. About 20% of the population are Anglicans and about 24% belong to other Protestant groups such as the

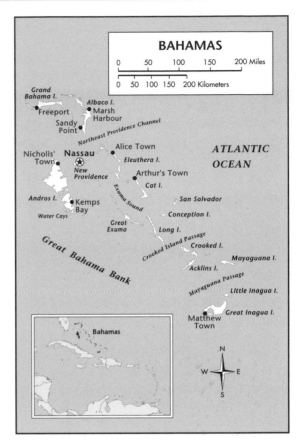

Location: 20°50′ to 27°25′N; 72°37′ to 82°32′W. **Total Coastline:** 3,542 kilometers (2,201 miles) **Territorial Sea Limit:** 3 miles.

Methodists (6%), the Church of God (6%), Presbyterians, Seventh-day Adventists, and the Salvation Army. About 19% of the population are Roman Catholics. There is also a strong Greek Orthodox community. Smaller groups include Jews, Baha'is, Muslims, Hindus, and Rastafarians. More traditional practices related to witchcraft and known to scholars as voodoo or *obeah* continue to be observed in some areas.

Biographical Profile

Name: Perry Gladstone Christie
Position: Prime Minister of a constitutional parliamentary democracy
Took Office: 3 May 2002
Birthplace: Nassau, The Bahamas
Birthdate: 21 August 1943
Religion: Anglican
Education: University Tutorial College in London, Inner Temple, and the University of Birmingham, UK, L.L.B. degree with honors in 1969
Spouse: Bernadette Hanna, an accountant and lawyer
Children: Two sons, Steffan and Adam, and a daughter, Alexandra
Of interest: Christie set up his own law practice, Christie Ingraham and Company. He enjoys gardening.

Perry Gladstone Christie

Religion, with a focus on Christianity, is considered an academic subject in government schools. Although students may freely choose not to participate in religious instruction or observances outside of their own faith, the topic is included in mandatory standardized tests.

11 ■ Transportation

In 2002, there were about 2,693 kilometers (1,673 miles) of highways, of which 1,546 kilometers (961 miles) were paved. There were 80,000 passenger cars and 24,283 commercial vehicles in 2000. There are no railways.

In 2002, this archipelago nation had a merchant fleet of 1,076 ships of 1,000 GRT or over, with a total volume capacity of 31,309,9187 GRT and a deadweight capacity of 45,859,485 tons. Nassau is a major port of call for cruise ships, which visit Freeport as well. Airports in 2001 totaled sixty-seven, of which thirty had paved runways. There are international airports at Nassau and Freeport, with frequent connections to the United States, Canada, and the United Kingdom. In 2001, scheduled domestic and international airline flights carried 1,625,700 passengers. Bahamas Air, a state-owned enterprise, is the national airline.

12 ▉ History

The first permanent European settlement was established in 1647 by a group of religious refugees from England. They and later settlers imported blacks as slaves during the seventeenth century.

The British established a crown colony on the islands in 1717. After the end of slavery in 1838, the Bahamas served only as a source of sponges and occasionally as a strategic location. During the U.S. Civil War (1861–65), Confederate blockade runners operated from the islands. After World War I (1914–18), Prohibition rumrunners used the islands as a base. During World War II (1939–45), the United States used them for naval bases.

The Bahamas achieved independence in stages, with full independence granted on 10 July 1973. The country's first prime minister, Lynden O. Pindling, ruled for nearly twenty years, during which the Bahamas benefited from tourism and foreign investment. By the early 1980s, the islands also had become a major center for the drug trade. In August 1992, the Bahamas had its first transfer of political power, when Hubert Ingraham became prime minister. Ingraham was reelected in 1997 to another four-year term.

In 1999, Hurricane Floyd did extensive damage in the Abacos and Eleuthra, hurting tourism revenues in those areas.

In the elections of May 2002, Perry Christie became the new prime minister. Christie promised to bring more diversified development to the tourism-dependent economy. He also vowed to further develop the country's fast-growing financial industry.

Susan D Rock

Government buildings in Nassau, the capital city of the Bahamas.

13 ▉ Government

The Bahamas has a republican form of government, formally headed by the British sovereign, who is represented by a governor-general. A prime minister and a cabinet have executive authority. The two-chamber legislature consists of a sixteen-member Senate appointed by the governor-general and an elected forty-member House of Assembly. The prime minister is the leader of the majority party in the House. There are twenty-one administrative districts, consisting of various islands and groups of islands.

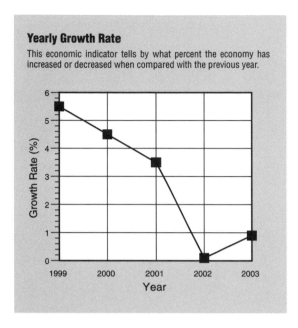

Yearly Growth Rate

This economic indicator tells by what percent the economy has increased or decreased when compared with the previous year.

one of the eight Caribbean nations that ratified a treaty establishing the Caribbean Court of Justice to handle some cases formerly heard by the Privy Council.) Lower courts include three magistrates' courts on New Providence and one on Freeport. Police abuse of suspects has been a serious problem. In 1993, a coroner's court was established to investigate cases in which criminal suspects die while in police custody.

16 ▪ Armed Forces
The Royal Bahamas Defense Force of 860 sailors is responsible for external security. Defense expenditures were less than 0.7% of the gross domestic product (GDP) in 1999.

14 ▪ Political Parties
The Progressive Liberal Party (PLP) emerged as the Bahamas' majority party in the early 1970s. The Free Progressive Liberal Party, a splinter group formed in 1970, merged with another opposition group, the United Bahamian Party, to form the Free National Movement (FNM). After years of loyal opposition, the FNM took power in 1992, winning thirty-two seats, compared to seventeen for the PLP. Its majority was increased to thirty-four seats in the 1997 elections. In 2002, however, the PLP won twenty-nine seats in the forty-member legislature, enough to command majority control once again.

15 ▪ Judicial System
The highest court is the Court of Appeal, consisting of three judges. Ultimate appeals go to the Privy Council of the United Kingdom. (In 2003, the Bahamas was not

17 ▪ Economy
Tourism, the mainstay of the economy, directly or indirectly involves most of the population. Because there is no direct taxation, the Bahamas also has become a haven for a variety of financial companies. The economy grew by 3.5% in 2001. Steady economic growth has brought a steady decline in unemployment, from 11.5% in 1996 to an estimated 6.9% in 2001. Inflation has remained low, averaging 1.3% from 1996 to 2001.

18 ▪ Income
In 2001, the Bahamas' gross domestic product (GDP) was $5 billion, or $16,800 per person. The annual growth rate of the GDP was estimated at 3.5%. The average inflation rate in 2001 was 1.5%.

19 ▪ Industry
Refined petroleum, cement, and rum production are important, and enterprises

Components of the Economy

This pie chart shows how much of the country's economy is devoted to agriculture (includes forestry, hunting, and fishing), industry, or services.

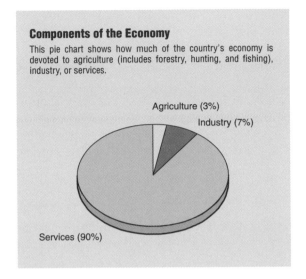

Agriculture (3%)

Industry (7%)

Services (90%)

producing pharmaceuticals, sea salt, and steel pipe have been developed. The Commonwealth Brewery in Nassau produces Heineken, Guinness, and Kalik beers.

20 ■ Labor

The total number of workers was estimated at 149,900 in 1999, with the overwhelming majority employed in tourism or tourist-related activities. About 25% of the labor force was unionized in 2001. Unemployment in 2001 stood at 6.9%.

In the Bahamas, children under the age of fourteen are prohibited from industrial work, work during school hours, or work at night.

21 ■ Agriculture

Agriculture is carried out on small plots throughout most of the islands. Only about 1% of the land area is cultivated. The main crops are onions, okra, and tomatoes. Inadequate production has necessitated the import of about 80% of the islands' food supply. Orange, grapefruit,

and cucumber production in Abaco is mainly for exports. Agricultural products include about 45,000 tons of sugarcane, 14,000 tons of grapefruit, and 22,000 tons of vegetables annually.

22 ■ Domesticated Animals

The livestock population includes some 1,000 head of cattle, 6,000 sheep, 14,000 goats, 16,000 hogs, and 4 million poultry. Each year about 1,000 tons of cow's milk, 1,000 tons of goat's milk, and 1,000,000 tons of eggs are produced. Poultry production (11,000 tons) accounts for almost all domestic meat production. In December 1991, the government banned foreign chicken, in order to protect local poultry producers from cheaper imports, mainly from the United States.

23 ■ Fishing

The 2000 catch amounted to 10,500 tons, over 78% of which was spiny lobsters (crayfish). Crayfish and conch exports are commercially important. There is excellent sport fishing for wahoo, dolphin fish, and tuna in Bahamian waters. In 2000, fisheries exports totaled $89.9 million. Since the Bahamas imports 80% of its food, the government is interested in expanding the role of domestic commercial fishing.

24 ■ Forestry

Caribbean pine and cascarilla bark are the major forestry products, but there is no commercial forestry industry. About 32% of the total land area consists of forests and woodlands. Roundwood production in 2000 totaled 17,000 cubic meters (600,000 cubic feet). That year, the Bahamas imported $30.3 million in wood and forest products.

25 ▪ Mining

Salt and aragonite stone, a component in glass manufacture, were the two most commercially important mineral products, with estimated 2000 production figures of 900,000 tons for salt and 1.2 million tons for aragonite. The major salt producer on the islands was Morton Bahamas Salt Company, the only major industry and the largest employer on the island of Inagua. Limestone sand was produced by Freeport Aggregate Ltd. for the local construction industry.

26 ▪ Foreign Trade

Exports include pharmaceuticals, cement, rum, crawfish, and aragonite. Imports are primarily composed of foodstuffs, manufactured goods, crude oil, vehicles, and electronics. About 91% of imports arrive from the United States. The Bahamas' major trade partners are the United States, France, United Kingdom, Canada, Mexico, Switzerland, Germany, and Japan.

27 ▪ Energy and Power

Electricity production totals more than 1,000 million kilowatt hours per year. Fossil fuel accounts for all power production. New gas turbines were added to the Blue Hill Power Station, and were becoming operational in late 2002 and early 2003.

28 ▪ Social Development

Workers' compensation and retirement, maternity, survivors', and funeral benefits are provided. Bahamian women are well represented in business, the professions,

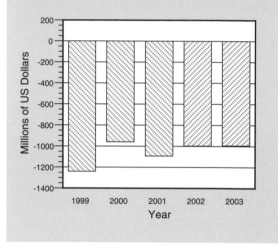

Yearly Balance of Trade

The balance of trade is the difference between what a country sells to other countries (its exports) and what it buys (its imports). If a country imports more than it exports, it has a negative balance of trade (a trade deficit). If exports exceed imports there is a positive balance of trade (a trade surplus).

and government. The constitution does not allow foreign-born husbands of Bahamian women to become citizens. Inheritance laws also discriminate against women. The government has authorized establishment of two battered women's shelters and a toll-free domestic violence hotline.

29 ▪ Health

The government operates the 436-bed Princess Margaret Hospital in Nassau and two other hospitals, the Sandilands Rehabilitation Center and the 82-bed Rand Memorial Hospital. In addition, 57 clinics and 54 satellite clinics are maintained throughout the islands, with emergency air links to Nassau. In 1995, there were 417 physicians and 80 dentists. In the same year, there were 653 registered nurses.

Selected Social Indicators

The statistics below are the most recent estimates available as of 2003. For comparison purposes, data for the United States and averages for low-income countries and high-income countries are also given. About 15% of the world's 6.4 billion people live in high-income countries, while 40% live in low-income countries.

Indicator	Bahamas	Low-income countries	High-income countries	United States
Per capita gross national income (GNI)*	$15,300	$2,110	$28,480	$36,110
Population growth rate	0.8%	2.1%	0.7%	1.1%
People per square kilometer of land	31	77	31	31
Life expectancy in years: *male*	62	58	75	75
female	69	60	81	80
Number of physicians per 1,000 people	1.4	1.0	3.0	2.8
Number of pupils per teacher (primary school)	21	40	17	15
Literacy rate (15 years and older)	95.6%	66%	>95%	97%
Television sets per 1,000 people	227	91	735	938
Internet users per 1,000 people	57	10	364	551
Energy consumed per capita (kg of oil equivalent)	6,781	550	5,366	7,937

* The GNI is the total of all goods and services produced by the residents of a country in a year. The per capita GNI is calculated by dividing a country's GNI by its population and adjusting for relative purchasing power.

n.a. = data not available   > = greater than   < = less than

SOURCES: International Telecommunication Union (ITU). *World Telecommunication Development Report 2003.* Geneva, Switzerland: ITU, 2003; World Bank. *World Development Indicators.* Washington, D.C.: The World Bank, 2004; Central Intelligence Agency. *The World Factbook.* Washington, D.C.: Government Printing Office, 2003.

In 1999, the infant mortality rate was 18 per 1,000 live births. In 2000, low birth weight babies accounted for an estimated 10.4% of all births. Average life expectancy in 2003 was sixty-six years, down from seventy-four years in 1999.

In 2000, 28% of all deaths were attributed to diseases of the circulatory system, 20% to communicable diseases, 14% to cancer, and the remainder to other causes. As of the end of 2000, a total of 5,648 people were living with human immunodeficiency virus/acquired immunodeficiency syndrome (HIV/AIDS), including 1,111 who had shown symptoms of AIDS. Between 1996 and 2000, HIV/AIDS was the leading cause of death among males and among the general population.

30 ■ Housing

Overcrowding is a problem on New Providence, and decent low-cost housing is in short supply. The Bahamas Housing Authority was established in 1983 to develop housing for low-income people.

As of 2001, the government had also launched a "new birth" program to renovate dwellings in traditional communities and to create new housing in urban centers, particularly for low or middle-class residents.

31 ■ Education

Education is free in all government-maintained schools. English is the official language. Primary education begins at age five and lasts for six years. Secondary education begins at age eleven and consists of two cycles, each of three years' duration.

Education is compulsory for children aged five to fourteen.

Post-secondary training is provided by the government primarily through the College of the Bahamas, which provides a two-year or three-year program leading to an associate's degree. It also offers a bachelor of arts degree in education. Other schools of continuing education offering academic and vocational courses include the Bahamas Hotel Training College, the Catholic Continuing Education College of Saint Barnabas, and the Industrial Training College. In addition, the Bahamas has been affiliated with the University of the West Indies since 1960.

As of 2003, the adult illiteracy rate was estimated at about 4% (males, 5%; females, 3%).

32 ■ Media

All telephone, telegraph, and teletype service is provided by the Bahamas Telecommunications Corp. In 1997, there were 96,000 mainline telephones in service. The same year, there were about 6,152 cellular phones in use.

In 2001, there were six radio stations, with only one owned and operated by the government. The only television station, which was established in 1996, is state owned. In 1997 there were 215,000 radios and 67,000 television sets in use nationwide.

Three daily newspapers are published in the country. The *Nassau Daily Tribune* had a circulation of 12,000 in 2002 while *The Nassau Guardian* had a circulation of 14,100. The daily *Freeport News* has a circulation of 4,000. All three papers are privately owned. There are also several weekly papers.

33 ■ Tourism and Recreation

In 2000, 1.59 million tourists visited the islands; the vast majority came from the United States. In the same year, tourists spent a total of $1.8 billion in the islands, and there were 14,701 hotel rooms and 29,402 beds, with a 67% occupancy rate.

Visitors are attracted to the Bahamas' excellent climate, beaches, and recreational and resort facilities. Water sports (including excellent deep-sea fishing) are the favorite pastimes.

34 ■ Famous Bahamians

Lynden Oscar Pindling (1930–2000), a lawyer and leader of the PLP, became the Bahamas' first prime minister following independence in 1973. He was succeeded by Hubert Ingraham (1947–) in 1992. American-born actor Sidney Poitier (1924–) was appointed Bahamian ambassador to Japan in 1997.

35 ■ Bibliography

Barlas, Robert. *Bahamas.* New York: Marshall Cavendish, 2000.

Craton, Michael. *Islanders in the Stream: A History of the Bahamian People.* Athens, GA: University of Georgia Press, 1992.

Hintz, Martin. *The Bahamas.* New York: Children's Press, 1997.

Johnson, Howard. *The Bahamas: From Slavery to Servitude.* Gainesville, FL: University Press of Florida, 1996.

Williams, Colleen Madonna Flood. *Bahamas.* Philadelphia, PA: Mason Crest Publishers, 2004.

Bahrain

State of Bahrain
Dawlat al-Bahrayn

Capital: Manama (Al-Manamah).

Flag: Red with a white vertical stripe on the hoist, the edge between them being saw-toothed.

Anthem: Music without words.

Monetary Unit: The Bahrain dinar (BD) is divided into 1,000 fils. There are coins of 5, 10, 25, 50, and 100 fils and notes of 500 fils and 1, 5, 10, and 20 dinars. BD1 = $2.6596 (or $1 = BD0.376; as of January 2003).

Weights and Measures: The metric system is used; local measures also are used.

Holidays: New Year's Day, 1 January; National Day, 16 December. Movable Muslim religious holidays include Hijra (Muslim New Year), 'Ashura, Prophet's Birthday, 'Id al-Fitr, and 'Id al-'Adha'.

Time: 3 PM = noon GMT.

1 Location and Size

The Middle Eastern State of Bahrain consists of a group of 33 islands (6 inhabited) in the western Persian Gulf, with a total area of 620 square kilometers (239 square miles), slightly less than 3.5 times the area of Washington, D.C. Bahrain, the main island, is linked by bridges to Al Muharraq and Sitra islands and to Saudi Arabia. Other islands include the Hawar group (off the west coast of Qatar), Nabih Salih, Umm an-Na'san, and Jidda. The total coastline is 161 kilometers (100 miles). Bahrain's capital, Manama, is located on the northeastern coast.

2 Topography

The north coast of Bahrain is irrigated by natural springs and artesian wells. South of this fertile area, the land is barren, with low rolling hills, numerous rocky cliffs, and wadis (dry river beds). From the shoreline the surface rises gradually toward the center, where it drops into a basin surrounded by steep cliffs. Toward the center of the basin is Jabal ad-Dukhan, a steep, rocky hill that rises to 122 meters (400 feet) above sea level, the highest point in the nation. Most of the lesser islands are flat and sandy. The lowest point in the country is at sea level.

Geographic Profile

Geographic Features

Size ranking: 175 of 193
Highest elevation: 122 meters (400 feet) at Jabal ad-Dukhan
Lowest elevation: Sea level at the Persian Gulf

Land Use*

Arable land: 1%
Permanent crops: 1%
Forests: 0%
Other: 98%

Weather**

Average annual precipitation: 7.6 centimeters (3.0 inches)
Average temperature in January: 17.4°c (63.3°F)
Average temperature in July: 33.8°c (92.8°F)

---

* *Arable Land: Land used for temporary crops, like meadows for mowing or pasture, gardens, and greenhouses.*

Permanent crops: Land cultivated with crops that occupy its use for long periods, such as cocoa, coffee, rubber, fruit and nut orchards, and vineyards.

Forests: Land containing stands of trees.

Other: Any land not specified, including built-on areas, roads, and barren land.

** *The measurements for precipitation and average temperatures were taken at weather stations closest to the country's largest city.*

Precipitation and average temperature can vary significantly within a country, due to factors such as latitude, altitude, coastal proximity, and wind patterns.

3 ▪ Climate

Summers in Bahrain are hot and humid, and winters are relatively cool. Daily average temperatures in July range from a minimum of 29°c (84°F) to a maximum of 37°c (99°F). In January, the minimum is 14°c (57°F); the maximum is 20°c (68°F). Rainfall averages less than 10 centimeters (4 inches) annually.

4 ▪ Plants and Animals

Outside the cultivated areas, numerous wild desert flowers appear, most noticeably after rain. Desert shrubs, grasses, and wild date palms are also found. Mammalian life is limited to the jerboa (desert rat), gazelle, mongoose, and hare. About 14 species of lizard and 4 types of land snake are also found. Bird life is especially varied. Larks, song thrushes, swallows, and terns are frequent visitors, and residents include the bulbul, hoopoe, parakeet, and warbler.

5 ▪ Environment

Bahrain's principal environmental problems are scarcity of fresh water, desertification (fertile land turning to desert), and pollution from oil production.

A wildlife sanctuary established in 1980 is home to threatened Gulf species, including the Arabian oryx, gazelle, zebra, giraffe, Defassa waterbuck, addax, and lesser kudu. Bahrain has also established captive breeding centers for falcons and for the rare Houbara bustard. The goitered gazelle, the greater spotted eagle, and the green sea turtle are considered endangered species.

6 ▦ Population

In 2003, the population was estimated at 724,000. The population projection for the year 2015 is 900,000. Population density was 971 per square kilometer (2,515 per square mile) in 2002. Manama, the capital, had a 2001 estimated population of 162,000.

7 ▦ Migration

The proportion of immigrants increased from 20% of the total population in 1975 to an estimated 40% in 2000. Most of them are temporary workers from other Arab countries, Iran, Pakistan, India, and the Republic of Korea. Many skilled workers are Europeans. In 2003, the estimated net migration rate was 1.07 migrants per 1,000 population.

8 ▦ Ethnic Groups

About 63% of the population consists of native Bahrainis, the vast majority of whom were of northern Arab (Adnani) ancestry, with some black racial traits. Asians accounted for 19% of the population. Other Arab groups (principally Omanis) accounted for 10%; Iranians, 8%.

9 ▦ Languages

Arabic (the Gulf dialect) is the universal language. English is widely understood. A small number of people speak Farsi and Urdu.

10 ▦ Religions

In 2002, an estimated 98% of the population was Muslim, with about two-thirds belonging to the Shi'a branch and the others Sunni. Foreigners make up 38% of the total population. Roughly half of them are

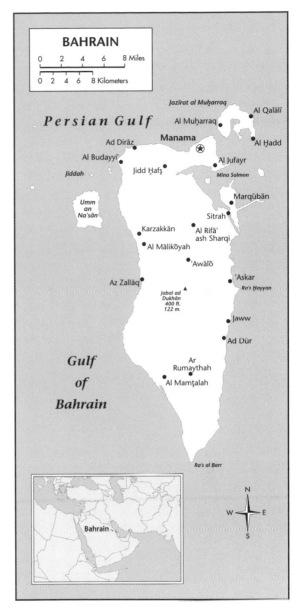

Location: 25°47′10° to 26°17′3°N; 50°22′45° to 50°40′20′E. **Total Coastline:** 161 kilometers (100 miles). **Territorial Sea Limit:** 3 miles.

non-Muslim, including Christians, Jews, Hindus, Buddhists, Sikhs, and Baha'is. All are free to practice their own religions,

Biographical Profile

Name: Sheikh Hamad bin 'Isa al-Khalifa
Position: Emir of a traditional monarchy
Took Office: 6 March 1999
Birthdate: 28 January 1950
Religion: Islam
Education: Sandhurst Military Academy; US Army Command and General Staff College, Fort Leavenworth, Kansas, 1973
Children: Three sons, two daughters
Of interest: He is an experienced military officer and became a qualified helicopter pilot in 1978

Sheikh Hamad bin 'Isa al-Khalifa

keep their own places of worship, and display the symbols for their religions. Islam, however, is the official religion.

11 ■ Transportation

There are 3,103 kilometers (1,928 miles) of bituminous surfaced highways. Bahrain's main port is Mina Salman. In 2001, Bahrain had a merchant fleet of eight ships with 228,273 gross registered tons. The international airport near Al-Muharraq can handle large jet aircraft and serves more than two dozen international airlines. In 2001, scheduled domestic and international flights carried 1,250,100 passengers.

12 ■ History

Known as Dilmun, Bahrain was a thriving trade center around 2000 B.C. The islands were visited by the ships of Alexander the Great in the third century B.C. Bahrain accepted Islam in the seventh century A.D.

The Portuguese occupied Bahrain from 1522 to 1602. The present ruling family, the Khalifa, who are related to the Sabah family of Kuwait and the Saudi royal family, captured Bahrain in 1782. Contact with the British followed in the nineteenth century, concluding in an 1861 treaty of protection. After a plan to federate the nine sheikhdoms of the southern Gulf failed, Bahrain became a sovereign state on 15 August 1971.

Owing to its small size, Bahrain, a founding member of the Gulf Cooperation

Council, generally takes its lead in foreign affairs from its Arab neighbors on the Gulf. During the Iran-Iraq War (1980–88), Bahrain joined most other Arab states in supporting Iraq. However, when Iraq invaded Kuwait in 1990, Bahrain stood with the United States and its Middle Eastern allies, contributing military support and facilities to the defeat of Iraq. Bahrain has long assisted the American naval presence in the Persian Gulf. In 1991, the United States signed an agreement giving the Department of Defense access to facilities on the island.

On 6 March 1999, Sheikh 'Isa bin Salman al-Khalifa, who had ruled his country since independence, died of a heart attack. He was succeeded on the throne by his son, Sheikh Hamad bin 'Isa al-Khalifa. The new ruler took a more liberal approach to government. By February 2001, the emir had pardoned and released all political prisoners, detainees, and exiles.

On 14 February 2001, a referendum was held that endorsed a return to constitutional rule. Under the constitution amended 14 February 2002, the country is no longer an emirate, but a constitutional monarchy. The emir was replaced by a king. A two-house National Assembly was established, along with an independent judiciary.

On 16 March 2001, the International Court of Justice (ICJ) resolved a territorial dispute between Bahrain and Qatar over the potentially oil- and gas-rich Hawar Islands. The dispute had lasted for decades and almost brought the two nations to the brink of war in 1986. The ICJ awarded Bahrain the largest disputed islands, the Hawar Islands, while Qatar was given sovereignty over Janan Island and Fasht ad Dibal.

Parliamentary elections, the first in nearly thirty years, were held in October 2002. In 2003, demonstrations took place in Bahrain in opposition to the U.S.-led war with Iraq.

13 ■ Government

The constitution was amended in 2002, and Bahrain became a constitutional monarchy headed by a king, after having been an emirate. The legislature is called the National Assembly. It consists of two houses, an appointed 40-member Consultative Council and an elected 40-member Chamber of Deputies. The first legislative elections since 1973 were held in October 2002. Under the new constitution, there are five municipal councils. The first local elections since 1957 were held in May 2002.

14 ■ Political Parties

Political parties are illegal in Bahrain. Several underground groups, including pro-Iranian militant Islamic groups, have been active and are vigorously opposed by the government.

Beginning with municipal elections in May 2002, candidates from a wide variety of political groups formed a more tolerant political culture in Bahrain. These groups are not officially designated as political parties. However, they are similar to democratic parties in the West. They can field candidates in elections, organize their activities, and campaign freely. There are seven main political groups: the Arab-Islamic Wasat (Center) Society (AIWS); the Democratic Progressive Forum (DPF); the Islamic National Accord (INA); the National Action Charter Society (NACS); the National Democratic Action Society (NDAS); the National Democratic

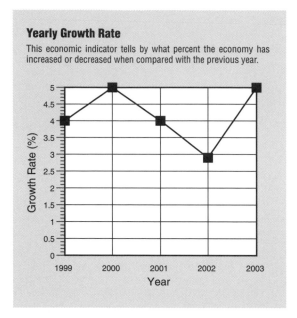

Yearly Growth Rate

This economic indicator tells by what percent the economy has increased or decreased when compared with the previous year.

Gathering Society (NDGS); and the National Islamic Forum (NIF).

The partially elected bicameral (two-chamber) parliament that was approved in a referendum in 2001 held its first session in December 2002 after elections were held that October. In the forty-member directly elected House of Deputies, independents took twenty-one seats, Sunni Islamists won nine seats, and other groupings held ten seats.

15 ▪ Judicial System

The law of Bahrain combines Islamic religious law (Shari'ah), tribal law, and other civil laws and regulations. A new constitution promises an independent judiciary. A Constitutional Court is appointed by the king. Military courts are confined to military offenses only. The new constitution provides for some women's political rights. In ordinary civil and criminal courts there are open trials, a right to counsel (includ-ing legal aid when determined to be necessary), and a right to appeal.

16 ▪ Armed Forces

The Bahrain armed forces in 2002 had 10,700 personnel. Bahrain sent troops to Saudi Arabia during the 1991 Gulf War. Defense expenditures in 2001 were $526.2 million, or 6.7% of the gross domestic product (GDP).

17 ▪ Economy

Bahrain's economy has been based on oil since the 1920s. However, the oil supply appeared to be running out as of the early 2000s. As a result, the government was encouraging development in other areas, such as petroleum refining, aluminum production, natural gas production, and offshore banking. Still, the oil industry accounted for 60% of export earnings and about 30% of the gross domestic product (GDP) in 2001. The banking sector has assets of $100 billion. Services accounted for 64% of all economic activity.

18 ▪ Income

In 2001, the gross domestic product (GDP) was $8.4 billion, or $13,000 per person. The average inflation rate in 2001 was 1.5%.

19 ▪ Industry

Petroleum refining, begun modestly in 1942, was Bahrain's first modern industrial enterprise. In 1999, a seven-year, $800 million modernization plan was begun to upgrade Bahrain's refinery. In January 2002, refinery capacity was estimated at 248,900 barrels per day. Aluminum production was 500,000 tons in 1998.

20 ▪ Labor

The number of people in the labor force in 1998 was 295,000, of whom some 44% were non-Bahrainis. The majority of workers were employed in community, social, and personal services. Although the constitution permits workers to organize, the government bans trade unions.

The minimum age for employment is fourteen. Young people between the ages of fourteen and sixteen may not be employed in hazardous conditions. Child labor in the industrial sector is well monitored. Some young people work in family-owned businesses.

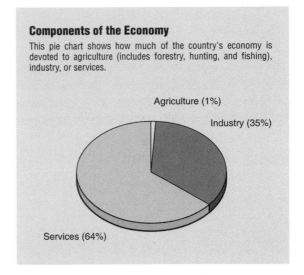

Components of the Economy

This pie chart shows how much of the country's economy is devoted to agriculture (includes forestry, hunting, and fishing), industry, or services.

Agriculture (1%)

Industry (35%)

Services (64%)

21 ▪ Agriculture

Only 2.9% of the land is arable (suitable for farming) and agriculture accounts for only about 1% of the gross domestic product (GDP). Ninety farms and small holdings produce fruit and vegetables, as well as alfalfa for fodder. Annual crop production includes 12,000 tons of vegetables and 22,000 tons of fruit. The government's goal is for output to meet 16% of demand.

22 ▪ Domesticated Animals

Most domestic meat consumption is supplied through imports of live cattle, goats, and sheep. About 13,000 head of cattle, 17,000 sheep, and 16,000 goats are kept for milk and meat production. A thriving poultry industry provides 5,000 tons of meat and 3,000 tons of eggs per year. Dairy farming has recently been expanded. Also, a national dairy pasteurization plant has been established in order to centralize all milk processing and distribution. Milk production from some 7,000 cows totals around 14,000 tons per year.

23 ▪ Fishing

The more than three hundred species of fish found in Bahraini waters are an important food source for much of the population. However, local fishing has declined because of industrial pollution. The catch totaled 11,718 tons in 2000. The government operates a fleet of seven trawlers. By encouraging traditional fishing methods, giving incentives to fishermen, improving fishing and freezing equipment, and establishing cooperatives, the government is attempting to increase the annual catch. There is a modern fishing harbor at Al-Muharraq.

24 ▪ Forestry

There are no major forested areas in Bahrain. In 2000, roundwood imports amounted to 32,000 cubic meters (1.1 million cubic feet) and imports of wood-based panels totaled 20,000 cubic meters (700,000 cubic feet). Bahrain's imports of forest products amounted to $25.8 million that year.

Yearly Balance of Trade

The balance of trade is the difference between what a country sells to other countries (its exports) and what it buys (its imports). If a country imports more than it exports, it has a negative balance of trade (a trade deficit). If exports exceed imports there is a positive balance of trade (a trade surplus).

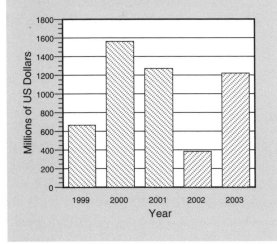

25 ■ Mining

Bahrain's oil-based economy produced few minerals other than crude oil and natural gas. Other minerals in 2000 accounted for $211 million of export earnings. Cement production was reported at 88,806 tons in 2000. Sulfur production was estimated at 66,400 tons.

26 ■ Foreign Trade

Refined oil products account for more than 70% of the island's exports. Refined aluminum, apparel, iron, and chemicals are other export earners. Imports in 2000 were crude oil, followed by industrial supplies, machinery, transportation equipment, food, and consumer goods. The principal markets for Bahrain's exports in 2000 were the United States, Saudi Arabia, Japan, the United Arab Emirates, and South Korea.

The major sources of imports were Saudi Arabia, the United States, Japan, the United Arab Emirates, India, Italy, Germany, China, and the United Kingdom.

27 ■ Energy and Power

In 1995, an estimated 90% of export revenues came from petroleum exports. Total crude petroleum production in 2001 was 35,000 barrels per day. Proven oil reserves in Bahrain were estimated by the government at 125 million barrels in 2002. Production of natural gas totaled 8.5 billion cubic meters (300 billion cubic feet) in 2000. That year, Bahrain had a total electrical power output of 5.9 billion kilowatt hours.

28 ■ Social Development

Impoverished families receive survival allowances from the government. A social security fund provides old age, disability, survivor, and accident insurance.

Islamic law, either Shi'a or Sunni, dictates the legal rights of Bahraini women. Women may initiate divorce proceedings, own and inherit property, and represent themselves in legal matters. However, men retain legal rights over children, even in case of divorce. Women are permitted to work, drive cars, and wear Western-style clothing. Women make up over 20% of the labor force, and their employment is encouraged by the government.

29 ■ Health

Bahrain sponsors a free national health service, available to both foreign and native members of the population. Bahraini patients who require sophisticated surgery or treatment are sent abroad at government expense. Health care centers are accessible to the population free of charge. In 1990, there were four government-operated hospitals (including a psychiatric hospital and a geriatric hospital), five maternity hospitals, nineteen health centers, six environment health centers, and sixteen maternity and child welfare centers. In 1991, Bahrain had 668 physicians, 123 pharmacists, and 66 dentists.

The effects of the 1991 Gulf War have endangered the health of many of Bahrain's people. Acute asthmatic attacks increased during the years after the war.

In 1999, infant mortality was 14.8 per 1,000 live births. Life expectancy in 1994 was seventy-one years. There were twenty-eight new cases of acquired immunodeficiency syndrome (AIDS) in 1996. Malaria was reported in 258 people while polio, measles, and tetanus in newborns were nonexistent.

30 ▪ Housing

At the 2001 government census, there were 105,686 housing units within the country. About 18% were private villas (single-family, independent structures). About 72% of all units were connected to the public water system. About 14.8% of homes relied on bottled water.

31 ▪ Education

The official language is Arabic, but English is widely spoken.

Bahrain introduced a free public education system to the Gulf region in 1919. The government aims to provide free educational opportunities for all children. Education was only recently made compulsory. School education is in three stages: primary lasts for six years, intermediate for three

AP/Wide World Photos

A young Arab woman, wearing a black abaya and aerobic shoes, arrives at a hotel fitness club in Bahrain. Physical fitness is a sensitive subject in the Arab world, where religion and custom decree that women's bodies and faces be covered.

years, and secondary—general, industrial, or commercial—for three years. The primary and secondary course of study includes nine years of religious studies. Nearly 100% of primary-school-age children are enrolled in school, while about 85% attend secondary school.

Bahrain's principal university is the University of Bahrain. It consists of five colleges and an English language center. The Arabian Gulf University has programs in science, engineering, and medicine. It is a joint venture project among the six Gulf Cooperation Council members and Iraq. Each nation

Selected Social Indicators

The statistics below are the most recent estimates available as of 2003. For comparison purposes, data for the United States and averages for low-income countries and high-income countries are also given. About 15% of the world's 6.4 billion people live in high-income countries, while 40% live in low-income countries.

Indicator	Bahrain	Low-income countries	High-income countries	United States
Per capita gross national income (GNI)*	**$15,100**	$2,110	$28,480	$36,110
Population growth rate	**1.6%**	2.1%	0.7%	1.1%
People per square kilometer of land	**983**	77	31	31
Life expectancy in years: *male*	**71**	58	75	75
female	**76**	60	81	80
Number of physicians per 1,000 people	**n.a.**	1.0	3.0	2.8
Number of pupils per teacher (primary school)	**21**	40	17	15
Literacy rate (15 years and older)	**89.1%**	66%	>95%	97%
Television sets per 1,000 people	**433**	91	735	938
Internet users per 1,000 people	**210**	10	364	551
Energy consumed per capita (kg of oil equivalent)	**9,716**	550	5,366	7,937

* The GNI is the total of all goods and services produced by the residents of a country in a year. The per capita GNI is calculated by dividing a country's GNI by its population and adjusting for relative purchasing power.

n.a. = data not available   > = greater than   < = less than

SOURCES: International Telecommunication Union (ITU). *World Telecommunication Development Report 2003.* Geneva, Switzerland: ITU, 2003; World Bank. *World Development Indicators.* Washington, D.C.: The World Bank, 2004; Central Intelligence Agency. *The World Factbook.* Washington, D.C.: Government Printing Office, 2003.

is allocated 10% of the seats for a total of 70% of all seats. The remaining 30% are given to other countries. Also important is the Bahrain Training Institute, which has more than 50% female students.

There are also sixty-seven adult education centers in Bahrain, which have helped to reduce the illiteracy rate of the country. All institutions of higher learning enroll between 7,000 and 9,000 students.

As of 2003, the adult illiteracy rate was estimated at 11% (males, 8%; females, 15%).

32 ■ Media

In 1997, there were 152,400 mainline telephones and 58,543 cellular phones in use nationwide.

In 1998, there were two AM and three FM radio stations and four broadcast television stations. All of them were owned and operated by the government. In 1997 there were 499 radios per 1,000 population. In 2003, there were 433 television sets per 1,000 population. Internet service is provided through the national phone company, with 105,000 subscribers counted in 2001. The government restricts access to some web sites with content that is considered anti-Islamic or antigovernment.

Bahrain's first daily newspaper in Arabic, *Akhbar al-Khalij* (circulation 17,000 in 2002), began publication in 1976, and the first English daily, the *Gulf Daily News* (50,000), was established in 1991. *Al Ayam*, an Arabic daily founded in 1989, had a 2002 circulation of 37,000.

Though the Bahraini constitution has provisions for freedom of expression, the press is not allowed to criticize the ruling family or government policy.

33 ■ Tourism and Recreation

In 2000, there were 3.8 million tourist arrivals, mostly from Saudi Arabia and other Arab countries, and tourism earnings totaled $469 million. Tourist attractions include Qal-at Al-Bahrain (The Portuguese Fort), the National Museum, and the Heritage Center.

34 ■ Famous Bahrainis

Sheikh 'Isa bin Salman al-Khalifa (1933–1999) ruled his nation from independence in 1971 until his death.

35 ■ Bibliography

Cooper, Robert. *Bahrain.* New York: Marshall Cavendish, 2000.

Fakhro, Munira A. (Munira Ahmed). *Women at Work in the Gulf.* New York: Kegan Paul International, 1990.

Fox, M. *Bahrain.* Chicago, IL: Children's Press, 1992.

Gillespie, Carol Ann. *Bahrain.* Philadelphia, PA: Chelsea House, 2002.

Holes, Clive. *Dialect, Culture, and Society in Eastern Arabia.* Boston, MA: Brill, 2001.

Bangladesh

People's Republic of Bangladesh
Gana-Prajatantri Bangladesh

Capital: Dhaka (formerly Dacca).

Flag: The national flag is a red circle against a dark-green background.

Anthem: *Amar Sonar Bangla (My Golden Bengal).*

Monetary Unit: The taka (т) of 100 poisha is a paper currency set on a par with the Indian rupee. There are coins of 1, 2, 5, 10, 25, and 50 poisha, and notes of 1, 5, 10, 20, 50, and 100 taka. т1 = $0.0173 (or $1 = т58.00; as of May 2003).

Weights and Measures: Bangladesh adopted the metric system as of 1 July 1982. Customary numerical units include the lakh (equal to 100,000) and the crore (equal to 10 million).

Holidays: New Year's Day, 1 January; National Mourning Day (Shaheel Day), 21 February; Independence Day, 26 March; May Day, 1 May; Victory Day, 16 December; Christmas, 25 December; Boxing Day, 26 December. Movable religious holidays include Good Friday, Jamat Wida, Shab-i-Bharat, 'Id al-Fitr, 'Id al-'Adha', and Durga Puja.

Time: 6 PM = noon GMT.

1 ▪ Location and Size

Located in South Asia, Bangladesh, before it became an independent state, was the eastern province of Pakistan. It was known as East Bengal and, later, as East Pakistan. Bangladesh is slightly smaller than the state of Iowa, with a total area of 144,000 square kilometers (55,598 square miles). It has a total land boundary length of 4,246 kilometers (2,638 miles), sharing borders with India and Myanmar. The coastline on the Bay of Bengal is 580 kilometers (360 miles). Bangladesh's capital city, Dhaka, is located near the center of the country.

2 ▪ Topography

Bangladesh is a tropical country, situated mainly on the deltas of large rivers flowing from the Himalayas. The Brahmaputra River, known locally as the Jamuna, unites with part of the Ganges to form the Padma, which, after its juncture with a third large river, the Meghna, flows into the Bay of Bengal. The Brahmaputra (which originates in the Himalayas outside of the country) is the longest river with a total distance of 2,900 kilometers (1,700 miles). The largest lake is the Karnaphuli reservoir in the southeast portion of the country, with a total area of 655 square kilometers (253 square miles).

Geographic Profile

Geographic Features

Size ranking: 91 of 193

Highest elevation: 1,230 meters (4,034 feet) at Keokradong

Lowest elevation: Sea level at the Indian Ocean

Land Use*

Arable land: 62%

Permanent crops: 3%

Forests: 10%

Other: 25%

Weather

Average annual precipitation: 119–145 centimeters (47–57 inches). Nearly 80% of annual precipitation falls between June and October. Total winter rainfall (November to February) averages just 18 centimeters (7 inches) in the east and 8 centimeters (3 inches) in the northwest.

Average temperature in January: 7°C (45°F)

Average temperature in July: 31°C (88°F)

---

* *Arable Land: Land used for temporary crops, like meadows for mowing or pasture, gardens, and greenhouses.*

Permanent crops: Land cultivated with crops that occupy its use for long periods, such as cocoa, coffee, rubber, fruit and nut orchards, and vineyards.

Forests: Land containing stands of trees.

Other: Any land not specified, including built-on areas, roads, and barren land.

During the rainy season floodwater covers most of the land surface, damaging crops and hurting the economy. The northwestern section of the country, drained by the Tista (Teesta) River, is somewhat higher and less flat. The only really hilly regions are in the east, especially in the Chittagong Hill Tracts to the southeast and the Sylhet District to the northeast. Near the Myanmar border, in the extreme southeast, is the Keokradong, which at 1,230 meters (4,034 feet) is the highest peak in Bangladesh. The lowest point is at sea level (Indian Ocean).

3 ■ Climate

Bangladesh has a tropical monsoon climate. Annual rainfall is high, averaging from about 119 centimeters (47 inches) up to 145 centimeters (57 inches). There are three distinct seasons. The winter, which lasts from October through early March, is cool and dry, with temperature ranges from 5 to 22°C (41 to 72°F); total winter rainfall averages about 18 centimeters (7 inches) in the east and less than 8 centimeters (3 inches) in the northwest. Temperatures rise rapidly in March. During the summer season, March through May, they average about 32°C (90°F). For parts of the year, tropical cyclones, accompanied by high seas and heavy flooding, are common. Storms and floods in 1970, 1974, 1980, and 1983 devastated the country and caused many deaths. In 1993, a cyclone killed more than 131,000 people and caused $2.7 billion in damages.

4 ■ Plants and Animals

Bangladesh has the plant and animal life typical of a tropical and riverine swamp. The landscape, which for most of the year is a lush green, is dotted with palms and flowering trees. The large forest area, the Sunderbans in the southwest, is home to the endangered Bengal tiger; there are also cheetahs, leopards, crocodiles, elephants, spotted deer, monkeys, boars, bears, pheasants, and many other varieties of birds and waterfowl.

5 ■ Environment

Overpopulation has severely strained Bangladesh's limited natural resources. Bangladesh's environmental problems have been complicated by natural disasters that add to the strain on an agricultural system that supports one of the world's most populous countries. Water supply is also a major problem because of population size, lack of purification procedures, and the spread of untreated contaminants into the usable water supply by floodwaters.

Despite passage of the Wildlife Preservation Act of 1973, wildlife continues to suffer from human settlement. Only 0.7% of the country's total land area is protected. In 2001, endangered wildlife included 18 species of mammals, 30 species of birds, and 18 plant species, including the Asian elephant, pygmy hog, Sumatran rhinoceros, Bengal tiger, estuarine crocodile, gavial, and river terrapin.

6 ■ Population

Bangladesh is one of the world's most densely populated nations, and controlling population growth is a major government priority. The population in 2003 was estimated at 146.8 million. A population of 181.4 million is projected for the year 2015. The population is heavily rural, with the great majority living in more

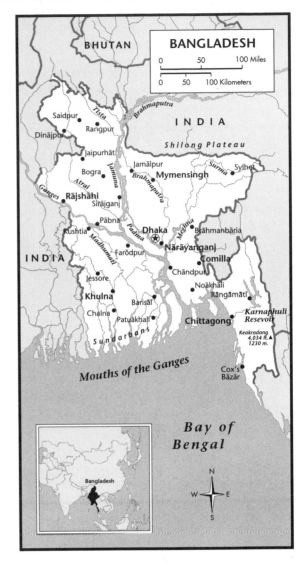

Location: 20°34' to 26°38'N; 88°1' to 92°41' E.
Boundary Lengths: India, 4,053 kilometers (2,553 miles); Myanmar, 193 kilometers (122 miles); Bay of Bengal coastline, 580 kilometers (324 miles).
Territorial Sea Limit: 12 miles.

than 85,000 villages. Dhaka, the capital, had a 2000 population of 10.9 million; Chittagong, 2.5 million; and Khulna, 1.2 million.

A Bangladeshi family, holding their livestock, leaves their flooded home for a shelter in the northeastern district of Sylhet.

7 ▧ Migration

Since 1947 there has been a regular interchange of population between India and what is now Bangladesh, with Hindus moving to India and Muslims leaving India. As of 1999, around 22,000 Myanmar refugees still resided in two camps in southern Bangladesh. The number of returns has been very limited due to procedural difficulties. As of 2000, there were approximately 988,000 migrants living in Bangladesh. The estimated net migration rate in 2003 was -0.72 per 1,000 population.

8 ▧ Ethnic Groups

About 98% of the people are Bengalis (or Banglas). There are about 12 tribes inhabiting the Chittagong Hill Tracts, collectively totaling less than 1 million people, who are ethnically distinct from the Bengalis. Their facial features and language are closer to the Burmese. About 250,000 inhabitants of Bangladesh are Biharis, non-Bengali Muslims who migrated from India to what was then East Pakistan. In the coastal areas of Bangladesh, Arab, Portuguese, and Dutch settlers have gradually come to adopt the Bengali lifestyle.

9 ▧ Languages

Bengali (Bangla), part of the Indo-European language family, is the official language of Bangladesh and is spoken by about 98% of the population. Non-Bengali migrants from India still speak Urdu (and Hindi) today, and this language is widely understood in urban areas. A few tribal groups, notably the tribal peoples of the Chittagong Hill Tracts, also speak distinct Tibeto-Burmese languages, akin to Burmese and Assamese. Among those speaking Bangla there are differences of dialect according to region. The people of Chittagong, Noakhali, and Sylhet are known for their distinctive dialects. Although today Bangla is the official language, English is also used for official and legal purposes and widely used in business.

10 ▧ Religions

Nearly 88% of the population are believers in Islam (mostly Sunni), making Bangladesh one of the world's largest Muslim countries. Most of the remaining population, about 10%, are Hindu. The remaining 2% are mainly Buddhist or Christian. There are small numbers of Shi'a Muslims, Sikhs, Baha'is, Ahmadis, and animists. Although Islam was established as the state religion in 1988, freedom of worship continues to be guaranteed under the constitution.

11 ▪ Transportation

The large number of rivers and the annual flooding hazard make it difficult to build and maintain adequate transportation facilities in Bangladesh. Railways and waterways are the chief means of transportation. The Bangladesh Railway operates 2,745 kilometers (1,706 miles) of track.

The country has two deepwater ports: Chittagong and Chalna. There are five main river ports—Dhaka, Narayanganj, Chandpur, Barisal, and Khulna—and more than 1,500 smaller ports.

There are 25,095 kilometers (15,594 miles) of paved roads. Because of the difficulties of land travel, the number of motor vehicles remains comparatively small. Bangladesh had eighteen airports in 2001, fifteen with paved runways. Bangladesh Biman, the national airline, operates international flights from Dhaka airport. In 2001, airlines carried 1,450,000 domestic and international passengers.

12 ▪ History

The area now known as Bangladesh was home to a flourishing civilization in the fourth century B.C. The region, then called Bengal, was eventually conquered by the Hindu Maurya empire that reached its height under Emperor Asoka around 207 B.C. From this time onward, the history of Bengal was part of the wider history of the Indian subcontinent.

Islam came to South Asia in the years following A.D. 800 but did not reach Bengal until Muslim invaders from the west secured a foothold there around A.D. 1200. In the thirteenth and fourteenth centuries, after waves of Turkish, Persian, and Afghan invaders, the religion began to take a firm hold in the area, which became known for its industries based on the weaving of silk and cotton cloth.

By the middle of the eighteenth century, the British established themselves in Calcutta and expanded quickly into all of what is now Bangladesh. British traders and officials gained control of most of the Indian subcontinent by 1859. In general, Hindus in Bengal prospered under the British. The Muslim aristocracy of eastern Bengal, on the other hand, resisted British rule. However, by the turn of the twentieth century, both communities united in anti-British feeling.

The subcontinent's demand for independence from Britain grew under the leadership of Mahatma Gandhi in the early 1930s. Finally, in 1947, Britain granted independence to the Indian subcontinent. British India was partitioned into a predominantly Hindu India and a predominantly Muslim Pakistan.

However, the new state of Pakistan was made up of Muslim-majority districts at both the eastern and western ends of formerly British India. These two distinct territories were separated by 1,600 kilometers (1,000 miles) of predominantly Hindu India. The division cut across long-established lines of trade and communication, divided families, and started a mass move-

AP/Wide World Photos

A woman examines the produce in a bustling market in the hill tracts that border India.

ment of millions of refugees caught on the "wrong" side of the partition markers.

In language, culture, and ethnic background, East and West Pakistan were totally different, the main bonds being Islam and a fear of potential Indian (Hindu) expansion. Pakistan's early years as a nation were dominated by unsuccessful attempts to create a nation that would somehow bridge these differences. The differences persisted, and demands for a separate state in the east began to mount.

Bangladesh Is Established: After continued refusal by West Pakistan to grant East Pakistan's requests for independence, civil war broke out in 1971. Swamped with a

million refugees from the fighting, India intervened militarily on behalf of those seeking a separate state. India's intervention helped create the independent nation of Bangladesh in 1972. Sheikh Mujibur (Mujib) Rahman, a leader of the fight for autonomy, was released from prison in West Pakistan and became prime minister of the new nation.

The civil war was a disaster for Bangladesh, undoing much of the limited progress East Pakistan had made in recovering from the social disruption of the 1947 partition. The nation's new leader faced a task for which his administrative and political experience was not enough. He fought and won a massive victory in the 1973 election, but two years later, he suspended the political process and took power into his own hands.

With this move, public opinion turned against Mujib. On 15 August 1975, a group of young military officers seized power. They killed Mujib and many of his family members and imposed martial law. A succession of military takeovers and new governments followed until General Hussain Mohammad Ershad seized power in 1981. Ershad gained support by cracking down on corruption and opening up the economy to foreign trade.

In 1982, Ershad declared Bangladesh an Islamic republic. This move angered the Hindu minority. Ershad remained in power until the end of 1990, when he was forced to resign the presidency.

In the February 1991 elections (described as the fairest ever held in the country), the Bangladesh National Party (BNP) won control of the government. The main opposition groups boycotted the February 1996 elections and the BNP won the majority. After charges of vote-rigging, Prime

Minister Khaleda Zia resigned and the BNP dissolved the parliament. New elections were held in June 1996, and the Awami League gained control of the parliament.

In August 1998, Bangladesh saw some of the worst flooding in its history. More than 1,000 people died, and floodwaters covered some 60% of the country. Total damage was estimated at more than $2 billion. In March 2000, Bill Clinton became the first U.S. president to visit Bangladesh.

A series of bombings beset Bangladesh in April, June, and September of 2001. In total, 155 people were killed and more than 2,500 were injured in violence leading up to the October 2001 parliamentary elections. Former Prime Minister Khaleda Zia won a landslide victory on 1 October 2001. The Awami League boycotted Parliament, protesting alleged rigging of elections and the persecution of religious minorities.

In June 2002, the Awami League ended its boycott of Parliament. Also in June 2002, President Badruddoza Chowdhury resigned, after being criticized for not visiting the grave of the BNP's founder, Zia-ur Rahman.

Bangladesh's history of political violence continued in 2002, when bomb explosions in four movie theaters killed seventeen people and injured three hundred among families celebrating the end of Ramadan. The government arrested thirty-nine members of the Awami League in connection with the explosions.

13 ▪ Government

The constitution of December 1972 (amended in 1991) established a democratic republic, with an indirectly elected president as official head of state and a prime minister as head of government and chief executive. The prime minister and the administration are responsible to a single-chamber legislature, the National Assembly, composed of three hundred members.

Bangladesh is divided into twenty-one regions, also referred to as districts. Regions are grouped into six divisions. In 1997, Bangladesh reorganized its local government structure in rural areas. There is now a four-tier local government system: gram (village), union (collection of villages), upazila (subdistrict), and zila (district) councils. The purpose of this reorganization was to make government at the local levels more democratic by increasing popular participation.

14 ▪ Political Parties

The June 1996 elections brought Sheikh Hasina Wajid and the Awami League (AL) to a majority role in the parliament, with 140 of 330 seats. The Jatiya Party (JP) withdrew from the governing coalition in March 1997. Following the October 2001 elections, the Bangladesh National Party (BNP), led by Khaleda Zia, came to power, ousting the Awami League of Hasina Wajid. Concern was raised over the political stance of one of Zia's coalition partners, the Jamaat-e-Islami Party, which voiced support for Osama bin Laden, the leader of the al-Qaeda terrorist network. The BNP's coalition partners—Jamaat-e-Islami, Islami Oikya Jote, and the Naziur faction of the Jatiya Party—were all Islamic parties advocating a return to Islamic law, or Shari'ah. Sheikh Hasina's Awami League supports secularism.

Biographical Profile

Name: Begum Khaleda Zia-ur Rahman
Position: Prime Minister of a republic
Took Office: 10 October 2001
Birthdate: 15 August 1945
Religion: Muslim
Spouse: Zia-ur Rahman, former president of Bangladesh
Children: Two sons
Of interest: Zia entered political life after the assassination of her husband in 1981

Begum Khaleda Zia-ur Rahman

15 ■ Judicial System

The judicial system consists of a Low Court and a Supreme Court, both of which hear civil and criminal cases. The Low Court consists of administrative courts (magistrate courts) and session judges. The Supreme Court also has two divisions, a high court that hears original cases and reviews decisions of the low court, and an appellate court that hears appeals from the high court.

In 2001, the World Bank announced $30.6 million in credit would be granted to Bangladesh to help it make its judicial system more efficient and accountable. A Law Commission reforms and updates existing laws.

16 ■ Armed Forces

In 2002, Bangladesh had an army of 120,000 men, a navy of 10,500, and an air force of 6,500. Paramilitary forces of border guards, armed police, and security guards totaled 63,200. The military budget accounts for about 2% of the gross domestic product (GDP).

17 ■ Economy

Bangladesh is a poor country with few natural resources and an economy dominated by agriculture. Bangladesh has suffered from the 1971 war with Pakistan, a severe famine in 1971, and a series of weather-related disasters, including a devastating cyclone in April 1991. However, measures taken by the government in 1991 allowed

Bangladesh to weather the combined effects of the 1991 Gulf War, domestic political disturbances, and the 1991 cyclone, and to bring inflation to a record low of 1.4% in 1993. Political instability and a lack of economic reforms pushed inflation to 5.2% in 1995, but as stability returned the gross domestic product (GDP) grew by 4.7% in 1996. The economy grew strongly during 1998 thanks to foreign aid in the wake of recent flooding.

Severe flooding also occurred in 1999, and growth slowed 3.4% in 2000. The following year economic growth was hurt by the global economic slowdown, continuing internal political turmoil, and the aftereffects of the 11 September 2001 terrorist attacks on the United States, including the war on terrorism. Growth was expected to revive in 2004, however, to approximately 5%.

18 ▪ Income
In 2001, Bangladesh's gross domestic product (GDP) was $230 billion, or $1,750 per person. The annual growth rate of the GDP was estimated at 5.6%. The average inflation rate in 2000 was 5.8%.

19 ▪ Industry
Major industries include the manufacture of jute, textiles, garments, cotton yarn, cotton cloth, and fertilizer. Paper, newsprint, tea, and sugar also are manufactured. The industrial growth rate was a high 8.1% in 1998. Currently, 40% of industry is government owned.

The garment industry, which employs 1.5 million workers, about 80% of whom are women, has been hurt since 2000 by United States grants of quotas and duty-free access to Sub-Saharan African countries.

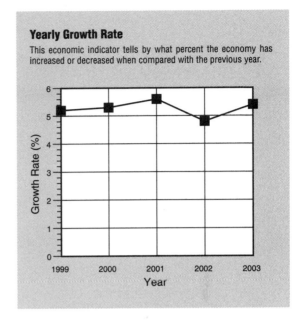

Yearly Growth Rate

This economic indicator tells by what percent the economy has increased or decreased when compared with the previous year.

The leading manufactured exports in 2000 and 2001 were ready-made garments, knitwear, frozen food, leather products, and jute products. Raw jute exports brought in $66 million, and tea exports earned $24 million in 2000 and 2001.

Recent discoveries of large natural gas reserves and plans for new power plants throughout the country were set to spur economic growth in the early twenty-first century. However, as of late 2002, plans for the development of natural gas resources continued to be delayed by political infighting over the participation of foreign companies.

20 ▪ Labor
The civilian labor force in 1998 was estimated at approximately 64 million. In 1996 approximately 11% of the civilian labor force was employed by industry. The unemployment rate in 2001 was estimated at 35%. In 2002, 6.6 million children between the ages of 5 and 14 were said to

Components of the Economy

This pie chart shows how much of the country's economy is devoted to agriculture (includes forestry, hunting, and fishing), industry, or services.

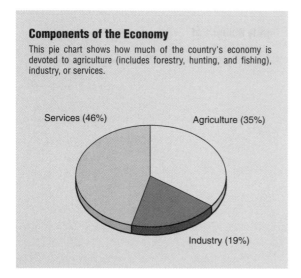

Services (46%) Agriculture (35%)

Industry (19%)

be working in all types of employment activities, many that were harmful to their well-being.

21 ▪ Agriculture

Agriculture accounts for 35% of the gross domestic product (GDP) and employs 63% of all workers. Most of the farmers own only a few acres of land. Rice is the dominant crop, accounting for about 60% of all farmland in Bangladesh. Aman rice is the main variety. Aus and Boro rice are also grown. To meet the challenge of the food shortages, the government of Bangladesh and international aid programs introduced a high-yielding variety of rice called IRRI with considerable success. Total rice production is 29.85 million tons per year.

Jute is the main cash crop of Bangladesh, which produces about one-quarter of the total jute supply of the world. Grown in most parts of the country, jute is harvested from July to September. Its strong fibers are used to produce carpets, burlap bags, mats,

upholstery, and other products. Jute is also used to manufacture textiles for clothes. Annual jute production is approximately 813,000 tons (25% of world production).

Although tea is the second most important agricultural export, it accounts for only 1% of export earnings. Most tea plantations are in the Sylhet Region and the Chittagong Hill Tracts. Much of the tea is consumed domestically. Total annual production is around 51,000 tons.

Agricultural exports accounted for 1.1% of total exports in 2001. Annual crop output includes about 6.95 million tons of sugarcane, 1.9 million tons of wheat, 1.7 million tons of potatoes, 398,000 tons of sweet potatoes, 37,000 tons of tobacco, 6,000 tons of barley, and 668,000 tons of pulses. Fruit production includes approximately 625,000 tons of bananas, 187,000 tons of mangoes, 149,000 tons of pineapples, and 89,000 tons of coconuts.

22 ▪ Domesticated Animals

Livestock provide most of Bangladesh's rural transportation, manure, and fuel, in addition to meat, milk, eggs, hides, and skins. Buffalo milk is an important item for consumption, especially in the form of clarified butterfat. Small dairy farms (with 5–20 crossbred cows) have been growing fast in recent years. Total milk production in 1999 was 2.1 million tons. That year, there were about 23.4 million head of cattle, 820,000 buffalo, 33.5 million goats, 1.1 million sheep, and 138 million chickens.

Much of the cattle stock is smuggled from India because of the reduced local availability of cows and bulls, especially during the midyear Muslim holiday of Eid Ul Azha, when cattle are sacrificed throughout the country. The cattle brought in from India may account for up to 30% of beef production.

23 ■ Fishing

Fish is a staple food of Bangladesh and the main source of protein in the Bangladeshi diet. There are hundreds of varieties, including carp, salmon, pomfret, shrimp, catfish, and many local varieties. Dried fish is considered a delicacy in many parts of the country. About 1,004,164 tons of fish were produced in 2000. While much of the fish is consumed domestically, Bangladesh exports a sizable quantity of freshwater fish to India and other neighboring countries. Freshwater shrimp and lobster are exported to a number of countries. Exports of fish products in 2000 amounted to $371.5 million. Bangladesh is also a major source of frogs' legs, which are "farmed" commercially.

24 ■ Forestry

Bangladesh has about 1 million hectares (2.4 million acres) of forest, covering about 7.8% of the land area. The main forest zone is the Sunderbans area in the southwest, consisting mostly of mangrove forests. Two principal species dominate the Sunderban forests: sundari trees, which are of tough timber, and gewa trees, a softer wood used for making newsprint. Teak and bamboo are grown in the central forests. Roundwood production in 2000 came to 28.5 million cubic meters (1 billion cubic feet). Over 98% of the timber cut is used for firewood.

25 ■ Mining

Aside from its large natural gas reserves, Bangladesh has few mineral resources.

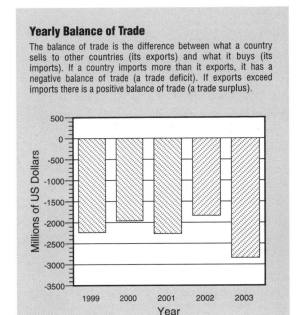

Yearly Balance of Trade

The balance of trade is the difference between what a country sells to other countries (its exports) and what it buys (its imports). If a country imports more than it exports, it has a negative balance of trade (a trade deficit). If exports exceed imports there is a positive balance of trade (a trade surplus).

Bangladesh had reserves of high-quality coal in the northern districts, but extraction has been difficult since many deposits are located at a depth of more than 900 meters (2,952 feet). Production estimates for mineral commodities in Bangladesh in 2000 included hydraulic cement (980,000 tons), marine salt (350,000 tons), and limestone (28,000 tons).

26 ■ Foreign Trade

Exports of ready-made garments are Bangladesh's leading earner of money from abroad. Leather goods and frozen seafood have also become important exports. Major imports are industrial supplies, machinery, food, and petroleum. In 1998, Bangladesh's main export purchasers were the United States, Germany, the United Kingdom, France, Italy, and the Nether-

Selected Social Indicators

The statistics below are the most recent estimates available as of 2003. For comparison purposes, data for the United States and averages for low-income countries and high-income countries are also given. About 15% of the world's 6.4 billion people live in high-income countries, while 40% live in low-income countries.

Indicator	Bangladesh	Low-income countries	High-income countries	United States
Per capita gross national income (GNI)*	$1,770	$2,110	$28,480	$36,110
Population growth rate	2.1%	2.1%	0.7%	1.1%
People per square kilometer of land	1042	77	31	31
Life expectancy in years: *male*	62	58	75	75
female	63	60	81	80
Number of physicians per 1,000 people	0.2	1.0	3.0	2.8
Number of pupils per teacher (primary school)	55	40	17	15
Literacy rate (15 years and older)	43.1%	66%	>95%	97%
Television sets per 1,000 people	59	91	735	938
Internet users per 1,000 people	2	10	364	551
Energy consumed per capita (kg of oil equivalent)	159	550	5,366	7,937

* The GNI is the total of all goods and services produced by the residents of a country in a year. The per capita GNI is calculated by dividing a country's GNI by its population and adjusting for relative purchasing power.

n.a. = data not available   > = greater than   < = less than

SOURCES: International Telecommunication Union (ITU). *World Telecommunication Development Report 2003*. Geneva, Switzerland: ITU, 2003; World Bank. *World Development Indicators*. Washington, D.C.: The World Bank, 2004; Central Intelligence Agency. *The World Factbook*. Washington, D.C.: Government Printing Office, 2003.

lands. Imports came mainly from India, China, Japan, and the United Kingdom.

27 ■ Energy and Power

A substantial portion of Bangladesh's electrical supply is met by the country's only hydroelectric plant, at Kaptai, which has a capacity of 230 megawatts. The rest of the country's power is produced by burning coal, gas, and oil. Total power production was 15 billion kilowatt hours in 2000, of which 7.5% was hydroelectric. In 2002, there were an estimated 0.4 to 1.4 trillion cubic meters (14 to 49 trillion cubic feet) of reserves of natural gas in twenty fields. Production was estimated at 9 million cubic meters (319 million cubic feet) in 1999.

28 ■ Social Development

While women have and exercise full voting rights, they receive unequal treatment in many areas, including education, employment, and family matters such as divorce and inheritance.

There is evidence that children are sold for their labor to the Middle East, India, Pakistan, and Southeast Asia. The use of child labor within Bangladesh is the result of widespread poverty and economic deprivation; there may be as many as 10 million child laborers. Discrimination against Hindus has led to violence and conflict.

29 ■ Health

Malaria, tuberculosis, and other serious diseases remain widespread, and public health problems are aggravated by wide-

AP/Wide World Photos

Bangladesh is a tropical country, situated mainly on river deltas flowing from the Himalayas.

spread malnutrition and periodic natural disasters.

In 1990, there were 8,566 doctors, 2,630 pharmacists, 523 dentists, and 5,074 nurses. In 2003, there were 0.2 physicians per 1,000 people.

In 2000, average life expectancy at birth was sixty-one years. The government pays the majority of vaccination costs, which has helped increase participation. The infant mortality rate was 60 per 1,000 live births in 2000.

As of 1999 an estimated 13,000 people were living with human immunodeficiency virus/acquired immunodeficiency syndrome (HIV/AIDS).

30 ▪ Housing

The government maintains an urban housing program but does not have any housing development program for villages. Housing units are made of straw, bamboo, mud, unburnt brick, and cement or wood roofed with iron sheets. The government operates programs focusing on poverty and homelessness.

31 ▪ Education

Primary education, extending over five years, is free and compulsory, although rural girls are exempted from this law. Secondary education covers six grades, divided into three two-year cycles. Most educational institutions are supported by the government either fully or partially. As of 2000, an estimated 70% of primary-school-age children were enrolled in school, while only 18% of those eligible were enrolled in secondary school. The language of instruction is Bangla.

There are seven universities, ten medical colleges, and ten teacher-training colleges. Research institutions include the Bangla Academy (which sponsors translations of scientific and literary works into Bangla), the Asiatic Society, and the National Institute of Public Administration's Institute of Law and International Affairs. There are between 400,000 and 600,000 students at all higher-level institutions. For the year 2003, the adult illiteracy rate was estimated at 57% (males, 46%; females, 68%).

32 ▪ Media

There were 500,000 mainline telephones in use in 2000, with an additional 283,000 cellular phones in use throughout the country. In 1999, Bangladesh had twelve AM and twelve FM radio broadcasting stations and fifteen television stations, which were accessible to about 90% of the population. Color television was introduced in 1980. In 2003, there were 59 television sets for every 1,000 people. In 2000, there were 49 radios for every 1,000 people. The same year, there were 10 Internet service providers serving about 30,000 subscribers.

The major Bengali daily newspapers (with 2002 circulations), all in Dhaka, are *Ittefaq* (200,000), *Dainik Inqilab* (180,000), *Sangbad* (71,050), *Dainik Bangla* (65,000), and *Dainik Sangram* (45,000). The largest English dailies, also in Dhaka, are the *Bangladesh Observer* (43,000), *Bangladesh Times* (35,000), and *Daily Star* (30,000).

The government generally respects the freedom of speech and press. On occasion, however, the government has censored stories that are critical of Islam.

33 ▪ Tourism and Recreation

In 2000, Bangladesh had 199,211 foreign visitors, nearly half from South Asia. There were 4,550 hotel rooms with a 49% occupancy rate. Tourism revenues totaled $50 million. The main tourist attractions include the old Mughal capital at Dhaka, nearby Sonargaon with its ancient architecture, the Buddhist cultural center of Mainamati, and the beach resort of Cox's Bazar.

34 ▪ Famous Bangladeshis

H. S. Suhrawardy (1895–1964), another former premier of Bengal, served for a time as premier of Pakistan and was a mentor to the next generation of Bengali leaders. Sheikh Mujibur Rahman (1920–1975) led the successful fight for the independence of East Pakistan and was the first premier of Bangladesh (1972–75).

35 ▪ Bibliography

Barter, James. *The Ganges*. San Diego, CA: Lucent Books, 2003.

Baxter, Craig. *Historical Dictionary of Bangladesh*. Lanham, MD: Scarecrow Press, 1996.

Cumming, David. *The Ganges*. Milwaukee, WI: World Almanac Library, 2003.

Lauré Jason. *Bangladesh*. Chicago, IL: Children's Press, 1992.

Nuget, Nicholas. *Pakistan and Bangladesh*. Austin, TX: Raintree/Steck-Vaughn, 1992.

Shrestha, Nanda R. *Nepal and Bangladesh: A Global Studies Handbook*. Santa Barbara, CA: ABC-Clio, 2002.

Whyte, Mariam. *Bangladesh*. New York: Marshall Cavendish, 1999.

Barbados

Capital: Bridgetown.

Flag: The national flag has three equal vertical bands of ultramarine blue, gold, and ultramarine blue and displays a broken trident in black on the center stripe.

Anthem: *National Anthem of Barbados,* beginning "In plenty and in time of need, when this fair land was young. . . ."

Monetary Unit: Officially introduced on 3 December 1973, the Barbados dollar (BDS$) of 100 cents is a paper currency officially pegged to the US dollar. There are coins of 1, 5, 10, and 25 cents and 1 dollar, and notes of 1, 2, 5, 10, 20, 50, and 100 dollars. BDS$1 = US$0.50 (or US$1 = BDS$2.0; as of January 2003).

Weights and Measures: The metric system is used.

Holidays: New Year's Day, 1 January; Errol Barrow Day, 23 January; May Day, 1 May; Kadooment Day, first Monday in August; CARICOM Day, 1 August; UN Day, first Monday in October; Independence Day, 30 November; Christmas Day, 25 December; Boxing Day, 26 December. Movable religious holidays are Good Friday, Easter Monday, and Whitmonday.

Time: 8 AM = noon GMT.

1 ■ Location and Size

Barbados is the most easterly of the Caribbean islands. Barbados has an area of 430 square kilometers (166 square miles), slightly less than 2.5 times the area of Washington, D.C., and a total coastline of 97 kilometers (60 miles). The capital city of Barbados, Bridgetown, is located on the country's southwestern coast.

2 ■ Topography

The coast is almost entirely encircled by coral reefs. The only natural harbor is Carlisle Bay on the southwest coast. The land rises to 340 meters (1,115 feet) at Mount Hillaby in the parish of Saint Andrew. In most other areas, the land falls in a series of terraces to a coastal strip or wide flat area. The lowest point is at sea level (Atlantic Ocean).

3 ■ Climate

The tropical climate is tempered by an almost constant sea breeze. Temperatures range from 21 to 30°C (70 to 86°F). Annual rainfall ranges from about 100 centimeters (40 inches) to 230 centimeters (90 inches).

Geographic Profile

Geographic Features

Size ranking: 181 of 193
Highest elevation: 340 meters (1,115 feet) at Mount Hillaby
Lowest elevation: Sea level at the Atlantic Ocean

Land Use*

Arable land: 37%
Permanent crops: 0%
Forests: 12%
Other: 51%

Weather**

Average annual precipitation: 127.3 centimeters (50.1 inches)
Average temperature in January: 25.2°c (77.4°F)
Average temperature in July: 26.8°c (80.2°F)

---

* Arable Land: Land used for temporary crops, like meadows for mowing or pasture, gardens, and greenhouses.

  Permanent crops: Land cultivated with crops that occupy its use for long periods, such as cocoa, coffee, rubber, fruit and nut orchards, and vineyards.

  Forests: Land containing stands of trees.

  Other: Any land not specified, including built-on areas, roads, and barren land.

** The measurements for precipitation and average temperatures were taken at weather stations closest to the country's largest city.

  Precipitation and average temperature can vary significantly within a country, due to factors such as latitude, altitude, coastal proximity, and wind patterns.

4 ▪ Plants and Animals

Palms, casuarina, mahogany, and almond trees are found on the island, but no large forest areas exist, most of the level ground having been turned over to sugarcane. The wide variety of flowers and shrubs includes wild roses, carnations, lilies, and several cacti. Natural wildlife is restricted to a few mammals and birds; finches, blackbirds, and moustache birds are common.

5 ▪ Environment

Soil erosion and coastal pollution from oil slicks are among the most significant environmental problems. The government of Barbados created a marine reserve to protect its coastline in 1980. As of 2000, the most pressing environmental problems resulted from the uncontrolled handling of solid wastes, which contaminate the water supply. Barbados is also affected by air and water pollution from other countries in the area. Despite its pollution problems, 100% of Barbados's urban and rural populations have safe water.

The Barbados yellow warbler, Eskimo curlew, tundra peregrine falcon, and Orinoco crocodile are endangered species. In addition, one plant species is considered endangered. The Barbados raccoon has become extinct.

6 ▪ Population

The population in 2003 was estimated at 270,000. The projected population for the year 2005 is 261,000. The population density was 626 persons per square kilometer (1,620 persons per square mile). Barbados is one of the most densely populated countries in the Western hemisphere. Bridgetown, the capital, and its suburbs had a population of about 133,000 in 2001.

7 ■ Migration

To meet the problem of overpopulation, the government encourages emigration. Most emigrants now resettle in the Caribbean region or along the eastern U.S. coast. As of 1999, Barbados did not host any refugees. The estimated net migration rate for Barbados in 2003 was -0.31 migrants per 1,000 population.

8 ■ Ethnic Groups

About 90% of all Barbadians (also called Bajans) are the descendants of former African slaves. Some 4% are Europeans and 6% are Asian and/or mixed.

9 ■ Languages

English, the official language, is spoken universally, with local pronunciations.

10 ■ Religions

Christianity is the dominant religion. About 67% of the total population is Protestant, with about 40% Anglican, 8% Pentecostal, 7% Methodist, and 12% of various other denominations including Moravian, Seventh-day Adventist, Jehovah's Witnesses, Baptist, and the Church of Jesus Christ of Latter-day Saints. Roman Catholics make up approximately 4% of the population, 17% claim no religious affiliation, and about 12% profess other faiths, including Islam, Baha'i, Judaism, Hinduism, and Rastafarianism.

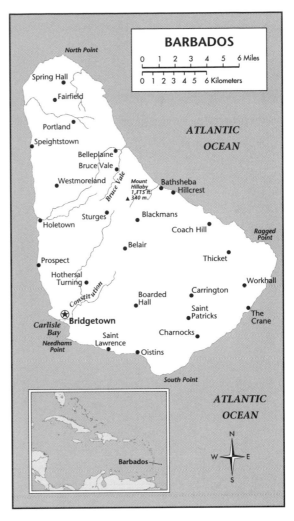

Location: 13°2′ to 13°20′N; 59°25′ to 59°39′W. **Total Coastline:** 101 kilometers (63 miles). **Territorial Sea Limit:** 12 miles.

11 ■ Transportation

The highway system had a total length of 1,650 kilometers (1,205 miles) in 2002. There were 44,300 passenger cars and 15,600 commercial vehicles registered in 2000. Barbados is served through Grantley Adams International Airport by 14

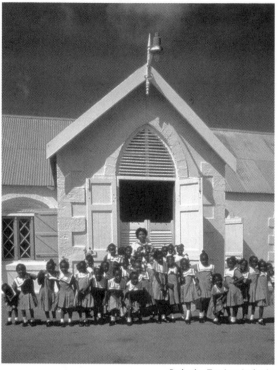

Children gather in front of their school

During the following one hundred years, the economic fortunes of Barbados rose and fell with alternating booms and slumps in the sugar trade. In the 1930s, the dominance of plantation owners and merchants was challenged by a labor movement. The gradual introduction of social and political reforms led to the granting of universal adult suffrage in 1950.

The island was proclaimed an independent republic on 30 November 1966. Political stability has been maintained since that time. In 1973, the nation began issuing its own currency. The country was a staging area in October 1983 for the U.S.-led invasion of Grenada, in which Barbadian troops took part.

Laws enacted in the early 1980s led to the development of Barbados as an offshore business center. The international recession of the early 1990s negatively affected the economy, which led to a lack of support for the government. In June 1994, Prime Minister Erskine Sandiford dissolved the House of Assembly, the first time since independence that such an action had been taken.

Economic recovery in the mid-to-late 1990s helped Prime Minister Owen S. Arthur lead the Barbados Labor Party (BLP) to a landslide victory in the 1999 elections, as the country prepared for the launch of a single CARICOM economic market in the Caribbean in 2005.

international airlines and one local airline. There is a deepwater harbor at Bridgetown, with docking facilities for cruise ships and freighters. In 2002, Barbados had a merchant fleet of 41 ships of 1,000 GRT or over, totaling 629,987 GRT.

12 ■ History

When the British landed on Barbados in 1625, the island was uninhabited. Almost 2,000 English settlers landed in 1627 and 1628. Soon afterward, the island developed a sugar-based economy, supported by a slave population. Slavery was abolished in 1834, and the last slaves were freed in 1838.

13 ■ Government

Barbados has a crown-appointed governor-general (who in turn appoints an advisory Privy Council) and independent executive, legislative, and judicial bodies. The two-chamber legislature consists of a twenty-one-member appointed Senate and a twenty-eight-member elected House

Biographical Profile

Name: Owen Arthur

Position: Prime Minister of a parliamentary democracy

Took Office: 6 September 1994

Birthplace: Barbados

Birthdate: 17 October 1949

Education: Harrison College; University of the West Indies (UWI), bachelors degree in economics

Of interest: He is the first and only professional economist to become prime minister in the English-speaking Caribbean

Owen Arthur

of Assembly. Voting is universal at age eighteen. The governor-general appoints as prime minister a member of the House of Assembly. The country is divided into eleven parishes and the city of Bridgetown for electoral and administrative purposes, but local governments were abolished in 1969.

14 ■ Political Parties

The leading parties are the Barbados Labor Party (BLP), the Democratic Labor Party (DLP), and the National Democratic Party (NDP). The BLP swept the May 2003 elections, winning twenty-three of the thirty House seats, while the DLP claimed only seven.

15 ■ Judicial System

The Supreme Court of Judicature sits as a high court and court of appeal. Magistrate courts have both civil and criminal jurisdiction. Final appeals are brought to the Committee of Her Majesty's Privy Council in the United Kingdom.

In 2003, Caribbean leaders met in Jamaica to establish a Caribbean Court of Justice (CCJ) to hear many of the cases formerly brought to the Privy Council in the United Kingdom. Barbados was one of the nations that approved the CCJ.

16 ■ Armed Forces

In 2000 the Barbados Defense Force included 610 active troops and 430 reserves, of which 500 were in the army and 110 in

Yearly Growth Rate

This economic indicator tells by what percent the economy has increased or decreased when compared with the previous year.

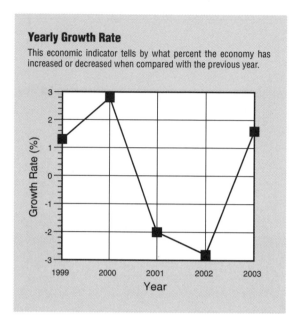

the navy. The defense budget was $11 million in 1998.

17 ■ Economy

The economy has traditionally been dependent on the production of sugar, rum, and molasses. In recent years, however, tourism and manufacturing have surpassed the sugar industry in importance.

The gross domestic product (GDP) grew by 5% in 2000, compared to an annual average of 3.4% during 1994 and 1995. Barbados was in an economic recession from 1990 to 1994.

In 2001, with the decline in tourism following the 11 September 2001 terrorist attacks on the United States and the global economic slowdown that had already taken hold, the Barbadian economy experienced its first contraction (-2.75%) after eight straight years of growth.

18 ■ Income

In 2001, Barbados's gross domestic product (GDP) was $4 billion, or $14,500 per person. The annual growth rate of the GDP was estimated at -2%. The average inflation rate in 2001 was 3.5%.

19 ■ Industry

Traditionally, sugar production and related enterprises were Barbados's primary industry, but light industry also has become more important. Items manufactured for export include soap, glycerine, pharmaceuticals, furniture, household appliances, plastic products, fabricated metal products, and cotton garments. Sugar production increased by close to 10% in 2000. Offshore banking has become increasingly popular in Barbados.

20 ■ Labor

The total labor force as of 2001 was 128,500. In 1997, services accounted for over 75% of the labor force; manufacturing, 9%; mining and construction, 8%; agriculture, 6%; and other areas for the rest. Unemployment, traditionally high, was reported at 19.7% in 1995 but fell to 10% in 2001. The legal minimum working age is 16. About 30% of the workforce was unionized in 2001.

21 ■ Agriculture

About 37.2% of the total land area is arable (suitable for farming). About 500,000 tons of sugarcane are produced per year. In 2001, sugar exports amounted to $22 million, or 8.4% of total exports. Major food crops are yams, sweet potatoes, corn, eddo, cassava, and several varieties of beans. Some cotton is also grown.

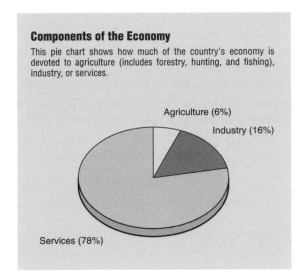

Components of the Economy

This pie chart shows how much of the country's economy is devoted to agriculture (includes forestry, hunting, and fishing), industry, or services.

Agriculture (6%)

Industry (16%)

Services (78%)

22 ▪ Domesticated Animals

The island must import large quantities of meat and dairy products. Most livestock is owned by individual households. Estimates show 23,000 head of cattle, 41,000 sheep, 33,000 hogs, 5,000 goats, and 4 million chickens. Poultry production includes approximately 9,000 tons of meat and 1,000 tons of hen eggs annually.

23 ▪ Fishing

The fishing industry employs about 2,000 persons and consists of more than 500 powered boats. The catch in 2000 was 3,100 metric tons. Flying fish, dolphinfish, tuna, turbot, kingfish, and swordfish are among the main species caught. There is a fisheries terminal complex at Oistins.

24 ▪ Forestry

There are an estimated 5,000 hectares (12,350 acres) of forested land, covering about 12% of the total land area. Roundwood production in 2000 totaled 5,000

cubic meters (176,500 cubic feet) and imports amounted to 3,000 cubic meters (106,000 cubic feet). Also in 2000, Barbados imported $35.3 million in wood and forest products.

25 ▪ Mining

Deposits of limestone and coral are quarried to meet local construction needs. Production of limestone in 2000 amounted to 1.5 million tons. Clays and shale, sand and gravel, and carbonaceous deposits provided limited yields. Hydraulic cement production totaled 267,659 tons in 2000.

26 ▪ Foreign Trade

Main exports include sugar, honey, and sugar-processing byproducts (including molasses and rum), electronic components, medications, printed matter, and pesticides and disinfectants. Barbados's main imports were foodstuffs, fuels and lubricants, consumer goods, industrial supplies, machinery, and transportation equipment. Main trade partners in 2000 were the United States, Trinidad and Tobago, the United Kingdom, Canada, and Japan.

27 ▪ Energy and Power

Electricity production in 2000 totaled 740 million kilowatt hours. Oil accounts for 95% of energy usage. Crude oil production in 2002 was about 1,200 barrels per day. Natural gas production was 28 million cubic meters (988 million cubic feet) in 1998.

28 ▪ Social Development

A national social security system provides old age and survivors' pensions, as

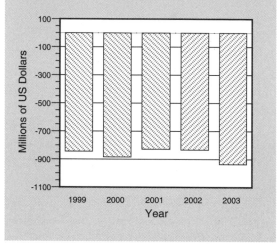

Yearly Balance of Trade

The balance of trade is the difference between what a country sells to other countries (its exports) and what it buys (its imports). If a country imports more than it exports, it has a negative balance of trade (a trade deficit). If exports exceed imports there is a positive balance of trade (a trade surplus).

30 ■ Housing

The Barbados Housing Authority constructs housing projects and redevelops overcrowded areas. At the last estimate, 90% of all housing consisted of detached homes and more than 5% of apartments.

The government has been looking at new ways to help private owners finance land and home purchases. The government also put a new building code into effect to improve existing structures, focusing particularly on renovations that could prevent destruction from hurricanes.

31 ■ Education

Primary education begins at the age of five. Secondary education begins at the age of eleven and lasts for five to six years. Education is compulsory for children between the ages of five and sixteen. The education program in Barbados is administered by the Ministry of Education and is free in all government-run schools. As of 2000, children in 93 government primary schools numbered 26,900; a small number attend private primary schools. Secondary education was provided in twenty-two government secondary schools, fifteen assisted private schools, and seven senior schools for students ages fourteen to sixteen. Scholarships are awarded for study in the United Kingdom and in Caribbean institutions.

The Barbados branch of the University of the West Indies opened at Cave Hill in 1963. It has over 250 teachers and more than 2,000 students. The government pays the fees of all Barbadian students at the Cave Hill Campus of the University of West Indies. The Barbados Community College was established in 1968.

well as sickness, disability, maternity, and employment injury benefits. A domestic violence law requires a police response to violence against women and children. The government has also formed a Child Care Board to monitor and protect the rights of children.

29 ■ Health

Barbados has a national health service. As of 1990, 100% of the population has access to health care services. As of the mid-1990s, there were 355 doctors, 48 dentists, and 898 nurses. Life expectancy as of 2003 was seventy-two years. The infant mortality rate was 17 per 1,000 live births in 1999. In the same year, the number of people living with human immunodeficiency virus/acquired immunodeficiency syndrome (HIV/AIDS) was estimated at 1,800 and deaths from AIDS were estimated at 130.

Selected Social Indicators

The statistics below are the most recent estimates available as of 2003. For comparison purposes, data for the United States and averages for low-income countries and high-income countries are also given. About 15% of the world's 6.4 billion people live in high-income countries, while 40% live in low-income countries.

Indicator	Barbados	Low-income countries	High-income countries	United States
Per capita gross national income (GNI)*	$15,000	$2,110	$28,480	$36,110
Population growth rate	0.4%	2.1%	0.7%	1.1%
People per square kilometer of land	626	77	31	31
Life expectancy in years: *male*	70	58	75	75
female	74	60	81	80
Number of physicians per 1,000 people	1	1.0	3.0	2.8
Number of pupils per teacher (primary school)	n.a.	40	17	15
Literacy rate (15 years and older)	99.7%	66%	>95%	97%
Television sets per 1,000 people	276	91	735	938
Internet users per 1,000 people	25	10	364	551
Energy consumed per capita (kg of oil equivalent)	1,007	550	5,366	7,937

* The GNI is the total of all goods and services produced by the residents of a country in a year. The per capita GNI is calculated by dividing a country's GNI by its population and adjusting for relative purchasing power.

n.a. = data not available   > = greater than   < = less than

SOURCES: International Telecommunication Union (ITU). *World Telecommunication Development Report 2003*. Geneva, Switzerland: ITU, 2003; World Bank. *World Development Indicators*. Washington, D.C.: The World Bank, 2004; Central Intelligence Agency. *The World Factbook*. Washington, D.C.: Government Printing Office, 2003.

There is also advanced education for adults at the Extramural Center of the University of West Indies, the Erdiston Teachers Training College, and the Samuel Jackman Prescod Polytechnic. There are special schools for the deaf, blind, and mentally retarded, including two residential institutions for disabled persons.

Barbados's adult illiteracy rate in 1995 (the most recent year for which statistics were available as of 2004) was estimated at 2.6% (males, 2%; females, 3%).

32 ▨ Media

There were about 108,000 mainline telephones in use as of 1997, with an additional 8,013 cellular phone subscribers.

Barbados has a government-controlled television and radio broadcasting service (the Caribbean Broadcasting System/ CBS) and a commercial service that broadcasts over a cable network. In 2001, there were six radio stations, two of which were owned by CBS. The country's only television station is also owned by CBS. In 1997, there were about 237,000 radios and 76,000 television sets in use throughout the country.

There are two major daily newspapers (both independently operated in Bridgetown), the *Advocate* (circulation 15,000 in 2002) and the *Daily Nation* (32,000), as well as some periodicals, including a monthly magazine, the *New Bajan*.

The constitution of Barbados provides for freedom of expression and the government is said to uphold freedom of speech and press. The government does, however, prohibit the production of pornographic materials.

Cory Langley

Barbados, with its fine beaches, sea bathing, and pleasant climate, has long been a popular holiday retreat.

33 ■ Tourism and Recreation

Barbados, with its fine beaches, sea bathing, and pleasant climate, has long been a popular holiday retreat. In 2000, 544,695 tourists visited Barbados, with 41% of travelers coming from the United Kingdom. Tourist spending was an estimated $711 million in 2000. There were 6,456 hotel rooms with a 57% occupancy rate. Cricket is the national sport, followed by surfing, sailing, and other water sports.

34 ■ Famous Barbadians

Grantley Adams (1898–1971) was premier of the Federation of the West Indies (1958–62). Erskine Sandiford (1938–) was prime minister from 1987 until 1994. Barbados-born Edwin Barclay (1882–1955) was president of Liberia from 1930 to 1944. George Lamming (1927–) is a well-known West Indian novelist. Sir Garfield Sobers (1936–) has gained renown as the "world's greatest cricketer."

35 ■ Bibliography

Beckles, Hilary. *A History of Barbados: From Amerindian Settlement to Nation-State.* New York: Cambridge University Press, 1990.

Broberg, Merle. *Barbados.* Philadelphia, PA: Chelsea House, 1999.

Elias, Marie Louise. *Barbados.* New York: Marshall Cavendish, 2000.

Kinas, Roxan. *Barbados.* Maspeth, NY: APA, 2002.

Orr, Tamra. *Barbados.* Philadelphia, PA: Mason Crest Publishers, 2004.

Philpott, Don. *Barbados.* Edison, NJ: Hunter Pub., 2000.

Belarus

Republic of Belarus
Respublika Belarus

Capital: Minsk.

Flag: Two horizontal bands of red (top) and green, with the red band twice as wide as the green. At the hoist is a vertical band showing a traditional Belarussian ornamental pattern.

Anthem: *Maladaya Belarus.*

Monetary Unit: The Belarus ruble (BR) circulates along with the Russian rouble (R). The government has a varying exchange rate for trade between Belarus and Russia. BR1 = $0.0004938 (or $1 = BR2025; as of May 2003).

Weights and Measures: The metric system is in force.

Holidays: New Year's Day, 1 January; Orthodox Christmas, 7 January; International Women's Day, 8 March; Labor Day, 1 May; Victory Day, 9 May; Independence Day, 27 July; Day of Commemoration, 2 November; Christmas, 25 December.

Time: 2 PM = noon GMT.

1 ◼ Location and Size

Belarus is a landlocked nation located in eastern Europe, between Poland and Russia. Comparatively, the area occupied by Belarus is slightly smaller than the state of Kansas, with a total area of 207,600 square kilometers (80,154 square miles). Belarus shares boundaries with Latvia, Russia, Ukraine, Poland, and Lithuania. The boundary length of Belarus totals 3,098 kilometers (1,925 miles).

The capital city of Belarus, Minsk, is located near the center of the country.

2 ◼ Topography

The topography of Belarus is generally flat and contains much marshland. The Belarussian Ridge (Belorusskya Gryda) stretches across the center of the country from the southwest to the northeast. The highest elevation, at Dzerzhinskaya Gora, is 346 meters (1,135 feet). The lowest point is along the Nyoman River at 90 meters (295 feet). The Dneiper is the longest river in the country with a length of 2,290 kilometers (1,420 miles). Lake Naroch, in the northwest, is the largest lake, with an area of 80 square kilometers (30 square miles).

Geographic Profile

Geographic Features

Size ranking: 83 of 193
Highest elevation: 346 meters (1,135 feet) at Dzerzhinskaya Gora (Dzyarzhynskaya Hara)
Lowest elevation: 90 meters (295 feet) at the Nyoman River

Land Use*

Arable land: 30%
Permanent crops: 1%
Forests: 45%
Other: 24%

Weather**

Average annual precipitation: 57–61 centimeters (22.5–26.5 inches)
Average temperature in January: -5°C (23°F)
Average temperature in July: 19.4°C (67°F)

* *Arable Land: Land used for temporary crops, like meadows for mowing or pasture, gardens, and greenhouses.*

   Permanent crops: Land cultivated with crops that occupy its use for long periods, such as cocoa, coffee, rubber, fruit and nut orchards, and vineyards.

   Forests: Land containing stands of trees.

   Other: Any land not specified, including built-on areas, roads, and barren land.

** *The measurements for precipitation and average temperatures were taken at weather stations closest to the country's largest city.*

   Precipitation and average temperature can vary significantly within a country, due to factors such as latitude, altitude, coastal proximity, and wind patterns.

3 ■ Climate

The mean temperature is 19.4°C (67°F) in July and -5°C (23°F) in January. Rainfall averages between 57 centimeters (22.5 inches) and 61 centimeters (26.5 inches) annually.

4 ■ Plants and Animals

One-third of the country is forest, which is home to mammals that include deer, brown bears, rabbits, and squirrels. The southern region is a swampy expanse. The marshes are home to ducks, frogs, turtles, archons, and muskrats.

5 ■ Environment

Belarus's main environmental problems are chemical and nuclear pollution. Belarus was the republic most affected by the accident at the Chernobyl nuclear power plant in April 1986. Northerly winds prevailed at the time of the accident; therefore, most of the fallout occurred over farmland in the southeastern section of the country (primarily in the Gomel and Mogilev *oblasts*). Most experts estimate that 25% to 30% of Belarus's farmland was exposed to radiation and should not be used for agricultural production or to collect wild berries and mushrooms, although it continues to be used for these and other purposes.

   In addition, Belarus has significant air and water pollution from industrial sources. The most common pollutants are formaldehyde, carbon emissions, and petroleum-related chemicals. In 1992, Belarus was among the world's top fifty nations in industrial emissions of carbon dioxide. The soils also contain unsafe levels of lead, zinc, copper, and the agricultural chemical DDT.

As of 2001, Belarus had over 2,000 species of plants, 74 mammal species, and 221 breeding bird species. Four mammal species and four bird species were listed as threatened that year. Endangered species include the European bison and the European mink. Belarus has 88 UNESCO World Heritage Sites.

6 ■ Population

The population of Belarus was estimated at 9.9 million in 2003. The projected population for 2005 is 10.4 million. At the start of 2001, Minsk, the capital, had an estimated population of 1.8 million.

7 ■ Migration

With the breakup of the Soviet Union in 1991, about 2 million Belarussians were among the various nationality groups who found themselves living outside the borders of their new republics. Most of the Belarussians who have returned to Belarus fled other former Soviet republics, including Azerbaijan, Kyrgyzstan, Kazakhstan, and Tajikistan, because of fighting or ethnic tensions.

As of 1999, Belarus had an estimated 13,000 asylum seekers. There were 131,200 persons who had lost their homes due to the ecological effects of the Chernobyl, Ukraine, nuclear plant accident in 1986. The country also had 160,000 "returnees," ethnic Belarussians who had returned to Belarus from other former Soviet republics. The estimated net migration rate of Belarus in 2003 was 2.66 per 1,000 population.

8 ■ Ethnic Groups

In 2003, an estimated 81% of the total population was native Belarussian. Russians

Location: 53°53′N; 28°0′E **Boundary Lengths:** Total boundary lengths, 3,098 kilometers (1,925 miles); Latvia 141 kilometers (88 miles); Lithuania 502 kilometers (312 miles); Poland, 605 kilometers (376 miles); Russia 959 kilometers (596 miles); Ukraine, 891 kilometers (554 miles).

made up about 11% of the populace; Poles, Ukrainians, and other groups combined to make up about 8% of the population.

9 ■ Languages

Belarussian belongs to the eastern group of Slavic languages and is very similar to Russian. It is written in the Cyrillic alphabet but has two letters that are not in Russian, and a number of distinctive sounds. The vocabulary borrows from Polish, Lithuanian, German, Latin, and Turkic. Russian and other languages are also spoken.

10 ■ Religions

As of 2001, approximately 80% of the population were Russian Orthodox, a faith that enjoys a favored status with the government. About 15% to 20% are Roman Catholics. Between 50,000 and 90,000 people are Jewish. Other minority religions include the Greek Rite Catholic Church, the Belarus Autocephalous Orthodox Church, Seventh-day Adventist Church, Calvinism, Lutheranism, Jehovah's Witnesses, the Apostolic Christian Church, and Islam.

11 ■ Transportation

About 5,523 kilometers (3,432 miles) of railways traverse Belarus, connecting it to Russia, Ukraine, Lithuania, Poland, and Latvia. Belarus had 98,200 kilometers (61,021 miles) of highways in 2002; of these, 66,100 kilometers (41,075 miles) were hard-surfaced. There are 136 airports in the country, 33 of which have paved runways. In 2001, scheduled airline traffic carried 221,700 domestic and international passengers.

12 ■ History

The Belarussians are the descendants of Slavic tribes that migrated into the region in the ninth century A.D. They trace their distinct identity from the thirteenth century when the Mongols conquered Russia and parts of Ukraine. During this period, Belarus managed to maintain its identity as part of the Grand Duchy of Lithuania. The merger of the Grand Duchy with Poland in 1569 put the territory of Belarus under Polish rule. After the division of Poland in the late eighteenth century, Belarus fell to the Russian Empire.

The Belarussian National Republic was formed in March 1918 with German military assistance. However, after the German government collapsed in November 1918, Bolshevik troops moved in and set up the Byelorussian Soviet Socialist Republic in January 1919. In 1922, the Belarus SSR became one of the 15 socialist republics to form the Union of Soviet Socialist Republics. Belarus, located between Germany and Russia, was devastated by World War II (1939–45).

During the decades of Soviet rule, Belarus's leaders generally complied with Soviet policy. However, after extensive nuclear contamination by the 1986 Chernobyl accident in neighboring Ukraine, Belarussian nationalists, acting from exile in Lithuania, organized the Belarussian People's Front.

Throughout the early 1990s the Belarussian leadership wanted to keep the Soviet Union intact. However, shortly after the failed August 1991 takeover attempt against Mikhail Gorbachev, the independence of Belarus was declared on 26 August 1991.

Since independence, Belarus has made very little progress toward economic and political reform. The economy is failing and Soviet-era party bosses are struggling to hold power. President Aleksandr Lukashenko has stopped economic and political reform since his election in 1994. In 1996, Lukashenko signed into law a new constitution that expanded his power. Despite widespread protests, Lukashenko remained in power. In July 1999 opposition leaders held an alterna-

Biographical Profile

Name: Aleksandr Lukashenka
Nickname: "Belarussian Zhirinovsky"
Position: President of a republic
Took Office: 20 July 1994
Birthplace: Vitebsk oblast, Belarus
Birthdate: 30 August 1954
Education: Mohylev Pedagogical Institute;
   Belarussian Agricultural Academy
Children: Two children
Of interest: Lukashenka spent two years as
   a Soviet border guard. He also suffers
   from a serious back condition that has
   required frequent hospitalization.

Aleksandr Lukashenka

tive presidential election prompting a new crackdown by Lukashenko.

Plans by Belarus and Russia to form an economic union remained stalled throughout the late 1990s. As of 2000, though, the leaders of both countries reaffirmed their intention of strengthening their bilateral ties.

Parliamentary elections were held in October 2000, and were criticized by election observers as being neither free nor fair. Turnout was so low that a rerun was necessary (it was held in March 2001). On 9 September 2001, Lukashenko was reelected president, with 75.6% of the vote.

In June 2002, Russian president Vladimir Putin refused to follow the path to integration that Belarus had sketched out for the two nations, saying it would lead to the re-creation of "something along the lines of the Soviet Union." Lukashenko pledged not to give up Belarus's sovereignty in the union with Russia. The issue was unresolved as of 2003.

In November 2002, 14 European Union (EU) states (minus Portugal) imposed a travel ban on Lukashenko and several of his government ministers as a way of protesting Belarus's poor human rights record. In April 2003, the travel ban was lifted, but the United States and the EU remained critical of the country's human rights record.

13 ■ Government

A new constitution was adopted on 15 March 1994. Until mid-1994, Belarus was the only former Soviet republic not to have a president. In elections held on 19 July 1994, Aleksandr Lukashenko was elected after promising to clear out the communist establishment ruling Belarus. However, in 1996 Lukashenko signed into law a new constitution that gave the presidency greater power. Under the new constitution, the president has the power to select the heads of the Constitutional Court, Central Bank, and Supreme Court. The president also has the power to dissolve parliament and veto its decisions. The 2-chamber parliament, called the National Assembly, is composed of a 64-member Council of the Republic and a 110-member House of Representatives. Lukashenko also increased restrictions on freedoms of speech, the press, and peaceful assembly.

Under the new constitution, Belarus is divided into six regions or provinces (*oblasts*).

14 ■ Political Parties

The Communist Party was declared illegal after the failed August 1991 takeover attempt, but was relegalized in February 1993. It and two other procommunist parties merged into one political party called the People's Movement of Belarus in May 1993.

The primary progovernment party is the Belarussian Popular Patriotic Union. The primary opposition party is the Belarussian Popular Front. As of 2002, there were 18 political parties registered in Belarus. In the parliamentary elections held in October 2000, 81 of the 110 seats in the House of Representatives were won by independents.

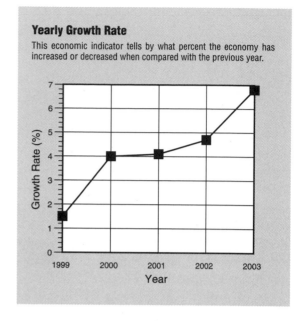

Yearly Growth Rate

This economic indicator tells by what percent the economy has increased or decreased when compared with the previous year.

15 ■ Judicial System

The court system consists of district courts, regional courts, and the Supreme Court. There are also economic courts, and a Supreme Economic Court. A Constitutional Court rules on serious constitutional issues, but has no power to enforce its decisions. The president appoints all district level and military judges. The judicial system is not independent and operates under the influence of the government.

16 ■ Armed Forces

The active armed forces of Belarus numbered 79,800 in 2002, including 4,000 women. The army numbered 29,300 with approximately 1,608 main battle tanks. The Air Force and Air Defense Force numbered 22,000 and had 212 combat aircraft and 58 attack helicopters. In 2001 the defense budget was approximately 1% of the gross domestic product (GDP).

17 ■ Economy

Belarus's economy has been geared toward industrial production, mostly in machinery and metallurgy with a significant weapons industry. Trade and services account for an increasing share of economic activity, however.

Belarus's economy is closely tied in with those of Eastern Europe and the other republics of the former Soviet Union. The breakup of the Soviet Union was highly disruptive to it.

The government has failed to stabilize the economy. The annual inflation rate was 2,220% in 1994, but it dropped to 244% in 1995. An overvalued Belarussian ruble has limited Belarus's exports. During 1998, the Belarus ruble lost half its value during a five-month period. The government stopped accepting payment of its own currency for exports.

Belarus's products remain noncompetitive on the world market. Losses from state-owned businesses are often written off, which prevents those businesses from going bankrupt and keeps unemployment artificially low. There are no legal provisions for regulating business matters. However, as of 2003, the country had six free economic zones, which attracted foreign investment.

18 ■ Income

In 2001, the gross domestic product (GDP) was $84.4 billion, or $8,200 per person. The annual growth rate of the GDP was estimated at 4.1%. The average inflation rate in 2001 was 46.1%.

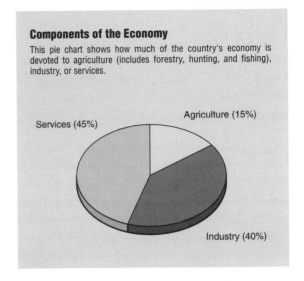

Components of the Economy

This pie chart shows how much of the country's economy is devoted to agriculture (includes forestry, hunting, and fishing), industry, or services.

Services (45%)

Agriculture (15%)

Industry (40%)

19 ■ Industry

Belarus's main industries are engineering, machine tools, agricultural equipment, fertilizer, chemicals, defense-related products, prefabricated construction materials, motor vehicles, motorcycles, textiles, threads, and some consumer goods, such as refrigerators, watches, televisions, and radios. Industry accounted for 42% of the gross domestic product (GDP) in 2000.

While there had been an increase in industrial production as of 2002, a high volume of unsold industrial goods remain stocked in warehouses, due to high operating costs that make Belarussian products non-competitive on the world market. Belarus has taken few steps to privatize state-owned industries: it was estimated that around 10% of all Belarussian enterprises were privatized as of 2000.

20 ■ Labor

There were 4.8 million persons employed in 2000. In 1998, 19% were engaged in agriculture, 41% in services, and 40% in

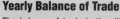

Yearly Balance of Trade

The balance of trade is the difference between what a country sells to other countries (its exports) and what it buys (its imports). If a country imports more than it exports, it has a negative balance of trade (a trade deficit). If exports exceed imports there is a positive balance of trade (a trade surplus).

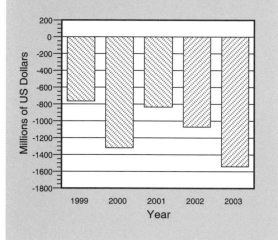

industry and construction. In 2000, the number of registered unemployed was 2.1%, but there was a large segment of the population that was underemployed.

The minimum age for employment is sixteen. As of 2001, the minimum wage was $30 a month, which does not provide a decent standard of living.

Although the constitution provides for the right of workers to form and join independent unions, these rights are not respected in practice.

21 ▨ Agriculture

About 30.4% of the land is arable (suitable for farming). In 2000, agriculture employed about 14% of the economically active population and accounted for 15% of the gross domestic product (GDP). Production levels include about 8 million tons of potatoes, 1.25 million tons of barley, 1 million tons of rye, 1.2 million tons of sugar beets, 376,000 tons of oats, and 600,000 tons of wheat.

22 ▨ Domesticated Animals

About 15% of the land area is devoted to pastureland. There are about 4.5 million cattle, 3.6 million pigs, 122,000 sheep, and 39 million chickens. Of the 652,000 tons of meat produced annually, beef and veal account for 40%; poultry, 11%; pork, 48%, and other meats, 1%. Belarus produces more dairy products than any other former Soviet republic except Russia, with approximately 1.9 million tons of milk, 73,000 tons of butter and ghee, and 59,000 tons of cheese produced annually. Egg production amounts to about 188,000 tons and honey production totals 3,000 tons.

23 ▨ Fishing

As Belarus is a landlocked nation, fishing is confined to the system of rivers that cross the country, including the Pripyat, Byarezina, Nyoman, Zach Dvina, Sozh, and Dnieper. The total catch in 2000 was 553 tons, with common carp accounting for 28% of that amount.

24 ▨ Forestry

In 2000, about 45% of the total land area was covered by forests and woodlands. Radioactive contamination from the 1986 Chernobyl, Ukraine, nuclear disaster has severely restricted timber output. In 2000, Belarus produced 6.1 million cubic meters (215 million cubic feet) of roundwood, of which 945,000 cubic meters (33.4 million cubic feet) were exported for a value of $21 million.

Selected Social Indicators

The statistics below are the most recent estimates available as of 2003. For comparison purposes, data for the United States and averages for low-income countries and high-income countries are also given. About 15% of the world's 6.4 billion people live in high-income countries, while 40% live in low-income countries.

Indicator	Belarus	Low-income countries	High-income countries	United States
Per capita gross national income (GNI)*	$5,500	$2,110	$28,480	$36,110
Population growth rate	0.1%	2.1%	0.7%	1.1%
People per square kilometer of land	48	77	31	31
Life expectancy in years: *male*	63	58	75	75
female	74	60	81	80
Number of physicians per 1,000 people	4.4	1.0	3.0	2.8
Number of pupils per teacher (primary school)	17	40	17	15
Literacy rate (15 years and older)	99.6%	66%	>95%	97%
Television sets per 1,000 people	362	91	735	938
Internet users per 1,000 people	82	10	364	551
Energy consumed per capita (kg of oil equivalent)	2,614	550	5,366	7,937

* The GNI is the total of all goods and services produced by the residents of a country in a year. The per capita GNI is calculated by dividing a country's GNI by its population and adjusting for relative purchasing power.

n.a. = data not available   > = greater than   < = less than

SOURCES: International Telecommunication Union (ITU). *World Telecommunication Development Report 2003*. Geneva, Switzerland: ITU, 2003; World Bank. *World Development Indicators*. Washington, D.C.: The World Bank, 2004; Central Intelligence Agency. *The World Factbook*. Washington, D.C.: Government Printing Office, 2003.

25 ■ Mining

Potash is the one significant mineral resource possessed by Belarus, which ranked second in world output of potash in 2000. Total production in 2000 was 3.79 million tons (more than 8% of which was exported). Two plants produced 1.85 million tons of cement in 2000.

26 ■ Foreign Trade

In 2000, Belarus's main exports were machinery and transport equipment, chemicals, petroleum products, and manufactured goods. Imports included fuel, natural gas, industrial raw materials, textiles, and sugar. Russia, Ukraine, Poland, and Germany were the major trade partners.

27 ■ Energy and Power

Domestic electricity is produced by four thermal plants. Belarus also imports electricity generated by nuclear and hydroelectric plants. In 2000, consumption of electricity totaled 26.8 billion kilowatt hours, while domestic generation totaled only 24.6 billion kilowatt hours. As of 2002, Belarus had oil reserves estimated at 198 million barrels. About 37,000 barrels of oil were produced per day in 2001.

28 ■ Social Development

Old age, disability, survivors, sickness, maternity, work injury, family allowance, and unemployment insurance benefits have been revised and updated in recent years. The government has provided inhabitants with food and other basic goods

Svetlana Belaia

Belarusans in traditional dress.

April 1986, an estimated 2.2 million Belarussians were directly affected by radioactive fallout. Since then, the population is constantly subject to increased amounts of background radiation that weaken the immune systems of individuals in contaminated areas. Many are said to suffer from "Chernobyl AIDS."

In 2000, life expectancy was sixty-eight years. The infant mortality rate in 2000 was 11 per 1,000 live births.

As of 1999, the number of people living with human immunodeficiency virus/acquired immunodeficiency syndrome (HIV/AIDS) was estimated at 14,000, and deaths from AIDS that year were estimated at 400.

30 ■ Housing

The lack of adequate, affordable housing continues to be a problem for Belarus, but certain advances have been made. New homes and apartments were built to house people displaced as a result of the Chernobyl disaster. The government has been reforming housing laws so that citizens may acquire, build, reconstruct, or lease housing facilities.

31 ■ Education

Education is compulsory for children between the ages of six and fifteen. Secondary education lasts for five to seven years, beginning at age twelve. The government is now putting more emphasis on replacing Russian with Belarussian as the official language for education. Approximately 97% of primary-school-age children are enrolled in school. There are over 4,000 preschools, more than 4,500 general-education schools, about 250 vocational and

to preserve social stability. Many factories have given workers mandatory unpaid vacations and four-day workweeks to avoid laying them off or closing down. There are no legal restrictions on women's participation in public life. However, social customs discourage active participation by women in politics and business.

29 ■ Health

As of 1999, there were an estimated 4.4 physicians and 12.2 hospital beds per 1,000 people.

As a result of the accident at the Chernobyl, Ukraine, nuclear power plant in technical schools, and 150 state-run specialized secondary schools.

There are three universities in Belarus. The largest is the Belarussian State University, which is located in Minsk. Along with these universities, there are four polytechnical institutes and nineteen educational institutes. All higher-level institutions have a combined enrollment of between 325,000 and 500,000 students.

As of 2003, the adult illiteracy rate was estimated at 0.4% (males, 0.2%; females, 0.5%).

32 ■ Media

There were approximately 2,313,000 mainline telephones in service in 1997, with an additional 8,167 mobile cellular phones in use.

In 1997, there were 3,020,000 radios and 2,520,000 television sets. The government operates the only nationwide television station; however, there are over 40 local stations. In 1998, there were 65 radio stations (28 AM and 37 FM).

The most widely read newspapers (with 2002 circulation figures) are: *Sovetskaya Belorussiya* (*Soviet Belorussia,* 330,000); *Narodnaya Hazeta* (*People's Newspaper,* 259,597); *Respublika* (*Republic,* 130,000); *Vechernii Minsk* (*Evening Minsk,* 111,000); *Svaboda* (*Liberty,* 90,000); *Zvyazda* (*Star,* 90,000); and *Belorusskaya Niva* (*Belarusian Cornfield,* 80,000).

As of 2002, there were 23 Internet service providers serving about 180,000 customers. All ISPs are controlled by the state.

Though freedom of the press is granted in the 1996 constitution, government authorities reserve the right to ban and censor publications presenting critical reports on national issues.

33 ■ Tourism and Recreation

In 1998, there were 355,342 tourist arrivals in Belarus, and Russians accounted for over half of all visitors. Scenery, architecture, and cultural museums and memorials are primary attractions in Belarus. The Belavaezhskaja Puscha Nature Reserve features a variety of wildlife and a nature museum. The city of Hrodna is home to the baroque Farny Cathedral, the Renaissance Bernadine church and monastery, and the History of Religion Museum, which is part of a renovated eighteenth-century palace. There are also two castles in the area, both housing museums.

34 ■ Famous Belarussians

Frantsky Sharyna, who lived in the first quarter of the sixteenth century, translated the Bible into Belarussian. Naksim Bahdanovich was an important nineteenth-century poet. Modern writers include Uladzimir Dubouka (1900–1976) and Yazep Pushcha, both poets. Kuzma Chorny and Kandrat Krapiva (1896–1991) were writers of fiction during the outpouring of Belarussian poetry and literature during the 1920s. Famous modern composers from Belarus included Dzmitry Lukas, Ryhor Pukst, and Yauhen Hlebau (1929–2000).

35 ■ Bibliography

Belarus. Minneapolis, MN: Lerner, 1993.

Levy, Patricia. *Belarus.* New York: Marshall Cavendish, 1998.

The Modern Encyclopedia of Russian, Soviet and Eurasian History. Gulf Breeze, FL: Academic International Press, 1994.

Zaprudnik, I.A. *Belarus: At a Crossroads in History.* Boulder, CO: Westview Press, 1993.

Zaprudnik, I.A. *Historical Dictionary of Belarus.* Lanham, MD: Scarecrow, 1998.

Belgium

Kingdom of Belgium
Dutch: *Koninkrijk België*; French: *Royaume de Belgique*

Capital: Brussels (Brussel, Bruxelles).

Flag: The flag, adopted in 1831, is a tricolor of black, yellow, and red vertical stripes.

Anthem: *La Brabançonne (The Song of Brabant),* named after the Duchy of Brabant.

Monetary Unit: The euro replaced the Belgian franc in 2002. The euro is divided into 100 cents. There are coins in denominations of 1, 2, 5, 10, 20, and 50 cents and 1 euro; and 2 euros. There are notes of 5, 10, 20, 50, 100, 200, and 500 euros. As of May 2003, €1 = $1.0977 (or $1 = €0.911).

Weights and Measures: The metric system is the legal standard.

Holidays: New Year's Day, 1 January; Labor Day, 1 May; Independence Day, 21 July; Assumption Day, 15 August; All Saints' Day, 1 November; Armistice Day, 11 November; Dynasty Day, 15 November; and Christmas, 25 December. Movable holidays are Easter Monday, Ascension, and Whitmonday.

Time: 1 PM = noon GMT.

1 ▪ Location and Size

Situated in northwestern Europe, Belgium has an area of 30,510 square kilometers (11,780 square miles), about the same size as the state of Maryland. Belgium has a total land boundary length of 1,385 kilometers (859 miles), sharing borders with the Netherlands, Germany, Luxembourg, and France. The country has a coastline of 66 kilometers (41 miles) on the North Sea. Belgium's capital city, Brussels, is located in the north central part of the country.

2 ▪ Topography

The coastal region consists mostly of sand dunes, flat pastureland, and polders (land reclaimed from the sea and protected by dikes). Eastward, this region gradually gives way to a gently rolling central plain, whose many fertile valleys are irrigated by an extensive network of canals and waterways. The Ardennes, a heavily wooded plateau, is located in southeast Belgium and continues into France. It reaches an altitude of 694 meters (2,277 feet) at Mount Botrange, the country's highest point. The lowest point is at sea level (North Sea).

Geographic Profile

Geographic Features

Size ranking: 136 of 193
Highest elevation: 694 meters (2,277 feet) at Signal de Botrange
Lowest elevation: Sea level at the North Sea

Land Use*

Arable land: 26%
Permanent crops: 1%
Forests: 22%
Other: 51%

Weather**

Average annual precipitation: 76.6 centimeters (30.2 inches)
Average temperature in January: 2.2°C (36°F)
Average temperature in July: 18°C (64°F)

---

* Arable Land: Land used for temporary crops, like meadows for mowing or pasture, gardens, and greenhouses.

Permanent crops: Land cultivated with crops that occupy its use for long periods, such as cocoa, coffee, rubber, fruit and nut orchards, and vineyards.

Forests: Land containing stands of trees.

Other: Any land not specified, including built-on areas, roads, and barren land.

** The measurements for precipitation and average temperatures were taken at weather stations closest to the country's largest city.

Precipitation and average temperature can vary significantly within a country, due to factors such as latitude, altitude, coastal proximity, and wind patterns.

Chief rivers are the Schelde and the Meuse. The Meuse is the longest river with a length of 933 kilometers (580 miles).

3 ■ Climate

In the coastal region, the climate is mild and humid. Except in the highlands, rainfall is seldom heavy. The average annual temperature is 8°C (46°F); in Brussels, the mean temperature is 10°C (50°F), ranging from 3°C (37°F) in January to 18°C (64°F) in July. Average annual rainfall is between 70 and 100 centimeters (28 to 40 inches).

4 ■ Plants and Animals

The digitalis, wild arum, hyacinth, strawberry, goldenrod, lily of the valley, and other plants common to temperate zones grow in abundance. Beech and oak are the predominant trees. Among mammals still found in Belgium are the boar, fox, badger, squirrel, weasel, marten, and hedgehog. The many varieties of aquatic life include pike, carp, trout, eel, barbel, perch, smelt, chub, roach, bream, shad, sole, mussels, crayfish, and shrimp.

5 ■ Environment

As of 2000, Belgium's most significant environmental problems were air, land, and water pollution due to the large number of industrial facilities in the country. The sources of pollution range from nuclear radiation and mercury from industry to pesticides from agricultural activity. The country's water supply is threatened by hazardous levels of heavy metals, mercury, and phosphorous. Air pollution reaches dangerous levels due to high concentrations of lead and hydrocarbons. Belgium is also among the 50 nations that emit the

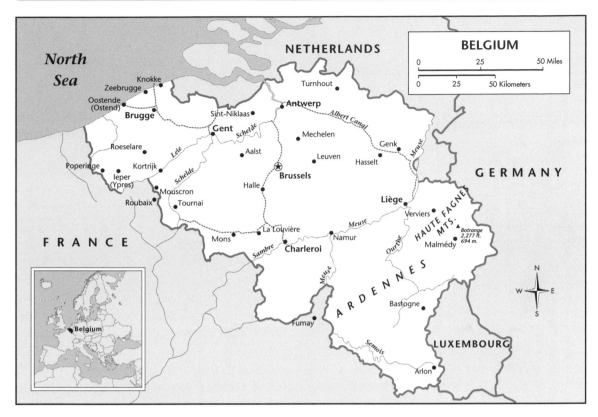

Location: 49°29′52° to 51°30′21″N; 2°32′48° to 6°25′38°E. **Boundary Lengths:** Netherlands, 450 kilometers (280 miles); Germany, 162 kilometers (101 miles); Luxembourg, 148 kilometers (92 miles); France, 620 kilometers (385 miles); North Sea, 66 kilometers (41 miles). **Territorial Sea Limit:** 12 miles.

highest levels of carbon dioxide from industrial sources. Belgium's problems with air pollution have also affected neighboring countries by contributing to the conditions that cause acid rain.

As of 2001, six species of mammals and three species of birds were endangered. The Mediterranean mouflon, the Atlantic sturgeon, and the black right whale are listed as endangered.

6 Population

One of the most densely populated countries in the world, Belgium had an esti-

mated population of 10.3 million in 2003, with a density of 315 persons per square kilometer (817 persons per square mile). The population projection for the year 2005 is slightly less at 10.1 million. The Belgian government uses a population registry to annually determine the total number of inhabitants. In 2001, the population of Brussels (including suburbs) was 1.1 million.

7 Migration

At the end of 2001, 862,000 persons of foreign nationality were living in Belgium.

Susan D Rock

People stroll along the Schelde River in Antwerp.

About 65% were those of other European Union (EU) countries, primarily Italy, France, the Netherlands, and Spain. There were also a considerable number of Moroccans and Turks living in Belgium that year.

As of 2000, Belgium hosted approximately 18,000 refugees. The estimated net migration rate of Belgium was 0.97 migrants per 1,000 population in 2003. In 2001, there were 24,550 asylum applications, mostly from Russia and Yugoslavia.

8 ■ Ethnic Groups

The Salian Franks, who settled there during the fourth century A.D., are considered the ancestors of Belgium's present popu-

lation. Among the native population, the ratio of Flemings (Dutch speakers) to Walloons (French speakers) is about 5 to 3. In 2003, the Flemings constituted about 58% of the total population; Walloons accounted for 31%. The remaining 11% was made up of those with mixed ancestry or other groups.

9 ■ Languages

According to a 1970 constitutional revision, there are three official languages in Belgium: French, Dutch (also called Flemish), and German. Dutch is the language of the four provinces of Antwerp, Limburg, East Flanders (Oost-Vlaanderen), and West Flanders (West-Vlaanderen), which form the northern half of the country. French is the language of the four southern Walloon provinces of Hainaut, Liège, Luxembourg, and Namur. The central province of Brabant is divided into three districts, one French-speaking (Nivelles, or Nijvel), one Dutch-speaking (Leuven, or Louvain), and one bilingual (composed of the nineteen boroughs of the capital city, Brussels). The majority of people in the Brussels metropolitan area are French-speaking.

As a rule, French is studied in all secondary schools in the Flemish region, while Dutch is a required secondary-school subject in Wallonia. According to 2002 estimates, 60% of the total population speak Dutch (Flemish), 40% speak French, fewer than 1% speak German. Many people are bilingual, speaking both Dutch and French.

10 ■ Religions

According to a 2002 report, about 75% of the population are Roman Catholic and 25% are Protestant or other faiths. The Muslim population numbers about 350,000, of whom 90% are Sunni. Protestants number between 90,000 and 100,000. The Greek and Russian Orthodox number about 100,000. The Jewish community is approximately 40,000 and Anglicans number approximately 21,000. The largest unrecognized religions include the Jehovah's Witnesses, with 27,000 members, and Mormons, with about 3,000 members. About 350,000 people belong to "laics," the government's term for nondenominational philosophical organizations. Unofficial estimates report that up to 10% of the population do not practice any religion at all.

11 ■ Transportation

In 2002, Belgium had the densest railway network in the world, with 3,422 kilometers (2,126 miles) of track operated by the government-controlled Belgian National Railway Company. In addition, Belgium has a regional railway network of 27,950 kilometers (17,367 miles). The road network makes up 145,774 kilometers (90,584 miles) of paved highways, including 1,674 kilometers (1,040 miles) of expressways. All major European highways pass through Belgium. Motor vehicles in 1995 included 4,239,051 passenger cars and 405,603 trucks.

Inland waterways total 2,043 kilometers (1,270 miles) of rivers and canals, and are linked with those of France, Germany, and the Netherlands. The chief port, Antwerp, handles three-fourths of the country's foreign cargo.

Brussels's National Airport is served by more than thirty major airlines. In 2001, 8,489,000 passengers flew on scheduled domestic and international flights.

12 ■ History

Belgium is named after the Belgae, a Celtic people whose territory Julius Caesar conquered in 57 B.C. and ruled as Gallia Belgica. In the fifth century A.D., it was overrun by the Franks, and in the eighth century, it became part of Charlemagne's empire. By the tenth century this empire had declined, and feudal powers ruled the land. During the next three centuries, trade flourished. Antwerp, Bruges, Ypres, and Ghent became especially prosperous.

The territories that currently form Belgium, the Netherlands, and Luxembourg, now called the Benelux countries, have been called the Low Countries. Beginning in the fifteenth century, these territories, or parts of them, were ruled at various times by France, Austria, and Spain for about four hundred years.

On 4 October 1830, Belgium was declared independent. The following year its parliament chose Prince Leopold of Saxe-Coburg-Gotha (Leopold I) as ruler of the new kingdom. In 1865, Leopold I was followed by Leopold II (ruled 1865–1909), who financed exploration and settlement in the Congo River Basin of Africa, laying the foundations of Belgium's colonial empire.

When World War I (1914–18) broke out, German troops invaded Belgium (4 August 1914). The Belgian army offered fierce resistance, but by the end of November 1914, most of the country was occupied by the Germans. Belgium, on the side of the Allies, continued to struggle against the occupation. Ypres, in particular, was the scene of fierce fighting. Nearly 100,000 men lost their lives at a battle near there in April and May 1915.

The Allies won the war, and under the Treaty of Versailles (1919), Belgium acquired the German-speaking districts of Eupen, Malmédy, Saint Vith, and Moresnet. The country made a remarkable recovery from the war, and by 1923, manufacturing industries were nearly back to normal.

Leopold III Surrenders: Belgium was again attacked early in World War II (1939–45). On 10 May 1940, without warning, the Germans invaded the country and bombed Belgian airports, railroad stations, and communications centers. King Leopold III surrendered unconditionally on 28 May and was taken prisoner of war. The country was liberated from the Germans in 1944, and the Belgian government returned to Brussels in September of that year.

The country was economically better off after World War II than after World War I. However, a split had developed during the war years between Leopold III, who had surrendered to the Germans, and the Belgian government-in-exile, operating from London. The government-in-exile had rejected the king's surrender to Germany. On 22 July 1950, Leopold came back from exile, but much of the country opposed his return. On 1 August 1950, he agreed to give up the throne in favor of his son, Baudouin I.

In 1960, the Belgian Congo (later known first as Zaire and then the Democratic Republic of the Congo), a major portion of Belgium's colonial empire, became independent. The event was followed by two years of brutal civil war, involving mercenaries from Belgium and other countries. Another Belgian territory in Africa, Ruanda-Urundi, became independent as the two states of Rwanda and Burundi in 1962.

Belgium shared fully in the European prosperity of the first three postwar decades. However, domestic political conflict during this period centered on the unequal distribution of wealth and power between Flemings (Dutch speakers) and Walloons (French speakers). Today, the country is divided into three regions (Flanders, Wallonia, and Brussels) and three linguistic communities (Flemish, French, and German).

Labor unrest and political violence have erupted in recent years. Vigorous trade-union protests have taken place to protest the freezing of wages and cuts in social security payments. Belgium has one of the largest national debts in Western Europe. In 1994, the government began an environment tax on a range of goods based on the amount of pollution caused in their production.

King Baudouin died suddenly on 31 July 1993, while vacationing in Spain. Since he had no children, he was succeeded by his brother, Prince Albert of Liège. King Baudouin had abdicated (given up power) for a day in April 1990 to avoid having to sign legislation legalizing abortion.

Belgium joined the European economic and monetary union in January 1999.

Belgium by 2003 had legalized euthanasia and the use of marijuana, and had approved gay marriages. Under Belgium's "universal jurisdiction" law, Belgian courts can hear cases involving war crimes and crimes against humanity even if the crimes were not committed in Belgium and did not involve Belgian citizens. Israeli prime minister Ariel Sharon and former U.S. president George H. W. Bush were charged with war crimes under the law, relating to the 1982 Sabra and Shatila massacres in Lebanon, and the bombing of a civilian shelter in the 1991 Gulf War, respectively.

Biographical Profile

Name: Guy Verhofstadt

Position: Prime Minister of a federal
    parliamentary democracy under a
    constitutional monarch

Took Office: 13 July 1999

Birthplace: Dendermonde, Belgium

Birthdate: 11 April 1953

Education: Rijksuniversiteit in Ghent, law
    degree, 1975

Spouse: A professional opera singer

Children: One son, one daughter

Of interest: He became highly interested in
    the environment while in Italy

Guy Verhofstadt

13 ■ Government

Belgium is a hereditary monarchy governed under the constitution of 1831. This document has been frequently amended in recent years to grant recognition and autonomy to the Dutch- and French-speaking communities. Executive power is held by the king, who also holds legislative power jointly with the two-chamber parliament. The Chamber of Representatives has 150 members, and the Senate, 71 members.

In the constitutional reform of 1980, three communities, the Dutch-, the French-, and the German-speaking, were established. Each has independent responsibility for cultural affairs and for matters concerning the individual. There also are three regions in the northwest that have partial responsibility for economic, energy, housing, environmental, and other matters.

Belgium is divided into ten provinces. Each has a council of fifty to ninety members and a governor appointed by the king.

14 ■ Political Parties

The Belgian political system operates through "twin" sets of French- and Dutch-speaking parties. Each French-speaking group has a Dutch-speaking counterpart. The three major political alliances are the Christian Social parties, consisting of the Parti Social Chrétien (PSC) and the Christian Democrats and Flemish (CD and V), formerly the Christelijke Volkspartij

Yearly Growth Rate

This economic indicator tells by what percent the economy has increased or decreased when compared with the previous year.

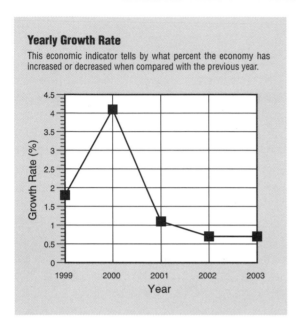

In 2002, the PSC was renamed the Democratic Humanistic Center (CDH), and the PRL, FDF, and the MCC or Movement of Citizens for Change (created in 1998 by a former leader of the French-speaking Christian Democrats) formed a new alliance called the Reform Movement (MR). These changes have not had a serious effect on the Belgian political landscape, however. In the 18 May 2003 elections, the party strength was distributed as follows: VLD, twenty-five seats; SP.A-Spirit, twenty-three seats; CD and V, twenty-one seats; PS, twenty-five seats; VB, eighteen seats; MR, twenty-four seats; CDH, eight seats; NVA, one seat; Ecolo, four seats; and FN, one seat. Liberal Guy Verhofstadt was appointed prime minister.

(CVP); the Socialist parties, the Parti Socialiste (PS) and Socialist Progressive Alternative Party (SP.A); and the Liberal parties, the Francophone Reformist Movement (MR) and Flemish Liberal Party (VLD).

The People's Union (Volksunie, or VU) was the Flemish nationalistic party, while the French-speaking Democratic Front (Front Démocratique des Francophones-FDF) affirms the rights of the French-speaking population of Brussels. (The VU later broke apart, to be replaced by the New Flemish Alliance [NVA] and the Spirit parties.) Ecology, or "green," parties (ECOCO/AGALEV) have become important political actors by gaining seats in the Chamber and Senate. The Flemish Block (Vlaams Blok-VB) is separatist and antiforeigner while the much smaller far-right National Front (Front Nationale; FN) is openly racist and intolerant of foreigners.

15 ■ Judicial System

Belgian law is modeled on the French legal system. The judiciary is an independent branch of government on an equal footing with the legislative and the executive branches.

Minor offenses are dealt with by justices of the peace and police tribunals. More serious offenses and civil lawsuits are brought before district courts of first instance. Other district courts are commerce and labor tribunals. Verdicts given by these courts may be appealed before five regional courts of appeal or the five regional labor courts in Antwerp, Brussels, Gent, Mons, and Liège.

The highest courts are five civil and criminal courts of appeal and the Supreme Court of Cassation, which must verify that the law has been properly applied and interpreted. A system of military tribunals, including appellate courts, handles both military and common law offenses involving military personnel.

16 ■ Armed Forces

Belgium's active armed forces in 2002 numbered 39,260, including 3,230 women and a 1,860-member medical service. Army personnel numbered 26,400. The air force, with 8,600 personnel, had 13 squadrons and operated 90 combat aircraft. The navy had only 2,400 personnel and manned 3 frigates and 11 mine warfare craft. In 1994, Belgium abolished the draft. In 2001–02 Belgium spent $3.1 billion on defense, or 1.4% of the gross domestic product (GDP).

17 ■ Economy

In relation to its size and population, Belgium is among the most highly industrialized countries in Europe. Poor in natural resources, it imports raw materials in great quantity and processes them largely for export. Belgium's highly developed transportation systems are closely linked with those of its neighbors. Its chief port, Antwerp, is one of the world's busiest. Belgium has a highly skilled and productive workforce, and the economy is diversified. By 2002, the service sector accounted for approximately 70% of the gross domestic product (GDP). Real growth averaged 2.6% between 1984 and 1991 and was 2.8% in 1998. Economic growth was expected to rise to some 3% in 2004 as a result of a recovery from the global economic downturn existing in 2001–03 (GDP growth in 2001 was estimated at 1.1%).

A UN study in 2002 listed Belgium as having the fourth-highest standard of living in the world.

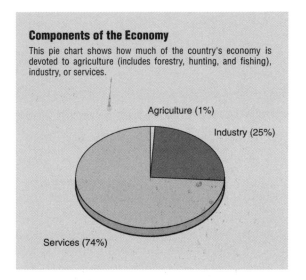

Components of the Economy

This pie chart shows how much of the country's economy is devoted to agriculture (includes forestry, hunting, and fishing), industry, or services.

Agriculture (1%)

Industry (25%)

Services (74%)

18 ■ Income

In 2002, Belgium's gross domestic product (GDP) was $297.6 billion, or $29,000 per person. The annual growth rate of the GDP was estimated at 0.6%. The average inflation rate in 2002 was 1.7%.

19 ■ Industry

Industrial production rose in the late 1990s. Industry accounted for 24% of the gross domestic product (GDP) in 2001.

Steel production is the single most important type of industry, with Belgium ranking high among world producers of iron and steel. In 1998, Belgium produced 342,000 tons of crude copper, as well as significant amounts of crude zinc and lead. The automotive industry is strong: Belgium produced 1,187,257 automobiles in 2001, a 15% increase over 2000. It also manufactured 30,499 heavy trucks in 2000, an increase of 20% over 1999. An important shipbuilding industry is centered in Temse, south of Antwerp. Belgian engineering and construction firms have built steel plants, chemical works, power stations, port facilities, and office buildings throughout the world.

The textile industry, dating from the Middle Ages, produces cottons, woolens, linens, and synthetic fibers. Brussels and Bruges are noted for fine linen and lace.

The chemical industry manufactures a wide range of products, from heavy chemicals and explosives to pharmaceuticals and photographic supplies.

The diamond-cutting industry in Antwerp supplies most of the U.S. industrial diamond requirements. Belgium has one of the largest glass industries in the world, and is especially known for its fine crystal glassware.

20 ▪ Labor

As of 2001, the Belgian workforce (people available to work) totaled 4.44 million. In 1999, 73% of employed persons worked in services, and most of the rest in industry. Unemployment in 2002 was at 7.2%.

Approximately 60% of workers are union members. Children under the age of fifteen years are prohibited from working. Those between the ages of fifteen and eighteen may engage in part-time work-study programs, or work during school vacations. In 2001, the national minimum wage was $1,050 per month, which provides a decent standard of living for workers and their families.

21 ▪ Agriculture

About 2% of the employed population work on farms. About 80% of the country's food needs are covered domestically. The richest farm areas are in Flanders and Brabant. About 45% of Belgium's total area is under cultivation. About 25% of the land is used for the production of cereals. Total production of grains is around 2.3 million tons, of which wheat accounts for about 65%; barley, 16%; corn, 11%; and spelt, triticale, oats, rye, and other grains, 8%.

Increased emphasis is being placed on horticulture (growing fruits and vegetables) and nearly all fruits found in temperate climates are grown in Belgium. Chief among these are apples, pears, and cherries.

Belgium imports considerable quantities of bread and feed grains and fruits. Its only agricultural exports are processed foods and a few specialty items such as endive, chicory, flower bulbs, sugar, and chocolates. In 2001, agricultural products amounted to 9.6% of exports. There was an agricultural trade surplus of $2.6 billion that year.

22 ▪ Domesticated Animals

Livestock raising is the most important single sector of Belgian agriculture, accounting for more than 60% of agricultural production. There are about 3.2 million head of cattle, 7.6 million hogs, 155,000 sheep, and 22,000 horses. Belgian farmers breed some of the finest draft horses in the world, including the famous Percherons.

The country produces all the butter, milk, meat, and eggs it needs. Some cheese is imported, mainly from the Netherlands. Milk production amounts to 3.3 million tons.

23 ▪ Fishing

The chief fishing ports are Zeebrugge and Ostend, from which a fleet of 156 boats sail the North Atlantic from the North Sea to Iceland. The total catch in 2000 was 29,800 tons, with exports valued at $469 million. Principal species caught that year were plaice, sole, turbot, and cod.

24 ■ Forestry

Forests cover 21% of Belgium's total area. Commercial production of timber is limited. Industrial roundwood production in 2000 was estimated at 2.78 million cubic meters (98 million cubic feet) and construction timber production was at 1.06 million cubic meters (37 million cubic feet). The most common trees are beech and oak, but considerable plantings of conifers have been made in recent years. Belgium serves as a large shipping center for temperate hardwood logs, softwood lumber, and softwood plywood. Large quantities of timber for the woodworking industry are typically imported from the Democratic Republic of the Congo.

The total value of exports of forest products in 2000 was $3.57 billion, with imports of $4.31 billion. Belgium's wood processing industry consists of over 2,000 businesses, over half of which are furniture manufacturers.

25 ■ Mining

Belgium's only active mining operations in 2001 were for the production of sand and gravel and the quarrying of stone, including specialty marbles and the Belgian blue-gray limestone called "petit granite." The mineral-processing industry was a significant contributor to the Belgian economy in 2001. The refining of copper, zinc, and minor metals and the production of steel (all from imported materials), were the most developed mineral industries in Belgium. The country possessed Europe's largest electrolytic copper and zinc refineries and one of the continent's largest lead refineries. In addition, Belgium retained its position as the world's

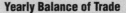

Yearly Balance of Trade

The balance of trade is the difference between what a country sells to other countries (its exports) and what it buys (its imports). If a country imports more than it exports, it has a negative balance of trade (a trade deficit). If exports exceed imports there is a positive balance of trade (a trade surplus).

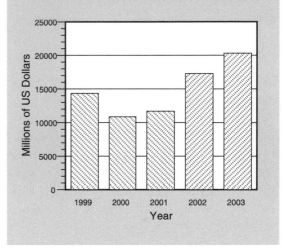

diamond capital. Estimated production figures for 2001 included 139,000 tons of secondary copper, 230,000 tons of primary zinc, and 8 million tons of hydraulic cement.

26 ■ Foreign Trade

Foreign trade plays a greater role in the Belgian economy than in any other EU (European Union) country except Luxembourg. In 2000, exports constituted 81% of the gross domestic product (GDP). Belgium's chief exports are iron and steel (semifinished and manufactured), foodstuffs, textiles, machinery, road vehicles and parts, nonferrous metals, and diamonds. Its imports are general manufactures, foodstuffs, diamonds, metals and metal ores, petroleum and petroleum products, chemicals, clothing, machinery, electrical equipment, and motor vehicles.

In 2000, more than 64% of Belgium's foreign trade was carried on with EU countries. France was the leading customer in 2000. Germany was the chief supplier from 1953 to 1999, but in 2000, the Netherlands took over that position from Germany.

27 ■ Energy and Power

In 1998, there were about 120 power stations operating in Belgium. Of a total power output of 78.2 billion kilowatt hours in 2000, 40% was conventional thermal, 57.7% was nuclear (compared to 25% in 1981), and less than 1% was hydroelectric. The principal sources of primary energy for conventional power production are low-grade coal and byproducts of the oil industry. Belgium is heavily dependent on imports of crude oil.

28 ■ Social Development

Belgium has a highly developed social security system dating back to mutual benefit societies begun in 1894. The central coordinating agency for welfare is the National Social Security Office. It collects all workers' and employers' contributions for old age pensions and life insurance. It also collects management's payments for family allowances, paid vacations, and other benefits. The government actively promotes women's and children's rights. Sexual harassment is banned in both the public and private sectors. Child protection laws are extensive, and children have the right to take concerns or complaints directly to a judge.

Although minority rights are well protected in Belgium, extreme-right political parties with beliefs that discriminate against foreigners have gained ground in recent years.

29 ■ Health

Every city or town in Belgium has a public assistance committee that is in charge of health and hospital services in its community. These committees organize clinics and visiting nurse services, run public hospitals, and cover expenses for patients in private hospitals who can't afford to pay. There is a national health insurance plan that covers practically the whole population.

Belgium had 287 hospitals at the beginning of 1997. The infant mortality rate in 2000 was 5 per 1,000 live births. Average life expectancy in 2000 was seventy-eight years.

As of 1999, the number of people living with human immunodeficiency virus/acquired immunodeficiency syndrome (HIV/AIDS) was estimated at 7,700 and deaths from AIDS that year were estimated at fewer than 100.

30 ■ Housing

Belgium no longer has a housing shortage. Public funds have been made available in increasing amounts to support the construction of low-cost housing, with low-interest mortgages. At least 85% of all dwellings have access to safe water and sanitation systems.

31 ■ Education

Education is free and compulsory for children between the ages of six and eighteen. The teaching language is that of the region—French, Dutch, or German.

Selected Social Indicators

The statistics below are the most recent estimates available as of 2003. For comparison purposes, data for the United States and averages for low-income countries and high-income countries are also given. About 15% of the world's 6.4 billion people live in high-income countries, while 40% live in low-income countries.

Indicator	Belgium	Low-income countries	High-income countries	United States
Per capita gross national income (GNI)*	$28,130	$2,110	$28,480	$36,110
Population growth rate	0.2%	2.1%	0.7%	1.1%
People per square kilometer of land	315	77	31	31
Life expectancy in years: *male*	75	58	75	75
female	82	60	81	80
Number of physicians per 1,000 people	3.9	1.0	3.0	2.8
Number of pupils per teacher (primary school)	12	40	17	15
Literacy rate (15 years and older)	98%	66%	>95%	97%
Television sets per 1,000 people	541	91	735	938
Internet users per 1,000 people	328	10	364	551
Energy consumed per capita (kg of oil equivalent)	5,719	550	5,366	7,937

* The GNI is the total of all goods and services produced by the residents of a country in a year. The per capita GNI is calculated by dividing a country's GNI by its population and adjusting for relative purchasing power.

n.a. = data not available   > = greater than   < = less than

SOURCES: International Telecommunication Union (ITU). *World Telecommunication Development Report 2003*. Geneva, Switzerland: ITU, 2003; World Bank. *World Development Indicators*. Washington, D.C.: The World Bank, 2004; Central Intelligence Agency. *The World Factbook*. Washington, D.C.: Government Printing Office, 2003.

Belgium has two complete school systems operating side by side. One is organized by the state or by local authorities and is known as the official school system. The other, the private school system, is largely Roman Catholic. Private school enrollment accounts for about 55% of all primary enrollment and 65% of secondary enrollment. For a long time, the rivalry between the public and private systems and the question of subsidies to private schools were the main issues in Belgian politics. The controversy was settled in 1958, and both systems are presently financed with government funds along more or less identical lines.

Schools in Wallonia and Flanders provide compulsory primary education for children from ages six through twelve, followed by six years of secondary education.

The pupil-teacher ratio at the primary level averages 12 to 1.

There are eight main universities. The higher-level institutions have a combined enrollment of between 350,000 and 500,000 students.

The adult illiteracy rate is about 2%.

32 ■ Media

There were 4,769,000 mainline telephones in use in 1997 and 974,494 mobile cellular phones.

National radio and television service is organized into Dutch and French branches. There are two national stations, one broadcasting in French, the other in Dutch. In addition, there are five Dutch-language and three French-language regional stations. Three shortwave transmitters are used for

Susan D Rock

A view of the Old City of Antwerp.

overseas broadcasts. As of 1999, there were five AM and seventy-seven FM radio stations and twenty-four television stations. Cable television subscribers can receive up to thirteen additional stations, from the United Kingdom and Belgium's continental neighbors. In 1997 there were 8 million radios and 4.7 million television sets.

The Belgian press has full freedom of expression as guaranteed by the constitution of 1831. Newspapers are published in French and Dutch and generally reflect the views of one of the major political parties. Agence Belga is the official news agency. Principal Belgian dailies with their 2002 circulations were: *De Standaard,* 372,000; *Het Laatste Nieuws,* 308,808; *Le Soir,* 178,500; *De Gazet*

van Antwerpen, 148,000; and *La Lanterne,* 129,800. About 500 weeklies appear in Belgium, most of them in French or Dutch and a few in German or English. Their overall weekly circulation is estimated to exceed 6.5 million copies.

As of 2000, there were 61 Internet service providers (with 2.8 million Internet users in 2001).

33 ■ Tourism and Recreation

Belgium has three major tourist regions: the seacoast, the old Flemish cities, and the Ardennes Forest in the southeast. Ostend is the largest North Sea resort. Among Flemish cities, Brugge, Gent, and Ypres stand out, while Antwerp also has many sightseeing attractions. Brussels, home of the European Union headquarters, is a modern city with historic and cultural landmarks including the Grand Place, the Palais des Beaux-Arts, the Théâtre Royal de la Monnaie, and Notre Dame du Sablon. There were 6.4 million tourist arrivals in 2000; receipts from tourism amounted to $7.4 billion.

34 ■ Famous Belgians

Belgium has produced many famous artists, including Jan van Eyck (c.1390–1441), Hans Memling (c.1430–1494), and Pieter Brueghel the Elder (c.1525–1569), the ancestor of a long line of painters. Generally considered the greatest of Flemish painters are Peter Paul Rubens (1577–1640) and Anthony van Dyck (1599–1641). René Magritte (1898–1967) was a famous twentieth-century artist. Belgium made contributions to the development of music through the works of such outstanding fifteenth- and sixteenth-century composers as Johannes Ockeghem (c.1430–1495), Josquin des Prés (c.1450–1521), and Roland de Lassus (known originally as Roland de Latre and later called Orlando di Lasso, 1532–94). César Franck (1822–1890) was a well-known nineteenth-century composer.

Three Belgians have won the Nobel Peace Prize: Auguste Beernaert (1829–1912) in 1909, Henri Lafontaine (1854–1943) in 1913, and Father Dominique Pire (1910–1969) in 1958.

35 ■ Bibliography

Burgan, Michael. *Belgium.* New York: Children's Press, 2000.

Carrick, Noel. *Belgium.* Philadelphia, PA: Chelsea House, 2000.

Cook, Bernard A. *Belgium: A History.* New York: Peter Lang, 2002.

Pateman, Robert. *Belgium.* New York: Marshall Cavendish, 1995.

Stallaerts, Robert. *Historical Dictionary of Belgium.* Lanham, MD: Scarecrow Press, 1999.

Belize

Capital: Belmopan.

Flag: The national flag consists of the Belize coat of arms on a white disk centered in a blue rectangular field with a narrow red stripe at the top and the bottom.

Anthem: *Land of the Free.*

Monetary Unit: The Belize dollar (B$), formerly tied to the UK pound sterling and now pegged to the US dollar, is a paper currency of 100 cents. There are coins of 1, 5, 10, 25, 50 cents and 1 dollar, and notes of 1, 5, 10, 20, 50, and 100 dollars. B$1= US$0.50 (or US$1= B$2.00; as of February 2003).

Weights and Measures: Imperial weights and measures are used. The exception is the measuring of petroleum products, for which the US gallon is standard.

Holidays: New Year's Day, 1 January; Baron Bliss Day, 9 March; Labor Day, 1 May; Commonwealth Day, 24 May; National Day, 10 September; Independence Day, 21 September; Columbus Day, 12 October; Garifuna Day, 19 November; Christmas, 25 December; Boxing Day, 26 December. Movable holidays are Good Friday and Easter Monday.

Time: 6 AM = noon GMT.

1 ▪ Location and Size

Belize (formerly British Honduras), on the Caribbean coast of Central America, has an area of 22,966 square kilometers (8,867 square miles). The country is slightly smaller than the state of Massachusetts. Belize has a total boundary length of 516 kilometers (320 miles) and a coastline on the Caribbean Sea of 386 kilometers (240 miles). The country shares borders with Guatemala and Mexico. The capital city of Belize, Belmopan, is located in the center of the country.

2 ▪ Topography

The country north of Belmopan is mostly level land interrupted only by the Manatee Hills. To the south, the land rises sharply toward a mountainous interior from a flat and swampy coastline heavily indented by many lagoons. The Maya and the Cockscomb Mountains reach a high point of 1,120 meters (3,675 feet) at Victoria Peak and form the backbone of the country, which is drained by 17 rivers. The lowest point is at sea level (Caribbean Sea).

The longest river is the Belize, with

Geographic Profile

Geographic Features

Size ranking: 147 of 193
Highest elevation: 1,120 meters (3,675 feet) at Victoria Peak
Lowest elevation: Sea level at the Caribbean Sea

Land Use*

Arable land: 2%
Permanent crops: 1%
Forests: 92%
Other: 5%

Weather**

Average annual precipitation: 164.8 centimeters (64.9 inches)
Average temperature in January: 23.5°C (74.3°F)
Average temperature in July: 27.6°C (81.7°F)

---

* *Arable Land: Land used for temporary crops, like meadows for mowing or pasture, gardens, and greenhouses.*

Permanent crops: Land cultivated with crops that occupy its use for long periods, such as cocoa, coffee, rubber, fruit and nut orchards, and vineyards.

Forests: Land containing stands of trees.

Other: Any land not specified, including built-on areas, roads, and barren land.

** *The measurements for precipitation and average temperatures were taken at weather stations closest to the country's largest city.*

Precipitation and average temperature can vary significantly within a country, due to factors such as latitude, altitude, coastal proximity, and wind patterns.

---

a distance of 288 kilometers (180 miles). The coastal waters are sheltered by a line of reefs. Beyond are numerous islands and cays, notably Ambergris Cay, the Turneffe Islands, Columbus Reef, and Glover Reef.

3 ■ Climate

The climate is tempered by northeast trade winds that keep temperatures between 16 and 32°C (61 and 90°F) in the coastal region. Annual rainfall averages vary from 127 centimeters (50 inches) to more than 380 centimeters (150 inches). There is a dry season from February to May and another dry spell in August. Hurricanes occur from July to October.

4 ■ Plants and Animals

Most of the forest cover consists of mixed hardwoods—mainly mahogany, cedar, and sapodilla (the source of chicle). In the flat regions there are extensive tracts of pine. The coastal land and the cays are covered with mangrove. Indigenous fauna (animals) include armadillo, opossum, deer, and monkeys; common reptiles include iguana and snakes.

5 ■ Environment

Due to its low population density, Belize has suffered less than its neighbors from such problems as soil erosion and pollution. However, substantial deforestation has occurred and water quality remains a problem because of the seepage of sewage, along with industrial and agricultural chemicals, into the water supply. Pollutants also threaten Belize's coral reefs. Removal of coral, picking orchids in forest reserves, spear fishing, and overnight camping in any public area (including forest reserves) are prohibited.

Approximately 21% of Belize's total land area is protected. Natural hazards to Belize's environment include hurricanes and coastal flooding. Endangered species in Belize include the tundra peregrine falcon, hawksbill, green sea and leatherback turtles, American crocodile, and Morelet's crocodile. In 2001, there were 5 endangered species of mammals out of 125. Of 356 breeding bird species, one is threatened. Endangered species include the iguana, Larpy eagle, spoonbill, wood stork, and hawksbill turtle.

6 ■ Population

The estimated 2003 population was 256,000. In 2002, the population density was 11 persons per square kilometer (29 persons per square mile), the lowest in Central America. Belmopan, the capital, had an estimated population of 6,000 in 2001. Belize City had a population of 46,342 in that year.

7 ■ Migration

Due to its high emigration rate, Belize encourages immigration. The population of Belize increased significantly in 1993, with 40,000 Central American refugees and other immigrants, mostly from Guatemala and El Salvador. This offset the heavy Creole emigration to North America. As of 1995, Belize still had 6,000 refugees from El Salvador and 2,000 refugees from Guatemala. In 2000, the net migration rate was -2.3 migrants per 1,000 population. The estimated net migration rate in 2003 was zero. The total number of migrants in Belize in 2000 was 17,000.

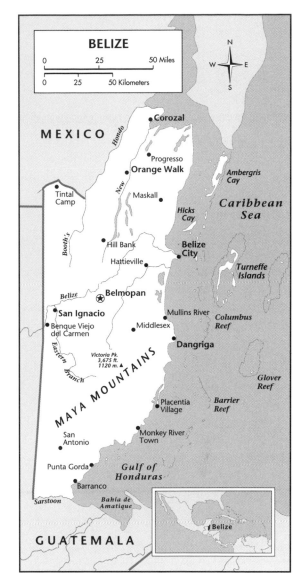

Location: 15°53' to 18°31'N; 87°16' to 89°8'W.
Boundary Lengths: Mexico, 250 kilometers (155 miles); Caribbean coastline, 386 kilometers (240 miles); Guatemala, 266 kilometers (165 miles).
Territorial Sea Limit: 3 miles.

8 ■ Ethnic Groups

According to the latest estimates, 49% of the population is mestizo (mixed White and Maya); nearly 25% is Creole (of African descent); another 10% is Maya; 6% is Garifuna (Carib); and nearly 10% is comprised of various other groups, including those of Arab, European, Chinese, Asian Indian, North American, and Syrian-Lebanese ancestry. Residents of Belize are called Belizeans.

9 ■ Languages

The official language is English. At least 80% of the people can speak standard English and/or a Creole patois (dialect). Spanish is spoken by approximately 60% of the population. Although English is the language of instruction, other languages spoken include Garifuna (Carib), Mayan and other Amerindian languages, and, in the Mennonite colony, Low German.

10 ■ Religions

About 58% of all inhabitants are Roman Catholic. Only 7% are Anglican and 6% are Pentecostal. Other faiths and denominations generally have fewer than 10,000 members each. These include Methodists (4.2%), Seventh-day Adventists (4.1%), and Mennonites (4%). There are approximately 5,000 Hindus and Nazarenes and smaller numbers of Baha'is, Baptists, Buddhists, Jehovah's Witnesses, Mormons, Muslims, Rastafarians, and Salvation Army members. About 6% of the population claim to be nonbelievers or to have no religious affiliation.

There is no state religion. However, the preamble to the constitution recognizes the religious history of the country by asserting that the nation "shall be founded upon principles which acknowledge the supremacy of God." Spirituality is a required topic in public schools as part of the social studies curriculum. All schools, both public and private, are required to provide 220 minutes per week of religious education or chapel services for students in kindergarten to sixth grade. However, students are not forced to participate in such instruction. The faith of the individual student, or their parents, is generally respected.

11 ■ Transportation

In 2002, Belize had 2,880 kilometers (1,789 miles) of roads, of which 490 kilometers (304 miles) were paved. In 2000, there were 8,500 registered motor vehicles, 3,400 of which were passenger cars. The country had no railways. In 2002, Belize's merchant marine was comprised of 315 ships, totaling 1,240,551 GRT. Several shipping lines provide regular services to North America, the Caribbean, and Europe. Belize City is the main port. In 2001, airports totaled 44, only four of which had paved runways. International airports at Belize City and Punta Gorda handle service to the United States and Central America.

12 ■ History

The area now called Belize was once heavily populated by Maya Indians, whose civilization collapsed around A.D. 900. The first permanent European settlement was established in 1638 by shipwrecked English seamen. Later immigrants included African slaves and British sailors.

England struggled with Spain over possession of the area, with the British winning by the nineteenth century. In 1862, they created the colony of British Honduras. For the next century, forestry was the main

Biographical Profile

Name: Said Musa

Position: Prime Minister of a parliamentary democracy

Took Office: 27 August 1998

Birthplace: San Ignacio, Belize

Birthdate: 19 March 1944

Education: Manchester University, law degree, 1967

Spouse: Joan Pearson

Of interest: Musa made the colony's history accessible to school children in social studies textbooks for the first time

Said Musa

enterprise until eventually replaced by the sugar industry.

After attaining self-government on 1 January 1964, the country adopted Belize as its official name in 1973, although not fully independent yet. The United Kingdom granted Belize independence as of 21 September 1981. Guatemala, which claimed the southern quarter of the area, refused to recognize the new nation and severed diplomatic relations with the United Kingdom. In December 1986, the United Kingdom and Guatemala resumed full diplomatic ties, but an 1,800-member British garrison remained in Belize. The United Kingdom withdrew its troops in 1994.

Tensions with Guatemala over territorial disputes not settled in 1991 continued into early 2000, when Belize's ambassador was expelled from Guatemala. But a hurricane in 2001 hurt both Belize and Guatemala and helped reduce tensions between the two countries.

13 ■ Government

Governmental authority is vested in a governor-general appointed by the UK monarch, a cabinet headed by a prime minister, and a two-chamber National Assembly. The National Assembly consists of a twenty-nine-member House of Representatives elected by universal adult voting, and a Senate of eight members appointed by the governor-general. The voting age is eighteen and parliamentary elections are held at least once every five years. Belize

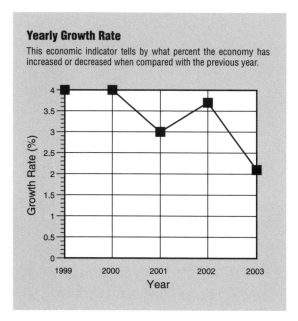

Yearly Growth Rate

This economic indicator tells by what percent the economy has increased or decreased when compared with the previous year.

is divided into six administrative districts. Local government at the village level is through village councils.

14 ■ Political Parties

The two major parties in Belize are the current majority United Democratic Party (UDP) and the People's United Party (PUP). Following the 2003 elections, the PUP held 21 and the UDP had 8 seats in the National Assembly.

15 ■ Judicial System

There is a Supreme Court and a Court of Appeal. Final appeal until 2003 was to the Privy Council of the United Kingdom. Six summary jurisdiction courts (criminal) and six district courts (civil) are presided over by magistrates.

In 2003, Caribbean leaders met in Jamaica to establish the Caribbean Court of Justice (CCJ). Eight nations, including Belize, approved the CCJ.

16 ■ Armed Forces

The Belize Defense Force consisted of 1,050 active personnel in 2002, supported by 700 reserves. The defense budget was $7.7 million in 2000–2001, or 1.9% of the gross domestic product (GDP).

17 ■ Economy

By 1995, tourism had surpassed the sugar industry as the leading source of foreign exchange. The economy also relies on agriculture and fishing. Garment manufacturing has gained in importance in the late 1990s and early 2000s. The country continues to import most of its consumer goods, including much of its food and all of its petroleum requirements. In 1997 and 1998, Belize's gross domestic product (GDP) growth hovered around 3%, but it was forecast at 1.5% for 2003.

18 ■ Income

In 2001 Belize's gross domestic product (GDP) was estimated at $830 million, or $3,250 per person. The annual growth rate of the GDP was estimated at 3%. The average inflation rate in 2001 was 1.7%.

19 ■ Industry

Industrial activities include sugar, citrus, and banana processing, textiles and garments, and fertilizers. Other industries include plywood and veneer manufacturing, matches, beer and other beverages, furniture, boat-building, and batteries.

Construction projects in 2001 included a multimillion-dollar housing project designed to build 10,000 units, a $14.7

Components of the Economy

This pie chart shows how much of the country's economy is devoted to agriculture (includes forestry, hunting, and fishing), industry, or services.

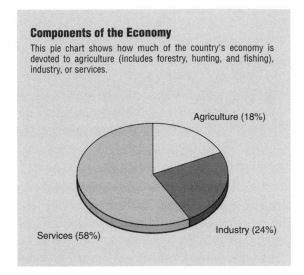

Agriculture (18%)

Industry (24%)

Services (58%)

million project to rehabilitate the country's southern highway, and a $9.5 million project to upgrade health centers and hospitals.

20 ▪ Labor

The labor force is estimated at about 90,000. In 2001, about 27% of the labor force was employed in agriculture, forestry, and fishing, 18% in industry, and 55% in services. Labor legislation covers minimum wages, work hours, employment of young persons, and workers' safety and compensation. Unemployment averaged 11.5% in 2000.

The minimum age for employment is fourteen, except in jobs involving dangerous machinery, where the minimum age is seventeen.

21 ▪ Agriculture

Only 3% of the total land area is used for the production of seasonal and permanent crops. Most Mayans still practice the traditional slash-and-burn method of farm-

ing. More efficient agricultural colonies have been established by Mennonite immigrants. Sugar and citrus are the leading agricultural exports. Sugarcane production totals 1.1 million tons. Rice paddy production totals about 9,000 tons and corn production is about 38,000 tons. Dry bean production is 5,000 tons.

The U.S.-based Hershey Foods Corp. has invested $2 million in cacao cultivation in El Cayo. In 1985, a consortium that included Coca-Cola paid $6 million for 383,000 hectares (946,400 acres) northwest of Belmopan for a citrus farming project. Citrus thus displaced bananas as the country's second most important crop. Citrus production includes 170,000 tons of oranges and 41,000 tons of grapefruit. Banana production is at 78,000 tons. Papaya exports total over 4,535 kilograms (10,000 pounds) monthly, and mango, peanut, pineapple, and winter vegetable exports are also on the rise.

Because agriculture is not sufficiently diversified, the country relies heavily on food imports. Export earnings from sugar in 2001 exceeded $35 million.

22 ▪ Domesticated Animals

Farms established by Mennonites (a religious sect) account for much of Belize's dairy and poultry output. The nation has an estimated 23,000 hogs, 5,000 horses, 4,000 mules, 3,000 sheep, and 1,000,000 chickens. Cattle suited for breeding or crossbreeding with local cattle are Red Poll, Jamaica Black, Hereford, and Brahman (zebu). There are 58,000 head of cattle. Some 8,000 tons of poultry meat and 8,000 tons of milk are produced.

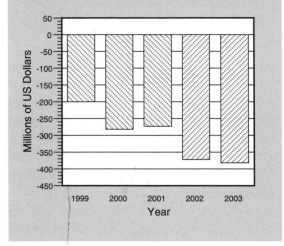

Yearly Balance of Trade

The balance of trade is the difference between what a country sells to other countries (its exports) and what it buys (its imports). If a country imports more than it exports, it has a negative balance of trade (a trade deficit). If exports exceed imports there is a positive balance of trade (a trade surplus).

23 ■ Fishing

In 2000, the total catch was 61,059 tons. Lobster is the leading product. In the mid-1990s, shrimp production increased by 75% as a result of three new shrimp farms opening in 1992. Whiteleg shrimp and spiny lobster are the leading species by volume.

24 ■ Forestry

About 92% of Belize's land area is covered with forests and woodlands. Timber cutting is usually done during the short dry season. Total roundwood production in 2000 was 188,000 cubic meters (6.64 million cubic feet). The principal varieties of trees cut are mahogany, pine, cedar, and rosewood. In 2000, timber exports were valued at $5.6 million.

25 ■ Mining

Clays, limestone, marble, and sand and gravel for construction are the mainstay of Belize's minerals industry. The Belize, Sibun, and Monkey Rivers, as well as North and South Stann Creeks, were the sites of clay, limestone, and sand and gravel operations. Clay production amounted to 2.6 million tons in 2001. Other product totals included 31,000 tons of dolomite, 320,000 tons of limestone, 360,000 tons of sand and gravel, and 6 kilograms (13 pounds) of gold, obtained by stream panning.

26 ■ Foreign Trade

Belize's most important imports are machinery, food, fuels, consumer goods, industrial supplies, and transportation equipment. The country's major exports include sugar, fruits, nuts, clothing, shellfish, wood, and vegetables. Belize's major trade partners are the United States, the United Kingdom, Mexico, and Denmark.

27 ■ Energy and Power

Electric power is supplied by ten diesel-powered generators and is inadequate. Production for 2000 totaled 192 million kilowatt hours. As of 2000, fossil fuels accounted for 58.3% of Belize's power generation, and hydropower 41.7%.

28 ■ Social Development

Workers' compensation covers agricultural workers. A social security system is in effect. Employed persons aged fourteen to sixty-four are eligible to make contributions for old age, disability, survivor, and health benefits. Women are active in all areas of national life, but they face do-

Selected Social Indicators

The statistics below are the most recent estimates available as of 2003. For comparison purposes, data for the United States and averages for low-income countries and high-income countries are also given. About 15% of the world's 6.4 billion people live in high-income countries, while 40% live in low-income countries.

Indicator	Belize	Low-income countries	High-income countries	United States
Per capita gross national income (GNI)*	$4,900	$2,110	$28,480	$36,110
Population growth rate	2.4%	2.1%	0.7%	1.1%
People per square kilometer of land	11	77	31	31
Life expectancy in years: *male*	65	58	75	75
female	70	60	81	80
Number of physicians per 1,000 people	5	1.0	3.0	2.8
Number of pupils per teacher (primary school)	26	40	17	15
Literacy rate (15 years and older)	94.1%	66%	>95%	97%
Television sets per 1,000 people	165	91	735	938
Internet users per 1,000 people	68	10	364	551
Energy consumed per capita (kg of oil equivalent)	411	550	5,366	7,937

* The GNI is the total of all goods and services produced by the residents of a country in a year. The per capita GNI is calculated by dividing a country's GNI by its population and adjusting for relative purchasing power.

n.a. = data not available   > = greater than   < = less than

SOURCES: International Telecommunication Union (ITU). *World Telecommunication Development Report 2003*. Geneva, Switzerland: ITU, 2003; World Bank. *World Development Indicators*. Washington, D.C.: The World Bank, 2004; Central Intelligence Agency. *The World Factbook*. Washington, D.C.: Government Printing Office, 2003.

mestic violence and discrimination in the business sector.

29 ▪ Health

Belize is relatively free of endemic (widespread) diseases. Cardiovascular disease, mental illness, external trauma, and human immunodeficiency virus/acquired immunodeficiency syndrome (HIV/AIDS) are significant public health problems. In 1995, 9,413 malaria cases were diagnosed.

There are eight public hospitals. The Cayo and Belize districts have two hospitals each, and all the remaining districts have one. There are forty health centers and thirty-five rural satellites.

In 1999, the life expectancy was 69 years and the infant mortality rate was 32 per 1,000 live births.

As of 1999, the number of people living with HIV/AIDS was estimated at 2,400, and deaths from AIDS that year were estimated at 170. The government has implemented a strategic program to deal with the AIDS epidemic.

30 ▪ Housing

Housing is inadequate, and the situation has been aggravated by hurricane devastation. The government has put aside small sums for low-cost housing programs. The vast majority of houses are made of wood, while the rest are made of concrete or adobe.

In 2000, it was estimated that nearly 100% of all urban homes had access to safe drinking water. About 71% of city dwellers

Mary A. Dempsey

A view of the Mayan site of Xunantunich.

and 25% of rural areas had access to modern bathrooms.

31 ■ Education

Primary education is free and compulsory for children between the ages of five and fourteen and includes eight grade levels. Secondary education covers four years and consists of either a general course of study or classes at a vocational or trade school. Most schools are church-affiliated but still supported by the government. It is estimated that 97% of primary-school-age children are enrolled in school and approximately 36% of eligible children are in secondary school. The pupil-teacher ratio in primary schools averages 26 to 1.

Belize's first university, the University College of Belize, was opened in 1986. The University of the West Indies maintains a School for Continuing Education (SCE) in Belize. There are also several colleges providing specialized training, such as the Belize Technical College; Belize Teachers' College; Belize College of Agriculture; and the Belize Vocational Training Center. There are also two special schools maintained by the government for children with mental and physical disabilities. Although government statistics claim that the adult illiteracy rate is at 7%, UNESCO estimated that the rate was at 29.7% in 1995 (the most recent year for which statistics were available as of 2004).

32 ▪ Media

Belize is connected by radiotelegraph and telephone with Jamaica, Guatemala, Mexico, and the United States. In 1997, Belize had 31,000 mainline telephones and 3,023 cellular phones in use.

The Belize National Radio Network, a government station in Belize City, transmits in English and Spanish. The first privately owned commercial radio station began broadcasting in 1990. As of 1998 there were one AM and twelve FM radio stations. In 2001, there were eight privately owned television stations and several cable stations. In 1997, there were 133,000 radios and 41,000 television sets in use nationwide. In 2000, two Internet service providers were serving 15,000 subscribers.

There are no daily newspapers. The largest weeklies in 2002 were *Amandala* (*Black Power,* circulation 45,000) and *The Reporter* (6,500), both published in Belize City. *Belize Today,* a monthly publication out of Belmopan, has a circulation of 17,000.

Though Belize's constitution assures freedom of speech and the press, there is a law forbidding citizens from questioning financial statements submitted by public officials. The Supreme Court has also warned journalists that questioning the integrity of the Court or of its members could result in criminal charges.

33 ▪ Tourism and Recreation

Belize is attracting growing numbers of tourists to its Mayan ruins, its barrier reef (the longest in the Western Hemisphere), and its beaches, forests, and wildlife. Tourist arrivals totaled 373,995 in 2000, with most from the Americas. That same year, tourist expenditures totaled $121 million. There were 4,106 hotel rooms and 7,045 beds.

34 ▪ Famous Belizeans

George C. Price (1919–), leader of the PUP, became the country's first premier in 1964. Manuel Esquivel (1940–), leader of the UDP, was prime minister from 1984 to 1998.

35 ▪ Bibliography

Crandell, Rachel. *Hands of the Maya: Villagers at Work and Play.* New York: Henry Holt, 2002.

Hennessy, Huw, ed. *Guatemala, Belize, and the Yucatán.* Maspeth, NY: Langenscheidt, 2000.

Jermyn, Leslie. *Belize.* New York: Marshall Cavendish, 2001.

Morrison, Marion. *Belize.* New York: Children's Press, 1996.

Shields, Charles J. *Belize.* Philadelphia, PA: Mason Crest Publishers, 2003.

Benin

Republic of Benin
République du Bénin

Capital: Porto-Novo.

Flag: Two equal horizontal bands of yellow (top) and red with a vertical green band on the hoist side.

Anthem: *L'Aube Nouvelle (The New Dawn).*

Monetary Unit: The Communauté Financière Africaine franc (CFA Fr), which was originally pegged to the French franc, has been pegged to the euro since January 1999 with a rate of 655.957 CFA francs to 1 euro. The CFA franc has coins of 1, 2, 5, 10, 25, 50, 100, and 500 CFA francs, and notes of 50, 100, 500, 1,000, 5,000, and 10,000 CFA francs. CFA Fr1 = $0.00167 (or $1 = CFA Fr597.577; as of May 2003).

Weights and Measures: The metric system is the legal standard.

Holidays: New Year's Day, 1 January; Anniversary of Mercenary Attack on Cotonou, 16 January; Labor Day, 1 May; Independence Day, 1 August; Armed Forces Day, 26 October; National Day, 30 November; Harvest Day, 31 December. Most religious holidays have been abolished, but Good Friday, Easter Monday, Christmas, 'Id al-Fitr, and Id al-'Adha' remain public holidays.

Time: 1 PM = noon GMT.

1 ▪ Location and Size

The People's Republic of Benin is situated in West Africa on the northern coast of the Gulf of Guinea. It has an area of 112,620 square kilometers (43,483 square miles). Comparatively, Benin is slightly smaller than the state of Pennsylvania. It shares borders with Niger, Nigeria, Togo, and Burkina Faso, with a total land boundary length of 1,989 kilometers (1,233 miles) and a coastline of 121 kilometers (75 miles). The capital city of Benin, Porto-Novo, is located in the southeastern corner of the country.

2 ▪ Topography

The coast of Benin is difficult to reach because of sandbanks. There are no natural harbors, river mouths, or islands. Behind the coastline is a network of lagoons. The Ouémé is the longest river located entirely within the country and is navigable for some 200 kilometers (125 miles) of its total of 459 kilometers (285 miles). Besides the Ouémé, the only other major river in the south is the Kouffo, which flows into Lake Ahémé, the largest lake in the country with an area of 100 square kilometers (39 square miles). Benin's northern rivers,

Geographic Profile

Geographic Features

Size ranking: 99 of 193
Highest elevation: 658 meters (2,159 feet) at Mount Sokbaro
Lowest elevation: Sea level at the Atlantic Ocean

Land Use*

Arable land: 18%
Permanent crops: 2%
Forests: 24%
Other: 56%

Weather**

Average annual precipitation: 134 centimeters (52.7 inches)
Average temperature in January: 27.1°C (80.8°F)
Average temperature in July: 25.2°C (77.4°F)

---

* *Arable Land: Land used for temporary crops, like meadows for mowing or pasture, gardens, and greenhouses.*

Permanent crops: Land cultivated with crops that occupy its use for long periods, such as cocoa, coffee, rubber, fruit and nut orchards, and vineyards.

Forests: Land containing stands of trees.

Other: Any land not specified, including built-on areas, roads, and barren land.

** *The measurements for precipitation and average temperatures were taken at weather stations closest to the country's largest city.*

Precipitation and average temperature can vary significantly within a country, due to factors such as latitude, altitude, coastal proximity, and wind patterns.

---

the Mékrou, Alibori, and Sota, are tributaries of the Niger. They are torrential and broken by rocks.

North of the narrow belt of coastal sand is a region of lateritic clay intersected by a marshy depression between Allada and Abomey that stretches east to the Nigerian frontier. In the north, the Atakora Mountains stretch in a southwesterly direction into Togo. The highest point in the country is Mount Sokbaro at 658 meters (2,159 feet). The lowest point is at sea level (Atlantic Ocean).

3 ■ Climate

Southern Benin's climate is typically equatorial—hot and humid, with a long dry season from December to March, in which a dry desert wind, the *harmattan,* blows in a northeasterly to southwesterly direction. Temperatures range between 22°C (72°F) and 35°C (95°F), averaging 27°C (81°F). Heavy rains fall from March to July.

Northern Benin has only one wet season (May to September, with most rain in August) and a hot dry season in which the *harmattan* blows for three or four months. Temperatures range from a maximum of 40°C (104°F) in January to a minimum of 13°C (56°F) in June.

4 ■ Plants and Animals

Apart from small isolated patches, little true forest remains. The coconut plantations of the coastal strip give way to oil palms and ronier palms growing as far north as Abomey. These are in turn succeeded by savanna woodland, which combines the vegetation of the Guinea forest and the southern Sudan, and then by typical Sudan savanna. Trees include coconut, oil palm, ronier palm, ebony, shea nut, kapok, fromager, and Senegal mahogany. Among the mammals in Benin are the elephant, lion, panther, monkey, and wild pig, as well as many kinds of antelope. Crocodiles and many species of snakes (including python, puff adder, and mamba) are widely distributed. Partridge, guinea fowl, and wild duck, as well as many kinds of tropical birds, are common. Insects include varieties of tsetse fly and other carriers of epidemic diseases.

5 ■ Environment

Benin has two national parks and several game reserves. In addition, the government has set aside 5,900 hectares (14,580 acres) for nurseries to foster reforestation. As of 2000, 6.9% of Benin's natural areas were protected. The main environmental issues facing the people of Benin are desertification (fertile land turning to desert), deforestation, wildlife endangerment, and water pollution. The spread of the desert into agricultural lands in the north is hastened by regular droughts. Benin has also lost 59% of its forests from uncontrolled agricultural practices and fires.

Factors that contribute to the endangerment of the wildlife in Benin are the same as those which threaten the forests. As of 2000, threatened species included 9 of the 188 species of mammals, 1 of 307 bird species, and 2 of the 2,000 plant species. As of 1994, the chimpanzee was extinct.

6 ■ Population

Total population in 2003 was estimated at 6.7 million. A population of 7.7 million is projected for the year 2005. Almost three-fourths of the population are clustered in

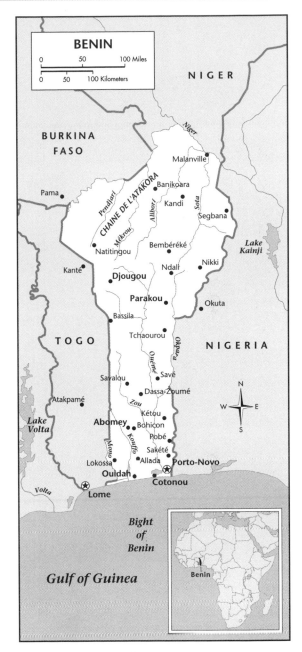

Location: 0°47′°to 3°47′ᴇ; 6°15′ to 12°25′ɴ. **Boundary Lengths:** Niger, 190 kilometers (118 miles); Nigeria, 750 kilometers (466 miles); Atlantic coastline, 125 kilometers (78 miles); Togo, 620 kilometers (385 miles); Burkina Faso, 270 kilometers (168 miles). **Territorial Sea Limit:** 200 miles.

the southern half of the country. An estimated 42% of the population lived in cities in 2002. Porto-Novo, the capital, had a population of about 213,000 in 2001.

7 ■ Migration

Many Beninese migrate to Nigeria and Ghana for seasonal labor. In 1995, there were 70,000 refugees from Togo in Benin. The total number of migrants living in Benin in 2000 was 101,000. The net migration rate for 2000 was -3.2 per 1,000 population, amounting to a loss of approximately 19,000 individuals. The estimated net migration rate in 2003 was zero.

8 ■ Ethnic Groups

The population of Benin (where residents are called Beninese) is 99% African. However, there are at least forty-two different ethnic groups represented. The largest ethnic group is that of the Fon or Dahomeyans (about 25%), the closely related Adja (about 6%), and the Aizo (about 5%), who live in the south of the country and are predominantly farmers. The Goun (about 11%), who are related to the Adja, are concentrated around Porto-Novo. The Bariba (about 12%) are the dominant people in northern Benin. The Yoruba (more than 12%), essentially a farming people, came from Nigeria and are settled along the eastern boundary of the country. In the northeast, the Somba (more than 4%) subdivide into a number of distinct groups. The Fulani (about 6%), traditionally nomadic herders, gradually are becoming settled. Other African groups include the Holli, the Dendi, and the Pilapila (or Yowa). The remaining 1% of the population is largely European, numbering about 5,500.

9 ■ Languages

The official language is French. However, many African languages are spoken. Fon and Yoruba are the most important in southern Benin. In the north there are at least six major tribal languages, including Bariba (a subgroup of the Voltaic group) and Fulani.

10 ■ Religions

An estimated 60% of the population follow traditional African religions. Even some who identify themselves as Christian or Muslim are likely to observe some traditional indigenous customs as well. The most common indigenous religion is Vodoun. Vodoun spread to the Americas with slavery and later became a source for African-inspired religions such as Santeria (in the Spanish-speaking Caribbean), voodoo (in Haiti), and Candomble (in Brazil). The Vodoun religion is based on a belief in one supreme being who rules over a number of lesser dieties, spirits, and saints.

About 30% of the population are Christian, with a majority belonging to the Roman Catholic Church. Other groups include Methodists, Baptists, Assemblies of God, Jehovah's Witnesses, the Church of Jesus Christ of the Latter-day Saints, Celestial Christians, Seventh-day Adventists, Rosicrucians, the Unification Church, Eckankas, and the Baha'i faith. About 20% of the population are Sunni Muslim. Certain Christian and Muslim holidays are officially observed, along with one traditional indigenous holiday.

11 ▪ Transportation

In 2002, Benin had 578 kilometers (359 miles) of meter-gauge railroad. Of Benin's 6,787 kilometers (4,217 miles) of roads, only about 1,357 kilometers (843 miles) are tarred. In 2000, Benin had about 103,400 passenger cars and 96,600 commercial vehicles.

Cotonou is Benin's one deepwater port, capable of handling 3 million tons of cargo annually. There is an international airport at Cotonou and another major airport at Parakou. In 2001, domestic and international flights carried 46,400 passengers .

12 ▪ History

The modern borders of Benin (formerly called Dahomey) were determined by England and France in the late-nineteenth-century partition of Africa. The Portuguese, the first Europeans to establish trading posts on the West African coast, founded the trading post of Porto-Novo on what is now the Benin coast. They were followed by English, Dutch, Spanish, and French traders as the slave trade developed. In the mid-nineteenth century, the slave trade was gradually replaced by trade in palm oil. Rivalry between England and France in Porto-Novo, in which a series of local kings took different sides, eventually ended with a French protectorate being established in 1882.

From 1892 to 1898, the territory took its modern shape with the exploration and extension of French control in the north. The construction of the railroad to the north was begun in 1900. Dahomey became a colony of the federation of French West Africa in 1904. The French ruled the country until 1

Cory Langley

A woman in Benin carries wood on her head through a local market.

August 1960, when Dahomey proclaimed its independence.

After independence, the country suffered from extreme political instability, with military coups in 1963, 1965 (twice), 1967, 1969, and 1972. The coup on 26 October 1972 established Major Mathieu Kérékou as the leader of a military regime. It represented a clear break with all earlier Dahomeyan governments, introducing revolutionary changes in the political and economic life of the country. In late 1974, Kérékou said that the national revolution would follow a Marxist-Leninist course, and the state took over many industries. On 1 December 1975, the

AP/Wide World Photos

A rural youth club leader encourages the children to salvage even the smallest amount of cotton clinging to the stalks. Frugality is important in a country where the population must depend on the land for its living.

country's name was changed to the People's Republic of Benin.

In 1980, Kérékou made an official visit to Libya. During the visit, he converted to the Islamic faith in the presence of the Libyan leader, Colonel Mu'ammar al-Qadhafi and took the first name Ahmed. The two countries then signed a major bilateral cooperation agreement.

Through the years, hundreds of government opponents have been imprisoned, often without trial. Opposition came mostly from the banned Communist Party (Parti Communiste du Dahomey; PCT) and stu-

dent protesters. However, in 1989, Kérékou announced that the country would no longer follow a Marxist-Leninist philosophy. Democratic reforms were instituted and on 2 December 1990, a new constitution was adopted by popular referendum. The country's name was changed from People's Republic of Benin to Republic of Benin. Benin's first free elections in thirty years, for both president and parliament, were held on 10 March 1991. Kérékou lost the presidential election to his opponent Nicephore Soglo. However, no one party was able to gain control of the National Assembly. A working coalition was formed to run the government. In September 1996, Soglo was narrowly defeated in a runoff presidential election by his old rival Kérékou (who was once again reelected in March 2001).

Despite deteriorating security in both urban and rural areas, Benin made significant political progress in the 1990s. It established an independent electoral commission, a Constitutional Court and a High Court of Justice, and kept the armed forces under government control.

In May 2002, Niger and Benin submitted a boundary dispute to the International Court of Justice in the Hague. At issue were sectors of the Niger and Mékrou Rivers and islands in them.

In December 2002 elections, 3 million people went to the polls in Benin to elect mayors and municipal councilors, who were previously appointed by the government. They were the first municipal and communal elections since the end of one-party rule in 1990.

13 ■ Government

The 1990 constitution led to multiparty elections. The president is elected by pop-

Biographical Profile

Name: Mathieu Kérékou
Position: President of a republic under multiparty democratic rule
Took Office: 4 April 1996
Birthplace: Koufra, Natitingou, Benin
Birthdate: 2 September 1933
Religion: Islam (converted in 1980)
Education: Officers School, Frejus, France
Of interest: Kérékou served in the French Army until 1961

Mathieu Kérékou

ular vote for a five-year term. A directly elected National Assembly of eighty-three members has a maximum term of four years.

The country is divided into twelve provinces, which are in turn divided into districts. There are elected provincial, district, commune, town, and village councils.

14 ■ Political Parties

Benin's partisan politics (firm adherence to a particular party) are characterized by frequent splits and mergers. As of 1996, there were more than eighty recognized political parties. Party allegiances in the National Assembly are constantly changing. The 1999 multiparty general elections produced a 70% turnover in the National

Assembly, with opposition candidates winning a slim majority to hold forty-two of eighty-three seats, while forty-one seats were held by supporters of Kérékou.

15 ■ Judicial System

Each district has a court with the power to try cases, and each province has a court to handle appeals. At the lowest level, each commune, village, and city ward has its own court. The highest court is the Supreme Court. A Constitutional Court is responsible for reviewing the constitutionality of laws and for deciding disputes between the president and National Assembly. Under the 1990 constitution, people who are arrested must be brought

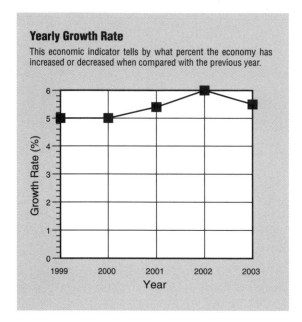

Yearly Growth Rate

This economic indicator tells by what percent the economy has increased or decreased when compared with the previous year.

for some 36% of the gross domestic product (GDP) in 2001. About 90% of this output is produced on family farms using little modern technology. They mainly produce domestically consumed crops such as maize, sorghum, millet, paddy rice, cassava, yams, and beans. Benin is self-sufficient in food. Cotton, palm oil, and groundnuts are grown and exchanged for cash.

Livestock, forestry, and fishing make up another 10% of the GDP. Not enough wood is produced to meet the national demand for fuel. The fishing sector is in decline due to overfishing.

Benin's mineral resources are limited. Limestone, marble, and petroleum reserves are exploited commercially. Gold is produced only by independent prospectors.

In the early 2000s, rapid population growth, inefficient state-owned enterprises, and high civil service salaries continued to offset economic growth. Corruption remains a major obstacle to economic development.

before a magistrate (judge) within forty-eight hours.

16 ■ Armed Forces

In 2002, the armed forces had 4,550 personnel. The army of 4,300 included 3 infantry battalions. There were 150 personnel in the air force, which had 1 attack helicopter and 14 support helos and aircraft. There was a navy of 100 personnel and 1 patrol boat. A paramilitary police force totaled 2,500.

17 ■ Economy

Benin's economy is recovering from the economic problems that led to the collapse of the socialist government in power between 1974 and 1989. Companies that were state-owned are being returned to private ownership.

Agriculture is the most important sector in the Benin economy, accounting

18 ■ Income

In 2001, Benin's gross domestic product (GDP) was $6.8 billion, or $1,040 per person. The annual growth rate of the GDP was estimated at 5.4%. The average annual inflation rate was 3%.

19 ■ Industry

Benin's industrial sector, which accounted for about 14% of the gross domestic product in 2001, centers primarily on construction materials and the processing of agricultural products. Benin's industrial electricity needs are met by hydroelectric power from the Akosombo Dam in Ghana and the Nangbeto Dam on the Mono River.

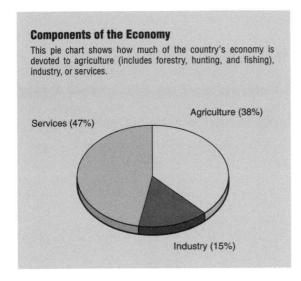

Components of the Economy

This pie chart shows how much of the country's economy is devoted to agriculture (includes forestry, hunting, and fishing), industry, or services.

Services (47%)

Agriculture (38%)

Industry (15%)

Benin is one of the countries involved in the planned $500 million, 620-kilometer (385-mile) West African natural gas pipeline to run from Nigeria to Côte d'Ivoire. Gas delivery from the pipeline was expected to begin in 2005.

Sonapra is the state-owned cotton enterprise, and revenues from the cotton sector of the economy are large. There are no plans to privatize Sonapra. The state-owned oil company, Sonacop, was privatized in 1999. Cement, textile, tobacco, breweries, and public transportation enterprises have been privatized (turned over from public to private ownership) in recent years.

20 ▮ Labor

Benin had a labor force of around 2 million people in 2000; slightly more than half were engaged in agriculture. Less than 2% of the labor force was salaried. As of 2002, around 75% of wage earners were unionized, but the percentage is much smaller in the private sector. The minimum wage was $34 per month in 2000, but was only enough to provide minimal food and shelter for a family. The Labor Code of Benin prohibits child labor (under the age of fourteen) in any form, but the code is not well enforced. An estimated 75% of apprentices working as seamstresses, hairdressers, carpenters, and mechanics were under the legal employment age in 2000.

21 ▮ Agriculture

Benin is predominantly an agricultural country. In 2000, about 55% of workers were employed in the agricultural sector, which accounted for 38% of the gross domestic product that year. Small, independent farmers produce 90% of agricultural output, but only about 17% of the total area is cultivated. Agricultural development has been hindered by a lack of transportation, poor utilization of credit, and inefficient and insufficient use of fertilizer, insecticides, and seeds.

The main food crops are manioc, yams, corn, sorghum, beans, rice, sweet potatoes, pawpaws, guavas, bananas, and coconuts. Annual production estimates are 1.77 million tons of yams, 2.37 million tons of manioc, 823,000 tons of corn, 154,000 tons of sorghum, 36,000 tons of rice, 94,000 tons of dry beans, 67,000 tons of sweet potatoes, and 34,000 tons of millet. Benin generally produces all the food crops it needs to feed its people.

Cotton production has increased in importance. Total cotton yield is about 175,000 tons. Peanut production has also recently become important, with about 121,000 tons of shelled groundnuts produced annually. Palm oil production is 10,000 tons and palm kernel output is 14,000 tons. Other annual crop production includes 10,000 tons of

Yearly Balance of Trade

The balance of trade is the difference between what a country sells to other countries (its exports) and what it buys (its imports). If a country imports more than it exports, it has a negative balance of trade (a trade deficit). If exports exceed imports there is a positive balance of trade (a trade surplus).

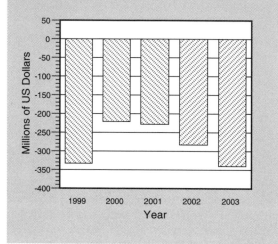

cashews, 13,000 tons of bananas, 12,000 tons of mangoes, and 20,000 tons of coconuts.

22 ▧ Domesticated Animals

There are an estimated 1.3 million head of cattle, 634,000 sheep, 1 million goats, 470,000 hogs, and 29 million chickens. Most of Benin's cattle are in the north, but there is also a small hardy type in the lagoon area. Horses are rare because of the ravages of trypanosomiasis (sleeping sickness). Poultry are mainly confined to the south of the country.

Estimated annual output of livestock products includes 23,000 tons of beef and veal, 6,000 tons of sheep and goat meat, and 6,000 tons of pork.

23 ▧ Fishing

Ocean fishing, which had been carried on largely by fishermen from Ghana, is gaining importance at Cotonou and other coastal centers. In 2000, exports of fish commodities amounted to nearly $2.6 million. Lagoon and river fishing remain of primary importance. Out of an estimated catch of 32,324 tons in 2000, about 26,400 tons were from inland waters.

24 ▧ Forestry

There are about 3.4 million hectares (nearly 8.4 million acres) classified as forest and woodland, accounting for about 31% of the total land area. Most forests are in northern Benin and their use is subject to public control. Timber production is small. Firewood, charcoal, and building wood for local use are the most important forest products. In 2000, an estimated 6.2 million cubic meters (218 million cubic feet) of roundwood were produced.

25 ▧ Mining

With the exception of oil, Benin is relatively poor in mineral resources. Sedimentary phosphate deposits have been located along the Mekrou River in the north. There is low-grade iron ore at Loumbou-Loumbou and Madekali. Limestone is quarried for use in cement plants. There is potential for small-scale gold mining in the Atacora gold zone, in the northwest. Other mineral resources included chromium, rutile, and diamonds; small quantities of industrial diamonds are exported. In 2000, the country produced 450,000 tons of hydraulic cement and 500 kilograms (1,102 pounds) of gold.

Selected Social Indicators

The statistics below are the most recent estimates available as of 2003. For comparison purposes, data for the United States and averages for low-income countries and high-income countries are also given. About 15% of the world's 6.4 billion people live in high-income countries, while 40% live in low-income countries.

Indicator	Benin	Low-income countries	High-income countries	United States
Per capita gross national income (GNI)*	$1,060	$2,110	$28,480	$36,110
Population growth rate	2.9%	2.1%	0.7%	1.1%
People per square kilometer of land	59	77	31	31
Life expectancy in years: *male*	51	58	75	75
female	55	60	81	80
Number of physicians per 1,000 people	0.1	1.0	3.0	2.8
Number of pupils per teacher (primary school)	53	40	17	15
Literacy rate (15 years and older)	40.9%	66%	>95%	97%
Television sets per 1,000 people	12	91	735	938
Internet users per 1,000 people	7	10	364	551
Energy consumed per capita (kg of oil equivalent)	377	550	5,366	7,937

* The GNI is the total of all goods and services produced by the residents of a country in a year. The per capita GNI is calculated by dividing a country's GNI by its population and adjusting for relative purchasing power.

n.a. = data not available   > = greater than   < = less than

SOURCES: International Telecommunication Union (ITU). *World Telecommunication Development Report 2003.* Geneva, Switzerland: ITU, 2003; World Bank. *World Development Indicators.* Washington, D.C.: The World Bank, 2004; Central Intelligence Agency. *The World Factbook.* Washington, D.C.: Government Printing Office, 2003.

26 ▪ Foreign Trade

Benin consistently runs a trade deficit. The leading exports are cotton, uranium and thorium ores, cottonseeds, and cigarettes. Leading imports are foodstuffs, petroleum products, beverages, tobacco, capital goods, and light consumer products. Brazil, India, and Indonesia are the leading export markets. Benin's imports come mainly from France, the United States, China, and Côte d'Ivoire.

27 ▪ Energy and Power

Production from the Sémé offshore oil field was begun in October 1982 by Saga Petroleum, a Norwegian firm working under a service contract. Oil reserves are estimated at 44 million barrels, but there is currently no refinery in Benin.

Installed electrical capacity in 2001 was an estimated 94,000 kilowatts. Total domestic power output in 2000 was 240 million kilowatt hours, of which hydropower accounted for 83.3% and fossil fuels for the rest.

28 ▪ Social Development

A social insurance system provides benefits to employed persons as well as pensions for old age, disability, and survivorship. Maternity benefits, worker's compensation, and family allowances are also offered. Because most people are self-employed or work in agriculture, they do not enjoy these benefits, however. Female circumcision is still legal and is practiced in Benin.

29 ▪ Health

Most serious epidemic diseases have been brought under control by mobile health units and other facilities. Estimated average life expectancy in 2000 was 53 years. The infant mortality rate in 1999 was 98 per 1,000 live births.

At the end of 2001, the number of people living with human immunodeficiency virus/acquired immunodeficiency syndrome (HIV/AIDS) was estimated at 120,000 (including 3.6% of the adult population).

30 ▪ Housing

In rural areas, the typical dwelling of northern Benin is a round hut of beaten mud with a cone-shaped thatch roof. In southern Benin, rectangular huts with sloping roofs of palm or straw thatch are more usual. Along the coastal lagoons, houses are often built on stilts.

The government has helped improve the overall appearance and sanitation facilities in towns and villages. Low-cost housing projects have been developed. Many residents have been looking to build more modern "Western-style" homes. However, most construction materials for such a structure need to be imported, making materials (and labor) too expensive for many residents to consider this an option.

31 ▪ Education

Since 1975, all education has been free, public, secular, and compulsory from ages six to eleven. Six years of primary education are followed by six years at a general, vocational, or technical secondary school. The pupil-teacher ratio for primary education averages 53 to 1.

AP/Wide World Photos

This mother and her sons have access to safe clean water from a well. Families like hers in Benin's arid north know frequent shortages of water.

The National University of Benin at Cotonou, founded in 1970, offers courses in agriculture, medicine, liberal arts, science, law, economics, and politics. The adult illiteracy rate for 2000 was estimated at 60% (44% for males and 73% for females).

32 ▪ Media

Virtually all media in Benin are controlled by the government. The state provides telegraph and telephone service. Government-owned radio and television services broadcast in French, English, and eighteen indigenous languages. In 2000, there were

51,000 mainline phones and 55,500 mobile cellular phones.

As of 2000, there were two AM and nine FM radio stations. In 2001, there was only one television station. In 2000, there were 439 radios for every 1,000 people. In 2003, there were 12 television sets for every 1,000 people. There were only two personal computers in use for every 1,000 people. In 2002, there were four Internet service providers serving about 50,000 users.

In 2002, there was only one daily newspaper. *Ehuzu* (also known as *La Nation*) is the primary government publication, with a daily circulation of about 12,000. Weeklies included *La Gazette du Golfe* (circulation 18,000) and *Le Forum de la Semaine*. Other publications included *L'Opinion* and *Tam-Tam Express* (8,000, every other week). All were published in Cotonou. There are also several general interest and a few special interest periodicals.

The constitution of Benin ensures freedom of expression, speech, and the press, and the government is said to respect this freedom.

33 ◼ Tourism and Recreation

Tourist attractions include the lake village of Ganvie, two game parks in the north, the ancient royal city of Abomey, several museums, and beaches. Hunting lodges have been built to promote safaris in the two national parks, where strong efforts have also been made to preserve wild game. In the south are picturesque villages built on stilts over the waters of the coastal lagoons. Benin had 575,000 visitors in 1998.

34 ◼ Famous Beninese

Perhaps the most famous historical ruler in the area now known as Benin was Béhanzin (d.1906), who was king from 1889 until he was defeated by the French in 1894.

35 ◼ Bibliography

Caulfield, Annie. *Show Me the Magic: Travels Round Benin by Taxi.* London: Penguin, 2003.

Decalo, Samuel. *Historical Dictionary of Benin.* Lanham, MD: Scarecrow Press, 1995.

Edgerton, Robert B. *Women Warriors: The Amazons of Dahomey and the Nature of War.* Boulder, CO: Westview, 2000.

Koslow, Philip. *Dahomey.* New York: Chelsea House, 1997.

Malaquais, Dominique. *The Kingdom of Benin.* New York: Franklin Watts, 1998.

Rich, Susan, Margot Volem, and Cynthia A. Black. *Africa South of the Sahara.* Austin, TX: Raintree Steck-Vaughn, 2000.

Sheehan, Sean. *Great African Kingdoms.* Austin, TX: Raintree Steck-Vaughn, 1999.

Bhutan

Kingdom of Bhutan
Druk-Yul

Capital: Thimphu (Tashi Chho Dzong).

Flag: The flag is divided diagonally into an orange-yellow field above and a crimson field below. In the center is a wingless white Chinese dragon.

Anthem: *Gyelpo Tenjur,* beginning "In the Thunder Dragon Kingdom, adorned with sandalwood."

Monetary Unit: The ngultrum (N) is a paper currency of 100 chetrum. There are coins of 5, 10, 25, and 50 chetrum and 1 ngultrum, and notes of 1, 5, 10, and 100 ngultrum. The ngultrum is at par with the Indian rupee (R), which also circulates freely. N1 = $0.0213 (or $1 = N46.97; as of May 2003).

Weights and Measures: The metric system is the legal standard, but some traditional units are still in common use.

Holidays: King's Birthday, 11–13 November; National Day, 17 December. Movable Buddhist holidays and festivals are observed.

Time: 5:30 PM = noon GMT.

1 ▨ Location and Size

Bhutan is a landlocked country in South Asia located on the Himalaya mountain range. It has an area of 47,000 square kilometers (18,147 square miles), slightly more than half the size of the state of Indiana, with a total boundary length of 1,075 kilometers (668 miles). It shares borders with India and China. The capital city, Thimphu, is located in the west central part of the country.

2 ▨ Topography

Bhutan is a mountainous country of extremely high altitudes and uneven terrain. Elevation generally increases from south to north. The mountains are a series of parallel north-south ranges. The highest peak is Kula Gangri at a height of 7,553 meters (24,783 feet). Bhutan has many rivers, including the Lhobrak, the Bumtang, the Drangme, the Tongsa, the Sankosh, and the Wong. Most of these empty into the Brahmaputra River in India. The lowest point in the country is on the Drangme Chhu at 97 meters (318 feet). The Tongsa is the longest river, with a distance of 350 kilometers (220 miles).

3 ▨ Climate

Rainfall is moderate in the central valleys, while the higher elevations are relatively

Geographic Profile

Geographic Features

Size ranking: 128 of 193
Highest elevation: 7,553 meters (24,783 feet) at Kula Gangri
Lowest elevation: 97 meters (318 feet) at Drangme Chhu

Land Use*

Arable land: 2%
Permanent crops: 0%
Forests: 66%
Other: 32%

Weather**

Average annual precipitation: 150–300 centimeters (60–120 inches)
Average temperature in January: 4°C (39°F)
Average temperature in July: 17°C (63°F)

* Arable Land: Land used for temporary crops, like meadows for mowing or pasture, gardens, and greenhouses.

Permanent crops: Land cultivated with crops that occupy its use for long periods, such as cocoa, coffee, rubber, fruit and nut orchards, and vineyards.

Forests: Land containing stands of trees.

Other: Any land not specified, including built-on areas, roads, and barren land.

** The measurements for precipitation and average temperatures were taken at weather stations closest to the country's largest city.

Precipitation and average temperature can vary significantly within a country, due to factors such as latitude, altitude, coastal proximity, and wind patterns.

dry. In general, the mountainous areas are cold most of the year. Temperatures in the mountains average 4°C (39°F) in January and 17°C (63°F) in July.

4 ■ Plants and Animals

Dense forest growth is characteristic at altitudes below 1,500 meters (5,000 feet). Above that height the mountain slopes are covered with forest, including beech, ash, birch, maple, cypress, and yew. At 2,400 to 2,700 meters (8,000 to 9,000 feet) are forests of oak and rhododendron. Above this level, firs and pines grow to the timber line. Primulas, poppies (including the rare blue variety), magnolias, and orchids abound.

The relative abundance of wild animals is attributed to the Buddhist reluctance to take life. In the lower parts of southern Bhutan, mammals include the cheetah, goral, sambar, bear, and rhinoceros; in the higher regions are snow deer, musk deer, and barking deer. Game birds include pheasants, partridges, pigeons, and quail.

5 ■ Environment

The most significant environmental problems in Bhutan are soil erosion and water pollution. The erosion of the soil occurs because 50% of the land in Bhutan is situated on mountainous slopes that are subject to landslides during the monsoon season. Other contributing factors are overcutting of timber, road construction, and the building of irrigation channels.

The Manas Game Sanctuary is located along the banks of the Manas River in southeastern Bhutan. Altogether, 21.2% of Bhutan's total land area was protected as of 2001. In the same year, there were twenty species of endangered mammals including the tiger, snow leopard, Asian elephant, and wild yak, and fourteen bird species were threatened with extinction, as well as five threatened species of plants and one endangered reptile.

6 ■ Population

The population of Bhutan was estimated by the United Nations at 2.3 million in 2003. The projected population for the year 2015 is 3.0 million. The capital, Thimphu, had an estimated population of 28,000 in 2001.

7 ■ Migration

Bhutan opposes immigration and forbids the entry of new settlers from Nepal. Since 1959, when about 4,000 Tibetan refugees entered Bhutan, the border with Tibet has been closed to immigration. By 1980, most of the refugees had become citizens of Bhutan, while the rest migrated to India. The border between Bhutan and India is open and citizens of Bhutan are free to live and work in India. In 2000, there were 10,000 migrants residing in Bhutan. The estimated net migration rate for 2003 was zero.

Cross-border attacks between Bhutan and Nepal through a narrow corridor of India have forced thousands of ethnic Nepalese-both illegal immigrants and Bhutanese citizens-to migrate in recent years. The fate of more than 100,000 of these refugees remained the subject of negotiations between Bhutan and Nepal as of 2003.

8 ■ Ethnic Groups

The Bhutanese people (also called the Bhote) are mainly of Tibetan ancestry

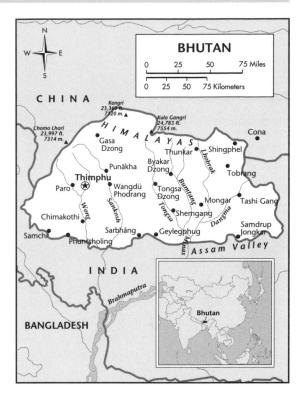

Location: 26°42′ to 28°21′N; 88°45′ to 92°8′E.
Boundary Lengths: India, 605 kilometers (378 miles); China, 470 kilometers (290 miles).

and account for approximately 50% of the population. They include the Sharchop, who inhabit the eastern regions and also have ethnic affinities with the people of China's Tibetan region. Aboriginal or indigenous tribal peoples live in villages scattered throughout Bhutan and account for approximately 15% of the population. The remaining peoples are Nepalese settlers (about 35% of the population), living mostly in the south.

9 ■ Languages

Four main languages are spoken in Bhutan. The official language is Dzongkha, a Tibetan dialect spoken mainly by the

Ngalop in the northern and western parts of the country. Bumthangkha, an aboriginal language, is spoken in central Bhutan, while Sharchopkha is spoken in eastern Bhutan. Both of these are used in primary schools in areas where their speakers predominate. The Nepalese largely retain their own language, Nepali.

10 ▪ Religions

About 75% of the Bhutanese practice Buddhism. While the law provides for religious freedom, the Drukpa sect of the Kagyupa School, a branch of Mahayana Buddhism, is the state religion and the law prohibits religious conversions to other faiths. The Drukpa (people of the dragon) came from Tibet in the twelfth century and now dominate the collective life of the Bhutanese through a large clerical body estimated at more than 6,000 lamas, or monks, centered in 8 major monasteries (*dzongs*) and 200 smaller shrines (*gompas*). This sect incorporates both the ideology of the classical Buddhist scriptures and the indigenous pre-Buddhist animistic (spirit worship) beliefs called Bon.

There are a few Hindu congregations and small numbers of Christians.

11 ▪ Transportation

Before the 1961–66 development plan, there were no surfaced roads in Bhutan. In 2002, there were about 3,285 kilometers (2,041 miles) of roads, including about 1,994 kilometers (1,239 miles) of surfaced roads. The national air carrier, Druk Airlines, began operations in 1983 with regular flights between Calcutta, India, and Bhutan's main airfield at Paro. In 2001,

scheduled domestic and international flights carried 35,100 passengers.

12 ▪ History

The ancestors of the Bhotes (or Bhotias) came from Tibet, probably in the ninth century. In the fifteenth century, Shabdung Ngawang Nangyal, a Tibetan lama (religious leader), united the country and built most of the fortified villages (*dzongs*). During the eighteenth and nineteenth centuries, British efforts to trade with Bhutan proved unsuccessful. In 1910, British India agreed explicitly not to interfere in Bhutanese internal affairs, while Bhutan accepted British "guidance" in handling foreign matters. After 1947, India took over this role.

In the 1960s, India helped Bhutan prepare economic plans to modernize the country and end its isolation. Relations with Nepal have grown difficult in recent years because of tensions surrounding ethnic Nepalese living in Bhutan.

Reforms introduced by King Jigme Singye Wangchuck in June 1998 marked a milestone in Bhutan's political and constitutional history. Bhutan in June 1999 took major steps toward modernization, legalizing television and the Internet. The first Internet cafe opened in 2000.

There are tensions between Bhutan and India's northeastern state of Assam. Two separatist groups from Assam maintain well-established bases in Bhutan. Bhutan was reluctant to take direct action against the Indian separatists for fear of attacks on its citizens, but in December 2002, Bhutan's government announced it would use military might to remove the separatists from bases within its borders.

Biographical Profile

Name: Jigme Singye Wangchuck
Position: King of a monarchy
Took Office: 24 July 1972 (following the death of his father)
Birthplace: 11 November 1955
Education: Ugyen Wangchuk Academy, Bhutan
Spouse: Four wives, all sisters
Children: Four sons, four daughters
Of interest: Wangchuck rarely travels outside of Bhutan

Jigme Singye Wangchuck

On 3 December 2002, the King of Bhutan issued a first draft of a constitution for his country.

13 ▪ Government

Bhutan has functioned as a limited monarchy since 1969. The king, who is chief of state and head of government, may be removed at any time by a two-thirds vote of the National Assembly. Following political reforms in 1998, the Royal Advisory Council and a Council of Ministers were combined to form a cabinet. The National Assembly, known as the Tsongdu, consists of 154 members. It meets twice a year at Thimphu, the capital. The country is divided into 4 regions, 20 districts (*dzongkhas*), and 202 blocks, or *gewog*.

14 ▪ Political Parties

Political parties are illegal in Bhutan. Opposition groups, composed mainly of ethnic Nepalese, include the Bhutan State Congress (BSC), the People's Forum for Democratic Rights, and the Bhutan People's Party (BPP), a militant group.

15 ▪ Judicial System

Local headmen and magistrates (*thrimpon*) hear original cases. Appeals may be made to a six-member High Court. From here, a final appeal may be made to the king.

There is no written constitution, although a draft for one was submitted in December 2002.

16 ■ Armed Forces

India is responsible for Bhutan's defense. The army and palace guard consist of about 4,000 lightly armed soldiers.

17 ■ Economy

Isolated Bhutan has one of the smallest economies in the world. Farming or herding supports 90% of the labor force, who produce 45% of the gross domestic product (GDP). The country supplies most of its food needs through the production of grains, fruits, some meat, and yak butter. Tourism is becoming important, however. In 2002, there were about 7,000 visitors to Bhutan. The overall GDP growth rate for 1988 to 1998 averaged an annual 6.1%. It dropped in 1999, but was estimated at 7.7% in 2002.

18 ■ Income

Bhutan's gross domestic product (GDP) was estimated at $2.5 billion in 2001, or $1,200 per person. The annual growth rate of GDP was estimated at 6%. The average inflation rate in 2000 was 7%.

19 ■ Industry

Manufacturing as a share of gross domestic product (GDP) rose from 3.2% in 1980 to 8.2% in 1990, followed by 12% in 1998 and an estimated 20% in 2001.

Crafts are the principal industrial occupation. Homespun textiles-woven and embroidered cottons, wools, and silks-are the most important products. Other Bhutanese handicrafts include daphne paper; swords; wooden bowls; leather objects; copper, iron, brass, bronze, and silverwork; wood carvings; and split-cane basketry. Also produced in Bhutan are cement, carbide, and

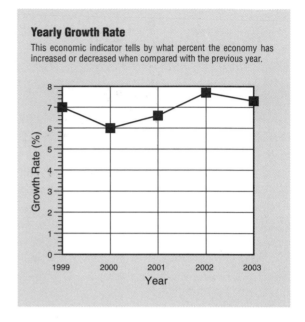

Yearly Growth Rate

This economic indicator tells by what percent the economy has increased or decreased when compared with the previous year.

particleboard. A large number of sawmills operate throughout the country. Hydroelectric power is an increasingly important sector of the economy.

20 ■ Labor

About 93% of all workers are farmers and herders. There is a severe shortage of skilled labor, and no health and safety standards. Most salaried workers are employed by the government. In 2002, Bhutan had a government-set minimum wage of approximately $2.50 per day, which provides a decent standard of living for a family.

The minimum work age is eighteen years for citizens (twenty years for noncitizens) although children as young as eleven are employed. Trade unions are illegal, and workers do not have the right to strike.

©Cynthia Bassett/EPD Photos

Children accompany their mothers to open-air vegetable market.

21 ▦ Agriculture

Only about 3.4% of the land area is used for seasonal and permanent crop production. In 2002, agriculture contributed about 45% to gross domestic product (GDP) and employed 93% of workers. Bhutan's near self-sufficiency in food permitted quantities of some crops to be exported to India in exchange for cereals. Since there is little level space available for cultivation, fields are generally terraced. Stone aqueducts carry irrigation water. The low-lying areas raise a surplus of rice. Output of paddy rice is estimated at 50,000 tons. Other crops include wheat, maize, millet, buckwheat, barley, potatoes, sugarcane, cardamom, walnuts, and oranges. Part of the crop yield is used in making beer and chong, a potent liquor distilled from rice, barley, and millet. Paper is made from the daphne plant, which grows wild. Walnuts, citrus fruits, apples, and apricots are grown in government orchards.

22 ▦ Domesticated Animals

Yaks, cattle, and some sheep graze in the lowland forests and, during the summer, in the uplands and high valleys. There are an estimated 435,000 head of cattle, 75,000 hogs, 59,000 sheep, and 42,000 goats. Draft animals include 30,000 horses, 18,000

Components of the Economy

This pie chart shows how much of the country's economy is devoted to agriculture (includes forestry, hunting, and fishing), industry, or services.

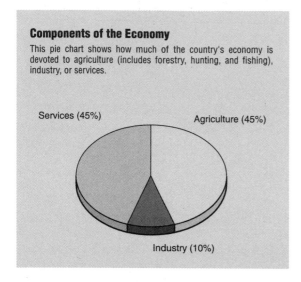

Services (45%) Agriculture (45%)

Industry (10%)

Yearly Balance of Trade

The balance of trade is the difference between what a country sells to other countries (its exports) and what it buys (its imports). If a country imports more than it exports, it has a negative balance of trade (a trade deficit). If exports exceed imports there is a positive balance of trade (a trade surplus).

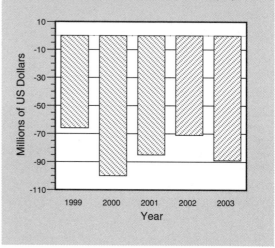

donkeys, and 10,000 mules. Meat production is estimated at 8,000 tons, of which about 75% is beef. Wool has been in short supply since its importation from Tibet was stopped by the government in 1960. About a ton of animal hides is produced annually.

23 ■ Fishing

The government has established a hatchery and started a program of stocking Bhutan's rivers and lakes with brown trout. Freshwater fish are found in most waterways. In 2000, the total catch was 330 tons.

24 ■ Forestry

In 2000, about 64% of Bhutan's land area was covered with forests. Although lack of transportation facilities has hampered forest development, timber has become a major export. Roundwood production in 2000 totaled 4.2 million cubic meters (148

million cubic feet), about 99% of which was used for fuel.

25 ■ Mining

The mineral industry of Bhutan is small and dominated by the production of cement, coal, dolomite, and limestone. Estimated production totals for 2001 were: limestone, 280,000 tons; dolomite, 265,000 tons; cement, 160,000 tons; gypsum, 55,000 tons; quartzite, 53,000 tons; ferrosilicon, 16,000 tons; and talc, 3,800 tons. In 2001, quarried stones included 4,000 square meters (43,055 square feet) of marble and 9,000 square meters (96,875 square feet) of slate. For centuries, silver and iron have been mined in Bhutan for handicrafts. Deposits of beryl, copper, graphite, lead, mica, pyrite, tin, tungsten, and zinc have also been found. A graphite-

Selected Social Indicators

The statistics below are the most recent estimates available as of 2003. For comparison purposes, data for the United States and averages for low-income countries and high-income countries are also given. About 15% of the world's 6.4 billion people live in high-income countries, while 40% live in low-income countries.

Indicator	Bhutan	Low-income countries	High-income countries	United States
Per capita gross national income (GNI)*	$1,300	$2,110	$28,480	$36,110
Population growth rate	2.1%	2.1%	0.7%	1.1%
People per square kilometer of land	18	77	31	31
Life expectancy in years: *male*	54	58	75	75
female	53	60	81	80
Number of physicians per 1,000 people	<1	1.0	3.0	2.8
Number of pupils per teacher (primary school)	31	40	17	15
Literacy rate (15 years and older)	42.2%	66%	>95%	97%
Television sets per 1,000 people	5	91	735	938
Internet users per 1,000 people	1	10	364	551
Energy consumed per capita (kg of oil equivalent)	33	550	5,366	7,937

*   The GNI is the total of all goods and services produced by the residents of a country in a year. The per capita GNI is calculated by dividing a country's GNI by its population and adjusting for relative purchasing power.

n.a. = data not available   > = greater than   < = less than

SOURCES: International Telecommunication Union (ITU). *World Telecommunication Development Report 2003*. Geneva, Switzerland: ITU, 2003; World Bank. *World Development Indicators*. Washington, D.C.: The World Bank, 2004; Central Intelligence Agency. *The World Factbook*. Washington, D.C.: Government Printing Office, 2003.

processing plant was established at Paro Dzong.

26 ▪ Foreign Trade

After the 1960 government ban on trade with Tibet, Bhutan came to trade almost exclusively with India. Trade with countries other than India has increased, however, especially with regard to imports. For 2000, the main export destinations were India (94%) and Bangladesh, and the main import sources were India (77%), Japan, the United Kingdom, Germany, and the United States.

Bhutan's principal exports include vegetables, dolomite, gypsum, timber, cement, coal, fruit, cardamom, some preserved food, precious stones, spices, alcoholic beverages, particle board, calcium carbide, handi-craft items, yak tails for fly whisks, and yak hair. The main imports from India are fuel and lubricants, motor vehicles, machinery and parts, cereals, rice, and fabrics.

27 ▪ Energy and Power

More than 95% of Bhutan's energy requirement is derived from firewood. Of commercial energy sources, petroleum accounts for 24%, coal 21%, and hydroelectric power 55%. In 2000, Bhutan produced 1,900 million kilowatt hours of electricity, 99% of it hydroelectric.

28 ▪ Social Development

There is no national social welfare system, except for a modest maternal and child welfare program begun in the early

AP/Wide World Photos

Two Bhutanese girls swing together at a playground.

1980s, which includes family planning. Bhutan's culture does not isolate or disenfranchise (deprive of voting and other rights) women. Polygamy is legal, but only with the consent of the first wife. Discriminatory policies against Nepalese Hindus in the 1980s led to the cultural repression of Hindus, but there are now a growing number of Nepalese employed in the public sector. Repatriation of exiled Nepalese deported from Bhutan is still an unresolved issue.

29 ▪ Health

Bhutan suffers from a shortage of medical personnel. Only 65% of the population

has access to medical care. In the 1990s, there were more than 120 doctors and 230 nurses, and about 70 midwives.

The life expectancy in 2003 was 53 years. The infant mortality rate was 109 per 1,000 live births.

Although smallpox has been wiped out, malaria, tuberculosis, and venereal disease remain widespread. Bhutanese refugees in the eastern Nepal region have high rates of measles, cholera, tuberculosis, malaria, diarrhea, beriberi, and scurvy.

30 ▪ Housing

Traditional houses are built of blocks or layers of stone set in clay mortar, with roofs formed of pine shingles kept in place by heavy stones.

Most of the population (an estimated 80% as of 2001) lives in rural areas, many on small family farms. It is, however, expected that the urban population will grow by about 50% over the next two decades, increasing the need for improved housing construction and utility services. All homeowners are eligible for assistance through subsidized timber purchases and group fire insurance.

As of 2000, some 80% of urban and 60% of rural dwellers had access to improved water supplies. That same year, 65% of urban and 70% of rural dwellers had access to sanitation services.

31 ▪ Education

Education is not compulsory and over 50% of school-age children do not attend. Community schools in remote rural areas often lack modern bathrooms, electricity, and drinking water, and students may have to walk several hours a day to get to them. Efforts have been made to improve the education of women, so that girls now account for 45% of primary school enrollment. However, the overall literacy rate for women is still very low and lags far behind that for men. Bhutan's estimated rate of adult illiteracy for the year 2000 stood at 52.7% (males, 38.9%; females, 66.4%). The official language for education is Dzongkha (written in the Tibetan script). However, English is widely used.

The educational system consists of seven years of primary schooling followed by four years of secondary school. The pupil-teacher ratio at the primary level averages 31 to 1.

Bhutan has 209 schools altogether, including 22 monastic schools, schools for Tibetan refugees, and 6 technical schools. At the highest level, Bhutan has one junior college, two teacher training colleges, and one degree college which is affiliated with the university at Delhi in India. Many teachers from India are employed in Bhutan.

32 ■ Media

In 1997, Bhutan had more than 6,000 mainline telephones. Telephone service is said to be very poor.

In 1998, there was only one radio station. It was government owned and included broadcasts in Dzongkha, Nepali, English, and Sharchop. From 1989 to 1999, the government had imposed a ban on private television reception. Television broadcasting was reintroduced to the country in 1999 through the government's creation of the Bhutan Broadcasting Service, which broadcasts locally produced and foreign programs. The same year, the government allowed for the licensing of cable companies. In 2001, there were about 10,000 cable subscribers. Druknet, the nation's first Internet service

©Cynthia Bassett/EPD Photos

A Bhutanese youngster sits inside a large basket and helps his mother sell her fruits and vegetables.

provider, was also established in 1999. By the end of 2000, there were about 1,820 subscribers, including Internet cafés in three major cities. In 1997, the country had an estimated 11 radios per 1,000 population.

A weekly government-subsidized newspaper, *Kuensel,* publishes simultaneous editions in Dzongkha, English, and Nepali, with a total circulation of about 11,162 as of 2002. Indian and other foreign publications are also available.

There are no legal provisions for the right of free expression in Bhutan. The government restricts criticism of the king and of the government policies of the national assembly.

33 ■ Tourism and Recreation

In 1974, Bhutan opened its door to tourists, but strict entry regulations and the country's remoteness have restricted the number of visitors. Income from tourism totaled approximately $10 million in 2000, when there were 7,559 foreign visitors. The beautiful Thimphu, Paro, and Punākha valleys, with their many monasteries, are accessible to tourists. The 1,200-year-old Takstsang Monastery near Paro was destroyed in an April 1998 fire. Archery is the national sport.

34 ■ Famous Bhutanese

Jigme Dorji Wangchuk (1928–1972) instituted numerous social reforms during his reign as king of Bhutan.

35 ■ Bibliography

Cooper, Robert. *Bhutan.* New York: Marshall Cavendish, 2001.

Dogra, R. C. *Bhutan.* Oxford, England; Santa Barbara, CA: ABC-Clio Press, 1990.

Foster, L. *Bhutan.* Chicago, IL: Children's Press, 1989.

Hellum, A. K. *A Painter's Year in the Forests of Bhutan.* Edmonton: University of Alberta Press, 2001.

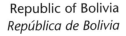

Bolivia

Republic of Bolivia
República de Bolivia

Capital: La Paz (administrative capital); Sucre (legal and judicial capital).

Flag: The flag is a horizontal tricolor of red, yellow, and green stripes, representing the animal, mineral, and vegetable kingdoms.

Anthem: *Himno Nacional,* beginning "Bolivianos, el hado propicio coronó nuestros volos anhelos" ("Bolivians, propitious fate crowned our outcries of yearning").

Monetary Unit: The boliviano (B) was introduced on 1 January 1987, replacing the peso at a rate of P1,000,000 = B1. There are coins of 2, 5, 10, 20, and 50 cents and 1 boliviano and notes of 2, 5, 10, 20, 50, 100, and 200 bolivianos. B1 = $0.1314 (or $1 = B7.61) as of May 2003.

Weights and Measures: The metric system is the legal standard, but some Spanish weights are still used in retail trade.

Holidays: New Year's Day, 1 January; Labor Day, 1 May; National Festival, 5–7 August; Columbus Day, 12 October; All Saints' Day, 1 November; Christmas, 25 December. Movable holidays include Carnival, Ash Wednesday, Holy Thursday, Good Friday, Holy Saturday, and Corpus Christi.

Time: 8 AM = noon GMT.

1 ■ Location and Size

Situated in South America just north of the Tropic of Capricorn, Bolivia has a total area of 1,098,580 square kilometers (424,164 square miles), slightly less than three times the size of the state of Montana. Completely landlocked, Bolivia shares borders with Brazil, Paraguay, Argentina, Chile, and Peru and has a total boundary length of 6,743 kilometers (4,190 miles).

The capital city of Bolivia, La Paz, is located in the west-central part of the country.

2 ■ Topography

Bolivia has three geographic zones: the Andean highlands in the southwest, running north to south; the moist slopes and valleys on the eastern side of the Andes, called the Yungas and Valles; and the eastern tropical lowland plains, or Oriente. In

Geographic Profile

Geographic Features

Size ranking: 27 of 193

Highest elevation: 6,542 meters (21,463 feet) at Nevado Sajama

Lowest elevation: 90 meters (295 feet) at the Rio Paraguay

Land Use*

Arable land: 3%

Permanent crops: 0%

Forests: 49%

Other: 48%

Weather**

Average annual precipitation: 10.5 centimeters (4.1 inches)

Average temperature in January: 25.4°C (77.7°F)

Average temperature in July: 19.7°C (67.5°F)

---

* *Arable Land: Land used for temporary crops, like meadows for mowing or pasture, gardens, and greenhouses.*

Permanent crops: Land cultivated with crops that occupy its use for long periods, such as cocoa, coffee, rubber, fruit and nut orchards, and vineyards.

Forests: Land containing stands of trees.

Other: Any land not specified, including built-on areas, roads, and barren land.

** *The measurements for precipitation and average temperatures were taken at weather stations closest to the country's largest city.*

Precipitation and average temperature can vary significantly within a country, due to factors such as latitude, altitude, coastal proximity, and wind patterns.

Bolivia, the Andes are divided into two chains. Between the Cordillera Occidental, forming the border with Chile, and the Cordillera Oriental lies a broad sedimentary plateau called the Altiplano, which contains about 28% of Bolivia's land area and more than half of its population. In the north of this plateau, astride the border with Peru, lies Lake Titicaca. With a surface area of 25,086 square kilometers (9,660 square miles) and an altitude of 3,805 meters (12,484 feet), it is the largest lake in the country and the highest navigable lake in the world.

Farther south are arid salt flats. The Cordillera Oriental has high habitable basins and valleys collectively referred to as the Puna. Bolivia's most majestic mountains are in the northern part of the Cordillera Oriental around Lake Titicaca, where the mountain sector is capped with snow. The highest mountain, Nevado Sajama at 6,542 meters (21,463 feet), is located south of this region.

The three important valleys of this region, Cochabamba, Sucre, and Tarija, are from 1,830 to 3,050 meters (6,000 to 10,000 feet) in altitude.

The Guaporé, the Mamoré, the Beni, and the Madre de Dios Rivers cross the often-flooded northern savanna and tropical forests, all converging in the northeast to form the Madeira, which flows into Brazil. The Mamoré is the longest river with a length of 1,931 kilometers (1,200 miles). The lowest point in the country is located along the Rio Paraguay at 90 meters (295 feet).

The plains become drier in the southeast, forming Bolivia's scrub-covered Chaco. Crossing the Chaco to the southeast, the Pilcomayo River leaves Bolivia to form the border between Paraguay and Argentina.

Location: 9°40' to 22°53's; 57°29' to 69°35'w. **Boundary Lengths:** Brazil, 3,400 kilometers (2,108 miles); Paraguay, 750 kilometers (465 miles); Argentina, 832 kilometers (516 miles); Chile, 861 kilometers (535 miles); Peru, 900 kilometers (558 miles).

3 ▪ Climate

Although Bolivia lies entirely in the tropics, extreme differences in altitude and rainfall give it a great variety of climates.

The mean annual temperature of La Paz, at 3,697 meters (12,130 feet), is about 8°C (46°F). That of Trinidad, in the eastern lowlands, is 26°C (79°F). Around Lake

Titicaca, rainfall is adequate, but there is less than 5 centimeters (2 inches) a year in the extreme southwest. The fertile valleys in the Cordillera Oriental have a warmer, drier Mediterranean climate.

The Yungas and Valles have a semi-tropical, moist climate. Rainfall is heavy in the northeast. The lowland plain becomes drier to the south, until it reaches drought conditions near the Argentine border.

4 ■ Plants and Animals

Because of the wide range in altitude, Bolivia has plants representative of every climatic zone, from arctic growth high in the sierra to tropical forests in the Amazon basin. On the high plateau above 3,050 meters (10,000 feet) grows a coarse bunch grass called ichu, used for pasture, thatching, and weaving mats. A reed called totora, which grows around Lake Titicaca, is used for making small fishing boats (balsas). The low bushlike tola and the resinous mosslike yareta are both used for fuel. The Lake Titicaca region is believed to be the original home of the potato.

In the tropical forest, the quinine-producing quina tree grows, as does the Pará rubber tree. There are more than 2,000 species of hardwoods. Aromatic shrubs are common, as are vanilla, sarsaparilla, and saffron plants. Useful native plants include palms, sweet potatoes, manioc, peanuts, and an astonishing variety of fruits. The Chaco region is covered with a prickly scrub collectively called monte. Tannin-producing quebracho trees also abound there.

On the Altiplano, the most important animal is the llama, one of the most efficient carrier animals known; alpaca and guanaco and several varieties of cavy (guinea pig) are found there, too. Lake Titicaca has

Anne Kalosh

A frontal view of the ornate San Francisco Church in La Paz.

several varieties of edible fish. In the tropical Amazon region are the puma, coati, tapir, armadillo, sloth, peccary, capiguara (river hog), and ant bear, as well as several kinds of monkeys. Bird life is rich and varied. Reptiles and an enormous variety of insects are found below 3,050 meters (10,000 feet).

5 ■ Environment

The chief environmental problem in the densely populated Altiplano is soil erosion, resulting from poor cultivation methods and overgrazing. Erosion currently affects 30% of the land in Bolivia. Inadequate sanitation and solid-waste disposal and waste from mining activities contribute to the Altiplano's declining water quality, which poses a threat both to fish life and to human health. The main sources of water pollution are fertilizers, pesticides, and mining.

As of 2001, 14.2% of Bolivia's total land area was protected. Endangered species in Bolivia include the puna rhea, South American river turtle, broad-nosed caiman, spectacled caiman, black caiman, jaguar, jaguarundi, margay, ocelot, emperor tamarin, and giant anteater. The llama and the alpaca are also threatened with extinction. In 2001, out of a total of 316 mammal species, 24 were considered endangered. There were 27 species of birds and 3 species of reptiles that were also threatened. Of 18,000-plus plant species, 107 were in danger of extinction.

6 ▓ Population

The population was estimated by the United Nations in 2003 at 8.9 million. The projected population for the year 2015 is 10.8 million. The population density in 2002 was 8 persons per square kilometer (21 per square mile). Three-fourths of the total population lives on the Altiplano or in the western mountain valleys. The southeastern lowlands are sparsely populated. In 2000, La Paz, the administrative capital, had an estimated population of 1.5 million. Santa Cruz, the next-largest city, had a population of 1.1 million. Sucre, the legal and judicial capital, had 152,000.

7 ▓ Migration

About 675,000 Bolivians were estimated to reside outside the country in the late 1980s, in search of employment and better economic opportunities. Since emigrants tend to have basic training or technical skills, a drain of important human resources is occurring. A number of Bolivian braceros (contract agricultural laborers) go to northwestern Argentina to work in rice and sugar harvests. Within the country, high unemployment among agricultural laborers and miners has caused significant migration to the cities.

As of 2000, the number of migrants in Bolivia totaled 61,000, including 400 refugees. The estimated net migration rate for 2003 was -1.37 migrants per 1,000 population.

8 ▓ Ethnic Groups

About 30% of all Bolivians are Quechua and 25% are Aymará. Cholos (Bolivians of mixed white and Amerindian lineage) make up another 30%, and those of wholly European background account for virtually all of the remainder. These estimates are not completely certain. Although the distinction between Amerindian, cholo, and white was at one time racial, it has gradually become at least partially social. Amerindians are sometimes called cholos when they abandon their native costumes, learn to speak Spanish, and acquire a skill or trade. Also, not all those classified as whites are without some Amerindian ancestry.

The rapidly disappearing Amerindians who populate the tropical plains in the southeast, the Chiriguanos, are believed to be a Guaraní tribe that moved west from Paraguay before the Spanish conquest. The Mojenos, Chiquitanos, and Sirionós inhabit the forest-grassland border in the far east. In all, Amerindians number about 100,000.

9 ▪ Languages

Spanish, Quechua, and Aymará are all official languages. About 40% of Bolivians speak Spanish as their first language. Approximately 37% of the population can speak Quechua and 24% speak Aymará, although an increasing number of Amerindians also speak Spanish.

10 ▪ Religions

Roman Catholicism is the dominant religion, and the constitution recognizes it as the official religion. As such, the Roman Catholic Church receives support from the state and exercises a certain degree of political influence. According to a 2001 survey, about 78% of the population are Roman Catholic. Between 16% and 19% of the population are Protestant. Missionary groups include Mennonites, Mormons, Seventh-day Adventists, Baptists, Pentecostals, and various evangelical groups. There is a small Jewish community with a synagogue in La Paz, as well as a Muslim community with a mosque in Santa Cruz. There is a Mormon temple in Cochabamba that is believed to serve more than 100,000 Mormons from across the country. There are small Buddhist and Shinto communities and a substantial number of Baha'is.

Indigenous beliefs and rituals are maintained by the Aymará, Quechua, Guaraní, and Chiquitano, as well as other indigenous groups, and many native superstitions persist. Common traditional beliefs include a focus on Pachamama, who is a mother earth figure, and Akeko, a god of luck, harvests, and abundance.

11 ▪ Transportation

The shortage of transportation facilities is one of the most serious barriers to economic development. Railroads are single-track meter gauge, totaling 3,691 kilometers (2,293 miles) in 2002. Of a total of 52,216 kilometers (32,447 miles) of roads, only about 2,872 kilometers (1,785 miles) were paved. In 2000, there were 120,494 motor vehicles, of which 35,788 were passenger cars, and 84,706 were commercial vehicles.

The hub of air traffic is El Alto airport near La Paz, the world's highest commercial airport. The other international airport is at Santa Cruz. Little use has been made of Bolivia's 10,000 kilometers (6,200 miles) of navigable waterways. The merchant marine had 36 vessels (1,000 GRT or over), totaling 196,399 GRT in 2002. Because Bolivia does not have access to the ocean, it has been granted port privileges at Antofagasta and Arica in Chile, at Mollendo in Peru, and at Santos in Brazil.

12 ▪ History

Before A.D.1300, there was a highly developed Tiahuanaco (native Amerindian) civilization. When this civilization went into decline, Quechua-speaking Incas conquered the region surrounding Lake Titicaca and colonized villages in most of what is now Bolivia. The Spanish explorer Francisco Pizarro led the Western conquest of the Inca Empire in 1532 and 1533.

In 1545, silver was discovered in the Andean region of Bolivia, then called Alto Peru, or Upper Peru, at a mine named the Cerro Rico (Rich Hill) de Potosí. The mines continued to produce vast amounts of wealth

Cory Langley

Modern skyscrapers can be found in Bolivia's major cities.

for the Spanish Empire, and for years Potosí was the largest city in the Western Hemisphere. In 1776, the region was added to the Viceroyalty of La Plata, a group of Spanish possessions with its center at Buenos Aires.

Upper Peru gained its freedom after Simón Bolívar's 1824 liberation of Peru. Bolívar sent his young general, Antonio José de Sucre, to free Upper Peru. Upper Peru was formally proclaimed the Republic of Bolívar on 6 August 1825 (the name was soon changed to Bolivia).

Sucre was chosen as the first president in 1826, and the capital city, Chuquisaca, was renamed Sucre in his honor. He was succeeded by General Andrés de Santa Cruz, who conquered Peru in 1836 and formed the Peruvian-Bolivian Confederation. In 1839, Chilean forces defeated and dissolved the confederation and ended the presidency of Santa Cruz.

A period of instability followed. The almost constant civil war slowed Bolivia's economic progress and resulted in the loss of much of its land. At the close of the War of the Pacific (1879–84), which pitted Chile against Bolivia and Peru, Chile seized what was then the Bolivian port of Antofagasta. Deprived of its only coastal territory, Bolivia was forever after a landlocked country.

After a silver boom in the late nineteenth century, silver production gave way to tin mining. The nation was controlled by a few wealthy mine and plantation owners,

Biographical Profile

Name: Carlos Diego Mesa Gisbert
Position: President of a republic
Took Office: 17 October 2003
Birthplace: La Paz, Bolivia
Birthdate: 12 August 1953
Religion: Catholic (Jesuit)
Spouse: Elvira Salinas
Children: Two children
Of interest: Before entering politics, Mesa was a noted historian and a journalist in radio, television, and newspapers

Carlos Diego Mesa Gisbert

allied with various foreign interests, while the Amerindians, excluded from the system, found their lot unchanged after almost four hundred years.

World War II (1939–45) brought further tensions to Bolivia. As world demand skyrocketed, the tin market boomed, but working conditions in Bolivia's mines remained miserable and wages remained low. In December 1943, a coalition of the army and the Nationalist Revolutionary Movement (Movimiento Nacionalista Revolutionario; MNR) engineered a successful takeover of the government. However, the tin market collapsed at the war's end, weakening the new government's power base. The new government, in turn, was overthrown, and a con-

servative government favoring the wealthy mine and land owners was installed.

The MNR returned to power in the early 1950s, dominating Bolivian politics from 1952 to 1964. Its first government, led by Víctor Paz Estenssoro, made dramatic moves to transform Bolivian society. The tin holdings of the three dominant families were taken over by the government, and a comprehensive land reform program was begun, along with large-scale welfare and literacy programs. Industry was encouraged, and the search for oil deposits was hastened.

In addition, a new policy gave Amerindians the right to vote and tried to integrate the Amerindian community more fully into the national economy. The right to vote, previously restricted to literate Bolivian males (who constituted less than 10% of the population), was made universal for all Bolivians over age twenty-one.

After his initial term in office, Paz became more and more dictatorial, and divisions within the MNR worsened. After Paz tried to rig the presidential elections in June 1964, he was removed from office by a military takeover. For the next twenty years, a series of military and civilian governments ruled Bolivia.

In 1985, former prime minister Paz, now seventy-seven, was returned to office. Faced with runaway inflation, which reached an annual rate of 14,000% in August 1985, the two leading parties agreed to cooperate, allowing a comprehensive economic reform package to pass through the legislature. Inflation and interest rates fell and the economy stabilized.

More importantly, Paz got competing political parties to cooperate in support of a continuing democracy. Paz's successor, Jaime Paz Zamora, who took office in 1989, was able to hold together a coalition and serve a full four-year presidential term.

Following the 1993 elections, Gonzalo Sánchez de Lozada assumed the presidency. His vice president, Victor Hugo Cárdenas, was the first Amerindian in Bolivian history to hold that office. The administration began a reform program that included selling public enterprises. State enterprises that were privatized included the national railroad, the state-owned airline, and electricity generation facilities.

In June 1997, General Hugo Banzer, the former dictator, won the presidential election and pledged to stop the privatization program. In March 2000, after 30 months in power, Banzer faced growing social unrest resulting from corruption, drug trafficking, and an economic crisis. Due to health reasons, Banzer resigned in 2001 and was replaced by his young vice president Jorge Quiroga. Quiroga served as a caretaking president until Gonzalo Sánchez de Lozada, the winner in the June 2002 election, took office for the second time in his life. Sánchez de Lozada's second term was marked by social and political upheaval. In October 2003, Sánchez de Lozada resigned following massive protests against his plan to export Bolivia's natural gas, which was seen to benefit the wealthy at the expense of Amerindians. Protests were also held against privatization and globalization in general. Sánchez de Lozada was replaced by his vice president, Carlos Mesa.

13 ▨ Government

The constitution of 3 February 1967 provides for a representative democracy, with its government divided into an executive branch, a two-chamber legislature (consisting of a Chamber of Deputies and a Senate), and the judiciary. Bolivia is divided into nine administrative departments but there are no local legislatures. The departments are subdivided into 94 provinces, which are further divided into 1,713 cantons.

In practice, the constitution has not been consistently observed. Military takeovers and states of siege have been frequent. Congress was dissolved by the armed forces from 1969 to 1979 and again between 1980 and 1982. Between 1966 and 1978, no presidential elections were held.

14 ▨ Political Parties

Numerous parties and coalitions have formed and dissolved over the years, usually tied to the personalities of the various leaders.

The right-wing Democratic Nationalist Alliance (Alianza Democrática Nacionalista; ADN) was closely tied to President Hugo Banzer Suarez until his death. After the June 1997 elections, the ADN formed a coalition government with the Movement of the Revolutionary Left (Movimiento de la Izquierda Revolucionaria; MIR), Civic Solidarity Union (UCS), and the far-right "Conscience of the Fatherland" party (CONDEPA).

In 2002, former president Sánchez de Lozada narrowly edged peasant activist Evo Morales in the presidential election. The strength of political parties in Bolivia has been weakened by the emergence of populist activists like Morales and by the resistance of aging party leaders like Sánchez de Lozada and Paz Zamora to retiring from politics. In addition to the center-left Nationalist Revolutionary Movement (MNR), the leftist MIR, and the center-right ADN, leading political parties include the New Republican Force (NFR) and Movement Toward Socialism (MAS), both populist parties created by presidential candidates Manfred Reyes and Evo Morales respectively.

Morales narrowly edged Reyes out in the 2002 presidential election to face Sánchez de Lozada in the runoff election in the electoral college. Because no candidate won a majority in the June 2002 election, Sánchez de Lozada was chosen president by Congress. He resigned the presidency in October 2003, and his vice president, Carlos Diego Mesa Gisbert, became president. Following the elections for Congress in 2002, the MNR held thirty-six seats in the Chamber of Deputies, the MAS held twenty-seven, MIR held twenty-six, NFR held twenty-five, and others held the sixteen remaining seats.

15 ▪ Judicial System

Judicial power is exercised by the Supreme Court, the superior district courts in each department, and the local courts. The Supreme Court, which sits at Sucre, is divided into four chambers: two deal with civil cases, one with criminal cases, and one with administrative, mining, and social cases.

The district courts usually hear appeals from the local courts. There also is a separate national labor court and an agrarian court.

16 ▪ Armed Forces

As of 2002, armed strength totaled 31,500 personnel (army, 25,000; a navy for lake and river patrol, 3,500; air force, 3,000), plus a paramilitary police force of 31,100 and a 6,000-member narcotics squad. Defense expenditures in 1999 were $147 million, or 1.8% of the gross domestic product (GDP).

17 ▪ Economy

As of 2003, Bolivia was in its second decade of democratic rule and was in a process of economic expansion. Market reforms are firmly in place, investment is growing steadily, and inflation is under control. Growth was led by energy, mining, and agriculture. Communications and the power industry had both received large amounts of foreign investment from privatization. Inflation was substantially reduced from the peak of 14,000% in 1985 to only 4.4% in 1998 and to a new low of 0.9% in 2002.

The success of the coca crop eradication program (coca is the product used in making cocaine) coupled with a lack of success in crop substitution caused growth to slow informally. An improvement to 2.4% growth in the gross domestic product (GDP) in 2000 was cut short by the worldwide economic slowdown in 2001, during which growth fell to 1.2%. Real GDP growth in 2002 was estimated at 2.5%.

18 ▪ Income

In 2001, Bolivia's gross domestic product (GDP) was $21.4 billion, or $2,600 per person. The annual growth rate of the GDP was estimated at 0%. The average inflation rate in 2001 was 2%.

19 ▪ Industry

Industrial development has been severely restricted by the small domestic market, the uncertain supply of raw materials, and the lack of technically trained labor. More than one-half of output is in nondurable consumer goods—food, beverages, tobacco, and coffee. Handicrafts and hydrocarbons account for much of the remainder.

In the late 1990s, Bolivia experienced a renaissance in the mining and hydrocarbons sectors due to privatization of the state-owned interests in these sectors. This attracted foreign interest in developing the energy and minerals potential of the country. In 2002, Bolivia had three oil refineries with a production capacity of 63,000 barrels per day.

The construction and manufacturing sectors were experiencing a slowdown in 2002, after three years of a stagnant economy. A gas pipeline to Brazil opened in 1999 was expected to take in much of Bolivia's natural gas production.

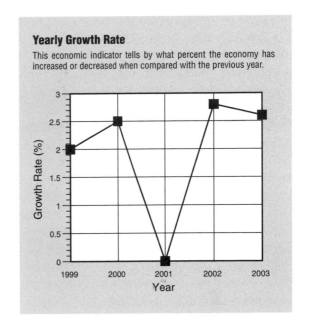

Yearly Growth Rate

This economic indicator tells by what percent the economy has increased or decreased when compared with the previous year.

20 ▪ Labor

Total employment was 2.5 million in 2002. In 1996, about 18% was in manufacturing, 20% in commerce, 8% in construction, and 2% in agriculture, and the rest in other sectors. Total unemployment was officially estimated at 7.6% in 2000.

Workers may form and join unions, but the labor code undermines this right. The Bolivian Labor Federation represents all workers, but only one-half of the employees actually belong.

The law prohibits child labor under age fourteen, but this is generally ignored. Approximately one in four children between the ages of seven and fourteen were employed in some way as of 2002. The minimum wage in 2002 was set at $59 per month. This does not provide a decent standard of living, and most workers earn more than the minimum.

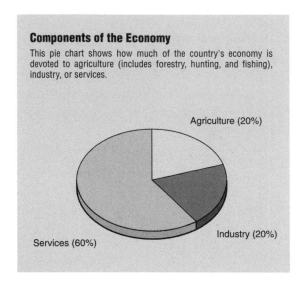

Components of the Economy

This pie chart shows how much of the country's economy is devoted to agriculture (includes forestry, hunting, and fishing), industry, or services.

Agriculture (20%)

Industry (20%)

Services (60%)

21 ■ Agriculture

An estimated 3% of Bolivia's land area is devoted to farming. About 60% of Bolivian agriculture is focused on markets and 40% on subsistence farming (living off the land).

The most important crops are potatoes, corn, barley, quinoa (a milletlike grain), habas (broad beans), wheat, alfalfa, and oca (a tuber). The potato is the main staple. The most lucrative crop in the Yungas is coca, which is chewed by the local population and from which cocaine is extracted. In 2001, the net production of coca leaf was estimated at 20,200 tons. Coca leaf produced in Bolivia represents about 20% of world production. Coffee, cacao, bananas, yucca, and aji (a widely used chili pepper) are also important. The Tarija area is famous for grapes, olives, and fruit.

The leading commercial crops are soybeans, cotton, sugar, and coffee. Annual production includes 762,000 tons of soybeans, 56,000 tons of seed cotton, 95,000 tons of sunflowers, 141,000 tons of wheat, 24,000 tons of coffee, 4.15 million tons of sugar, and 189,000 tons of rice.

22 ■ Domesticated Animals

There are an estimated 6.5 million head of cattle, 8.6 million sheep, 1.5 million goats, 2.7 million hogs, 631,000 donkeys, 322,000 horses, and 85 million poultry.

The main cattle-raising department is El Beni, in the tropical northeast, which has about 30% of the nation's cattle. Cochabamba is the leading dairy center, and improved herds there supply a powdered-milk factory. Genetic development helped increase milk production from an average of 113,000 tons annually from 1989 to 1991 to 210,000 tons by 1999.

The Amerindians of the high plateau depend on the llama because it can carry loads at any altitude and provides leather, meat, and dung fuel. Leading animal product exports are hides, alpaca and vicuña wool, and chinchilla fur. Llamas and alpacas are grown for their wool and meat. In 1995, the llama population was about two million and the alpacas numbered 324,336.

23 ■ Fishing

Fishing is a minor activity in Bolivia. A few varieties of fish are caught in Lake Titicaca by centuries-old methods and sent to La Paz. In 2000, the catch was 6,106 tons. Bolivia has some of the world's largest rainbow trout and Bolivian lakes are well stocked for sport fishing.

24 ■ Forestry

Bolivia is potentially one of the world's most important forestry nations. About 49% of Bolivia's land area consists of forests and woodlands. Trees are mostly evergreens and deciduous hardwoods, with the richest forests on the Andes' eastern slope along the tributaries of the Amazon. Humid tropical and subtropical forests account for 37% of Bolivia's forests. More than 2,000 species of tropical hardwoods of excellent quality, such as mahogany, jacaranda, rosewood, palo de balsa, quina, ironwood, colo, and cedar, abound in this area. Sawmills are few, however, and the almost total lack of transportation facilities has made exploitation expensive. Most of the sawmills are in the eastern department of Santa Cruz.

Roundwood production in 2000 was 2.6 million cubic meters (92 million cubic feet). About 50% of Bolivia's exports are derived from forestry. Bolivia is one of South America's leading rubber exporters.

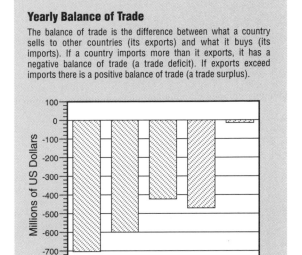

Yearly Balance of Trade

The balance of trade is the difference between what a country sells to other countries (its exports) and what it buys (its imports). If a country imports more than it exports, it has a negative balance of trade (a trade deficit). If exports exceed imports there is a positive balance of trade (a trade surplus).

25 ■ Mining

Bolivia is the fourth-largest tin-producing nation and has traditionally been a mining country producing bismuth, copper, gold, lead, silver, tungsten, and zinc. Zinc was the third-leading export commodity in 2002 and gold ranked fourth. Silver, tungsten, bismuth, lead, copper, and asbestos were also exported.

Production totals for 2000 were 149,134 tons of zinc, 12,000 kilograms (26,455 pounds) of gold, 433,592 kilograms (955,906 pounds) of silver, 12,464 tons of tin, 9,523 tons of lead, 382 tons of tungsten, 320 kilograms of rough amethyst, and 318 tons of arsenic.

26 ■ Foreign Trade

Bolivia depends primarily on its mineral exports, especially zinc and natural gas. Tin exports, however, have been gradually decreasing since 1946. Among Bolivia's imports are food, consumer goods, industrial supplies, machinery, transportation equipment, and fuels. Bolivia's major export markets are the United States, Colombia, the United Kingdom, Brazil, and Switzerland. Imports come mainly from the United States, Brazil, Chile, and Argentina.

27 ■ Energy and Power

Total electric power output in 2000 was 3.8 billion kilowatt hours, of which 50.1% was hydroelectric. In 2001, the total average daily production of crude oil was 43,000 barrels. An estimated 3.3 billion cubic meters (116 billion cubic feet) of natural gas was produced in 2000. Despite an official estimate of 680 billion cubic meters (24 trillion cubic feet) in 2002, Bolivia's natu-

Selected Social Indicators

The statistics below are the most recent estimates available as of 2003. For comparison purposes, data for the United States and averages for low-income countries and high-income countries are also given. About 15% of the world's 6.4 billion people live in high-income countries, while 40% live in low-income countries.

Indicator	Bolivia	Low-income countries	High-income countries	United States
Per capita gross national income (GNI)*	$2,390	$2,110	$28,480	$36,110
Population growth rate	2.3%	2.1%	0.7%	1.1%
People per square kilometer of land	8	77	31	31
Life expectancy in years: *male*	62	58	75	75
female	65	60	81	80
Number of physicians per 1,000 people	1.3	1.0	3.0	2.8
Number of pupils per teacher (primary school)	25	40	17	15
Literacy rate (15 years and older)	87.2%	66%	>95%	97%
Television sets per 1,000 people	121	91	735	938
Internet users per 1,000 people	32	10	364	551
Energy consumed per capita (kg of oil equivalent)	581	550	5,366	7,937

* The GNI is the total of all goods and services produced by the residents of a country in a year. The per capita GNI is calculated by dividing a country's GNI by its population and adjusting for relative purchasing power.

n.a. = data not available   > = greater than   < = less than

SOURCES: International Telecommunication Union (ITU). *World Telecommunication Development Report 2003*. Geneva, Switzerland: ITU, 2003; World Bank. *World Development Indicators*. Washington, D.C.: The World Bank, 2004; Central Intelligence Agency. *The World Factbook*. Washington, D.C.: Government Printing Office, 2003.

ral gas reserves are thought to be much larger, possibly the second largest in South America.

28 ■ Social Development

Social security coverage is compulsory for both salaried employees and rural workers. Those covered by the program receive medical, hospital, dental, and pharmaceutical care for themselves and their families. The government also provides old age pensions, survivors' benefits, maternity benefits, and family allowances.

Although women are guaranteed equal protection under the constitution, in most cases, they earn less than men for doing similar work. A law provides federal protection against sexual harassment, which is now considered a civil crime. The government has a program to prevent and treat child abuse.

29 ■ Health

Health conditions have been notably poor, owing to poor hygiene and an insufficient number of doctors and hospitals, especially in rural areas. The most common disorders are acute respiratory diseases, tuberculosis, malaria, hepatitis, and Chagas' disease. Malnutrition is a serious and growing problem, with 27% of children under five considered malnourished as of 2000.

In the mid-1990s, there were more than 4,000 physicians and nearly 2,000 nurses. As of 2002, Bolivia had 3,165 public and private health care facilities, with a total of 12,554 beds.

Anne Kalosh

A young woman poses with her llama near Lake Titicaca on Bolivia's border with Peru.

Infant mortality was 57 per 1,000 live births in 2000. Life expectancy in 2000 was estimated at 63 years.

The number of people living with human immunodeficiency virus/acquired immunodeficiency syndrome (HIV/AIDS) is estimated at 4,200, and deaths from AIDS are estimated at 380.

30 ▒ Housing

At last estimate, 67% of all housing units were detached private dwellings, 25% were detached rooms for rent with common facilities, 5% were huts, and fewer than 5% were apartments.

The government has attempted to provide safe drinking water and sanitation systems for all places with 2,000 or more inhabitants. Water systems remain inadequate in some areas, however.

31 ▒ Education

Primary education, which lasts for eight years, is compulsory and free of charge. Secondary education lasts for another four years. Approximately 91% of primary-school-age children are enrolled in school, while about one-third of those eligible attend secondary school. The pupil-teacher ratio at the primary level is roughly 25 to 1.

Bolivia has ten state-funded and twenty-three private universities. The University of San Andrés (founded in 1930) in La Paz is Bolivia's largest university; the University of San Francisco Xavier in Sucre, dating from 1624, is one of the oldest universities in Latin America.

As of 2003, the adult illiteracy rate was estimated at 13% (males, 7%; females, 18%).

32 ▒ Media

Bolivia had about 327,000 mainline telephones in 1996 with an additional 116,000 cellular phones in use in 1997.

There were 171 AM and 73 FM radio stations in 1999. There were forty-eight television stations as of 1997. In 2000, Bolivia had 676 radios for every 1,000 people. In 2003, there were 121 television sets for every 1,000 people. In 2000, there were 9 Internet service providers serving about 78,000 subscribers.

In 2002, there were about sixteen major daily newspapers. The largest La Paz daily newspapers, with their estimated circulations in 2002, were *El Diario,* 55,000; *La Razon,* 27,000; and *Presencia,* 20,000. Important provincial dailies are *Los Tiempos* (Cochabamba), with a circulation of 19,000; *El Deber* (Santa Cruz), 35,000; and *El Mundo* (Santa Cruz), with 15,000.

The constitution of Bolivia provides for freedom of speech and the press, and the government is said to allow free operation of electronic and print media.

33 ▪ Tourism and Recreation

In 2000, there were 15,795 rooms in hotels and other facilities, with 26,852 beds and a 24% occupancy rate. There were 306,000 international tourist arrivals in 2000. Tourism receipts totaled $160 million.

La Paz and Sucre have many colonial churches and buildings, and there are Inca ruins on the islands of Lake Titicaca, which also offers opportunities for fishing and sailing. The world's highest ski run is located at Chacaltaya, and mountain climbing and hiking are available on the country's Andean peaks.

34 ▪ Famous Bolivians

Pedro Domingo Murillo (1757–1810) was the first martyr of Bolivian independence. Andrés de Santa Cruz (1792–1865), who considered himself the "Napoleon of the Andes," dominated the early years of the independent nation. The most infamous of the nineteenth-century Bolivian dictators was Mariano Melgarejo (1818–1871).

Simón Patiño (1861–1947) was the richest of the "big three" tin barons and later became one of the world's wealthiest men.

Bolivia's outstanding literary figure is Gabriel René-Moreno (1836–1909), a historian, sociologist, and literary critic. The highly original poet and philosopher Franz Tamayo (1879–1956), although belonging to the landed aristocracy, was a champion of the downtrodden Amerindian. Tamayo was elected president in 1935, but an army revolt prevented him from taking power. Alcides Argüedas (1879–1946) achieved fame throughout Latin America with his historical works on Bolivia and his novels *Wata wara* and *Raza de bronce,* concerned with the plight of the Indian; his critical sociological study *Pueblo enfermo* provoked an enduring controversy.

35 ▪ Bibliography

Augustin, Byron. *Bolivia.* New York: Children's Press, 2001.

Gritzner, Mandy Lineback, and Jason M Gritzner. *Bolivia.* Philadelphia, PA: Chelsea House Publishers, 2004.

Hermes, Jules. *The Children of Bolivia.* Minneapolis, MN: Carolrhoda Books, 1996.

Klingel, Cynthia Fitterer, and Robert B. Noyed. *Bolivia.* Minneapolis, MN: Compass Point Books, 2002.

Morales, Waltraud Q. *A Brief History of Bolivia.* New York: Facts on File, 2003.

Glossary

A

abdicate: To formally give up a claim to a throne; to give up the right to be king or queen.

aboriginal: The first known inhabitants of a country. A species of animals or plants which originated within a given area.

acid rain: Rain (or snow) that has become slightly acidic by mixing with industrial air pollution.

adobe: A brick made from sun-dried heavy clay mixed with straw, used in building houses. A house made of adobe bricks.

adult literacy: The ability of adults to read and write.

agrarian economy: An economy where agriculture is the dominant form of economic activity. A society where agriculture dominates the day-to-day activities of the population is called an agrarian society.

air link: Refers to scheduled air service that allows people and goods to travel between two places on a regular basis.

airborne industrial pollutant: Pollution caused by industry that is supported or carried by the air.

allies: Groups or persons who are united in a common purpose. Typically used to describe nations that have joined together to fight a common enemy in war.

In World War I, the term Allies described the nations that fought against Germany and its allies. In World War II, Allies described the United Kingdom, United States, the USSR and their allies, who fought against the Axis Powers of Germany, Italy, and Japan.

aloe: A plant particularly abundant in the southern part of Africa, where leaves of some species are made into ropes, fishing lines, bow strings, and hammocks. It is also a symbolic plant in the Islamic world; anyone who returns from a pilgrimage to Mecca (Mekkah) hangs aloe over his door as a token that he has performed the journey.

Altaic language family: A family of languages spoken in portions of northern and eastern Europe, and nearly the whole of northern and central Asia, together with some other regions. The family is divided into five branches: the Ugrian or Finno-Hungarian, Smoyed, Turkish, Mongolian, and Tunguse.

althing: A legislative assembly.

amendment: A change or addition to a document.

Amerindian: A contraction of the two words, American Indian. It describes native peoples of North, South, or Central America.

amnesty: An act of forgiveness or pardon, usually taken by a government, toward persons for crimes they may have committed.

Anglican: Pertaining to or connected with the Church of England.

animal husbandry: The branch of agriculture that involves raising animals.

animism: The belief that natural objects and phenomena have souls or innate spiritual powers.

annex: To incorporate land from one country into another country.

annual growth rate: The rate at which something grows over a period of 12 months.

annual inflation rate: The rate of inflation in prices over the course of a year.

anthracite coal: Also called hard coal, it is usually 90 to 95 percent carbon, and burns cleanly, almost without a flame.

anti-Semitism: Agitation, persecution, or discrimination (physical, emotional, economic, political, or otherwise) directed against the Jews.

apartheid: The past governmental policy in the Republic of South Africa of separating the races in society.

appeasement: To bring to a state of peace.

appellate: Refers to an appeal of a court decision to a high authority.

aquaculture: The culture or "farming" of aquatic plants or other natural produce, as in the raising of catfish in "farms."

aquatic resources: Resources that come from, grow in, or live in water, including fish and plants.

aquifer: An underground layer of porous rock, sand, or gravel that holds water.

arable land: Land that can be cultivated by plowing and used for growing crops.

arbitration: A process whereby disputes are settled by a designated person, called the arbitrator, instead of by a court of law.

archipelago: Any body of water abounding with islands, or the islands themselves collectively.

archives: A place where records or a collection of important documents are kept.

arctic climate: Cold, frigid weather similar to that experienced at or near the north pole.

aristocracy: A small minority that controls the government of a nation, typically on the basis of inherited wealth.

armistice: An agreement or truce which ends military conflict in anticipation of a peace treaty.

artesian well: A type of well where the water rises to the surface and overflows.

ASEAN *see* Association of Southeast Asian Nations.

Association of Southeast Asian Nations (ASEAN): ASEAN was established in 1967 to promote political, economic, and social cooperation among its six member countries: Indonesia, Malaysia, the Philippines, Singapore, Thailand, and Brunei. ASEAN headquarters are in Jakarta, Indonesia. In January 1992, ASEAN agreed to create the ASEAN Free Trade Area (AFTA).

asylum: To give protection, security, or shelter to someone who is threatened by political or religious persecution.

atoll: A coral island, consisting of a strip or ring of coral surrounding a central lagoon.

atomic weapons: Weapons whose extremely violent explosive power comes from the splitting of the nuclei of atoms (usually uranium or plutonium) by neutrons in a rapid chain reaction. These weapons may be referred to as atom bombs, hydrogen bombs, or H-bombs.

austerity measures: Steps taken by a government to conserve money or resources during an economically difficult time, such as cutting back on federally funded programs.

Australoid: Pertains to the type of aborigines, or earliest inhabitants, of Australia.

Austronesian language: A family of languages which includes practically all the languages of the Pacific Islands—Indonesian, Melanesian, Polynesian, and Micronesian sub-families. Does not include Australian or Papuan languages.

authoritarianism: A form of government in which a person or group attempts to rule with absolute authority without the representation of the citizens.

autonomous state: A country which is completely self-governing, as opposed to being a dependency or part of another country.

autonomy: The state of existing as a self-governing entity. For instance, when a country gains its independence from another country, it gains autonomy.

average inflation rate: The average rate at which the general prices of goods and services increase over the period of a year.

average life expectancy: In any given society, the average age attained by persons at the time of death.

Axis Powers: The countries aligned against the Allied Nations in World War II, originally applied to Nazi Germany and Fascist Italy (Rome-Berlin Axis), and later extended to include Japan.

B

Baha'i: The follower of a religious sect founded by Mirza Husayn Ali in Iran in 1863.

Baltic states: The three formerly communist countries of Estonia, Latvia, and Lithuania that border on the Baltic Sea.

Bantu language group: A name applied to the languages spoken in central and south Africa.

Baptist: A member of a Protestant denomination that practices adult baptism by complete immersion in water.

barren land: Unproductive land, partly or entirely treeless.

barter: Trade practice where merchandise is exchanged directly for other merchandise or services without use of money.

bedrock: Solid rock lying under loose earth.

bicameral legislature: A legislative body consisting of two chambers, such as the U.S. House of Representatives and the U.S. Senate.

bill of rights: A written statement containing the list of privileges and powers to be granted to a body of people, usually introduced when a government or other organization is forming.

bituminous coal: Soft coal; coal which burns with a bright-yellow flame.

black market: A system of trade where goods are sold illegally, often for excessively inflated prices. This type of trade usually develops to avoid paying taxes or tariffs levied by the government, or to get around import or export restrictions on products.

bloodless coup: The sudden takeover of a country's government by hostile means but without killing anyone in the process.

boat people: Used to describe individuals (refugees) who attempt to flee their country by boat.

bog: Wet, soft, and spongy ground where the soil is composed mainly of decayed or decaying vegetable matter.

Bolshevik Revolution: A revolution in 1917 in Russia when a wing of the Russian Social Democratic party seized power. The Bolsheviks advocated the violent overthrow of capitalism.

bonded labor: Workers bound to service without pay; slaves.

border dispute: A disagreement between two countries as to the exact location or length of the dividing line between them.

Brahman: A member (by heredity) of the highest caste among the Hindus, usually assigned to the priesthood.

broadleaf forest: A forest composed mainly of broadleaf (deciduous) trees.

Buddhism: A religious system common in India and eastern Asia. Founded by and based upon the teachings of Siddhartha Gautama, Buddhism asserts that suffering is an inescapable part of life. Deliverance can only be achieved through the practice of charity, temperance, justice, honesty, and truth.

buffer state: A small country that lies between two larger, possibly hostile countries, considered to be a neutralizing force between them.

bureaucracy: A system of government that is characterized by division into bureaus of administration with their own divisional heads. Also refers to the inflexible procedures of such a system that often result in delay.

Byzantine Empire: An empire centered in the city of Byzantium, now Istanbul in present-day Turkey.

C

CACM *see* Central American Common Market.

canton: A territory or small division or state within a country.

capital punishment: The ultimate act of punishment for a crime, the death penalty.

capitalism: An economic system in which goods and services and the means to produce and sell them are privately owned, and prices and wages are determined by market forces.

Caribbean Community and Common Market (CARICOM): Founded in 1973 and with its headquarters in Georgetown, Guyana, CARICOM seeks the establishment of a common trade policy and increased cooperation in the Caribbean region. Includes 13 English-speaking Caribbean nations: Antigua and Barbuda, the Bahamas, Barbados, Belize, Dominica, Grenada, Guyana, Jamaica, Montserrat, Saint Kitts-Nevis, Saint Lucia, St. Vincent/Grenadines, and Trinidad and Tobago.

CARICOM *see* Caribbean Community and Common Market.

carnivore: Flesh-eating animal or plant.

carob: The common English name for a plant that is similar to and sometimes used as a substitute for chocolate.

cartel: An organization of independent producers formed to regulate the production, pricing, or marketing practices of its members in order to limit competition and maximize their market power.

cash crop: A crop that is grown to be sold rather than kept for private use.

cassation: The reversal or annulling of a final judgment by the supreme authority.

cassava: The name of several species of stout herbs, extensively cultivated for food.

caste system: One of the artificial divisions or social classes into which the Hindus are rigidly separated according to the religious law of Brahmanism. Membership in a caste is hereditary, and the privileges and disabilities of each caste are transmitted by inheritance.

Caucasian or Caucasoid: The white race of human beings, as determined by genealogy and physical features.

cease-fire: An official declaration of the end to the use of military force or active hostilities, even if only temporary.

censorship: The practice of withholding certain items of news that may cast a country in an unfavorable light or give away secrets to the enemy.

census: An official counting of the inhabitants of a state or country with details of sex and age, family, occupation, possessions, etc.

Central American Common Market (CACM): Established in 1962, a trade alliance of five Central American nations. Participating are Costa Rica, El Salvador, Guatemala, Honduras, and Nicaragua.

Central Powers: In World War I, Germany and Austria-Hungary, and their allies, Turkey and Bulgaria.

centrally planned economy: An economic system all aspects of which are supervised and regulated by the government.

centrist position: Refers to opinions held by members of a moderate political group; that is, views that are somewhere in the middle of popular thought between conservative and liberal.

cession: Withdrawal from or yielding to physical force.

chancellor: A high-ranking government official. In some countries it is the prime minister.

cholera: An acute infectious disease characterized by severe diarrhea, vomiting, and, often, death.

Christianity: The religion founded by Jesus Christ, based on the Bible as holy scripture.

Church of England: The national and established church in England. The Church of England claims continuity with the branch of the Catholic Church that existed in England before the Reformation. Under Henry VIII, the spiritual supremacy and jurisdiction of the pope were abolished, and the sovereign (king or queen) was declared head of the church.

circuit court: A court that convenes in two or more locations within its appointed district.

CIS *see* Commonwealth of Independent States.

city-state: An independent state consisting of a city and its surrounding territory.

civil court: A court whose proceedings include determinations of rights of individual citizens, in contrast to criminal proceedings regarding individuals or the public.

civil jurisdiction: The authority to enforce the laws in civil matters brought before the court.

civil law: The law developed by a nation or state for the conduct of daily life of its own people.

civil rights: The privileges of all individuals to be treated as equals under the laws of their country; specifically, the rights given by certain amendments to the U.S. Constitution.

civil unrest: The feeling of uneasiness due to an unstable political climate, or actions taken as a result of it.

civil war: A war between groups of citizens of the same country who have different opinions or agendas. The Civil War of the United States was the conflict between the states of the North and South from 1861 to 1865.

climatic belt: A region or zone where a particular type of climate prevails.

Club du Sahel: The Club du Sahel is an informal coalition which seeks to reverse the effects of drought and the desertification in the eight Sahelian zone countries: Burkina Faso, Chad, Gambia, Mali, Mauritania, Niger, Senegal, and the Cape Verde Islands. Headquarters are in Ouagadougou, Burkina Faso.

CMEA *see* Council for Mutual Economic Assistance.

coalition government: A government combining differing factions within a country, usually temporary.

coastal belt: A coastal plain area of lowlands and somewhat higher ridges that run parallel to the coast.

coastal plain: A fairly level area of land along the coast of a land mass.

coca: A shrub native to South America, the leaves of which produce organic compounds that are used in the production of cocaine.

coke: The solid product of the carbonization of coal, bearing the same relation to coal that charcoal does to wood.

cold war: Refers to conflict over ideological differences that is carried on by words and diplomatic actions, not by military action. The term is usually used to refer to the tension that existed between the United

States and the USSR from the 1950s until the breakup of the USSR in 1991.

collective bargaining: The negotiations between workers who are members of a union and their employer for the purpose of deciding work rules and policies regarding wages, hours, etc.

collective farm: A large farm formed from many small farms and supervised by the government; usually found in communist countries.

collective farming: The system of farming on a collective where all workers share in the income of the farm.

colloquial: Belonging to ordinary, everyday speech; often applied to common words and phrases which are not used in formal speech.

colonial period: The period of time when a country forms colonies in and extends control over a foreign area.

colonist: Any member of a colony or one who helps settle a new colony.

colony: A group of people who settle in a new area far from their original country, but still under the jurisdiction of that country. Also refers to the newly settled area itself.

COMECON *see* Council for Mutual Economic Assistance.

commerce: The trading of goods (buying and selling), especially on a large scale, between cities, states, and countries.

commercial catch: The amount of marketable fish, usually measured in tons, caught in a particular period of time.

commercial crop: Any marketable agricultural crop.

commission: A group of people designated to collectively do a job, including a government agency with certain law-making powers. Also, the power given to an individual or group to perform certain duties.

commodity: Any items, such as goods or services, that are bought or sold, or agricultural products that are traded or marketed.

common law: A legal system based on custom and decisions and opinions of the law courts. The basic system of law of England and the United States.

common market: An economic union among countries that is formed to remove trade barriers (tariffs) among those countries, increasing economic cooperation. The European Community is a notable example of a common market.

commonwealth: A commonwealth is a free association of sovereign independent states that has no charter, treaty, or constitution. The association promotes cooperation, consultation, and mutual assistance among members.

Commonwealth of Independent States (CIS): The CIS was established in December 1991 as an association of 11 republics of the former Soviet Union. The members include: Russia, Ukraine, Belarus (formerly Byelorussia), Moldova (formerly Moldavia), Armenia, Azerbaijan, Uzbekistan, Turkmenistan, Tajikistan, Kazakhstan, and Kyrgyzstan (formerly Kirghiziya). The Baltic states—Estonia, Latvia, and Lithuania—did not join. Georgia maintained observer status before joining the CIS in November 1993.

Commonwealth of Nations: Voluntary association of the United Kingdom and its present dependencies and associated states, as well as certain former dependencies and their dependent territories. The term was first used officially in 1926 and is embodied in the Statute of Westminster (1931). Within the Commonwealth, whose secretariat (established in 1965) is located in London, England, are numerous subgroups devoted to economic and technical cooperation.

commune: An organization of people living together in a community who share the ownership and use of property. Also refers to a small governmental district of a country, especially in Europe.

communism: A form of government whose system requires common ownership of property for the use of all citizens. All profits are to be equally distributed and prices on goods and services are usually set by the state. Also, communism refers directly to the official doctrine of the former USSR.

compulsory: Required by law or other regulation.

compulsory education: The mandatory requirement for children to attend school until they have reached a certain age or grade level.

conciliation: A process of bringing together opposing sides of a disagreement for the purpose of compromise. Or, a way of settling an international dispute in which the disagreement is submitted to an independent committee that will examine the facts and advise the participants of a possible solution.

concordat: An agreement, compact, or convention, especially between church and state.

confederation: An alliance or league formed for the purpose of promoting the common interests of its members.

Confucianism: The system of ethics and politics taught by the Chinese philosopher Confucius.

coniferous forest: A forest consisting mainly of pine, fir, and cypress trees.

conifers: Cone-bearing plants. Mostly evergreen trees and shrubs which produce cones.

conscription: To be required to join the military by law. Also known as the draft. Service personnel who join the military because of the legal requirement are called conscripts or draftees.

conservative party: A political group whose philosophy tends to be based on established traditions and not supportive of rapid change.

constituency: The registered voters in a governmental district, or a group of people that supports a position or a candidate.

constituent assembly: A group of people that has the power to determine the election of a political representative or create a constitution.

constitution: The written laws and basic rights of citizens of a country or members of an organized group.

constitutional monarchy: A system of government in which the hereditary sovereign (king or queen, usually) rules according to a written constitution.

constitutional republic: A system of government with an elected chief of state and elected representation, with a written constitution containing its governing principles. The United States is a constitutional republic.

consumer goods: Items that are bought to satisfy personal needs or wants of individuals.

continental climate: The climate of a part of the continent; the characteristics and peculiarities of the climate are a result of the land itself and its location.

continental shelf: A plain extending from the continental coast and varying in width that typically ends in a steep slope to the ocean floor.

copra: The dried meat of the coconut; it is frequently used as an ingredient of curry, and to produce coconut oil. Also written cobra, coprah, and copperah.

Coptic Christians: Members of the Coptic Church of Egypt, formerly of Ethiopia.

cordillera: A continuous ridge, range, or chain of mountains.

corvette: A small warship that is often used as an escort ship because it is easier to maneuver than larger ships like destroyers.

Council for Mutual Economic Assistance (CMEA): Also known as COMECON, the alliance of socialist economies was established on 25 January 1949 and abolished 1 January 1991. It included Afghanistan*, Albania, Angola*, Bulgaria, Cuba, Czechoslovakia, Ethiopia*, East Germany, Hungary, Laos*, Mongolia, Mozambique*, Nicaragua*, Poland, Romania, USSR, Vietnam, Yemen*, and Yugoslavia.

Nations marked with an asterisk were observers only.

counterinsurgency operations: Organized military activity designed to stop rebellion against an established government.

county: A territorial division or administrative unit within a state or country.

coup d'ètat or coup: A sudden, violent overthrow of a government or its leader.

court of appeal: An appellate court, having the power of review after a case has been decided in a lower court.

court of first appeal: The next highest court to the court which has decided a case, to which that case may be presented for review.

court of last appeal: The highest court, in which a decision is not subject to review by any higher court. In the United States, it could be the Supreme Court of an individual state or the U.S. Supreme Court.

cricket (sport): A game played by two teams with a ball and bat, with two wickets (staked target) being defended by a batsman. Common in the United Kingdom and Commonwealth of Nations countries.

criminal law: The branch of law that deals primarily with crimes and their punishments.

crown colony: A colony established by a commonwealth over which the monarch has some control, as in colonies established by the United Kingdom's Commonwealth of Nations.

Crusades: Military expeditions by European Christian armies in the eleventh, twelfth, and thirteenth centuries to win land controlled by the Muslims in the middle east.

cultivable land: Land that can be prepared for the production of crops.

Cultural Revolution: An extreme reform movement in China from 1966 to 1976; its goal was to combat liberalization by restoring the ideas of Mao Zedong.

Cushitic language group: A group of Hamitic languages that are spoken in Ethiopia and other areas of eastern Africa.

customs union: An agreement between two or more countries to remove trade barriers with each other and to establish common tariff and nontariff policies with respect to imports from countries outside of the agreement.

cyclone: Any atmospheric movement, general or local, in which the wind blows spirally around and in towards a center. In the northern hemisphere, the cyclonic movement is usually counter-clockwise, and in the southern hemisphere, it is clockwise.

Cyrillic alphabet: An alphabet adopted by the Slavic people and invented by Cyril and Methodius in the ninth century as an alphabet that was easier for the copyist to write. The Russian alphabet is a slight modification of it.

D

decentralization: The redistribution of power in a government from one large central authority to a wider range of smaller local authorities.

deciduous species: Any species that sheds or casts off a part of itself after a definite period of time. More commonly used in reference to plants that shed their leaves on a yearly basis as opposed to those (evergreens) that retain them.

declaration of independence: A formal written document stating the intent of a group of persons to become fully self-governing.

deficit: The amount of money that is in excess between spending and income.

deficit spending: The process in which a government spends money on goods and services in excess of its income.

deforestation: The removal or clearing of a forest.

deity: A being with the attributes, nature, and essence of a god; a divinity.

delta: Triangular-shaped deposits of soil formed at the mouths of large rivers.

demarcate: To mark off from adjoining land or territory; set the limits or boundaries of.

demilitarized zone (DMZ): An area surrounded by a combat zone that has had military troops and weapons removed.

demobilize: To disband or discharge military troops.

democracy: A form of government in which the power lies in the hands of the people, who can govern directly, or can be governed indirectly by representatives elected by its citizens.

denationalize: To remove from government ownership or control.

deportation: To carry away or remove from one country to another, or to a distant place.

depression: A hollow; a surface that has sunken or fallen in.

deregulation: The act of reversing controls and restrictions on prices of goods, bank interest, and the like.

desalinization plant: A facility that produces freshwater by removing the salt from saltwater.

desegregation: The act of removing restrictions on people of a particular race that keep them socially, economically, and, sometimes, physically, separate from other groups.

desertification: The process of becoming a desert as a result of climatic changes, land mismanagement, or both.

détente: The official lessening of tension between countries in conflict.

devaluation: The official lowering of the value of a country's currency in relation to the value of gold or the currencies of other countries.

developed countries: Countries which have a high standard of living and a well-developed industrial base.

development assistance: Government programs intended to finance and promote the growth of new industries.

dialect: One of a number of regional or related modes of speech regarded as descending from a common origin.

dictatorship: A form of government in which all the power is retained by an absolute leader or tyrant. There are no rights granted to the people to elect their own representatives.

dike: An artificial riverbank built up to control the flow of water.

diplomatic relations: The relationship between countries as conducted by representatives of each government.

direct election: The process of selecting a representative to the government by balloting of the voting public, in contrast to selection by an elected representative of the people.

disarmament: The reduction or depletion of the number of weapons or the size of armed forces.

dissident: A person whose political opinions differ from the majority to the point of rejection.

dogma: A principle, maxim, or tenet held as being firmly established.

domain: The area of land governed by a particular ruler or government, sometimes referring to the ultimate control of that territory.

domestic spending: Money spent by a country's government on goods used, investments, running of the government, and exports and imports.

dominion: A self-governing nation that recognizes the British monarch as chief of state.

dormant volcano: A volcano that has not exhibited any signs of activity for an extended period of time.

dowry: The sum of the property or money that a bride brings to her groom at their marriage.

draft constitution: The preliminary written plans for the new constitution of a country forming a new government.

Druze: A member of a Muslim sect based in Syria, living chiefly in the mountain regions of Lebanon.

dual nationality: The status of an individual who can claim citizenship in two or more countries.

duchy: Any territory under the rule of a duke or duchess.

due process: In law, the application of the legal process to which every citizen has a right, which cannot be denied.

durable goods: Goods or products which are expected to last and perform for several years, such as cars and washing machines.

duty: A tax imposed on imports by the customs authority of a country. Duties are generally based on the value of the goods (ad valorem duties), some other factors such as weight or quantity (specific duties), or a combination of value and other factors (compound duties).

dyewoods: Any wood from which dye is extracted.

dynasty: A family line of sovereigns who rule in succession, and the time during which they reign.

E

earned income: The money paid to an individual in wages or salary.

Eastern Orthodox: The outgrowth of the original Eastern Church of the Eastern Roman Empire, consisting of eastern Europe, western Asia, and Egypt.

EC *see* European Community.

ecclesiastical: Pertaining or relating to the church.

echidna: A spiny, toothless anteater of Australia, Tasmania, and New Guinea.

ecological balance: The condition of a healthy, well-functioning ecosystem, which includes all the plants and animals in a natural community together with their environment.

ecology: The branch of science that studies organisms in relationship to other organisms and to their environment.

economic depression: A prolonged period in which there is high unemployment, low production, falling prices, and general business failure.

economically active population: That portion of the people who are employed for wages and are consumers of goods and services.

ecotourism: Broad term that encompasses nature, adventure, and ethnic tourism; responsible or wilderness-sensitive tourism; soft-path or small-scale tourism; low-impact tourism; and sustainable tourism. Scientific, educational, or academic tourism (such as biotourism, archetourism, and geotourism) are also forms of ecotourism.

elected assembly: The persons that comprise a legislative body of a government who received their positions by direct election.

electoral system: A system of choosing government officials by votes cast by qualified citizens.

electoral vote: The votes of the members of the electoral college.

electorate: The people who are qualified to vote in an election.

emancipation: The freeing of persons from any kind of bondage or slavery.

embargo: A legal restriction on commercial ships to enter a country's ports, or any legal restriction of trade.

emigration: Moving from one country or region to another for the purpose of residence.

empire: A group of territories ruled by one sovereign or supreme ruler. Also, the period of time under that rule.

enclave: A territory belonging to one nation that is surrounded by that of another nation.

encroachment: The act of intruding, trespassing, or entering on the rights or possessions of another.

endangered species: A plant or animal species whose existence as a whole is threatened with extinction.

endemic: Anything that is peculiar to and characteristic of a locality or region.

Enlightenment: An intellectual movement of the late seventeenth and eighteenth centuries in which scientific thinking gained a strong foothold and old beliefs were challenged. The idea of absolute monarchy was questioned and people were gradually given more individual rights.

enteric disease: An intestinal disease.

epidemic: As applied to disease, any disease that is temporarily prevalent among people in one place at the same time.

Episcopal: Belonging to or vested in bishops or prelates; characteristic of or pertaining to a bishop or bishops.

ethnolinguistic group: A classification of related languages based on common ethnic origin.

EU *see* European Union.

European Community: A regional organization created in 1958. Its purpose is to eliminate customs duties and other trade barriers in Europe. It promotes a common external tariff against other countries, a Common Agricultural Policy (CAP), and guarantees of free movement of labor and capital. The original six members were Belgium, France, West Germany, Italy, Luxembourg, and the Netherlands. Denmark, Ireland, and the United Kingdom became members in 1973; Greece joined in 1981; Spain and Portugal in 1986. Other nations continue to join.

European Union (EU): The EU is an umbrella reference to the European Community (EC) and to two European integration efforts introduced by the Maastricht Treaty: Common Foreign and Security Policy (including defense) and Justice and Home Affairs (principally cooperation between police and other authorities on crime, terrorism, and immigration issues).

exports: Goods sold to foreign buyers.

external migration: The movement of people from their native country to another country, as opposed to internal migration, which is the movement of people from one area of a country to another in the same country.

F

faction: People with a specific set of interests or goals who form a subgroup within a larger organization.

fallout: The precipitation of particles from the atmosphere, often the result of a ground disturbance by volcanic activity or a nuclear explosion.

family planning: The use of birth control to determine the number of children a married couple will have.

Fascism: A political philosophy that holds the good of the nation as more important than the needs of the individual. Fascism also stands for a dictatorial leader and strong oppression of opposition or dissent.

federal: Pertaining to a union of states whose governments are subordinate to a central government.

federation: A union of states or other groups under the authority of a central government.

fetishism: The practice of worshipping a material object that is believed to have mysterious powers residing in it, or is the representation of a deity to which worship may be paid and from which supernatural aid is expected.

feudal estate: The property owned by a lord in medieval Europe under the feudal system.

feudal society: In medieval times, an economic and social structure in which persons could hold land given to them by a lord (nobleman) in return for service to that lord.

final jurisdiction: The final authority in the decision of a legal matter. In the United States, the Supreme Court would have final jurisdiction.

Finno-Ugric language group: A subfamily of languages spoken in northeastern Europe, including Finnish, Hungarian, Estonian, and Lapp.

fiscal year: The twelve months between the settling of financial accounts, not necessarily corresponding to a calendar year beginning on 1 January.

fjord: A deep indentation of the land forming a comparatively narrow arm of the sea with more or less steep slopes or cliffs on each side.

fly: The part of a flag opposite and parallel to the one nearest the flagpole.

fodder: Food for cattle, horses, and sheep, such as hay, straw, and other kinds of vegetables.

folk religion: A religion with origins and traditions among the common people of a nation or region that is relevant to their particular life-style.

foreign exchange: Foreign currency that allows foreign countries to conduct financial transactions or settle debts with one another.

foreign policy: The course of action that one government chooses to adopt in relation to a foreign country.

Former Soviet Union (FSU): The FSU is a collective reference to republics comprising the former Soviet Union. The term, which has been used as both including and excluding the Baltic republics (Estonia, Latvia, and Lithuania), includes the other 12 republics: Russia, Ukraine, Belarus, Moldova, Armenia, Azerbaijan, Uzbekistan, Turkmenistan, Tajikistan, Kazakhstan, Kyrgizstan, and Georgia.

fossil fuels: Any mineral or mineral substance formed by the decomposition of organic matter buried beneath the earth's surface and used as a fuel.

free enterprise: The system of economics in which private business may be conducted with minimum interference by the government.

free-market economy: An economic system that relies on the market, as opposed to government planners, to set the prices for wages and products.

frigate: A medium-sized warship.

fundamentalist: A person who holds religious beliefs based on the complete acceptance of the words of the Bible or other holy scripture as the truth. For instance, a fundamentalist would believe the story of creation exactly as it is told in the Bible and would reject the idea of evolution.

G

game reserve: An area of land reserved for wild animals that are hunted for sport or for food.

GDP *see* gross domestic product.

genocide: Planned and systematic killing of members of a particular ethnic, religious, or cultural group.

Germanic language group: A large branch of the Indo-European family of languages including German itself, the Scandinavian languages, Dutch, Yiddish, Modern English, Modern Scottish, Afrikaans, and others. The group also includes extinct languages such as Gothic, Old High German, Old Saxon, Old English, Middle English, and the like.

glasnost: President Mikhail Gorbachev's frank revelations in the 1980s about the state of the economy and politics in the Soviet Union; his policy of openness.

global greenhouse gas emissions: Gases released into the atmosphere that contribute to the greenhouse effect, a condition in which the earth's excess heat cannot escape.

global warming: Also called the greenhouse effect. The theorized gradual warming of the earth's climate as a result of the burning of fossil fuels, the use of man-made chemicals, deforestation, etc.

GMT *see* Greenwich (Mean) Time.

GNP *see* gross national product.

grand duchy: A territory ruled by a nobleman, called a grand duke, who ranks just below a king.

Greek Catholic: A person who is a member of an Orthodox Eastern Church.

Greek Orthodox: The official church of Greece, a self-governing branch of the Orthodox Eastern Church.

Greenwich (Mean) Time (GMT): Mean solar time of the meridian at Greenwich, England, used as the basis for standard time throughout most of the world. The world is divided into 24 time zones, and all are related to the prime, or Greenwich mean, zone.

gross domestic product (GDP): A measure of the market value of all goods and services produced within the boundaries of a nation, regardless of asset ownership. Unlike gross national product, GDP excludes receipts from that nation's business operations in foreign countries.

gross national product (GNP): A measure of the market value of goods and services produced by the labor and property of a nation. Includes receipts from that nation's business operation in foreign countries

groundwater: Water located below the earth's surface, the source from which wells and springs draw their water.

guano: The excrement of seabirds and bats found in various areas around the world. Gathered commercially and sold as a fertilizer.

guerrilla: A member of a small radical military organization that uses unconventional tactics to take their enemies by surprise.

gymnasium: A secondary school, primarily in Europe, that prepares students for university.

H

hardwoods: The name given to deciduous trees, such as cherry, oak, maple, and mahogany.

harem: In a Muslim household, refers to the women (wives, concubines, and servants in ancient times) who live there and also to the area of the home in which they live.

harmattan: An intensely dry, dusty wind felt along the coast of Africa between Cape Verde and Cape Lopez. It prevails at intervals during the months of December, January, and February.

heavy industry: Industries that use heavy or large machinery to produce goods, such as automobile manufacturing.

hoist: The part of a flag nearest the flagpole.

Holocaust: The mass slaughter of European civilians, the vast majority Jews, by the Nazis during World War II.

Holy Roman Empire: A kingdom consisting of a loose union of German and Italian territories that existed from around the ninth century until 1806.

home rule: The governing of a territory by the citizens who inhabit it.

homeland: A region or area set aside to be a state for a people of a particular national, cultural, or racial origin.

homogeneous: Of the same kind or nature, often used in reference to a whole.

Horn of Africa: The Horn of Africa comprises Djibouti, Eritrea, Ethiopia, Somalia, and Sudan.

housing starts: The initiation of new housing construction.

human rights activist: A person who vigorously pursues the attainment of basic rights for all people.

human rights issues: Any matters involving people's basic rights which are in question or thought to be abused.

humanist: A person who centers on human needs and values, and stresses dignity of the individual.

humanitarian aid: Money or supplies given to a persecuted group or people of a country at war, or those devastated by a natural disaster, to provide for basic human needs.

hydrocarbon: A compound of hydrogen and carbon, often occurring in organic substances or derivatives of organic substances such as coal, petroleum, natural gas, etc.

hydrocarbon emissions: Organic compounds containing only carbon and hydrogen, often occurring in petroleum, natural gas, coal, and bitumens, and which contribute to the greenhouse effect.

hydroelectric potential: The potential amount of electricity that can be produced hydroelectrically. Usually used in reference to a given area and how many hydroelectric power plants that area can sustain.

hydroelectric power plant: A factory that produces electrical power through the application of waterpower.

I

IBRD *see* World Bank.

illegal alien: Any foreign-born individual who has unlawfully entered another country.

immigration: The act or process of passing or entering into another country for the purpose of permanent residence.

imports: Goods purchased from foreign suppliers.

indigenous: Born or originating in a particular place or country; native to a particular region or area.

Indo-Aryan language group: The group that includes the languages of India; also called Indo-European language group.

Indo-European language family: The group that includes the languages of India and much of Europe and southwestern Asia.

industrialized nation: A nation whose economy is based on industry.

infanticide: The act of murdering a baby.

infidel: One who is without faith or belief; particularly, one who rejects the distinctive doctrines of a particular religion.

inflation: The general rise of prices, as measured by a consumer price index. Results in a fall in value of currency.

installed capacity: The maximum possible output of electric power at any given time.

insurgency: The state or condition in which one rises against lawful authority or established government; rebellion.

insurrectionist: One who participates in an unorganized revolt against an authority.

interim government: A temporary or provisional government.

interim president: One who is appointed to perform temporarily the duties of president during a transitional period in a government.

internal migration: Term used to describe the relocation of individuals from one region to another without leaving the confines of the country or of a specified area.

International Date Line: An arbitrary line at about the 180th meridian that designates where one day begins and another ends.

Islam: The religious system of Mohammed, practiced by Moslims and based on a belief in Allah as the supreme being and Mohammed as his prophet. The spelling variations, Muslim and Muhammad, are also used, primarily by Islamic people. Islam also refers to those nations in which it is the primary religion.

isthmus: A narrow strip of land bordered by water and connecting two larger bodies of land, such as two continents, a continent and a peninsula, or two parts of an island.

J

Judaism: The religious system of the Jews, based on the Old Testament as revealed to Moses and characterized by a belief in one God and adherence to the laws of scripture and rabbinic traditions.

Judeo-Christian: The dominant traditional religious makeup of the United States and other countries based on the worship of the Old and New Testaments of the Bible.

junta: A small military group in power of a country, especially after a coup.

K

khan: A sovereign, or ruler, in central Asia.

khanate: A kingdom ruled by a khan, or man of rank.

kwashiorkor: Severe malnutrition in infants and children caused by a diet high in carbohydrates and lacking in protein.

kwh: The abbreviation for kilowatt-hour.

L

labor force: The number of people in a population available for work, whether actually employed or not.

labor movement: A movement in the early to mid-1800s to organize workers in groups according to profession to give them certain rights as a group, including bargaining power for better wages, working conditions, and benefits.

land reforms: Steps taken to create a fair distribution of farmland, especially by governmental action.

landlocked country: A country that does not have direct access to the sea; it is completely surrounded by other countries.

least developed countries: A subgroup of the United Nations designation of "less developed countries;" these countries generally have no significant economic growth, low literacy rates, and per person gross national product of less than $500. Also known as undeveloped countries.

leeward: The direction identical to that of the wind. For example, a leeward tide is a tide that runs in the same direction that the wind blows.

leftist: A person with a liberal or radical political affiliation.

legislative branch: The branch of government which makes or enacts the laws.

leprosy: A disease that can effect the skin and/or the nerves and can cause ulcers of the skin, loss of feeling, or loss of fingers and toes.

less developed countries (LDC): Designated by the United Nations to include countries with low levels of output, living standards, and per person gross national product generally below $5,000.

literacy: The ability to read and write.

M

Maastricht Treaty: The Maastricht Treaty (named for the Dutch town in which the treaty was signed) is also known as the Treaty of European Union. The treaty creates a European Union by: (a) committing the member states of the European Economic Community to both European Monetary Union (EMU) and political union; (b) introducing a single currency (European Currency Unit, ECU); (c) establishing a European System of Central Banks (ESCB); (d) creating a European Central Bank (ECB); and (e) broadening EC integration by including both a common foreign and security policy (CFSP) and cooperation in justice and home affairs (CJHA). The treaty entered into force on 1 November 1993.

Maghreb states: The Maghreb states include the three nations of Algeria, Morocco, and Tunisia; sometimes includes Libya and Mauritania.

maize: Another name (Spanish or British) for corn or the color of ripe corn.

majority party: The party with the largest number of votes and the controlling political party in a government.

mangrove: A tree which abounds on tropical shores in both hemispheres. Characterized by its numerous roots which arch out from its trunk and descend from its branches, mangroves form thick, dense growths along the tidal muds, reaching lengths hundreds of miles long.

manioc: The cassava plant or its product. Manioc is a very important food-staple in tropical America.

maquis: Scrubby, thick underbrush found along the coast of the Mediterranean Sea.

marginal land: Land that could produce an economic profit, but is so poor that it is only used when better land is no longer available.

marine life: The life that exists in, or is formed by the sea.

maritime climate: The climate and weather conditions typical of areas bordering the sea.

maritime rights: The rights that protect navigation and shipping.

market access: Market access refers to the openness of a national market to foreign products. Market access reflects a government's willingness to permit imports to compete relatively unimpeded with similar domestically produced goods.

market economy: A form of society which runs by the law of supply and demand. Goods are produced by firms to be sold to consumers, who determine the demand for them. Price levels vary according to the demand for certain goods and how much of them is produced.

market price: The price a commodity will bring when sold on the open market. The price is determined by the amount of demand for the commodity by buyers.

Marshall Plan: Formally known as the European Recovery Program, a joint project between the United States and most Western European nations under which $12.5 billion in U.S. loans and grants was expended to aid European recovery after World War II.

Marxism *see* Marxist-Leninist principles.

Marxist: A follower of Karl Marx, a German socialist and revolutionary leader of the late 1800s, who contributed to Marxist-Leninist principles.

Marxist-Leninist principles: The doctrines of Karl Marx, built upon by Nikolai Lenin, on which communism was founded. They predicted the fall of capitalism, due to its own internal faults and the resulting oppression of workers.

massif: A central mountain-mass or the dominant part of a range of mountains.

matrilineal (descent): Descending from, or tracing descent through, the maternal, or mother's, family line.

Mayan language family: The languages of the Central American Indians, further divided into two subgroups: the Maya and the Huastek.

mean temperature: The air temperature unit measured by the National Weather Service by adding the maximum and minimum daily temperatures together and diving the sum by 2.

Mecca (Mekkah): A city in Saudi Arabia; a destination of pilgrims in the Islamic world.

Mediterranean climate: A wet-winter, dry-summer climate with a moderate annual temperature range.

mestizo: The offspring of a person of mixed blood; especially, a person of mixed Spanish and American Indian parentage.

migratory birds: Those birds whose instincts prompt them to move from one place to another at the regularly recurring changes of season.

migratory workers: Usually agricultural workers who move from place to place for employment depending on the growing and harvesting seasons of various crops.

military coup: A sudden, violent overthrow of a government by military forces.

military junta: The small military group in power in a country, especially after a coup.

military regime: Government conducted by a military force.

military takeover: The seizure of control of a government by the military forces.

militia: The group of citizens of a country who are either serving in the reserve military forces or are eligible to be called up in time of emergency.

millet: A cereal grass whose small grain is used for food in Europe and Asia.

minority party: The political group that comprises the smaller part of the large overall group it belongs to; the party that is not in control.

missionary: A person sent by authority of a church or religious organization to spread his religious faith in a community where his church has no self-supporting organization.

monarchy: Government by a sovereign, such as a king or queen.

money economy: A system or stage of economic development in which money replaces barter in the exchange of goods and services.

Mongol: One of an Asiatic race chiefly resident in Mongolia, a region north of China proper and south of Siberia.

Mongoloid: Having physical characteristics like those of the typical Mongols (Chinese, Japanese, Turks, Eskimos, etc.).

Moors: One of the Arab tribes that conquered Spain in the eighth century.

Moslem: A frequently used variation of the spelling of Muslim; a follower of Muhammad in the religion of Islam.

mosque: An Islam place of worship and the organization with which it is connected.

mouflon: A type of wild sheep characterized by curling horns.

Muhammad (or Muhammed or Mahomet): An Arabian prophet, known as the "Prophet of Allah" who founded the religion of Islam in 622, and wrote The Koran, the scripture of Islam. Also commonly spelled Mohammed.

mujahideen (mujahedin or mujahedeen): Rebel fighters in Islamic countries, especially those supporting the cause of Islam.

mulatto: One who is the offspring of parents one of whom is white and the other is black.

municipality: A district such as a city or town having its own incorporated government.

Muslim: A follower of the prophet Muhammad, the founder of the religion of Islam.

Muslim New Year: A Muslim holiday. Although in some countries 1 Muharram, which is the first month of the Islamic year, is observed as a holiday, in other places the new year is observed on Sha'ban, the eighth month of the year. This practice apparently stems from pagan Arab times. Shab-i-Bharat, a national holiday in Bangladesh on this day, is held by many to be the occasion when God ordains all actions in the coming year.

N

NAFTA (North American Free Trade Agreement): NAFTA, which entered into force in January 1994, is a free trade agreement between Canada, the United States, and Mexico. The agreement progressively eliminates almost all U.S.-Mexico tariffs over a 10–15 year period.

nationalism: National spirit or aspirations; desire for national unity, independence, or prosperity.

nationalization: To transfer the control or ownership of land or industries to the nation from private owners.

native tongue: One's natural language. The language that is indigenous to an area.

NATO *see* North Atlantic Treaty Organization.

natural gas: A combustible gas formed naturally in the earth and generally obtained by boring a well. The chemical makeup of natural gas is principally methane, hydrogen, ethylene compounds, and nitrogen.

natural harbor: A protected portion of a sea or lake along the shore resulting from the natural formations of the land.

naturalize: To confer the rights and privileges of a native-born subject or citizen upon someone who lives in the country by choice.

nature preserve: An area where one or more species of plant and/or animal are protected from harm, injury, or destruction.

neutrality: The policy of not taking sides with any countries during a war or dispute among them.

Newly Independent States: The NIS is a collective reference to 12 republics of the former Soviet Union: Russia, Ukraine, Belarus (formerly Byelorussia), Moldova (formerly Moldavia), Armenia, Azerbaijan, Uzbekistan, Turkmenistan, Tajikistan, Kazakhstan, Kyrgyzstan (formerly Kirghiziya), and Georgia. Following dissolution of the Soviet Union, the distinction between the NIS and the Commonwealth of Independent States (CIS) was that Georgia was not a member of the CIS. That distinction dissolved when Georgia joined the CIS in November 1993.

news censorship *see* censorship.

Nonaligned Movement (NAM): The NAM is an alliance of third world states that aims to promote the political and economic interests of developing countries. NAM interests have included ending colonialism/neo-colonialism, supporting the integrity of independent countries, and seeking a new international economic order.

Nordic Council: The Nordic Council, established in 1952, is directed toward supporting cooperation among Nordic countries. Members include Denmark, Finland, Iceland, Norway, and Sweden. Headquarters are in Stockholm, Sweden.

North Atlantic Treaty Organization (NATO): A mutual defense organization. Members include Belgium, Canada, Denmark, France (which has only partial membership), Greece, Iceland, Italy, Luxembourg, Netherlands, Norway, Portugal, Spain, Turkey, United Kingdom, United States, and Germany.

nuclear power plant: A factory that produces electrical power through the application of the nuclear reaction known as nuclear fission.

nuclear reactor: A device used to control the rate of nuclear fission in uranium. Used in commercial applications, nuclear reactors can maintain temperatures high enough to generate sufficient quantities of steam which can then be used to produce electricity.

O

OAPEC (Organization of Arab Petroleum Exporting Countries): OAPEC was created in 1968; members include: Algeria, Bahrain, Egypt, Iraq, Kuwait, Libya, Qatar, Saudi Arabia, Syria, and the United Arab Emirates. Headquarters are in Kuwait.

OAS (Organization of American States): The OAS (Spanish: Organizaciûn de los Estados Americanos, OEA), or the Pan American Union, is a regional organization which promotes Latin American economic and social development. Members include the United States, Mexico, and most Central American, South American, and Caribbean nations.

oasis: Originally, a fertile spot in the Libyan desert where there is a natural spring or well and vegetation; now refers to any fertile tract in the midst of a wasteland.

occupied territory: A territory that has an enemy's military forces present.

official language: The language in which the business of a country and its government is conducted.

oligarchy: A form of government in which a few people possess the power to rule as opposed to a monarchy which is ruled by one.

OPEC (Organization of Petroleum Exporting Countries): An organization created in 1961 open to all countries that are major exporters of oil. Members in 2004 included Algeria, Indonesia, Iran, Iraq, Kuwait, Libya, Nigeria, Qatar, Saudia Arabia, The United Arab Emirates and Venezuela.

open economy: An economy that imports and exports goods.

open market: Open market operations are the actions of the central bank to influence or control the money supply by buying or selling government bonds.

opposition party: A minority political party that is opposed to the party in power.

Organization of Arab Petroleum Exporting Countries *see* OAPEC.

Organization of Petroleum Exporting Countries *see* OPEC.

organized labor: The body of workers who belong to labor unions.

Ottoman Empire: A Turkish empire founded by Osman I in about 1603, that variously controlled large areas of land around the Mediterranean, Black, and Caspian Seas until it was dissolved in 1918.

overfishing: To deplete the quantity of fish in an area by removing more fish than can be naturally replaced.

overgrazing: Allowing animals to graze in an area to the point that the ground vegetation is damaged or destroyed.

overseas dependencies: A distant and physically separate territory that belongs to another country and is subject to its laws and government.

P

Pacific Rim: The Pacific Rim, referring to countries and economies bordering the Pacific Ocean.

pact: An international agreement.

Paleolithic: The early period of the Stone Age, when rough, chipped stone implements were used.

panhandle: A long narrow strip of land projecting like the handle of a frying pan.

papyrus: The paper-reed or -rush which grows on marshy river banks in the southeastern area of the Mediterranean, but more notably in the Nile valley.

paramilitary group: A supplementary organization to the military.

parasitic diseases: A group of diseases caused by parasitic organisms which feed off the host organism.

parliamentary republic: A system of government in which a president and prime minister, plus other ministers of departments, constitute the executive branch of the government and the parliament constitutes the legislative branch.

parliamentary rule: Government by a legislative body similar to that of Great Britain, which is composed of two houses—one elected and one hereditary.

parochial: Refers to matters of a church parish or something within narrow limits.

partisan politics: Rigid, unquestioning following of a specific party's or leader's goals.

patriarchal system: A social system in which the head of the family or tribe is the father or oldest male. Kinship is determined and traced through the male members of the tribe.

patrilineal (descent): Descending from, or tracing descent through, the paternal or father's line.

pellagra: A disease marked by skin, intestinal, and central nervous system disorders, caused by a diet deficient in niacin, one of the B vitamins.

per capita: Literally, per person; for each person counted.

perestroika: The reorganization of the political and economic structures of the Soviet Union by president Mikhail Gorbachev.

periodical: A publication whose issues appear at regular intervals, such as weekly, monthly, or yearly.

petrochemical: A chemical derived from petroleum or from natural gas.

pharmaceutical plants: Any plant that is used in the preparation of medicinal drugs.

plantain: The name of a common weed that has often been used for medicinal purposes, as a folk remedy and in modern medicine. Plaintain is also the name of a tropical plant producing a type of banana.

polar climate: Also called tundra climate. A humid, severely cold climate controlled by arctic air masses, with no warm or summer season.

political climate: The prevailing political attitude of a particular time or place.

political refugee: A person forced to flee his or her native country for political reasons.

potable water: Water that is safe for drinking.

pound sterling: The monetary unit of Great Britain, otherwise known as the pound.

prefect: An administrative official; in France, the head of a particular department.

prefecture: The territory over which a prefect has authority.

prime meridian: Zero degrees in longitude that runs through Greenwich, England, site of the Royal Observatory. All other longitudes are measured from this point.

prime minister: The premier or chief administrative official in certain countries.

private sector: The division of an economy in which production of goods and services is privately owned.

privatization: To change from public to private control or ownership.

protectorate: A state or territory controlled by a stronger state, or the relationship of the stronger country toward the lesser one it protects.

Protestant: A member or an adherent of one of those Christian bodies which descended from the Reformation of the sixteenth century. Originally applied to those who opposed or protested the Roman Catholic Church.

Protestant Reformation: In 1529, a Christian religious movement begun in Germany to deny the universal authority of the pope, and to establish the Bible as the only source of truth. (*Also see* Protestant)

proved reserves: The quantity of a recoverable mineral resource (such as oil or natural gas) that is still in the ground.

province: An administrative territory of a country.

provisional government: A temporary government set up during time of unrest or transition in a country.

pulses: Beans, peas, or lentils.

purge: The act of ridding a society of "undesirable" or unloyal persons by banishment or murder.

R

Rastafarian: A member of a Jamaican cult begun in 1930 as a semi-religious, semi-political movement.

rate of literacy: The percentage of people in a society who can read and write.

recession. A period of reduced economic activity in a country or region.

referendum: The practice of submitting legislation directly to the people for a popular vote.

reforestation: Systematically replacing forest trees lost due to fire or logging.

Reformation *see* Protestant Reformation.

refugee: One who flees to a refuge or shelter or place of safety. One who in times of persecution or political commotion flees to a foreign country for safety.

revolution: A complete change in a government or society, such as in an overthrow of the government by the people.

right-wing party: The more conservative political party.

Roman alphabet: The alphabet of the ancient Romans from which the alphabets of most modern western European languages, including English, are derived.

Roman Catholic Church: The designation of the church of which the pope or Bishop of Rome is the head, and that holds him as the successor of St. Peter and heir of his spiritual authority, privileges, and gifts.

romance language: The group of languages derived from Latin: French, Spanish, Italian, Portuguese, and other related languages.

roundwood: Timber used as poles or in similar ways without being sawn or shaped.

runoff election: A deciding election put to the voters in case of a tie between candidates.

Russian Orthodox: The arm of the Orthodox Eastern Church that was the official church of Russia under the czars.

S

sack: To strip of valuables, especially after capture.

Sahelian zone: Eight countries make up this dry desert zone in Africa: Burkina Faso, Chad, Gambia, Mali, Mauritania, Niger, Senegal, and the Cape Verde Islands. Also see Club du Sahel.

salinization: An accumulation of soluble salts in soil. This condition is common in desert climates, where water evaporates quickly in poorly drained soil due to high temperatures.

Samaritans: A native or an inhabitant of Samaria; specifically, one of a race settled in the cities of Samaria by the king of Assyria after the removal of the Israelites from the country.

savanna: A treeless or near treeless plain of a tropical or subtropical region dominated by drought-resistant grasses.

schistosomiasis: A tropical disease that is chronic and characterized by disorders of the liver, urinary bladder, lungs, or central nervous system.

secession: The act of withdrawal, such as a state withdrawing from the Union in the Civil War in the United States.

sect: A religious denomination or group, often a dissenting one with extreme views.

segregation: The enforced separation of a racial or religious group from other groups, compelling them to live and go to school separately from the rest of society.

seismic activity: Relating to or connected with an earthquake or earthquakes in general.

self-sufficient: Able to function alone without help.

separation of power: The division of power in the government among the executive, legislative, and judicial branches and the checks and balances employed to keep them separate and independent of each other.

separatism: The policy of dissenters withdrawing from a larger political or religious group.

serfdom: In the feudal system of the Middle Ages, the condition of being attached to the land owned by a lord and being transferable to a new owner.

Seventh-day Adventist: One who believes in the second coming of Christ to establish a personal reign upon the earth.

shamanism: A religion of some Asians and Amerindians in which shamans, who are priests or medicine men, are believed to influence good and evil spirits.

shantytown: An urban settlement of people in flimsy, inadequate houses.

Shia Muslims: Members of one of two great sects of Islam. Shia Muslims believe that Ali and the Imams are the rightful successors of Muhammad (also commonly spelled Mohammed). They also believe that the last recognized Imam will return as a messiah. Also known as Shiites. (*Also see* Sunni Muslims.)

Shiites *see* Shia Muslims.

Shintoism: The system of nature- and hero-worship which forms the indigenous religion of Japan.

shoal: A place where the water of a stream, lake, or sea is of little depth. Especially, a sand-bank which shows at low water.

sierra: A chain of hills or mountains.

Sikh: A member of a politico-religious community of India, founded as a sect around 1500 and based on the principles of monotheism (belief in one god) and human brotherhood.

Sino-Tibetan language family: The family of languages spoken in eastern Asia, including China, Thailand, Tibet, and Burma.

slash-and-burn agriculture: A hasty and sometimes temporary way of clearing land to make it available for agriculture by cutting down trees and burning them.

slave trade: The transportation of black Africans beginning in the 1700s to other countries to be sold as slaves—people owned as property and compelled to work for their owners at no pay.

Slavic languages: A major subgroup of the Indo-European language family. It is further subdivided into West Slavic (including Polish, Czech, Slovak and Serbian), South Slavic (including Bulgarian, Serbo-Croatian, Slovene, and Old Church Slavonic), and East Slavic (including Russian Ukrainian and Byelorussian).

social insurance: A government plan to protect low-income people, such as health and accident insurance, pension plans, etc.

social security: A form of social insurance, including life, disability, and old-age pension for workers. It is paid for by employers, employees, and the government.

socialism: An economic system in which ownership of land and other property is distributed among the community as a whole, and every member of the community shares in the work and products of the work.

socialist: A person who advocates socialism.

softwoods: The coniferous trees, whose wood density as a whole is relatively softer than the wood of those trees referred to as hardwoods.

sorghum (also known as Syrian Grass): Plant grown in various parts of the world for its valuable uses, such as for grain, syrup, or fodder.

Southeast Asia: The region in Asia that consists of the Malay Archipelago, the Malay Peninsula, and Indochina.

staple crop: A crop that is the chief commodity or product of a place, and which has widespread and constant use or value.

state: The politically organized body of people living under one government or one of the territorial units that make up a federal government, such as in the United States.

steppe: A level tract of land more or less devoid of trees, in certain parts of European and Asiatic Russia.

student demonstration: A public gathering of students to express strong feelings about a certain situation, usually taking place near the location of the people in power to change the situation.

subarctic climate: A high latitude climate of two types: continental subarctic, which has very cold winters, short, cool summers, light precipitation and moist air; and marine subarctic, a coastal and island climate with polar air masses causing large precipitation and extreme cold.

subcontinent: A land mass of great size, but smaller than any of the continents; a large subdivision of a continent.

subsistence economy: The part of a national economy in which money plays little or no role, trade is by barter, and living standards are minimal.

subsistence farming: Farming that provides the minimum food goods necessary for the continuation of the farm family.

subtropical climate: A middle latitude climate dominated by humid, warm temperatures and heavy rainfall in summer, with cool winters and frequent cyclonic storms.

Sudanic language group: A related group of languages spoken in various areas of northern Africa, including Yoruba, Mandingo, and Tshi.

suffrage: The right to vote.

Sufi: A Muslim mystic who believes that God alone exists, there can be no real difference between good and evil, that the soul exists within the body as in a cage, so death should be the chief object of desire, and sufism is the only true philosophy.

sultan: A king of a Muslim state.

Sunni Muslims: Members of one of two major sects of the religion of Islam. Sunni Muslims adhere to strict orthodox traditions, and believe that the four caliphs are the rightful successors to Mohammed, founder of Islam. (Mohammed is commonly spelled Muhammad, especially by Islamic people.) (*Also see* Shia Muslims.)

T

Taoism: The doctrine of Lao-Tzu, an ancient Chinese philosopher (about 500 B.C.) as laid down by him in the Tao-te-ching.

tariff: A tax assessed by a government on goods as they enter (or leave) a country. May be imposed to protect domestic industries from imported goods and/or to generate revenue.

temperate zone: The parts of the earth lying between the tropics and the polar circles. The northern temperate zone is the area between the tropic of Cancer and the Arctic Circle. The southern temperate zone is the area between the tropic of Capricorn and the Antarctic Circle.

terracing: A form of agriculture that involves cultivating crops in raised banks of earth.

terrorism: Systematic acts of violence designed to frighten or intimidate.

thermal power plant: A facility that produces electric energy from heat energy released by combustion of fuel or nuclear reactions.

Third World: A term used to describe less developed countries; as of the mid-1990s, it is being replaced by the United Nations designation Less Developed Countries, or LDC.

topography: The physical or natural features of the land.

torrid zone: The part of the earth's surface that lies between the tropics, so named for the character of its climate.

totalitarian party: The single political party in complete authoritarian control of a government or state.

trachoma: A contagious bacterial disease that affects the eye.

trade unionism: Labor union activity for workers who practice a specific trade, such as carpentry.

treaty: A negotiated agreement between two governments.

tribal system: A social community in which people are organized into groups or clans descended from common ancestors and sharing customs and languages.

tropical monsoon climate: One of the tropical rainy climates; it is sufficiently warm and rainy to produce tropical rainforest vegetation, but also has a winter dry season.

tsetse fly: Any of the several African insects which can transmit a variety of parasitic organisms through its bite. Some of these organisms can prove fatal to both human and animal victims.

tundra: A nearly level treeless area whose climate and vegetation are characteristically arctic due to its northern position; the subsoil is permanently frozen.

U

undeveloped countries *see* least developed countries.

unemployment rate: The overall unemployment rate is the percentage of the work force (both employed and unemployed) who claim to be unemployed.

UNICEF: An international fund set-up for children's emergency relief: United Nations Children's Fund (formerly United Nations International Children's Emergency Fund).

universal adult suffrage: The policy of giving every adult in a nation the right to vote.

untouchables: In India, members of the lowest caste in the caste system, a hereditary social class system. They were considered unworthy to touch members of higher castes.

urban guerrilla: A rebel fighter operating in an urban area.

urbanization: The process of changing from country to city.

V

veldt: In South Africa, an unforested or thinly forested tract of land or region, a grassland.

W

Warsaw Pact: Agreement made 14 May 1955 (and dissolved 1 July 1991) to promote mutual defense between Albania, Bulgaria, Czechoslovakia, East Germany, Hungary, Poland, Romania, and the USSR.

Western nations: Blanket term used to describe mostly democratic, capitalist countries, including the United States, Canada, and western European countries.

wildlife sanctuary: An area of land set aside for the protection and preservation of animals and plants.

workers' compensation: A series of regular payments by an employer to a person injured on the job.

World Bank: The World Bank is a group of international institutions which provides financial and technical assistance to developing countries.

world oil crisis: The severe shortage of oil in the 1970s precipitated by the Arab oil embargo.

Y

yaws: A tropical disease caused by a bacteria which produces raspberry like sores on the skin.

yellow fever: A tropical viral disease caused by the bite of an infected mosquito, characterized by jaundice.

Z

Zoroastrianism: The system of religious doctrine taught by Zoroaster and his followers in the Avesta; the religion prevalent in Persia until its overthrow by the Muslims in the seventh century.

Afghanistan

Albania

Algeria

Argentina

Armenia

Australia

Bahrain

Bangladesh

Barbados

Benin

Bhutan

Bolivia